HIKING AND TRAVELING
THE BLUE RIDGE PARKWAY

Other Books by Leonard M. Adkins

Wildflowers of the Blue Ridge and Great Smoky Mountains
(Joe Cook, photographer)

Wildflowers of the Appalachian Trail
(Joe Cook and Monica Sheppard, photographers)

The Best of the Appalachian Trail: Day Hikes
(with Victoria and Frank Logue)

The Best of the Appalachian Trail: Overnight Hikes
(with Victoria and Frank Logue)

The Appalachian Trail: A Visitor's Companion

All about the Appalachian Trail

50 Hikes in Northern Virginia: Walks, Hikes, and Backpacks
from the Allegheny Mountains to the Chesapeake Bay

50 Hikes in Southern Virginia: From the Cumberland Gap
to the Atlantic Ocean

50 Hikes in Maryland: Walks, Hikes, and Backpacks from the
Allegheny Plateau to the Atlantic Ocean

50 Hikes in West Virginia: From the Allegheny Mountains
to the Ohio River

Images of America: Along the Appalachian Trail: Georgia,
North Carolina, and Tennessee

Images of America: Along Virginia's Appalachian Trail

Images of America: Along the Appalachian Trail: West Virginia,
Maryland, and Pennsylvania

Images of America: Along the Appalachian Trail: New Jersey,
New York, and Connecticut

Images of America: Along the Appalachian Trail: Massachusetts,
Vermont, and New Hampshire

Postcards of America: Along Virginia's Appalachian Trail

Maryland: An Explorer's Guide

West Virginia: An Explorer's Guide

Adventure Guide to Virginia

The Caribbean: A Walking and Hiking Guide

Seashore State Park: A Walking Guide

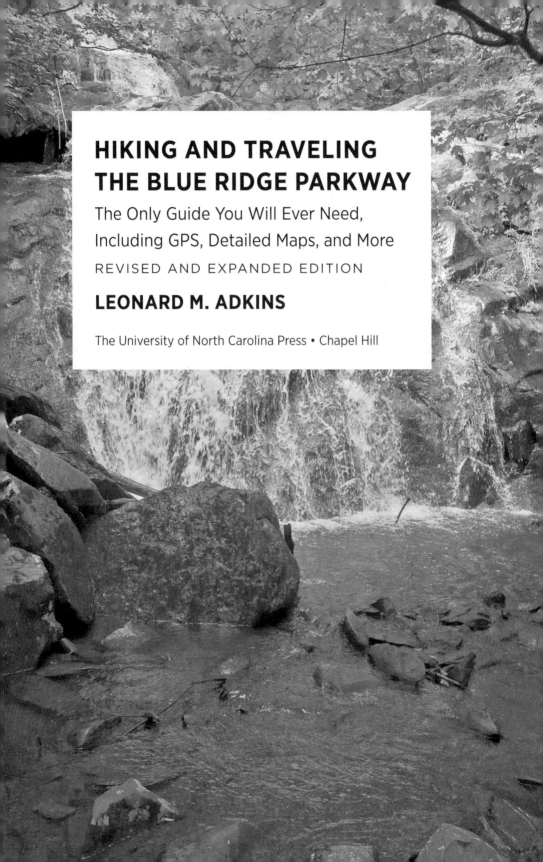

HIKING AND TRAVELING THE BLUE RIDGE PARKWAY

The Only Guide You Will Ever Need, Including GPS, Detailed Maps, and More

REVISED AND EXPANDED EDITION

LEONARD M. ADKINS

The University of North Carolina Press • Chapel Hill

Published with the assistance of the Wachovia Wells Fargo
Fund for Excellence of the University of North Carolina Press.

A Southern Gateways Guide
© 2018 Leonard M. Adkins
All rights reserved
Set in Caecilia and Gotham

Manufactured in the United States of America

The University of North Carolina Press has been a member of the
Green Press Initiative since 2003.

Cover illustration: *Scenic Sunrise over Fog-Filled Valley*, © iStockphoto.com/aheflin.

All photos are by the author.
ISBN 978-1-4696-4697-8 (pbk. alk. paper)
ISBN 978-1-4696-4698-5 (ebook)

The Library of Congress has catalogued the original edition as follows:

Library of Congress Cataloging-in-Publication Data
Adkins, Leonard M.
Hiking and traveling the Blue Ridge Parkway : the only guide
you will ever need, including GPS, detailed maps, and more /
by Leonard M. Adkins.
    p. cm. — (Southern gateways guide)
    Includes index.
    ISBN 978-1-4696-0819-8 (pbk : alk. paper)
    1. Hiking—Blue Ridge Parkway (N.C. and Va.)—Guidebooks.
2. Trails—Blue Ridge Parkway (N.C. and Va.)—Guidebooks.
3. Blue Ridge Parkway (N.C. and Va.)—Guidebooks.
I. Title.
GV199.42.B65A33 2013   917.55—dc23
2012046985

Southern Gateways Guide™ is a registered trademark
of the University of North Carolina Press.

To my parents
  for making everything possible
and to Laurie
  for making me happy

In the woods is perpetual youth.
—Emerson, Nature

CONTENTS

FOREWORD

Among my earliest and best childhood memories is one of riding in a 1954 Oldsmobile Super 88 with my father at the wheel, my mother up next to him, and my brother, sister, and me in the backseat.

This was Sunday afternoon, and we'd changed out of our church clothes and were headed to one of our favorite places—the Blue Ridge Parkway, not far from our home on South Turkey Creek Road outside of Asheville.

I knew that back in the trunk, the Kool-Aid was cold—no one made it better than our mom—and the picnic lunch was going to be as delicious as always.

As a boy of five or six, I was lucky to have some sense of what we were doing. Maybe it was my parents' enthusiasm and regularity in taking us out on those Sunday afternoon drives that rubbed off on me somehow.

Whatever it was, I understood that a wonder was about to unfold before me again, and that as it did, it would be both the same as and completely different from the last time we went.

That, I see these decades later, is why we love the Blue Ridge Parkway. It's supremely human to want to have things we depend on not change, and equally a part of our character to want variation within that dependability. It works that way with baseball.

With a good marriage.

With a fine meal made from recipes you've enjoyed many times before.

And with the Blue Ridge Parkway. Every time you're on it, there's a new vista there, a new caste of light back that way, a new look to the vegetation along that ridge.

And as you get older and move from the backseat to up front, you get more and more curious about all those vistas, overlooks, trails, trees, and so much more that are the Blue Ridge Parkway. You want to know more about that valley down there, about the wildflowers along the roadside, about where you might stop for a meal that's a little beyond a picnic.

That's where my longtime friend, colleague, and guide Leonard Adkins comes in. Leonard, who has walked these mountains like no one else, also simply cannot get enough of them. His sense of wonder, not just about every mile of the roadway, but about every inch of trail, every bloom and blossom, every birdcall and animal track, is unequalled.

In fact, open the book in your hands to just about any page. Look at the breakdown of every single trail that has any connection to the parkway. Look at those distance numbers. Not tenths of miles even, but often *hundredths*. And within those tiny distances, take a look at what Leonard looks at as he goes—the rhododendron tunnel, the 27-step climb, the rock facing, the 60-foot falls.

Equally marvelous is that he takes the same detailed, painstaking approach to all aspects of the parkway and its environs. He provides a bloom calendar, an elevation-change chart for cyclists, and a complete guide to campsites, not to mention information and insight on every overlook on the roadway.

A guidebook is a great thing to have for any undertaking. *The definitive guidebook* is really another thing altogether. And anyone setting out on a parkway excursion equipped with Leonard Adkins's *Hiking and Traveling the Blue Ridge Parkway: The Only Parkway Guide You Will Ever Need, including GPS, Detailed Maps, and More* is in possession of that entity.

Please enjoy and savor it. And pass along some of the wonderful details to those in the backseat.

J. Richard Wells
President Emeritus, FRIENDS of the Blue Ridge Parkway

ABBREVIATIONS

AT	Appalachian Trail
BRP	Blue Ridge Parkway
FS	Forest Service
FSR	Forest Service road (usually unpaved)
MST	Mountains-to-Sea Trail
NC RT	Roadway in North Carolina
VA RT	Roadway in Virginia
US RT	Branch of federal highway system

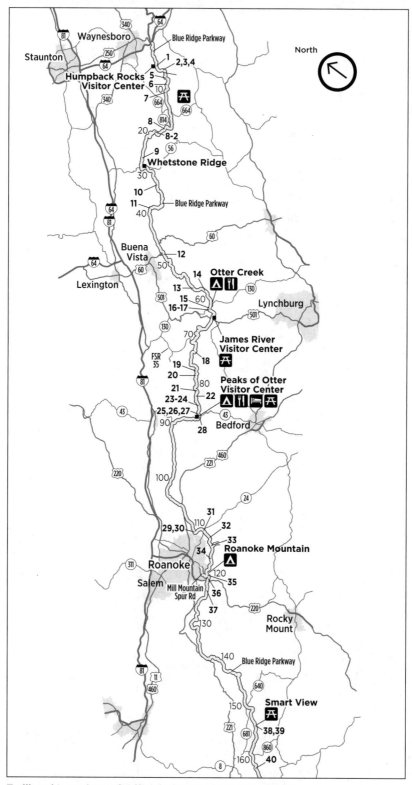

Trailhead Locations of Official Blue Ridge Parkway Trails

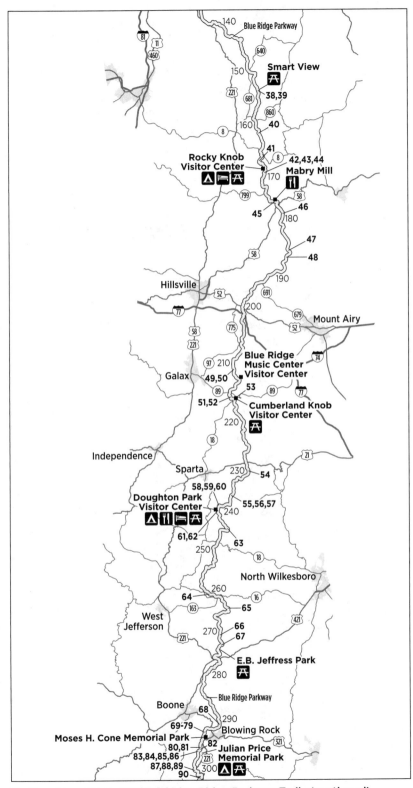

Trailhead Locations of Official Blue Ridge Parkway Trails (continued)

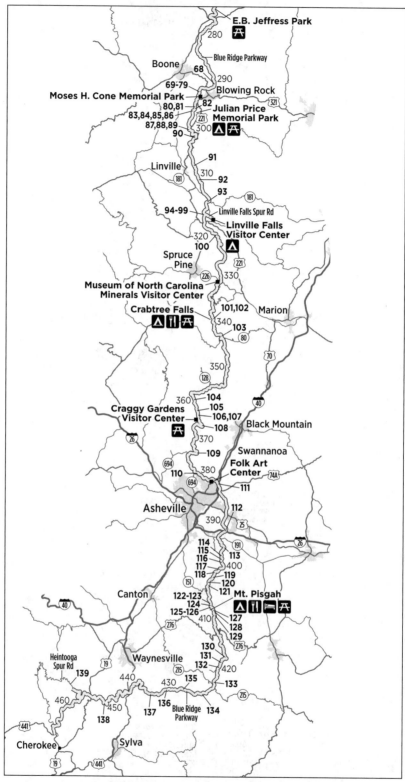

Trailhead Locations of Official Blue Ridge Parkway Trails (continued)

1.
Introduction

What is it about these Blue Ridge Mountains that continues to draw me to them time after time and year after year? I have now hiked their full length, from northern Georgia to central Pennsylvania, five times. I have driven each mile of the Skyline Drive and the Blue Ridge Parkway (BRP) numerous times. Yet, after each excursion to the Blue Ridge, I find the yearning to return stronger than before.

Maybe it is the sense of discovery I feel each time I venture into the mountains. The place names alone are a constant source of enticement and entertainment. How can I resist not trying to find out what happens in Bear Wallow Gap or what Rough Butt Bald really looks like? Will Graveyard Fields be as spooky as it sounds? Will tears come to my eyes when I walk over Onion Mountain? What the heck is The Lump? Does a rock castle actually exist in the gorge, and does anyone maintain the Craggy Gardens?

The idea of walking all of the trails of the parkway occurred to me while I was on one of these small, personal quests. Wanting to understand the geology of the mountains, I was on the Greenstone Self-Guiding Trail (BRP mile 8.8) trying to concentrate on the information presented on the trail signs. Yes, I was gaining knowledge on the origins of the mountains, but I was also being thrilled by the beauty of the surroundings. The bright sunshine, filtering through the leaf canopy of the oak and hickory trees, danced about to create varying shadows on the underbrush of mountain laurel and rhododendron. Warm air rising from the hazy green of the Shenandoah Valley wrapped around my skin like a welcomed shawl against the coolness of an early spring day. A couple of wildflowers were just beginning to break through the coarse, rocky soil next to the trail, adding a dash of color to the brown and gray forest floor.

If I could derive such pleasure from walking just one little .2-mile trail, how much more would I enjoy and get to know these mountains if I walked all of the trails on the parkway?

After more than eight months of hiking and measuring all of these pathways and spending a full year writing about them, the first-ever

Along the Greenstone Self-Guiding Trail.

guide to the trails of the parkway, *Walking the Blue Ridge*, was published by the University of North Carolina Press. I have returned to the parkway time and time again in the following years to keep the information up-to-date; the book you are holding in your hands is the newest edition of that original guidebook. Despite the appearance of competing books that provide only selected hikes or trails, *Hiking and Traveling the Blue Ridge Parkway* remains the most comprehensive and useful guide available.

The Blue Ridge Parkway, administered by the U.S. National Park Service, is 469.1 miles long. There are more than 100 park service trails along the parkway and dozens of U.S. Forest Service and state park pathways, along with those on municipal and private-property lands (on which the public is invited), that come in close contact—in other words, ample opportunities to explore, enjoy, and experience the mountains.

The park service has done an excellent job in making the Blue Ridge accessible to everyone, even the most casual of walkers. A large number of the trails are easy or moderately easy to walk. Many are self-guiding trails on which much information can be learned about the natural history of the Blue Ridge Mountains.

For those inclined to put forth a little more effort, the rewards are greater. Parkway trails will bring you along spiny ridgelines to views of verdant isolated valleys or out to soaring mountain peaks covered in the dark green growth of spruce, firs, and mountain laurel. Other trails can lead you through tunnels of rhododendron to end at rushing waterfalls tumbling over steep, precipitous mountainsides. Still others will deliver you onto gentle, rolling plateaus of open fields and meadows, where you may revel in warm sunshine and cool mountain breezes.

The parkway can be a lesson in human history, too. The ridges and valleys of the Blue Ridge Mountains were inhabited when the park service began to obtain land for the parkway. The (somewhat idealized) way of life of the mountain populace, their daily chores, and their hopes and aspirations may be discovered and studied by following some parkway trails to farms and outdoor exhibits restored or reconstructed by the park service. Even on trails secluded and far removed from where you would expect someone to have lived, you may stumble upon the foundation of a house or cabin no longer in existence or a crumbling stone wall once used to contain livestock. Pay attention when hiking; you might be walking through an old fruit orchard or by someone's long-abandoned flower garden.

Also, be willing to visit a trail more than once, and don't limit your excursions to just the warmer months. A trail walked in the spring will certainly look different in the fall. The cooler temperatures of winter will keep you from sweating as you huff and puff up a steep hill, and the absence of insects will be most welcomed. I had walked trails in the Peaks of Otter area so many times that I assumed I had seen everything they had to offer. But one winter afternoon, after a light snow had fallen, I came upon the tracks of a gray fox. Excited, I followed the small paw prints and caught a glimpse of the fox dashing across an open meadow above the Johnson Farm.

Another excellent way to enjoy your visit on the parkway is to take advantage of the interpretive programs offered by the park service. During the heaviest tourist months, park rangers (and knowledgeable volunteers) conduct guided walks on the parkway trails, focusing on a myriad of subjects ranging from endangered plants to old-time methods of farming. Campfire programs are also presented on an irregular basis at the campgrounds. I have been awestruck by stunning slide shows highlighting the beauty of the parkway, enjoyed concerts of mountain music on lap dulcimers and Autoharps, and been amused by the antics of a ranger dressed as an aged mountain woman imparting her knowledge of local medicinal plants.

Since that day a number of years ago when I stood on the Greenstone Self-Guiding Trail, I have walked all of the trails of the Blue Ridge Parkway (and was married on the Abbot Lake Trail at the Peaks of Otter!). It is my sincere hope that this guidebook will entice you to lace up those comfortable old walking shoes of yours, put one foot in front of the other, and begin your own love affair with the mountains by walking the Blue Ridge. Happy Trails!

A Short History of the Blue Ridge Mountains and the Parkway

At various times through the ages, the area now known as the Blue Ridge Mountains, stretching from northern Georgia to central Pennsylvania, has risen to great heights from the sea or has sunk to become the floor of a vast ancient ocean. For millions of years, along with the rest of the North American continent, the land has been alternately subjected to the effects of the movements of the earth's crustal plates, rising and falling seas, erosion from wind and water, and advancing and receding glaciers.

Each time the crustal plates collided, North America would take on a new face. Giant land masses grinding into each other would cause the earth's surface to break, crack, and fold upward, creating mountains. At the same time, large slabs of the lower portion of the crust were sliding underneath one another, raising the surface even higher.

About 200 million years ago, the plates began to split and drift apart, forming the Atlantic Ocean. Several theories maintain that, at that time, the Blue Ridge may have been as rugged and tall as the Rocky Mountains. What happened to create the Blue Ridge Mountains we see today? Erosion by wind and water has been wearing away these mountains bit by bit. Rock that was once part of a high, lofty peak has been washed down the mountainside and swept away in a spring thaw, violent summer thunderstorm, or gentle fall rain. The tiny particles of the mountains may be deposited in the valleys, move on to create the rich soil of the Piedmont, or even be carried out to sea. Some of the sand particles a child uses to build a sand castle on Virginia Beach may have once been part of a rock outcropping on the crest of the Blue Ridge.

Glaciers have also played an important role in the creation of the present-day landscape. Scientific theories suggest that as the great sheets of ice advanced from the north, they forced many plants to migrate southward. The Ice Age's cooler temperatures allowed northern trees, such as birch, beech, fir, and spruce, to begin to compete with, and even gain a foothold against, the traditional southern hardwoods like oak, poplar, and hickory. Once the glaciers began to recede and warmer air returned, most of the northern plants died out, unable to tolerate a southern climate. However, the cool temperatures on the higher peaks and ridgelines of the southern Blue Ridge have allowed many of these trees to remain and prosper, cut off from their relatives several hundred miles to the north.

No studies have established exactly when the first occupants arrived in the Blue Ridge Mountains. Archaeological evidence does show that the mountains were inhabited at least 10,000 years ago. These first Appalachians were hunters and nomads, gathering fruits and nuts during the warmer months only to retreat to the valleys and lowlands with the return of fall and winter. Not much else is known about these archaic Indians.

The Catawba, Algonquin, Iroquois, Shawnee, Delaware, and Cherokee Indians were all living in, or making use of, the Blue Ridge Mountains when European explorers first arrived in the New World. The Cherokee had large villages in northern Georgia and eastern Tennessee, but most of the tribes used the mountains as a rich and diverse hunting ground, taking advantage of the tremendous numbers of elk, deer, and buffalo.

Traveling southward from Pennsylvania or westward from the coast of North Carolina, the first European settlers began arriving in the 1700s. Their numbers increased after the Revolutionary War, and soon small communities were established throughout the mountains. These settlers and communities became proficient in the skills of self-sufficiency but did trade with urban centers to the east.

Owing to the rugged terrain, modern transportation methods developed slowly in the Southern Appalachians. Even as late as the 1920s and 1930s, most roadways were little more than narrow, rutted, hand-built dirt paths. Melting winter snows and spring rains would turn them into quagmires that could be best traversed on horseback or by oxcart.

In 1933, President Franklin Roosevelt made an inspection tour of the first Civilian Conservation Corps camp to be established in Virginia. The corps was helping to build the Skyline Drive and other facilities in Shenandoah National Park. Roosevelt not only enjoyed the beauty of the park but was pleased with the progress and potential of the Skyline Drive. A U.S. senator from Virginia, Harry F. Byrd, suggested to the president that a scenic highway be built linking Shenandoah National Park with the Great Smoky Mountains National Park in North Carolina and Tennessee.

(History does not record if Senator Byrd was the originator of the idea for the parkway. There were similar propositions at the same time, such as the Eastern National Park-to-Park Highway initiative that proposed to link Mammoth Cave, Great Smoky, and Shenandoah National Parks, along with other park service areas, via federal highways. Possibly the distinction should go to Colonel Joseph Hyde Pratt, whose construction of a "Crest of the Blue Ridge Highway" was halted by the outbreak of World War I.)

Roosevelt, who liked the idea that a parkway would bring immediate jobs and encourage future tourism, approved the parkway. After much arguing and maneuvering by the politicians of Virginia, North Carolina, and Tennessee (who realized its economic benefits), construction of the Blue Ridge Parkway began on September 11, 1935. Congress placed the parkway under the jurisdiction of the National Park Service in 1936.

The parkway was, of course, built in bits and pieces. The first portion was built near the North Carolina/Virginia border. Other stretches were added as the park service was able to obtain the necessary rights-of-way. In addition, scores of rivers and creeks had to be bridged and more than 20 tunnels blasted through the mountainsides.

With the construction of the Linn Cove Viaduct on the side of Grandfather Mountain and another small portion of roadway, the task was accomplished. On September 11, 1987, a gala ceremony on the viaduct officially declared the completion of the 469-mile Blue Ridge Parkway, 52 years after the project was started. Its design and engineering qualities have earned it honors from the American Society of Landscape Architects and the American Society of Civil Engineers.

According to U.S. National Park Service statistics, the parkway receives more visitors than any other unit of the park system.

How to Use This Book

More than just a guide to the trails of the parkway, this book does what no other BRP guide does. It provides you with everything you need for a visit to the parkway. There are details about what you will see at every overlook and other sites along the way (and how low a tunnel is if you are driving an RV); where to dine, lodge, shop, obtain water, or use a restroom; worthwhile side trips to interesting cities and towns and natural and cultural attractions off the BRP; where you may camp in a developed campground or on your own at a backcountry site; and specific locations where you may easily study wildflowers. In addition, it covers every trail along the parkway—not just "official" BRP trails, but also forest service, state park, municipal, and private property (open to the public) pathways. Often you will read in other guidebooks that the author has not included particular trails because they are not the kind of routes that the author feels will appeal to the average person. That is not the case with this book, as you are the best judge of what kind of experience you would like to have. In other words, if it is a trail and it comes in contact with the parkway, it is in this book; thus you can become the master of your own outdoor adventure.

The overlooks, attractions, and trails are presented in the order in which they appear geographically on the parkway—by milepost, beginning with mile 0, where US RT 250 intersects the BRP a few miles east of Waynesboro, Virginia. Over the course of each BRP trail and some of the side trails, I give descriptions and directions by decimal mile point.

Although the parkway does meander in all directions, it can be considered to be generally aligned in a north-south configuration. Directions are given assuming you are traveling south on the parkway. Therefore, trails or roadways identified to the west will be on the right side of the parkway, and those listed to the east will be on the left side. Additionally, overlooks will have a northern and southern end corresponding to the general north-south alignment.

Elevations (in feet above sea level) at the overlooks have been provided for those of you who like to know how high you are. The elevations of campgrounds are approximate, as a site can have an elevation range of possibly 50 feet or more because of its spread-out nature.

The GPS coordinates mark either where you will park to begin a hike or the point where you would turn off the BRP to drive to a described location not on the parkway.

In order to record as accurately as possible the full lengths and mile points of the parkway trails and those forest service trails that have descriptions, I pushed a measuring wheel while I walked them.

You may note that my mileages differ slightly from some parkway mileages or distances mentioned in other sources. It is always hard to get different sources to agree on the exact distance. The park service may have measured a trail from a visitor center, a trail sign, or some other point. Other sources may have begun measuring a trail at a parking area or a contact station. My distances are accurate in that they begin at the point I say to start walking at mile point .0.

The *one way* length is how far you will walk to arrive either at a point reachable by automobile or at an intersection with another pathway.

On the *out-and-back* length you walk to your destination and then return by the same route. If there is only an out-and-back length and not a one-way length listed, it means the hike will not arrive at a point reachable by automobile or intersect with another pathway.

On a *circuit* hike you will take a circular route to return to your starting point, rewalking very little, if any, of the same trail or trails.

Ranging from pleasant, easy nature strolls of 2 minutes to challenging climbs of 5,000- and 6,000-foot peaks to multiday backpacking trips, the trails along the Blue Ridge Parkway make it possible for anyone to enjoy the beauty and pleasures of the Blue Ridge Mountains. To help you choose the trails appropriate for your interests and ability, I have given each walk one of the following grades of difficulty:

An *easy leg stretcher* is a very short walk that simply gets you out of the car to enjoy a view, learn a little bit of history, or observe some significant feature.

A walk rated *easy* will last no more than a few minutes and have little or no change in elevation.

A *moderately easy* walk is an extended easy one with slight changes in elevation. (With a little effort, all of the easy and moderately easy trails should be within range of anyone—even those who are not in the best of shape.)

A trail rated *moderate* has either a number of gradual changes in elevation or a few steep ascents and descents. Also, the trail will probably be longer than those of the previous ratings.

A *moderately strenuous* trail will involve quite a number of ups and downs on a rough and/or rocky pathway.

A *strenuous* hike should be undertaken only by those in good physical condition with experience in negotiating steep ascents and descents on rocky, and possibly dangerous, terrain.

Please remember these ratings are just general guidelines. Individual perceptions of trail difficulties vary widely from person to person. What may be moderate to you may be strenuous to someone else. Also, you may be feeling especially vigorous one day and walk a strenuous trail rather easily. Another day an easy trail could become an arduous journey requiring more effort than you had imagined. Do not let all of this deter you from enjoying the enchantment of wandering through the mountains. The more you walk and hike, the better you will be able to determine your own abilities and limitations.

Side trails—those that intersect the main trails discussed—are marked with an arrow (▶). Pathways designated handicapped accessible are marked with the ⅋ icon.

This guidebook does not cover just the "official" trails of the Blue Ridge Parkway. In order to present as many walking opportunities as possible, I have also provided information on forest service, state park, municipal, and private property (open to the public) trails that come into close contact with the parkway or any of its trails. The park service does not list any of the parkway trails by letter or number. In order to simplify the identification of these trails, I have assigned them numbers in brackets (for example, [BRP 1]). These numbers are relevant to this guidebook only and will not correspond to any outside resources or information. The forest service, however, does assign numbers to their trails (for example, [FS 161]). These numbers will match up with those on forest service maps and in most other national forest trail guides. Please note that as a general rule, forest service and other trails are not as well maintained as the parkway trails.

To give mile-point information on every nonparkway trail is, of course, impossible. Enough information is provided to allow you to decide whether or not you wish to walk a particular trail. Information on additional resources is included. You will note, however, that I do present mile-point information on a number of the forest service trails. These detailed descriptions are included because those pathways possess a high degree of scenic value, are exceptionally isolated or secluded, present possible campsite opportunities, or are just personal favorites.

As you drive, walk, and hike the parkway, please keep in mind that the world is not a static place. Trails may have been relocated, a bench or other landmark may have deteriorated or been removed, or flowers or other plants may no longer grow at a specific site. The loss of most of the parkway's hemlock trees, due to infestations of the hemlock woolly adelgid, is a prime example of the changes that can occur.

Because the administration of the parkway is greatly underfunded and understaffed (more than 65 positions—about a third of full staffing—have gone unfilled for many years), you may find that some facilities have been closed or not maintained in a long time. One of the most conspicuous results of this understaffing is that a number of the overlooks have become overgrown and no longer present the vistas they had been constructed to provide. Fortunately, outside organizations have stepped in to help.

FRIENDS of the Blue Ridge Parkway is an award-winning, nonprofit, volunteer organization dedicated to preserving and protecting the Blue Ridge Parkway. Among its many activities are the Viewshed Protection Program (saving the parkway views and protecting natural habitats), Interpretive Parkway Exhibits, Volunteers in Parks Program, Adopt-a-Trail Program, Parkway Environmental Awareness and Outreach Programs, Parkway Information and Public Education, Preservation Initiatives for Historic Sites and Structures, and Save the Hemlock Project. You are urged to participate in one of these programs or, at the least, to join the organization to help it financially.

> FRIENDS of the Blue Ridge Parkway, Inc.
> P.O. Box 20986
> Roanoke, Va. 24018
> 800-228-7275
> www.blueridgefriends.org

The Blue Ridge Parkway Foundation is a nonprofit supporting foundation of the Blue Ridge Parkway authorized to request and receive funds on behalf of the BRP. It provides private funding for specific programs and projects that further the preservation, protection, and enhancement of the parkway. (One of those projects was the excellent expansion of the Museum of North Carolina Minerals at BRP mile 330.9.) Its many programs include preservation of the parkway's scenic quality, historic preservation, capital project funding, wildlife management studies, watershed preservation and water quality enhancement, and education and outreach.

Blue Ridge Parkway Foundation
717 South Marshall Street, Suite 105 B
Winston-Salem, NC 27101
866-308-2773
www.brpfoundation.org

The Mountains-to-Sea Trail

The Mountains-to-Sea Trail (MST) is one of the most exciting trail projects currently under way in North America. The idea was originally proposed in 1977 by Howard N. Lee, secretary of the North Carolina Department of Natural Resources and Community Development. His concept was further developed with the aid of the Department of Natural Resources and Community Development, the North Carolina Trails Committee, and the North Carolina Trails Association. The result of this collaboration is a proposed route that will someday stretch approximately 1,000 miles from spruce- and fir-covered Clingman's Dome high atop the Great Smoky Mountains National Park to the rolling surf and white sand beach of Nags Head on the Outer Banks jutting into the Atlantic Ocean.

Aided by the provisions of the 1973 North Carolina Trails System Act and a publicly funded state trails coordinator, volunteer citizen task forces are gradually building new pathways to connect with existing trails. As a result of a 1979 agreement between the State of North Carolina and the U.S. government, much of the route will be passing through federal lands such as the Great Smoky Mountains National Park, the Nantahala National Forest, the Pisgah National Forest, the Croatan National Forest, and the Cape Hatteras National Seashore.

Many local governments and agencies are helping the trail by arranging routes through numerous state parks and, possibly, county and city parks. As this book went to press, almost 700 miles of the trail have been completed. Beginning at BRP mile 235.7, well in excess of 300 of those miles are within proximity of the BRP. In fact, portions of the parkway's paths, such as the Shut-In Trail and the Watkins Carriage Road, are now considered components of the MST.

Obviously, with so many miles of the MST near the parkway, it would take another full-sized book to describe the route. However, since the trail is such an exciting project and worthy of some of your hiking time, this book lists many of the places where the MST comes in contact with the parkway or where short access trails connect to the MST. Please note that the MST does come in contact with the parkway in a number of additional places, but they are not listed because there may be no safe or designated parking areas or the contact points are relatively close together. Do keep in mind that the MST is still in the development stage and that changes and reroutes may have taken place since this book went to press.

The Friends of the Mountains-to-Sea Trail publishes guidebooks to the pathway and provides a great deal of detailed information about the route on its website.

If you wish to obtain more information about the Mountains-to-Sea Trail or to aid its development, contact

> Friends of the Mountains-to-Sea Trail
> 112 S. Bount St.
> Raleigh, NC 27601
> www.ncmst.org

Advice and Precautions

Emergencies

After making a call to 911, you should report an emergency to the nearest ranger station (see Appendix A) or to the parkwatch number (800-727-5928 or 800-PARKWATCH). It is important to know your location (BRP mile) so rangers may respond as quickly as possible.

Water

If you are going to be hiking much more than an hour, you should bring along some water. It is not wise to assume that the crystal clear mountain streams, or even the springs, will be safe without being treated. Gone are the days when a hiker could drink from such sources with impunity. The increase in the numbers of people visiting the natural areas of North Carolina and Virginia has brought a corresponding increase in the appearance of giardia. This waterborne parasite has varying effects on the human body—some people never feel any effects, others experience slight discomfort and maybe a mild case of diarrhea, while others are incapacitated to the point of requiring hospitalization.

Water sources can also become tainted by viruses, bacteria, and other pollutants, such as runoff from roadways.

If you are only out for day hikes, you have nothing to worry about—just bring enough water with you. If you're going to be out overnight, though, it will be tough to carry all of the water you need. Most water sources you encounter can be made potable by boiling. However, only a water purifier can effectively remove man-made chemical pollutants. A great variety of lightweight backpacking purifiers are available, but some work better than others. Talk to backpacking friends or consult a trusted retail outdoors outfitter before deciding which purifier will be best for you.

You can help not add to the water problems by camping at least 100 feet away from any source. Bury human waste at least 400 to 500 feet away.

Snakes

With a wide variety and large number of snakes living in the Blue Ridge Mountains, encountering one is a possibility. Only two, the copperhead and the rattlesnake, are poisonous. It would be wise to learn how to identify them.

There are a number of things you can do to reduce the possibility of an encounter. Stay on the authorized pathways. Avoid rocky areas. Do not put your hands into places you can't see into. Step on a log first instead of just walking over the top of it. Walking with a group will also reduce the possibility of encountering snakes. If you are hiking alone and want to avoid an encounter, tap the ground in front of you with a stick in order to alert any snakes of your presence. They're just as reluctant as you are to have an altercation and, given enough warning, time, and room, will usually be gone long before you arrive.

Remember, the mountains are a snake's natural habitat. Please refrain from killing one; just walk around it, giving it a wide berth, and continue on your way.

Important: All snakebites contain bacteria; seek medical attention for any type of bite.

Black Bears

The Blue Ridge Mountains are also the home of a large number of black bears. The chance of seeing one or more, especially on the longer and more remote trails, is a very real possibility. The best time of day to catch a glimpse of a bear is early morning or early evening, but bears are also known to be roaming about throughout the day.

Seeing a bear in its natural surroundings is definitely an exciting experience. This experience, however, brings some responsibility to you. Although black bear attacks on humans are extremely rare, there are several things you can and should do to keep it this way. Remember that bears are wild animals and do not like to be approached at close range (if you must take a photograph, do so from quite a distance away). Do not try to feed a bear. Not only does this endanger you, it also endangers the bear. Once a bear becomes used to close human contact, it may begin wandering into campsites or housing developments looking for free handouts. This often results in the bear having to be destroyed by the authorities.

Insects

Warm weather brings no-see-ums, gnats, fleas, mosquitoes, deer flies, ticks, and more. You should bring repellent.

To protect yourself, you should try to stay away from overhanging underbrush where the ticks are most likely to be encountered. Some authorities go so far as suggesting that you tuck your pants into your socks or boots and consider wearing a long-sleeved shirt and a cap. After each outing, it would be wise to check yourself closely or, better yet, have someone else check you. Remember, the things you are looking for are rather small, and they may attach themselves to you in the most inconvenient and immodest places.

Plants

Poison ivy is prolific throughout the Blue Ridge Mountains. You should definitely learn how to identify it. Unfortunately, it appears in a number of different forms. The most common is a woody shrub of up to 2 feet high that will grow in large patches, often lining or overtaking pathways. Almost as likely, it will grow as a hairy, root-covered vine that clings to the trunk of a tree, climbing far up into the branches.

All parts of the poison ivy plant contain the poison. This is true even in winter when it looks as if the plant has died a long time ago. Appearing in the fall, the poison ivy's white berry is especially toxic to certain people.

Poison oak also grows in the mountains, but less frequently than poison ivy.

Stinging nettle will grow in large patches and encroach upon pathways that are not well maintained. Brushing up against the plants will give the tiny hairs an opportunity to scratch your legs and deposit a poison that will probably make you itch for the rest of the day. One bout with this plant will teach you to be on the lookout for it from then on.

Waterfalls

An amazing number of the injuries and deaths that happen in national parks occur around waterfalls. The accidents usually happen because someone is trying to climb up or down the falls, gets too close to an edge to get a better look or photograph, or just does not use caution—or common sense.

Sun

By now we have all heard of the dangerous effects of the sun. More and more doctors are suggesting that you apply a high-strength sun-block lotion whenever you will be outdoors for an extended period of time.

Proper Clothing and Equipment

Like any large mountain range, the Blue Ridge Mountains are susceptible to wild fluctuations in weather. Warm sunny days can become cold and rainy in just minutes. Additionally, don't be surprised if a pleasant spring or fall day changes quickly to one with sleet or snow. Hypothermia, one of the major causes of death for campers and hikers, is a condition in which the body loses heat faster that it can produce it. Amazingly, hypothermia often strikes at temperatures in the 50s and 60s simply because many people do not anticipate changes in the weather. Be prepared for these conditions by carrying raingear and an insulating layer of clothing in your daypack. Winter hiking, of course, means you need to carry several layers of insulating clothing. (Layering is a more effective means of keeping warm than wearing just one thick or bulky garment.)

In addition to raingear and extra layers of clothes, your daypack should contain a small first-aid kit, a flashlight, a knife, a space blanket, toilet paper, and some waterproof matches.

Also, if you're camping, be prepared for cool nights, even in the summer.

There is really no reason to invest in a pair of heavy-duty mountaineering-type boots in order to enjoy the benefits of walking in the Blue Ridge. Excluding those people who have ankle or foot problems, sturdy and comfortable running, walking, or tennis shoes should be adequate for most day hikes. Unless you are carrying an extremely heavy pack (which you should not do) lightweight hiking boots or shoes will suffice for overnight backpacking trips. To assure a proper fit, wear the socks you will be hiking in when shopping for new footwear. Before embarking upon any extended hike, be sure to break in new boots or shoes so as to avoid any discomfort or blisters. Applying moleskin (available at most pharmacies and outdoors outfitters) to any "hotspots" on your feet will go a long way in preventing blisters from developing.

Obviously it is not within the scope of this guidebook to be a backpacking or hiking "primer." A number of books are available if you feel the need for further information. Currently, two of the most complete books on the subject of outdoor travel are *Be Prepared: Hiking and Backpacking*, by Karen Berger, and *Hiking and Backpacking: Essential Skills, Equipment, and Safety*, by Victoria Steele Logue. *The Complete Walker IV*, by Colin Fletcher and Chip Rawlins, is not only informative but also makes for some very entertaining reading.

Blue Ridge Parkway Regulations

All of these regulations apply while you are within parkway boundaries. The regulations in the national forests are not quite as rigid, but the parkway's rules are wise guidelines to follow anywhere.

Speed Limit

The Blue Ridge Parkway is not an interstate. The speed limit is 45 miles per hour but may be lower in some marked areas.

Natural Features

All of the plants and animals within the boundary of the parkway are protected by law. Picking flowers or digging plants is prohibited. Berries, nuts, and fruits can be picked, but only for personal consumption, and then only a gallon a day.

Please do not deface any natural features such as rock facings or road cuts. You should contact a park ranger before engaging in any rock climbing activities; rock climbing is prohibited on road cuts.

Pets

All pets must be kept under physical control (caged, carried, or on a leash) at all times. Pets are not permitted in the parkway's public buildings and on some trails.

Weapons

A federal law that became effective in 2010 allows people who can legally possess firearms under applicable federal, state, and local laws to legally possess firearms while on parkway property. Hunters may use parkway lands to access adjacent game lands (a permit is required to transport any game); however, hunting on parkway property, the use and discharge of firearms, and the possession of other weapons and traps are prohibited. Federal law does prohibit firearms in certain facilities; those places are marked with signs at all public entrances. Check state regulations for Virginia or North Carolina to make certain of your compliance.

Camping

Parkway campgrounds are usually open from early May through October. Call 828-271-4779 for the most up-to-date information. See Appendix C for a listing of the campgrounds on the parkway.

Camping is permitted only in the designated campgrounds. Drinking water and restrooms are provided. Shower and laundry facilities are not available, except at Mount Pisgah Campground. (There are plans to provide showers in other campgrounds as funds become available.) There are no hookups, but each campground does have a sanitary dumping station.

There are three backcountry campsites within parkway boundaries —BRP miles 169, 241.1, and 296. Permits are required and can be obtained free of charge at ranger stations nearby. Except for these three places, camping is prohibited along all of the "official" parkway trails. You are usually permitted to camp along the forest service trails, and I alert you to this fact in the descriptions of these pathways.

Fires

Fires are permitted only in designated areas such as picnic areas and campgrounds, must not be left unattended, and are to be completely extinguished after use. The parkway superintendent may issue a no-fire rule during periods of high fire danger.

Wood for campfires may be gathered only if it is dead, lying on the ground, and within .25 mile of the campground. Cutting trees that are dead but still standing is prohibited.

Unattended Vehicles

If you must park on the shoulder of the parkway, make sure that you are completely off the road but no farther than 10 feet from the pavement. Use an overlook or parking area whenever possible.

The parkway is part of the real world; vandalism and theft do occur, so it is wise to leave your valuables at home. Place whatever valuables you do have out of sight and lock the car.

If you're going to leave your vehicle at an overlook or parking area overnight, it may be best to give a park ranger your vehicle's make and license number, the length of time and place you will be leaving it, and the name of each person in your party.

Swimming

Swimming is prohibited in parkway waters.

Fishing

You must possess a valid state fishing license in order to fish along the parkway. Local fishing regulations do apply, and some parkway waters may be closed from time to time. Contact the nearest parkway facility or the main parkway office (828-271-4779) to be sure which regulations are in effect at any given time.

2.
Rockfish Gap to the Roanoke River
Blue Ridge Parkway Miles 0–114.8

Beginning just a few miles east of Waynesboro, Virginia, the parkway winds back and forth between the eastern and western sides of a single, narrow ridgeline that makes up the Blue Ridge Mountains from BRP mile 0 to mile 114.8. Spur ridges, stretching like knobby-knuckled fingers, descend into the valleys. Many places provide points where you may view all of this from just one spot—the Blue Ridge extends north to south as you peer over the flat lands of eastern Virginia or turn your gaze to the west and focus on the distant Allegheny Mountains in West Virginia.

Dictated by the narrow topography, the trails of this section have only two choices as to where they may go. They either closely parallel the parkway, rising and descending according to the whims of the undulating ridgeline, or they plummet quickly from the crest of the mountains onto the edge of the Piedmont or the Shenandoah Valley.

Ninety percent of this section is bounded by the George Washington and Jefferson National Forest. Extensive trail systems join up with many of the parkway's trails, allowing you to work out quite a number of extended, overnight excursions. Backcountry camping is allowed almost anywhere in the national forests, but please be aware that these trails may not be as regularly maintained as the parkway trails.

Except for the parkway's first few miles, the national forests and the steep mountainsides have kept modern civilization's encroachment to a minimum. It is possible to walk many of the trails without encountering any signs of present day inhabitation. Even the views into the Piedmont and various valleys show that the bulk of human activity is currently concentrated in areas quite some distance from the parkway. Often trails (such as the White Rock Falls Trail, BRP mile 18.5) stay within a half mile of the parkway, yet most sounds of the roadway are blotted out by dense forest growth, an obstructing knob, or a briskly moving stream.

These mountains were inhabited at one time, however—not in the distant past, but just a relatively short time ago. Certain trails (like the Humpback Rocks and Mountain Trail, BRP mile 6) go past crumbling stone walls, while a number of others will deliver you to cabins and farms reconstructed by the park service, where you can participate in living history demonstrations.

Not forgetting the natural world, the park service has provided self-guiding trails (BRP miles 8.8, 63.6, and 85.9), which give detailed but easily understood information on the natural history of the central Blue Ridge Mountains.

Mile 0. Rockfish Gap. US RT 250 and I-64 (1,909 feet)

Shenandoah National Park is located to the north of the Blue Ridge Parkway. The Skyline Drive, the main roadway through the park, joins the BRP here in Rockfish Gap. A number of guidebooks, including one of my own, *50 Hikes in Northern Virginia*, detail the vast hiking possibilities within the park.

A tourist information center is located just off the BRP. Waynesboro, 4 miles west, has complete services and a strong art presence with the P. Buckley Moss Museum and Shenandoah Arts Center. Charlottesville, 16 miles east, is home to the University of Virginia, Thomas Jefferson's Monticello, and the 20-mile Rivanna Trail, which encircles the city, passing through urban and natural areas.

Mile 0. Appalachian Trail (N 38°01.864 W 78°51.470). See Chapter 3.

Approximately 100 miles of the more than 2,000-mile Appalachian National Scenic Trail parallel the Blue Ridge Parkway. See Chapter 3 for details.

Mile 0.2. Afton Overlook (1,898 feet)

View of the small town of Afton, where VA 151 follows what was once a stage coach route of the 1800s.

Mile 1.5. Rockfish Valley Overlook (2,148 feet)

Millions of years ago, the Rockfish River began west of the Blue Ridge and flowed through Rockfish Gap toward the Atlantic Ocean. At the same time, the Shenandoah River was cutting through Shenandoah Valley limestone and eventually "captured" the Rockfish River, drying out the land and creating what is known as a wind gap.

Mile 2.2. Access to VA RT 610

Mile 2.9. Shenandoah Valley Overlook (2,354 feet)
The valley is a part of the Great Valley that runs from Canada to Alabama and was a natural route for settlers traveling southward and westward.

Mile 4.4. Access to VA RT 610

Mile 5.9. Humpback Rocks Visitor Center (2,353 feet)

Natural and human history displays. Living history demonstrations presented on special occasions. Water, restrooms, and small gift shop.

♿ **Mile 5.9. Mountain Farm Trail [BRP 1]** (N 37°58.369 W 78°53.953) Map 1

> *Length: .5 mile, out-and-back*
> *Difficulty: easy*
> *Handicapped accessible: gravel with slight inclines*
> *Highly recommended*

The Mountain Farm Trail is an easy, self-guiding pathway that begins at the Humpback Rocks Visitor Center. The farm is a representative site made up of a collection of buildings relocated from farther south along the parkway that allows you to sample some of the colorful aspects of life on a mountain farm in the late 1800s. Signposts along the way explain the various structures (including log cabins, weasel-proof chicken houses, and gear loft) and farm tools (such as maul and frow, beatlin block, and ash hopper). A garden is planted for the growing season, and live demonstrations are presented during the spring, summer, and fall. Check at the visitor center for times and dates.

This walk presents a good overview and introduction to a certain class of inhabitants of the Blue Ridge Mountains.

Mile 6. Humpback Gap parking area (2,360 feet)
The meadow below the summit, now kept open by mowing, was known as Coiner's Deadening. When settlers first moved into the mountains, they had to plant crops as quickly as possible, so they would girdle the bark of trees, thereby killing (deadening) the trees and permitting sunlight to reach the garden area.

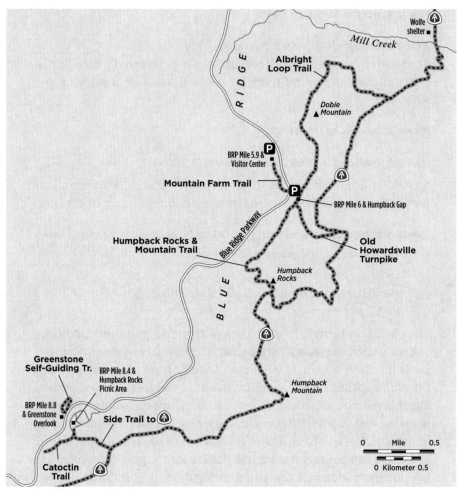

Map 1. Miles 5.9–8.8

Mile 6. Albright Loop Trail [BRP 2] (N 37°58.112 W 78°53.793) Map 1

*Length: 3.4 miles (3.8 miles with optional side trail to a viewpoint), circuit
Difficulty: moderate*

The Albright Loop Trail honors the memory of Dr. John S. Albright, a longtime volunteer editor of *The Appalachian Trail Guide: Central Virginia* and a member of the boards of the Appalachian Trail Conservancy and the Old Dominion Appalachian Trail Club. Encircling but never quite reaching the summit of Dobie Mountain, the trail, in some places, follows a former route of the Appalachian Trail, passing by an abundance of spring wildflowers. Although it does not have far-reaching vistas, the

The Mountain Farm Trail enables visitors to imagine life in the mountains around the late 1800s.

route can be a peaceful alternative to the throngs of people attracted to nearby Humpback Rocks [BRP 4] during nice weekends.

.0   Begin on the left side of the parking area by passing the Albright Loop Trail sign and ascending next to a few wild azalea bushes that will be blooming mid-spring.

.25   Arrive at the loop trail intersection and bear to the left, continuing to ascend, now on a narrower pathway.

.4   Note the large boulder balanced atop another rock formation. Since glaciers did not come this far south during the last Ice Age, it's somewhat of a mystery as to how this boulder came to rest here.

.65   After reaching a high point near the summit of Dobie Mountain, the pathway descends via switchbacks.

1.4   Bear right onto a nearly level woods road lined by small patches of mayapple and wild geranium.

2.0   Bear right to join and follow the white-blazed Appalachian Trail (see Chapter 3).

2.4   An optional side trail to the left leads 0.2 mile to a view of Glass Hollow.

3.2   Be alert! The Appalachian Trail continues to the left. Bear right and ascend along the Old Howardsville Turnpike. Built in the mid-1800s, this was an important carriage (toll) road that facilitated travel and trade from the Shenandoah Valley to Virginia's capitol, Richmond, many miles to the east.

3.4   Arrive back at the parking lot.

Mile 6. Appalachian Trail access via Old Howardsville Turnpike [BRP 3]
(N 37°58.112 W 78°53.793) Map 1. Also see Chapter 3.

Length: .2 mile, one way; .4 mile, out-and-back
Difficulty: moderately easy

Descending from the middle of the Humpback Rocks parking area, this route, which may or may not be signed, follows the bed of the Old Howardsville Turnpike for .2 mile to intersect the Appalachian Trail (left is northbound on the AT; right is southbound). This route enables you to complete a loop hike to Humpback Rocks of 4.1 miles by following the Old Howardsville Turnpike, the Appalachian Trail, and the Humpback Rocks and Mountain Trail [BRP 4].

Mile 6. Humpback Rocks and Mountain Trail [BRP 4]
(N 37°58.112 W 78°53.793) Map 1

Length: 3.75 miles, one way (plus .3 mile to reach Humpback Rocks
*   picnic area parking lot); 7.5 miles, out-and-back*
Difficulty: strenuous

A steep and rocky pathway climbs steadily for a view from Humpback Rocks and an even better view on the summit of Humpback Mountain. In addition to other views, the trail also passes a couple of mountain laurel thickets that, along with the azaleas, make for a colorful walk in late spring. In early spring, trillium may be abundant.

Humpback Rocks has been attracting visitors for generations; this is a very heavily used trail. Please stay on the designated pathway in order to prevent erosion and any further damage to the environment.

A blue-blazed side trail [BRP 5] gives access to the Humpback Rocks picnic area. You could have someone pick you up here if you don't want to walk back on the same path.

Some people prefer to walk out-and-back just to the Humpback Rocks, a hike of 2 miles.

.0   Begin an immediate ascent at the southern end of the parking lot, which is on the eastern side of the BRP.

.06   Here are good views overlooking the BRP and the Shenandoah Valley.

The view from Humpback Rocks makes the uphill climb worthwhile.

.15 Come to a bench and a final view over a meadow.

.2 Reach the ridgeline; continue to ascend at a more gradual rate. The fall flowers are particularly abundant here.

.5 Do not go left! To the left is the old trail—very steep, dangerous, and badly eroded. Please continue to the right on fairly level ground and let this land heal itself.

.55 Ascend on wooden steps.

.6 Begin a series of short switchbacks on a trail that is now steeper, rougher, and rockier.

.8 At a wonderful, old, double-trunked oak tree, the trail switches back and becomes even rockier and steeper.

.9 Intersection. To the left are Humpback Rocks and a commanding view of Shenandoah Valley (800 feet). Even though the rocks are marred by graffiti, this spot is still magnificent. After enjoying the rocks, return to the intersection and continue on the trail, joining the route of the white-blazed southbound Appalachian Trail.

1.1 Level out and pass through a mountain laurel thicket. Soon come to an old stone wall where there are good views from the rocks on the right side of the trail.

1.3 A large greenstone talus slope appears on the left; continue to ascend.

1.4 On top of the ridgeline, cross through an old stone wall and continue; good wintertime views into Rockfish River Valley.

1.7 Drop into, and ascend out of, a gap.

2.0 Arrive at the summit of Humpback Mountain, where there are good views of Rockfish Gap and Shenandoah National Park to the north, Shenandoah Valley to the west, and Rockfish River Valley to the east. Begin a gradual descent.

2.6 Note the old stone wall on the right.

3.0 The southward view from a rock ledge is of Wintergreen Ski Resort and Bald Mountain. Drop through mountain laurel.

3.2 Leave mountain laurel and drop more steeply.

3.75 Arrive at a trail junction and the end of the Humpback Rocks and Mountail Trail. The Appalachian Trail continues to the left for about 4 miles to arrive at the Three Ridges Overlook. To reach the Humpback Rocks picnic area parking lot, turn right onto the blue-blazed trail [BRP 5] for .3 mile.

Mile 8.4. Humpback Rocks picnic area (2,375 feet)

Water, restrooms. The azalea bushes burst forth in bloom in spring.

Mile 8.4. Blue-Blazed Side Trail to the Appalachian Trail from Humpback Rocks Picnic Area [BRP 5] (N 37°56.718 W 78°55.588) Map 1

See Catoctin Trail [BRP 6] for directions to the beginning of this trail.
Length: .3 mile, one way; .6 mile, out-and-back
Difficulty: moderate

This pathway goes through a mixed hardwood forest and passes by a fine example of the old "hogwall" stone fences used by farmers to keep their razorback pigs from wandering too far.

.0 Begin to the left of the Catoctin Trail [BRP 6] on the pathway identified by blue blazes and an Appalachian Trail symbol.

.1 Note how the builder of this stone wall incorporated the rock outcropping into the wall.

.26 Level out.

.3 Trail intersection joining the Appalachian Trail (see Chapter 3). To the left is the Humpback Gap parking lot (3.75 miles); to the right is the Three Ridges Overlook at BRP mile 13.1 (about 4 miles).

Mile 8.4. Catoctin Trail [BRP 6] (N 37°56.718 W 78°55.588) Map 1

Length: .4 mile, out-and-back
Difficulty: moderate

The Catoctin Trail is located at the farthest point in the Humpback Rocks picnic area parking lot. It may not be identified by a trail sign, but it is the obvious pathway that begins to the right of the blue-blazed Appalachian Trail access route [BRP 5]. This short trail is well worth the walk, for the payoff is a magnificent view into the Shenandoah Valley. A nice spot for a quiet, secluded picnic.

.0   Ascend slightly and cross small concrete bridge.

.13   Level out.

.2   Arrive at the rock outcropping overlook.

Mile 8.8. Greenstone Overlook (3,007 feet)

The view is of Big Levels, a large mountain mass that contains the St. Mary's Wilderness and Sherando Lake (see BRP mile 16). The village of Stuart's Draft is also visible.

Mile 8.8. Greenstone Self-Guiding Trail [BRP 7]

(N 37°56.836 W 78°55.676) Map 1

Length: .2 mile, circuit
Difficulty: moderately easy

Winding through an upland hardwood forest, the Greenstone Trail is a self-guiding circuit trail with signposts explaining the volcanic origins of the northern Blue Ridge Mountains. An easy pathway, this trail is one of the first you should walk. The information learned here will add greatly to your future walks and drives along the parkway.

.0   Start at the northern end of the parking lot and bear to the right.

.05   Passing by Virginia pine, mountain laurel, and rhododendron, drop down stone steps and continue to descend.

.1   Drop down again and begin to loop back.

.15   There are good views into the valley here. Begin to ascend on stone steps.

.2   Return to the parking lot.

Mile 9.2. Laurel Springs Gap (2,878 feet)

Laurel Springs is a tributary of the Rockfish River.

Mile 9.6. Dripping Rock parking area (2,878 feet)

The Appalachian Trail passes through the small parking lot, and the spring is a welcome sight to thirsty hikers.

Mile 9.6. Appalachian Trail (N 37°56.478 W 78°56.184). See Chapter 3.

Mile 10.4. Rockpoint Overlook (3,113 feet)

The view is of Torry Ridge and its rocky slopes.

Mile 10.7. Ravens Roost Overlook (3,200 feet)

An additional view of Torry Ridge. Picnic table.

Mile 11.7. Hickory Spring parking area (2,986 feet)

Several species of hickory trees grow in the forest around the parking area.

Mile 13.1. Three Ridges Overlook (2,697 feet)

The massif to the east is Three Ridges, whose slopes are traversed by the Appalachian Trail and whose summit is 3,900 feet above sea level. Picnic table.

Mile 13.1. Appalachian Trail (N 37°54.222 W 78°58.749). See Chapter 3.

Mile 13.7. Reids Gap (2,637 feet)

VA RT 664 with access to VA RT 814 and US RT 29.

Mile 13.7. Appalachian Trail and access to the trails of Three Ridges Wilderness, Crabtree Falls, and additional George Washington National Forest trails (N 37°54.090 W 78°59.131). See Chapter 3.

Trails of Wintergreen Resort, Blue Ridge Parkway Mile 13.7

Barely more than a mile to the east on VA RT 664 is Wintergreen, a four-season resort offering lodging, dining, skiing, snowboarding and snowtubing, golf, tennis, boating, biking, fishing, a spa, and more. Although the resort did displace several miles of the Appalachian Trail, it operates on a more environmentally friendly philosophy than many of its counterparts. Approximately 6,000 of its 11,000 acres have been set aside to be preserved in a natural state, never to be developed. A nonprofit organization, the Wintergreen Nature Foundation, has input into construction projects to help reduce the resort's impact on the natural world.

Wintergreen also sets itself apart from other resorts by having close to 30 miles of hiking trails that the public is permitted to explore and use. You do not have to be a resort guest or even report to anyone that you are taking advantage of the offer, but please remember to treat all of the land and property with respect so that this privilege will continue to be extended to everyone.

More information about the resort may be obtained from

Wintergreen Resort
P.O. Box 706
Wintergreen, VA 22958
434-325-2200
www.wintergreenresort.com

More information concerning the trails may be obtained from

The Wintergreen Nature Foundation
Route 1, Box 770
Roseland, VA 22967
434-325-8169
www.twnf.org

The following brief descriptions of the resort's trails, along with Map 2, will provide you with the information you need to decide which routes are suited to your tastes, fitness level, and time allotment. Portions of the first 12 trails (from Fortunes Ridge to Pond Hollow) make up what is known as the Perimeter Trail, which, along with short distances along two paved roads, provides a route of approximately 12 miles, taking in some of the resort's best sites and environments. Please be aware that a number of the trails are closed in winter.

Note: There are 4 additional resort trails not shown on Map 2—the .6-mile Pauls Creek, 1.7-mile Lower Shamokin Falls, .9-mile Stoney Creek Park, and .7-mile Allen Creek Nature Preserve trails—that are located on Wintergreen's property in the valley and many miles away from the parkway. All are easy to moderately easy hiking through gentle terrain.

Fortunes Ridge Trail Map 2

> *Length: 1.1 miles, one way; 2.2 miles, out-and-back*
> *Difficulty: moderately strenuous*
> *Accessed from Fortunes Ridge Drive, Laurel Ridge LoopTrail,*
>   *and Brimstone Trail*

After descending quickly along a cascading stream and passing a small waterfall, the pathway traverses a terrain of varying forest types, including lush mountain laurel bushes.

Brimstone Trail Map 2

> *Length: .8 mile, one way; 1.6 miles, out-and-back*
> *Difficulty: moderately strenuous*
> *Accessed from Fortunes Ridge Trail, Blackrock Drive,*
>   *The Plunge Trail, and Blackrock Trail*

Running along a rocky cliff that faces to the southwest, providing nice sunset views and that of Three Ridges Mountain, the Brimstone Trail is lined in places by fly poison and rock cap fern.

Blackrock Trail Map 2

> *Length: .8 mile, one way; 1.6 miles, out-and-back*
> *Difficulty: strenuous*
> *Accessed from Brimstone Trail, The Plunge Trail, Pedlars*
>   *Edge Drive, and Pedlars Edge Trail*

The Blackrock Trail runs along a southeast-facing mountainside that receives less rainfall than those slopes facing northwest. The reduced precipitation creates a dry, nutrient-poor soil. However, that doesn't mean this will be an unpleasant walk, as members of the heath family, such as blueberry, azalea, and mountain laurel, thrive in this environment.

Pedlars Edge Trail Map 2

> *Length: 1.6 miles, one way; 3.2 miles, out-and-back*
> *Difficulty: strenuous*
> *Accessed from Blackrock Trail, Blackrock Circle, Hemlock*
>   *Springs Trail, and Cedar Cliffs South Trail*

The trail gets its name from the geological formation known as pedlar, which was created close to 1 million years ago. With only one good view, that of Cedar Cliffs, the attraction here is the mixed hardwood forest and interesting rock patterns.

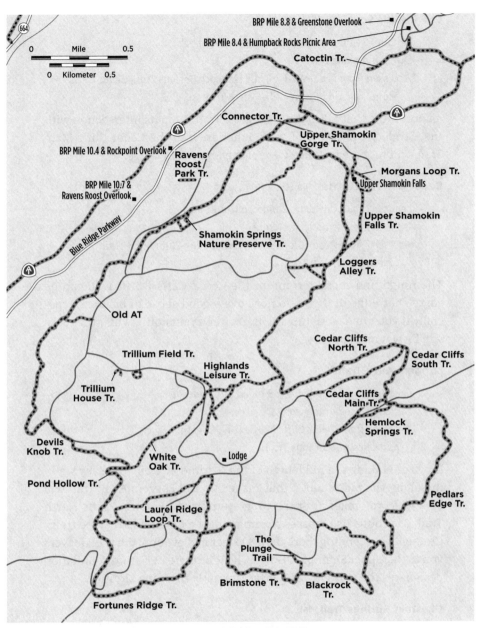

Map 2. Trails of Wintergreen Resort (miles 8.8-13.7)

Cedar Cliffs South Trail Map 2

Length: .2 mile, one way; .4 mile, out-and-back
Difficulty: moderate
Accessed from Pedlars Edge Trail, Hemlock Springs Trail, Cedar Cliffs
  Main Trail, and Cedar Cliffs North Trail

A short route that takes the "Perimeter Trail" from its intersection with the Hemlock Springs Trail to its junction with the Cedar Cliffs Main Trail, where there is a nice view of the Shamokin Gorge.

Cedar Cliffs North Trail Map 2

Length: 1 mile, one way; 2 miles, out-and-back
Difficulty: moderately strenuous
Accessed from Cedar Cliffs South Trail, Cedar Cliffs Main Trail,
  and Loggers Alley Trail

The rough and rocky terrain on the Cedar Cliffs North Trail can be somewhat difficult if you do not have a good sense of balance, especially if you are negotiating the trail after a rainstorm, when the rocks will be wet and slippery.

Loggers Alley Trail Map 2

Length: 1.5 miles, one way; 3 miles, out-and-back
Difficulty: moderately easy
Accessed from Cedar Cliffs North Trail, Chestnut Place,
  and Chestnut Springs Trail

If you are hiking the full length of the "Perimeter Trail," the easy walking along the old roadbed that makes up the Loggers Alley Trail will be a welcome relief after the rough terrain of the Cedar Cliffs North Trail. The route also crosses a number of the downhill ski slope trails. Gradually descending more than 800 feet in elevation, the trail delivers you to the Upper Shamokin Gorge. The Wintergreen Nature Foundation designates the pathway as "perfect for early morning birding."

Chestnut Springs Trail Map 2

Length: 1.1 miles, one way; 2.2 miles, out-and-back
Difficulty: moderate
Accessed from Chestnut Place, Loggers Alley Trail, Shamokin Springs
  Trail Road, and Upper Shamokin Gorge Trail

The streams along the Chestnut Stream Trail provide the needed moisture for an abundance of wildflowers, including violets, bloodroot, and wild ginger. The route connects with the Upper Shamokin Gorge Trail, a recommended route.

Upper Shamokin Gorge Trail Map 2

> *Length: .8 mile, one way; 1.6 miles, out-and-back*
> *Difficulty: strenuous*
> *Recommended*
> *Accessed from Chestnut Springs Trail, Upper Shamokin Falls Trail,*
> *   and the Old Appalachian Trail*

Following and crossing the headwaters of Stony Creek, the Upper Shamokin Gorge Trail is possibly the most strenuous trail at Wintergreen. It is also one of the most interesting, as the route is within the narrow confines of the gorge where the stream sometimes disappears but can still be heard flowing under the rocks.

Old Appalachian Trail Map 2

> *Length: 3.3 miles one way; 6.6 miles, out-and-back*
> *Difficulty: moderately strenuous*
> *Accessed from Upper Shamokin Gorge Trail, the Appalachian Trail*
> *   (see Chapter 3, mile 8.4), Shamokin Springs Nature Preserve Trail,*
> *   Laurel Springs Drive, Hemlock Lane, and Cedar Drive*

In 1983, Wintergreen sold 2,700 acres of land to the Appalachian Trail Conference (now Conservancy), and volunteers rerouted the Appalachian Trail away from resort property. The resort continues to keep the old route open, so you can still hike the rough and rocky section that newer AT hikers no longer traverse. Spring wildflowers and an occasional view make the effort worthwhile.

Devils Knob Trail Map 2

> *Length: .6 mile, one way; 1.2 miles, out-and-back*
> *Difficulty: moderate*
> *Accessed from Devils Knob Loop Road, White Oak Trail,*
> *   and Pond Hollow Trail*

Traversing Wintergreen's highest elevations, the rocky Devils Knob Trail has good views of Fortunes Ridge and Pond Hollow. Another good bird-watching route, according to the Wintergreen Nature Foundation.

Pond Hollow Trail Map 2

Length: 1 mile, one way; 2 miles, out-and-back
Difficulty: strenuous
Accessed from Devils Knob Trail, Wintergreen Drive, Fortunes Ridge
Drive, and Fortunes Ridge Trail

Do not underestimate the difficulty of the Pond Hollow Trail, which is constructed atop a geological fault line. The boulders that you need to negotiate mark the actual fault.

Laurel Ridge Loop Trail Map 2

Length: 1.6 miles, circuit
Difficulty: moderately strenuous
Accessed from the main parking areas just below the Mountain Inn on
Wintergreen Drive, Pond Hollow Trail, and Fortunes Ridge Trail

One of the resort's few self-contained circuit hikes, the loop trail passes through a rich mixed hardwood forest, with some steep ups and downs.

The Plunge Trail Map 2

Length: .3 mile, one way; .6 mile, out-and-back
Difficulty: moderately strenuous
Highly recommended
Accessed from Blackrock Circle, Brimstone Trail, and Blackrock Trail

Although it is one of the resort's shortest, steepest, and rockiest trails, The Plunge is highly recommend for its spectacular view of the surrounding topography and into Rockfish Valley. On clear days it is sometimes possible to make out the buildings of Lynchburg, about 45 miles away!

Hemlock Springs Trail Map 2

Length: .8 mile, circuit
Difficulty: moderately strenuous
Accessed from Grassy Ridge Drive, Pedlars Edge Trail,
and Cedar Cliffs South Trail

A route that traverses a mountain stream's headwaters, the trail is known for its abundance of lady's slipper flowers. (As beautiful as they are, please do not pick or try to harvest them. Picked flowers will only last a few hours at most, and those that are transplanted can only survive if the soil you plant them in has the same mix of fungi as that from which they came.)

Cedar Cliffs Main Trail Map 2

Length: .7 mile, one way; 1.4 miles, out-and-back
Difficulty: moderate
Accessed from Grassy Ridge Road, Cedar Cliffs South Trail,
*   and Cedar Cliffs North Trail*

One of the few resort trails that stays atop a ridge for its full length, the route terminates at a good view of the Shamokin Gorge.

Highlands Leisure Trail Map 2

Length: .5 mile, one way; 1 mile, out-and-back, with intersections onto
*   other short access trails*
Difficulty: moderately easy
Accessed from Blue Ridge Drive, Wintergreen Drive, Loggers Alley Trail,
*   and the roads above the Mountain Inn*

Constructed primarily to provide foot access from one of the main lodging areas to the Mountain Inn and skiing facilities, the trail passes through forestlands with views of the slopes.

Upper Shamokin Falls Trail Map 2

Length: .4 mile, one way; .8 mile, out-and-back
Difficulty: moderate
Highly recommended
Accessed from Laurel Springs Drive, Morgans Loop Trail, Loggers Alley
*   Trail, and Upper Shamokin Gorge Trail*

Do not miss this one. Without a doubt, one of the resort's loveliest and most interesting routes, as the trail parallels Stony Creek, where short side trails provide access to the stream as it descends the mountain in a series of pretty cascades. The moist soil is crowded with jack-in-the-pulpit and jewelweed. Be careful of the stinging nettle, which also likes this environment.

Ravens Roost Park Trail Map 2

Length: less than .2 mile, out-and-back
Difficulty: easy
Recommended
Accessed from Valley View Lane

It's only a short hike to reach Upper Shamokin Falls in Wintergreen Resort.

Barely long enough to even be called a "leg stretcher," the short route leads to a soaring vista of the Shenandoah Valley and is a great spot to be during the fall hawk migration, when thousands of raptors zip along the crest of the Blue Ridge Mountains.

Shamokin Springs Nature Preserve Trail Map 2

>*Length: .3 mile, circuit*
>*Difficulty: easy*
>*Recommended*
>*Accessed from Blue Ridge Drive, Shamokin Springs Trail Road,*
>   *and Old Appalachian Trail*

This preserve is an example of the role that the Wintergreen Nature Foundation has at the resort. The foundation successfully lobbied to save it from planned housing developments—and rightly so. This is one of the most diverse plots in the resort, as attested to by a brochure (available at the trailhead) that lists more than 120 species of plants existing within these 13 acres.

Trillium House Trail Map 2

>*Length: .1 mile, circuit*
>*Difficulty: easy*
>*Accessed from the Wintergreen Nature Foundation's Trillium House*
>   *headquarters off Wintergreen Drive*

You can learn much from this short loop whose interpretive signs provide information about the flora along the trail.

Trillium Field Trail Map 2

>*Length: .1 mile, circuit*
>*Difficulty: easy*
>*Highly recommended*
>*Accessed from Wintergreen Drive*

Come here in spring to be amazed by the abundance and variety of wildflowers, especially trillium. The profusion is even more amazing when you realize that it takes a trillium plant at least 6 years to blossom from the time its seed germinates in the ground.

Mile 15.4. Love Gap (2,597 feet)

Mile 16. VA RT 814 (N 37°52.974 W 79°01.233)

VA RT 814 descends to the west of the parkway to enter George Washington National Forest. The national forest around Sherando Lake and the St. Mary's Wilderness presents many opportunities for circuit hikes and, since camping is allowed throughout the area, the option for excursions of several days in length.

The trails are characterized by long, narrow ridgelines for ease of walking and good views, steep ascents and descents for challenging hiking, old mining areas to explore, and plenty of water to quench a hard-working walker's thirst. This is a highly recommended area in which to spend some time. See the narratives at BRP mile 22 for descriptions of these trails.

More information concerning Sherando Lake and St. Mary's Wilderness may be obtained by contacting

> Glenwood/Pedlar Ranger Districts
> 27 Ranger Lane
> Natural Bridge Station, VA 24579
> 540-291-2188

Mile 17.6. Priest Overlook (2,695 feet)

Straight across from the overlook is The Priest, whose slopes and summit (4,056 feet) are crossed by the Appalachian Trail. The mountain to the left is Three Ridges. In between the two is the Tye River Valley. Picnic table.

Mile 17.6. The Priest Overlook Trail [BRP 8]
(N 37°53.517 W 79°01.959) Map 3

> *Length: 600 feet, out-and-back*
> *Difficulty: easy leg stretcher*

A very short path begins on the south end of the parking lot, crosses a small field, and in 300 feet arrives at a bench overlooking (depending on recent maintenance) Torry Ridge. This leg stretcher is so short that no one should miss it. At the very least you can always boast to your friends that you actually got out of your automobile to walk one of the trails of the BRP.

Mile 18.5. White Rock Gap parking area (2,549 feet)

The area is named for the abundance of quartz, a "white" rock.

Mile 18.5. White Rock Falls Trail [BRP 8-2]

(N 37°53.782 W 79°02.708) Map 3

Length: 2.7 miles, one way; 5.4 miles, out-and-back
Difficulty: moderate

The first portion of the hike is an easy, gently sloping pathway to a cool, shaded spot beside a small stream. The pathway, built by the Youth Conservation Corps in 1979, then becomes rockier and steeper. However, once it reaches the falls, it ascends at a gradual rate. Parking for the trailhead is on the west side of the BRP in White Rock Gap.

A pleasant day hike of 5 miles could be accomplished by combining the White Rock Falls Trail with the Slacks Overlook Trail [FS 480A]. Also, the falls could be approached from the other end—Slacks Overlook, mile 20—in a hike of about 2 miles out-and-back.

.0   Cross the parkway from the White Rock Gap parking area and begin by descending gradually on the pathway.

.15   Cross 3 small footbridges and notice the jumble of large boulders in the valley below.

.3   Pass old, crumbling stone walls.

.5   The pathway joins an old roadbed.

.65   Be alert! The trail makes an abrupt turn to the right, off of the old road, and ascends gradually through mountain laurel and pine. Sassafras is particularly abundant.

.8   Continue with slight ups and downs.

1.2   Cross a small stream (nice spot for a rest break) and parallel it by ascending very steeply. Be sure to watch for the beginning of some switchbacks.

1.4   End of switchbacks and ascend more steeply along a ravine.

1.5   Pass under large boulders and walk below stone outcropping.

1.6   Trail intersection. Three hundred feet to the right along the rock wall leads to White Rock Falls—a most magical place. The sun, beaming through the mountain laurel, dances on the steep walls as the water cascades downward 30 to 40 feet. After stopping at this enjoyable spot, return to the intersection and continue to ascend.

1.8   Switch back to the right.

1.9   Reach the ridgeline and descend.

2.0   The rocks to the right afford good valley views. Cross a small footbridge and ascend gradually.

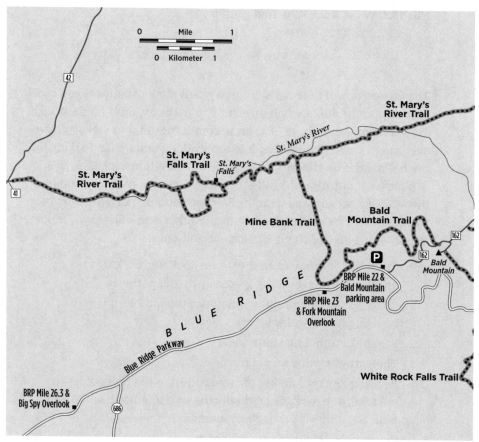

Map 3. Miles 13.7–26.3

2.2 Be alert! The trail does not enter the grove of trees to the left, no matter how inviting it looks; rather, the trail makes an abrupt right, crosses the creek, and ascends.

2.3 Cross the creek on a footbridge.

2.7 Arrive at BRP. The Slacks Overlook is 150 feet to the left (BRP mile 20).

Mile 18.5. The White Rock Gap Trail [FS 480]
(N 37°53.782 W 79°02.708) Map 3

> *Length: 2.5 miles, one way; 5 miles, out-and-back*
> *Difficulty: moderate*

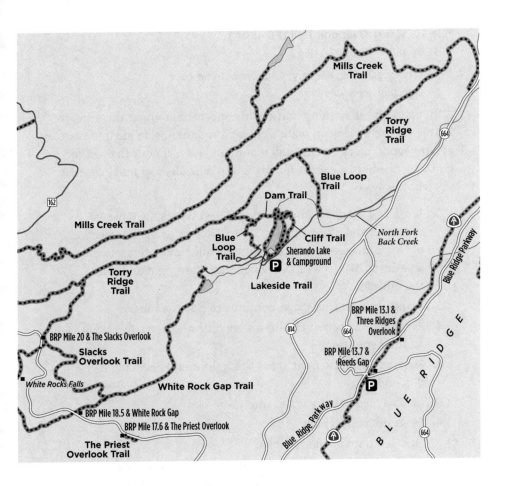

This trail descends from the western side of the BRP for .5 mile to an intersection with the Slacks Overlook Trail [FS 480a] (BRP mile 20). It continues another 2 miles to the Sherando Lake Recreation Area.

Mile 19. 20 Minute Cliff Overlook (2,715 feet)

A plaque at the overlook explains that a rock below it served the people who lived in the valley below. They knew that dusk would arrive in the valley 20 minutes after sunlight hit the cliff. Picnic table.

Mile 20. The Slacks Overlook (2,800 feet)

The view looks onto ridgelines descending to the valley that contains the forest service's Sherando Lake.

Mile 20. Slacks Overlook Trail [FS 480A]

(N 37°54.480 W 79°03.051) Map 3

> *Length: 2.2 miles, one way; 4.4 miles, out-and-back*
> *Difficulty: moderate*

Although there is nothing particularly spectacular about this trail, it is an extremely pleasant walk through a mountainside environment of hardwoods, berry bushes, and mountain laurel. If done in the direction described, it is, except for the final half mile, a gradual descent the whole way.

.0 Begin by taking the unmarked trail past the picnic table at the north end of the parking lot. In 250 feet, at the intersection of two unmarked trails, turn left downhill and intersect with a pathway blazed with blue diamonds. Turn right and slab the hillside.

.25 Walk around a spur ridge; continue to slab the hillside.

.4 Amid abundant berry bushes, walk onto and begin following another spur ridge.

.6 Switchback to the right, cross a ridgeline, and begin to descend.

1.0 Cross a (usually) dry water run.

1.4 Descend more rapidly.

1.6 Turn left onto an old roadbed.

1.8 Come to the White Rock Gap Trail [FS 480] with orange diamond blazes (to the left it is about 2 miles to Sherando Lake). Turn right and ascend through hemlock.

1.9 Arrive at an old homestead site where raspberries should be plentiful in season!

2.0 A sign here identifies the spring as the headwaters of North Fork Back Creek.

2.2 Arrive at BRP mile 18.5 in White Rock Gap.

Mile 22. Bald Mountain parking area and FSR 162 (3,250 feet)

The reference is to the Big Levels ridgeline that crests on the summit of Big Bald, named at a time when the mountain was less forested than it is now.

FSR 162 provides access to Torry Ridge Trail [FS 507], Slacks Overlook Trail [FS 480A], and Bald Mountain Trail [FS 500E].

**Mile 22. Torry Ridge Trail [FS 507] and Slacks Overlook Trail
[FS 480A]** (N 37°54.844 W 79°04.414) Map 3

Length: 1.9 miles, one way; 3.8 miles, out-and-back
Difficulty: moderate

The trailhead involves a little searching to find, but this hike is a standout because of its ease of walking, the numerous viewpoints, intimacy with a ridgetop environment, and a good feeling of isolation. The trailhead is about 1 mile up FSR 162 (near Bald Mountain Overlook, mile 22). The road may be gated, and it may be necessary to walk, gradually ascending, the 1 mile. At the first road intersection turn right, and in less than .1 mile, the yellow diamond-blazed trail begins on the left side of the road.

.0   Descend through a hardwood forest.

.16   A break in the vegetation reveals a good view of Torry Ridge dropping to the valley floor. Begin walking through rhododendron.

.25   At the top of a small knoll is a view back to the BRP.

.4   As you descend from the knoll, note the telegraph pole. Before radio, telegraph was the only means of communication for the fire tower on top of Bald Mountain.

.7   A rock slide provides a couple of nice views.

.8   With a telegraph pole on the right, descend through a large rock jumble. The trail is then less rocky, and mountain laurel and rhododendron are thicker.

1.2   Trail intersection.

▶ The Torry Ridge Trail continues to the left to descend along a ridgeline of oak trees, blueberry bushes, and groves of mountain laurel to arrive, in 2.9 miles, at the Blue Loop Trail [FS 507A], whose .7-mile length (in .3 is a nice view of the lake and a junction with the Dam Trail [FS 507B]) will bring you to the shore of Sherando Lake and other hiking options. Included near the lake are the Lakeside Trail [FS 300], which encircles the body of water for 1 mile, and the Cliff Trail [FS 301], which branches off of the Lakeside Trail and returns to that route in .7 mile.

▶ Staying to the left on the Torry Ridge Trail at its junction with the Blue Loop Trail opens up a wonderful loop hike that would make for a great overnight journey. About 1 mile beyond this junction, another section of the Blue Loop Trail [FS 507C] descends to the right for .8 mile for FSR 91. Staying on the Torry Ridge Trail, bear left onto the Mills Creek Trail [FS 518] in an additional 2.2 miles (the Torry Ridge Trail continues right for a short distance to terminate at VA RT 664). Follow Mills Creek Trail, lightly traveled and with some nice campsites, for 7 miles, turn left onto FSR 162, go .3 mile, make a left onto FSR 162C, continue another .1 mile, and bear left onto the Torry Ridge Trail. Another 2.9 brings you back to the junction with the Blue Loop Trail.

Turn right to continue on the Slacks Overlook Trail, with blue diamond blazing. After passing through so many thickets of rhododendron, you will notice that it is conspicuously absent on this gently sloping pathway.

1.4 Cross a small rock field.

1.5 Cross second rock field.

1.7 Pass a small gully. The hillside becomes much steeper, but the pathway remains wide and level.

1.9 Be alert! Look for double blue blazes, and just beyond them turn to the right (unmarked trail) to ascend to the Slacks Overlook parking area. (The Slacks Overlook Trail [FS 480A] continues straight for 2.2 miles to reach White Rock Gap at mile 18.5; see BRP mile 20.)

Mile 22. Bald Mountain Trail [FS 500E]

(N 37°54.844 W 79°04.414) Map 3

Length: 2.2 miles, one way; 4.4 miles, out-and-back
Difficulty: moderate

This wonderfully isolated hike passes through the St. Mary's Wilderness. It receives very little traffic, so there is a good possibility you won't see anyone for the full distance. Also, since it's in the wilderness, you can camp here.

The trailhead is located on FSR 162 (near Bald Mountain Overlook, mile 22). This road may be gated and therefore have to be walked. About .75 mile up the road are two horizontal yellow blazes. A sign on the left side of the road identifies the trail.

.0 Begin by entering the wilderness area and gradually descend.

.4 An open place in the vegetation offers the first view.

.5 Switchback to the right and enter the head of a valley. This isolated spot seems far away from the BRP and virtually undiscovered. Cross the creek and parallel it on a rocky, descending pathway.

.6 Cross the creek again as the valley begins to open up.

.7 Cross the creek once more and continue to descend through a thick growth of rhododendron.

1.0 At a pleasant campsite, leave the creek and begin the ascent on an old roadbed.

1.3 Cross over a water run. Enter a different world as the rhododendron gives way to a very open forest floor.

1.5 Reach a ridgeline; continue to ascend, but at a gentler pace.

1.9 Be alert! At the double blazes, the trail leaves the old road and makes an abrupt right turn onto a pathway lined with azaleas and sassafras.

2.2 Intersect the Mine Bank Trail and turn left; walk 300 feet to reach the BRP across from the Fork Mountain Overlook, BRP mile 23.

▶ The Mine Bank Trail [FS 500C] descends into the St. Mary's Wilderness to connect with other trails that would provide a nice loop hike with side trail options. In 2.2 miles from its intersection with the Bald Mountain Trail, the Mine Bank Trail terminates at the St. Mary's River Trail [FS 500]. (A left onto St. Mary's River Trail would lead, in 2.2 miles, to the St. Mary's Falls Trail [FS 500B]—a popular route because of the falls and swimming hole—and another 1.4 miles to FSR 41.) Make a right onto St. Mary's River Trail, follow it for 2.6 miles, and make a right onto FSR 162. Continue on the old dirt road for 3.6 miles, and turn right onto the Bald Mountain Trail to return to the Mine Bank Trail in another 2.2 miles.

Mile 23. Fork Mountain Overlook (3,294 feet)

Fork Mountain is the summit whose bulk is defined by the valleys of the north and south forks of the Tye River.

Mile 23. Access to Bald Mountain Trail [FS 500E], Mine Bank Trail [FS 500C], and the trails of the St. Mary's Wilderness
(N 37°54.719 W 79°05.211).

The trails are accessed just a few feet south of the Fork Mountain Overlook. See mile 22.

Mile 23.4 (3,333.7 feet)

Highest point on the BRP north of the James River.

Mile 25.6. Spy Run Gap and VA RT 686 (3,185 feet)

Mile 26.3. Big Spy Overlook (3,185 feet)

In the distance, you can see the stone dome of Big Spy Mountain. It offers a 360-degree view and was used as a lookout by soldiers during the Civil War.

Mile 26.3. Big Spy Mountain Overlook Trail [BRP 9]
(N 37°53.479 W 79°08.329) Map 3

> *Length: .1 mile, out-and-back*
> *Difficulty: easy leg stretcher*
> *Highly recommended*

This short trail ascends through clover to a grassy knob for good views of the Shenandoah and West River Valleys. It is especially good at sunrise and sunset and for stargazing.

Mile 27.2. Tye River Gap and VA RT 56 (2,969 feet)

Access to Vesuvius, Montebello, and Steele's Tavern, where Cyrus McCormick's reaper was demonstrated in 1831.

Mile 27.2. Crabtree Falls Trail [FS 526] (N 37°51.098 W 79°04.682).
See Map 12, Chapter 3.

> *Length: 2.9 miles, one way; 5.8 miles, out-and-back*
> *Difficulty: moderately strenuous*

Less than 7 miles eastward from the parkway on VA RT 56 is the not-to-be-missed Crabtree Falls.

Often you must go on an extended, arduous journey to reach and appreciate a waterfall of any significant or true scenic value, but not in the case of Crabtree Falls, a spectacular waterfall that descends in a series of 5 cascades. In fact, you can reach the first of the impressive cascades by a relatively easy walk of less than 10 minutes from a trailhead located off a paved roadway. From there, the forest service's first-rate pathway of graded switchbacks and wooden staircases winding over and around giant boulders helps ease the burden of gaining about 1,000 feet in 1.5 miles to reach the top of the upper falls. Observation decks of native stone and timber, overlooking different portions of the falls, seem to appear at convenient spots—just about the time you are looking for an excuse to pause and catch your breath.

There is also the opportunity to join up with the Appalachian Trail near the end of the hike.

.0 Take the bridge across the south fork of the Tye River to begin the hike.

.2 Moisture-laden air coming from the creek along with shade provided by the rich forest should make you notice a slight drop in temperature as you come to the first falls overlook. The water dropping in front of you makes a picturesque scene, but be sure to look upward to appreciate the full length of the falls you are viewing.

.4 Reach another platform, followed a short distance away by an excellent view of an approximately 70-foot cascade.

.7 Another vantage point, this one looking downstream. The cascades seem to get taller and more impressive the farther you progress along the route. Violets, wild geranium, and jewelweed are now common.

.9 The creek drops down a smooth vertical rock face.

1.5 Reach the base of the upper, and certainly most impressive, falls. The water splits and takes many different paths down the rocks, so be sure to walk around as much as possible (remember to stay on the path, though) to gain various perspectives on the falls.

1.7 Come to the top of the upper falls. The water drops at such a precipitous angle that it is hard to really see any great portion of the falls. For safety reasons, don't be tempted to walk to, or on, slippery rocks in order to peer over the edge in hopes of obtaining a better look. Rather, continue on a few feet and take the footbridge across Crabtree Creek to follow a side trail out to an observation platform. You still won't be able to see the falls from here, but you can tell how much elevation you have gained by gazing down into the narrow valley carved by the south fork of the Tye River. Fork Mountain is on the other side of the valley. Retrace your steps, cross the creek, and continue upstream.

2.0 Turn right onto a woods road. Mayapple, violets, wild geranium, and cinquefoil add their colors and shapes to the undergrowth near the road.

2.7 An old road comes in from the left; keep right.

2.9 Arrive at the end of the trail and the parking area on VA 826. Retrace steps. (The Appalachian Trail [see Chapter 3, mile 13.7] can be reached by following VA 826 uphill for about half a mile from the end of Crabtree Falls Trail.)

Mile 29. Whetstone Ridge (2,990 feet).

Ranger office and restrooms. VA RT 603.

Mile 29. Whetstone Ridge Trail [FS 523] (N 37°52.141 W 79°08.865) Map 4

Length: 11.8. miles, one way; 23.6 miles, out-and-back
Difficulty: moderately strenuous

The 11.8-mile pathway gradually descends along the crestline of Whetstone Ridge (named for the fine-grained sharpening stones it provided to early mountain settlers) from the ranger office parking lot to a parking area on VA RT 603. The far end of the trail is reached by automobile by driving across the parkway from the parking area onto Whetstone Ridge Road and, in .1 mile, turning right on Irish Creek Road (VA RT 603) and following it 9.3 miles to the small trailhead parking area on the right.

The trail, which much of the way is along the original route of the Appalachian Trail of the 1930s, has few vistas during the summer. Yet once the leaves drop off the trees in the fall, the views are almost continuous. This makes a nice weekend hike, since the route is on forest service property where camping is permitted. However, water sources are practically nonexistent, so be sure to carry plenty of fluids. Please note that the trail is open to mountain bikers, who must be thanked for their continuing maintenance efforts.

.0 Follow the yellow diamond–blazed trail from the north end of the parking area past a home, and parallel the parkway, gradually ascending.

.2 Switchback to the left and soon attain the ridgeline and forest service property where camping is now permitted. However, be conscious that the trail is along a property line (marked

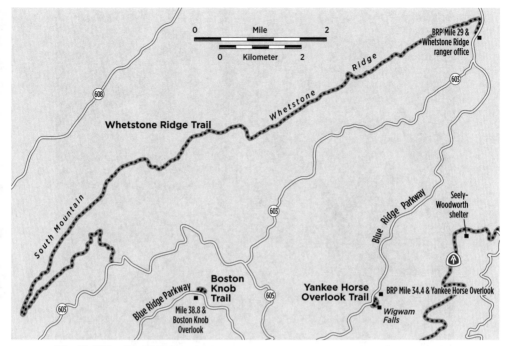

Map 4. Miles 29–38.8

      by yellow blazes), so be sure to set up your tent on public, and not private, land.

.9   There is a limited view to the south during the warmer months.

1.5   The trail swings to right of the main crest of the ridge to avoid a knob and goes by boulders covered with rock tripe.

2.1   The route bears right onto woods road.

2.3   Be alert! The trail veers right off the road and ascends a knob.

2.4   The trail returns to the woods road, but be alert as the route soon bears right again.

3.3   Ascend steeply to the top of a rocky knob on a narrow and rocky treadway.

4.0   The trail begins a downward trend, where sometimes the ridge would be wide enough to find a small tentsite.

4.7   Reach a low point on the cross ridge, which is taking the trail off Whetstone Ridge and bringing it to the South Mountain ridgeline.

5.7   Begin a steep and rocky descent.

The forest service's Whetstone Ridge Trail is lightly traveled and offers backcountry campsites on the ridgeline.

6.0 Reach a gap and ascend, sometimes steeply.

7.3 Attain the top of first steep knob; just beyond this is a good summertime view of the Shenandoah Valley.

8.2 The top of a second knob has views of the parkway snaking along the main crest of the Blue Ridge.

8.3 Pass between large rock formations.

8.9 A knob, whose openness is the result of a fire, has a view down into the valley (and a tiny! tentsite that someone spent hours constructing). Beyond this, the trail soon descends, following a woods road.

9.2   Do not take the road descending to the right; stay along the ridge.

9.5   Be alert! The trail leaves the woods road and begins its long descent on a narrow pathway.

10.0   Cross a spur ridge.

10.2   Cross a second spur ridge.

11.8   Arrive at the parking area on VA RT 603.

Mile 31.4. Still-House Hollow parking area (3,000 feet)

Local history states that there was a legal apple cider still near here in the days before Prohibition. Birdlife observed here has included black-billed cuckoo, flycatcher, northern parula, junco, and a variety of warblers. Picnic table.

Mile 31.9. VA RT 686

Mile 33. Yankee Fence Exhibit (3,210 feet)

The fence here is of a construction not often seen in the Blue Ridge and is credited to a settler who arrived in the area from the northern states.

Mile 34.4. Yankee Horse Overlook Trail [BRP 10] (3,140 feet)
(N 37°48.566 W 79°10.799) Map 4

> Length: .1 mile, circuit
> Difficulty: easy leg stretcher

A good place to visit on a hot summer afternoon. The pathway leads to a cool, shaded grotto in which Wigwam Falls plunges 30 feet over the rock facing. The trail makes use of a small portion of the bed of a narrow gauge railroad. At one time the Blue Ridge Mountains were laced by narrow gauge tracks, allowing the harvesting of timber and other resources in otherwise inaccessible areas.

.0   Ascend to the railroad tracks on steps, turn right, and cross the stream. Turn left uphill.

.06   Cross another stream on a footbridge and arrive at the water-fall. The water, hemlocks, and cool shades of green ferns and mosses make this an enchanting spot.

.1   Turn left onto the railroad tracks and return to the parking lot.

The lower portion of Wigwam Falls flows above the reconstructed tracks of an early 1900s narrow gauge railroad.

Mile 34.8. Yankee Horse Ridge

A Union soldier's horse fell along the ridge and had to be shot.

Mile 37.4. Irish Gap (2,261 feet)

Site of an old road that crossed the mountains and followed the route of Irish Creek to the west.

Mile 37.5. VA RT 605

Access to Irish Creek, Buena Vista (full services), Amherst, and US RT 60. Buena Vista is the western terminus of the easy, and highly recommended, Chessie Nature Trail, which follows the route of an old railroad grade next to the Maury River for approximately 7 miles to Lexington, home of Virginia Military Institute and Washington and Lee University.

Mile 38.8. Boston Knob Trail [BRP 11] (2,508 feet) (N 37°48.748 W 79°13.718)
Map 4

> *Length: .1 mile, circuit*
> *Difficulty: easy leg stretcher*

Abundant dogwood trees make walking this circular path a pleasure and a thing of beauty just about any time of year. Spring brings forth their pink and white leaf bracts and small yellow flowers, while in summer the trees provide some welcome shade. In autumn, the hillside is ablaze with the dogwood's bright red berries and rust-colored leaves.

Mile 40. Clarks Gap (2,177 feet)

Named for a family that received land for the service they performed during the War of 1812.

Mile 42.2. Irish Creek Valley parking area (2,665 feet)

Irish Creek is 500 feet below the parking area and has cut a gap through the mountains, which provides a view of the Shenandoah Valley. The ridgeline to the right contains a part of the Whetstone Ridge Trail [FS 523]—see BRP mile 29.

Mile 44.4. Whites Gap Overlook (2,567 feet)

Just north of the overlook is FSR 356, which follows a portion of the former Jordon toll road, once a major crossing of the Blue Ridge Mountains. Picnic table.

Mile 44.9. Chimney Rock parking area (2,485 feet)

The view takes in Chimney Rock (it's obvious as to why it received its name) and Silver Peak (on the left side of the vista).

Mile 45.6. Humphries Gap and US RT 60 (2,296 feet)

Access to Buena Vista (5 miles) and Amherst.

Mile 45.7. Buena Vista Overlook (2,325 feet)

If you visit the town visible from this overlook, be sure to pronounce its name as *BEW-na VIS-ta* and not *BWAY-na VIS-ta* or the locals will immediately recognize you as a tourist.

Mile 47.5. Indian Gap Trail [BRP 12] (2,093 feet)

(N 37°43.043 W 79°18.792) Map 5

> *Length: .2 mile, circuit*
> *Difficulty: easy leg stretcher*

Late spring and early summer is the time to best enjoy this quick trail. It twists and winds its way through a maze of rhododendron tunnels, and nothing quite equals the enjoyment of negotiating the maze when

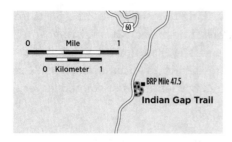

Map 5. Indian Gap Trail
(mile 47.5)

the plants are in full bloom. The interesting rock formation on top of the knoll is an added bonus.

.0 From the middle of the Indian Gap parking area, ascend on a stone walkway through mountain laurel.

.06 Cross over the ridgeline.

.1 Come to the balanced rocks and small caves of Indian Rocks. Go around the rocks and begin to descend through a tunnel of mountain laurel.

.2 Arrive back at the parking lot.

Mile 48.9. Licklog Spring Gap (2,481 feet)

Named for the practice of putting salt in the cut-out portion of a log for roaming livestock.

Mile 49.3. House Mountain Overlook (2,498 feet)

As seen from this overlook, House Mountain outside Lexington stands alone, rising abruptly from lowland valleys, with two distinct summits, each towering above the U-shaped saddle that separates them. A campaign in the late 1980s by volunteer members of the Rockbridge Area Conservation Council and the Virginia Outdoor Foundation proved successful, and the upper portion of House Mountain is now preserved, with hiking trails, for all to enjoy.

Mile 50.5. Robinson Gap (2,412)

Named for an Irish immigrant who fought for the colonies during the Revolutionary War.

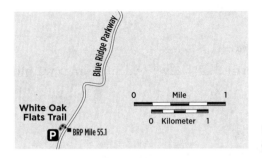

Map 6. White Oak Flats Trail (mile 55.1)

Mile 51.5. Punchbowl Mountain Overlook (2,136 feet)

There is no view here, but the maturing forest of towering beech and poplar trees along with an understory of dogwood looks especially pleasing when the early morning light filters through the leaf canopy.

Mile 51.5. Appalachian Trail and access to the trails of the James River Face Wilderness (N 37°40.428 W 79°20.074). See Chapter 3.

Mile 52.8. Bluff Mountain Overlook (1,850 feet)

The Appalachian Trail crosses over Bluff Mountain, which at one time was easier to identify as it had a fire tower on its summit.

Mile 53.1. Bluff Mountain Tunnel

The only BRP tunnel in Virginia, it measures 630 feet long. Be aware that two national park service sources provide different minimum heights. One states 13 feet, 7 inches; another says 13 feet.

Mile 53.6. Rice Mountain Overlook (1,755 feet)

Rice Mountain rises directly across from the overlook, blocking out any other ridgelines.

Mile 54.6. Brown's Creek (1,560 feet)

Mile 55.1. White Oak Flats Trail [BRP 13] (1,460 feet)
(N 37°38.641 W 79°19.824) Map 6

> Length: .2 mile, out-and-back
> Difficulty: easy leg stretcher

The White Oak Flats walk begins at the picnic tables and follows a small stream through a bottomland forest of white oaks, azalea, and mountain laurel. (The unmaintained trail across the creek ends in .25 mile at a gated forest service road.)

Mile 55.2. Otter Creek

Mile 55.9. Dancing Creek Overlook (1,300 feet)

Dancing Creek is a tributary of the Pedlar River, which in turn flows into the James River. Picnic table.

Mile 56.6 Otter Creek Bridge #1

Mile 57.6. Upper Otter Creek Overlook (1,085 feet)

The first good place to stop and observe the creek that will parallel the parkway to the James River at mile 63.6.

Mile 58.2. Otter Creek Flats Overlook (1,005 feet)

The flats are formed when the creek overflows it banks and erodes the surrounding soil. Picnic table.

Mile 58.5. Otter Creek Bridge #2

Mile 59.1. Otter Creek Bridge #3

Mile 59.6. Otter Creek Bridge #4

Mile 59.7. Otter Creek Overlook (885 feet)

The parkway is following the descending route of the creek and is at a mere 885 feet above sea level at the overlook.

Mile 59.8. Otter Creek Bridge #5

Mile 60.4. The Riffles Overlook (825 feet)

A view of Otter Creek as it drops via a 22-foot cascade.

Mile 60.8. Otter Creek campground (779 feet)

Restrooms and water are available for campers. Water and restrooms for other travelers are available at BRP mile 63.6. *Please Note:* As this book went to press, the former restaurant (with restrooms) and gift shop were closed, and questions remained as to if they would reopen. Contact the BRP offices for current information.

Mile 60.8. Otter Creek Trail [BRP 14] (N 37°34.574 W 79°20.293) Map 7

> *Length: 3.4 miles, one way; 6.8 miles, out-and-back*
> *Difficulty: moderate*

The trail begins right next to the campground, so if you are staying there, this makes a nice before-breakfast or after-dinner walk. Except for one steep ascent and descent, the pathway follows gradually descending Otter Creek as it winds its way to the James River at BRP mile 63.6. You will pass through a grand variety of vegetation and terrain—hemlock, oak, mountain laurel, rhododendron, and galax line the stream, which has quite a number of inviting wading pools. The trail also crosses hillsides and wide, flat bottomlands.

This trail is worth walking any time of the year. Spring provides an abundance of wildflowers; the creek offers flat rocks for sunbathing and cooling water in the summer; Otter Lake reflects the dazzling fall colors; and icicles sparkle on the hanging rocks in winter.

Since the Otter Creek Trail crosses the BRP or comes close to overlooks quite a number of times, you can make this walk as long or as short as you wish. (This can be a good activity to calm down an active group of young campers—send them on the trail and then follow on the parkway to meet them at prearranged spots.)

.0　Begin the hike in the parking lot downstream from the campground entrance.

.02　Side trail to the campground.

.1　Cross Otter Creek on large concrete stepping blocks. This may be a difficult crossing during times of high water.

.2　A side trail to the campground comes in from the left. There are a couple of nice pools to cool your feet in here.

.3　Cross under an eye-pleasing stone overpass of the BRP.

.4　Large, flat rocks in the creek are suitable for resting and sunbathing.

.6　Come to steps leading to Terrapin Hill Overlook (BRP mile 61.4) (760 feet) (N 37°34.462 W 79°20.876). Soon use a stone culvert to pass under the BRP.

.7　Go under VA RT 130 in a concrete tunnel and immediately cross Otter Creek. The imposing, fern-covered rock cliff is worth a moment's study.

.8　Cross the creek again and walk below the rock cliff, but soon ascend on a fern-lined trail through an evergreen forest.

1.0　The ascent steepens. (The park service has thoughtfully provided a bench to rest upon.) The hillside brings a new environment with it—mountain laurel, galax, and pine trees.

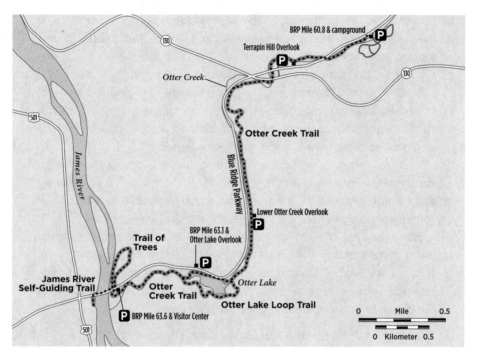

Map 7. Miles 60.8–63.6

1.2 Begin a very rapid and steep ascent.

1.3 Cross a creek on a handrailed footbridge; descend gradually to cross a spur ridge.

1.4 Take time to explore and enjoy the quiet coolness of the natural cave to the left. Just beyond, descend quite steeply. (Be careful!)

1.5 Return to Otter Creek.

1.6 Cross a side stream that in times of high water has some very pretty, small cascades.

1.9 Come to some picnic tables, cross Otter Creek on a footbridge, pass by the Lower Otter Creek Overlook (685 feet) (N 37°33.689 W 79°21.076) at BRP mile 62.5, and continue downstream next to the BRP.

2.0 Once again cross Otter Creek, this time on large boulders. The trail now meanders through a wide bottomland and soon enters an old pine plantation forest.

2.4 Junction with the Otter Lake Loop Trail [BRP 15] (.6 mile to the left leads to the Otter Lake Overlook; see BRP mile 63.1.).

Otter Creek Trail passes under the roadway via a culvert with a facade of native stone.

Turn right to continue on Otter Creek Trail; cross a ditch and a creek on footbridges.

2.5 Come to Otter Lake Overlook (655 feet) (N 37°33.398 W 79°21.357) at BRP mile 63.1 and continue to walk downstream next to the BRP.

2.7 Pass by the dam, go down the steps, cross Otter Creek on concrete stepping stones, and turn right. (To the left is the Otter Lake Loop Trail [BRP 15].)

2.8 Cross a side stream and walk onto an old railroad bed.

2.9 Turn right and leave the railroad bed.

3.0 Cross Otter Creek, which has some very inviting deep pools here.

3.1 Walk along a stone wall directly below the BRP. Honeysuckle is abundant, but so are greenbrier and poison ivy!

3.4 Arrive at the James River Visitor Center (668 feet) (N 37°33.323 W 79°21.933) at mile 63.6.

Mile 61. Otter Creek Bridge #6

Mile 61.4. Terrapin Hill Overlook and VA RT 130 (760 feet)

In a wooded area, steps from the overlook descend to the Otter Creek Trail [BRP 14]. VA RT 130 provides access to US RT 501 and Glasgow (8 miles), Natural Bridge (15 miles), and Lynchburg (22 miles; full services). The 215-foot-high and 900-foot-long Natural Bridge attracts thousands of visitors a year. Thomas Jefferson was so impressed that he purchased it in the early 1800s.

Mile 61.5. Otter Creek Bridge #7

Mile 61.6. Otter Creek Bridge #8

Mile 62.1. Otter Creek Bridge #9

Mile 62.5. Lower Otter Creek Overlook (685 feet)

Wooden bridges cross the creek, providing access to the Otter Creek Trail [BRP 14]. Picnic table.

Mile 63.1 Otter Lake Overlook (655 feet)

Casting a line for trout, carp, and bream is permitted with a Virginia fishing license.

Mile 63.1. Otter Lake Loop Trail [BRP 15] (N 37°33.398 W 79°21.357) Map 7

> *Length: 1 mile, circuit (includes the .2 mile that must be walked*
>   *along the BRP)*
> *Difficulty: moderate*

The Otter Lake Loop Trail has only one extended ascent and descent and offers glimpses of life in and around the lake. Results of the beavers' industrious lifestyle might be seen in quite a number of places, trout and carp inhabit the lake, and water snakes may be spotted slithering through the underbrush. The normally calm waters of the lake reflect the surrounding hillsides. Although the trail is not designed for wheelchairs, an observation deck ♿ beside the lake is handicapped accessible.

.0 Begin at the south end of the parking lot. Descend the steps below the dam, cross Otter Creek on concrete stepping stones, and ascend, rather steeply, to the left. (To the right is Otter Creek Trail [BRP 14].)

.1 You are now directly above the dam, where downed trees may be evidence of an active beaver population.

.15 Come around a bend for the first good view of the lake from this trail.

.2 Veer away from the lake and cross a small stream. Traffic noise from the BRP is muted as you ascend around the side of a knoll.

.3 A bench is on top of the ridgeline. Turn right. (To obtain an outstanding panoramic view of the lake, follow the trail to the left for 150 feet.)

.45 Come to another bench and begin the descent between two ridges.

.5 Cross a creek and wind through vine-choked bottomland. Soon cross a second creek.

.6 Pass by the ruins of an old homestead and intersect the Otter Creek Trail [BRP 14]. (To the right is the Otter Creek campground [2.4 miles].) Continue by bearing left and crossing two footbridges.

.8 Reach the BRP and the Otter Lake Overlook. (Your automobile is still some steps away—the parking lot is .2 mile long!)

Mile 63.2 (649.4 feet)

Lowest elevation on the parkway.

Mile 63.6. James River Overlook (668 feet)

Visitor center, small gift shop, and restrooms. Note: as this book went to press, the park service was considering closing the visitor center or reducing the hours it is open.

Trails of the James River Water Gap, Blue Ridge Parkway Mile 63.6

The water gap of the James River is a significant geological formation of the Blue Ridge Mountains. The following two trails offer excellent opportunities to comprehend the force and power of a river that can carve out such a channel for itself through these mountains. (A plaque on the Trail of Trees explains this geological phenomenon in layman's terms.)

Both walks are highly recommended. (As this book went to press, plans were to name the trails TRACK Trails; see page 76.) The information learned here will increase enjoyment of other BRP trails. A trip through the visitor center is also worthwhile.

Mile 63.6. Trail of Trees Self-Guiding Trail [BRP 16]

(N 37°33.323 W 79°21.933) Map 7

> *Length: .4 mile, circuit*
> *Difficulty: moderate*
> *Highly recommended*

Exhibits and signs along the loop trail explain the life cycles and interrelationships of more than forty identified plants and trees. (*Please Note*: As this book went to press, some of the signs had incorrect information, as many trees have died over the years. The park service plans to correct this as funding becomes available.)

.0   Begin at the visitor center, drop to the footbridge across the James River, but do not cross it. Instead, continue by ascending the steps straight ahead.

.06   Keep to the left and descend for a commanding view of the James River; eventually descend almost to the river.

.15   Cross a footbridge and ascend next to a large rock outcropping.

.2   Another good place to view the river. This one has an exhibit explaining the formation of a water gap. Soon cross another footbridge and come to a bench. Ascend on steps.

.25   Arrive at a cool, shaded spot (courtesy of a large red maple tree). You'll also find a bench for resting here.

.4   Descend the steps back to the beginning of the trail and return to the visitor center.

Mile 63.6. James River Self-Guiding Trail [BRP 17]

(N 37°33.323 W 79°21.933) Map 7

> *Length: .4 mile, out-and-back*
> *Difficulty: easy*
> *Highly recommended*

In the 1800s, a system of canals and locks was built that turned the James River into a vital link between the civilization of the East and the newer settlements west of the Blue Ridge Mountains. The coming of the railroads brought about the decline of the canals, but exhibits and a well-preserved lock on the James River Self-Guiding Trail bring those bygone days back to life.

.0   Begin at the visitor center, and in 200 feet turn left onto a concrete footbridge over the James River.

.1 The bridge ends; descend the steps and walk through an open field, enjoying your closeness to the river.

.15 Arrive at the canal, lock, and exhibits, which explain the history and workings of this nineteenth-century method of transporting people and goods across and through the mountains.

.2 The trail ends overlooking the river. Retrace steps.

Mile 63.7. James River Bridge and US RT 501

Access to Glasgow (9 miles), Natural Bridge (15 miles), and Lynchburg (22 miles; full services).

Mile 66.3. BRP maintenance facilities

Mile 66.6. Falling Rock Creek (1,230 feet).

Mile 67.1. Falling Rock Creek (1,250 feet)

Mile 67.9. Billy's Branch

Mile 68.7. Bellamy Creek

Mile 69.1. James River Valley Overlook (1,874 feet)

The view of the valley is only available when the leaves are off the trees. Picnic table. FSR 951.

Mile 71. Petites Gap (2,361 feet)

U.S. Forest Service Cave Mountain Lake Recreation Area is 8 miles away via FSR 35.

Mile 71. Appalachian Trail and access to trails of the James River Face Wilderness Area (N 37°33.564 W 79°27.524). See Chapter 3 (mile 51.5 for the wilderness area trails).

Mile 71. Glenwood Horse Trail (N 37°33.529 W 79°27.479).
See Map 13, Chapter 3.

The Glenwood Horse Trail, a network of well over 60 miles of pathways, is a cooperative effort between the U.S. Forest Service and local equestrian groups. The trail system comes in contact with the parkway at BRP miles 71, 80.5, and 93.1. Information on trailheads, distances, and

A concrete causeway below the Blue Ridge Parkway's bridge delivers hikers to a lock on a remnant of the James River and Kanawha Canal.

conditions of the trails may be obtained by contacting the Glenwood/Pedlar Ranger Districts, 27 Ranger Lane, Natural Bridge Station, VA 24579, 540-291-2188.

Mile 72.6. Terrapin Mountain parking area (2,884 feet)

Use your imagination and you will make out the shape of a terrapin, or turtle, on the ridgeline that rises out of the valley on the right side of the vista.

Mile 74.7. Thunder Ridge Overlook and Trail [BRP 18] (3,485 feet)
(N 37°32.385 W 79°29.425). See Map 13, Chapter 3.

> Length: .2 mile, circuit
> Difficulty: easy

This walk through a rocky mountaintop environment of rhododendron and hardwoods brings you to a view of Arnold Valley, a part of the Shenandoah Valley. The Thunder Ridge Trail and the Appalachian Trail are one and the same here, and if you start at one end of the parking lot and come around to the other, you can brag to your friends that you have now walked a portion of the famous 2,000-mile-long trail!

Mile 74.7. Appalachian Trail (N 37°32.385 W 79°29.425). See Chapter 3.

Mile 74.7. Hunting Creek Trail [FS 3] (N 37°32.385 W 79°29.425).
See Map 13, Chapter 3.

> Length: 2.4 miles, one way; 4.8 miles, out-and-back
> Difficulty: moderate

This is an extremely pleasant walk as the trail descends via gentle switchbacks through 2 miles of almost continual rhododendron tunnels. It is most delightful in late spring and early summer, when the rhododendron is in full bloom. Although campsites are few and far between, camping is allowed anywhere along this trail.

.0 Park at the Thunder Ridge Overlook, take the approach trail to the AT, and turn left.

.3 Cross the BRP (mile 74.9).

.4 Trail intersection. The Appalachian Trail continues to the right; bear left onto the Hunting Creek Trail.

.6 Enter a large rhododendron thicket.

.7 The rhododendron begins to form tunnels.

.8   The rhododendron is not quite so thick here, which allows great wintertime views into the valley. In the summer, you can behold the rhododendron in all of its magnificent glory.

1.0   Switchback to the left as mountain laurel becomes mixed in with the rhododendron.

1.1   Switchback to the right. A nice spot to watch the rising sun in the morning.

1.4   Leave the rhododendron and cross a rock field.

1.6   Reenter rhododendron tunnels.

1.7   Switchback to the left.

1.8   Switchback to the right.

1.9   Begin to parallel a creek lined by moss-covered rocks, hemlock, and rhododendron.

2.1   After two dry gullies, switchback to the right in a rock field. Trail becomes somewhat indistinct. Keep looking for the blue blazes; soon the trail begins to follow a very old road.

2.3   Follow a grassy woods road.

2.4   Cross a creek and arrive at FSR 45. This trailhead may be reached by automobile by following FSR 951 from BRP mile 69.1 to VA RT 602, which turns into FSR 45.

Mile 75.2. Arnold Valley north parking area (3,510 feet)

The valley is named for a settler of the mid-1700s. It's at the foot of the mountains and is a part of the Shenandoah Valley, which in turn is a part of the Great Valley. Snake Den Ridge is most prominent from the southernmost point of the overlook.

Mile 75.3. Arnold Valley south parking area (3,700 feet)

The view is so good that there is an additional parking area.

Mile 76.3. Appalachian Trail (N 37°31.312 W 79°30.238). See Chapter 3.

Mile 76.5. Apple Orchard parking area (3,922 feet)

The signpost explains that weather conditions have pruned the mountain's deciduous trees, giving the appearance of a cultivated orchard. The huge "golf ball" on the summit (seen as you drive southward on the BRP) is a radar once used during the Cold War and now employed by the FAA to monitor commercial air flights.

Mile 76.7 (3,950 feet)

Highest point on the BRP in Virginia.

Mile 78.4. Sunset Field Overlook (3,472 feet)

Aptly named, this is the place to be when the evening sun begins to spread its reddish rays across the Shenandoah Valley and the Allegheny Mountains in the distance.

A gated road across the parkway from the overlook leads to the site of the former Camp Kewanzee, a popular summer base for hikers and climbers. Owner Gus Welch was a full-blooded Chippewa and was on the Carlisle, Pennsylvania, Indian School football team at the same time as Jim Thorpe. Among his many accomplishments and jobs were his membership on the U.S. track and field team for the 1912 Olympics, 4 years of playing professional football for the Canton Bulldogs, his graduation from the Dickinson School of Law in 1917, and his position as head football coach for Randolph-Macon College. Welch purchased Camp Kewanzee in 1929 and ran it primarily as a youth camp. His clients named this overlook of the Shenandoah Valley for the many sunsets they enjoyed here.

Mile 78.4. FSR 812

Access to forest service's North Creek Campground.

Mile 78.4. Appalachian Trail (N 37°30.472 W 79°31.441). See Chapter 3.

Mile 78.4. Apple Orchard Falls Trail [BRP 19 and FS 17]
(N 37°30.472 W 79°31.441). See Map 14, Chapter 3.

> Length: 3.6 miles, one way; 7.2 miles, out-and-back, with the option
>   for an 8.2-mile circuit instead (see end of hike for description)
> Difficulty: strenuous

The Apple Orchard Falls Trail drops nearly 2,000 feet as it passes by the 150-foot falls and goes through a wonderfully isolated mountain valley. After .2 mile, the trail enters Jefferson National Forest. (Camping is allowed. However, this is a very popular trail, so please use common sense in setting up camp. Try to camp a good distance away from the pathway and avoid setting up in any overused areas.)

Many people simply go down to the falls and then retrace their steps back to Sunset Field Overlook, an out-and-back of 2.4 miles. Regaining the 1,000 feet in elevation makes even this shorter outing a strenuous hike. However, if a car shuttle can be arranged, it is possible to make this a one-way, all-downhill trip. Take FSR 812, which begins at the north end of the Sunset Field Overlook (BRP mile 78.4). This dirt road has only one lane but is well graded and has frequent turnouts. Follow it down the side of Wildcat Mountain to a major intersection with FSR 768. Turn left onto FSR 768 and continue to FSR 59. A left turn onto FSR 59 will lead to the Apple Orchard Falls and Cornelius Creek trailheads [FS 18].

An alternative, and one that provides the shortest hike to the falls, is to drive FSR 812 from the north end of Sunset Field Overlook for 2.9 miles from the BRP, make a left onto FSR 3035 (Apple Tree Road), and continue for another 2 miles to its end. Take the short trail from the parking area and, in about 100 yards, turn left onto the Apple Orchards Falls Trail. It will be an .8 mile (1.6 miles out-and-back) strenuous uphill climb to the falls from that point.

.0   Begin a gradual descent from the Sunset Field Overlook.

.2   Cross the Appalachian Trail (see Chapter 3) and begin a series of long switchbacks.

.6   Come to an old roadway.

.8   Cross a wide, old woods road, variously known as Apple Orchard Road, Apple Orchard Spur, or Cornelius Creek Spur Trail. Lined by an abundance of Dutchman's breeches, geraniums, trilliums, and violets, it goes about 1 mile to the left to meet up with the Cornelius Creek Trail [FS 18].

1.0   The trail parallels the creek.

1.1   Pass below a large rock outcropping. Soon descend steeply through rhododendron, and cross the creek on a footbridge, enjoying the small cascades upstream. The trail now veers away from the creek and soon descends steeply via a long set of steps.

1.2   Arrive at Apple Orchard Falls, which drops about 150 feet over a stone facing that is surrounded by a moss- and lichen-covered rocky grove. The water takes many paths down the rocks, so be sure to walk around to get a number of different perspectives of the falls. The trail beyond is rocky, and footing is unsure; it is obvious that many people turn around upon reaching the falls.

1.35 The trail switches back to the left—keep watching for the paint blazes.

1.55 Cross a creek.

1.7 The trail has been relocated to avoid a very steep incline; be on the lookout for the switchback to the right.

2.0 The route to the right goes about 100 yards to a trailhead on FSR 3034.

2.1 The continued descent becomes much more gradual. If you are on an overnight hike, you should notice that good campsites begin to appear.

2.7 You'll have an even better choice of campsites as the valley floor becomes flatter, wider, and more open with less underbrush.

3.6 Arrive at FSR 59 and the trailhead for the Cornelius Creek Trail. The forest service has reconstructed the bridge across Cornelius Creek to make it &. handicapped accessible. The bridge also now has platforms to enable people in wheelchairs to take advantage of the reportedly good native trout fishing available in the creek.

▶ The Apple Orchard Falls Trail may be combined with the Appalachian Trail and the blazed Cornelius Creek Trail [FS 18] for an enjoyable 8.2-mile circuit hike. After reaching FSR 59 via Apple Orchard Falls Trail, turn left and ascend along the Cornelius Creek Trail (traversing Backbone Ridge and gaining 1,700 feet in elevation) for about 3 miles to intersect the Appalachian Trail. Turn left onto the Appalachian Trail for 1.3 miles to return to the Apple Orchard Falls Trail, where a right turn will lead, in .2 mile, back to the Sunset Field Overlook. Because of the extensive loss and regain of elevation, this should be considered a strenuous hike. Camping is permitted on the Apple Orchard Falls Trail as well as on the Cornelius Creek and Appalachian Trails.

Mile 79.7. Onion Mountain Overlook (3,195 feet)

The view is to the east, across the Blue Ridge Mountains' lower peaks as the elevation drops to the Piedmont.

Mile 79.7. Onion Mountain Loop Trail [BRP 20] (N 37°29.791 W 79°32.260).
See Map 14, Chapter 3.

> *Length: .1 mile, circuit*
> *Difficulty: easy*

This loop trail winds through a maze of rhododendron and mountain laurel. It is an especially worthwhile walk in early summer when the pink, purple, and white blossoms are putting on their dazzling display. Onion was once the local name for the ramp that grows well in this area. The plant has a taste described as a cross between strong garlic and an onion. Picnic table.

Mile 79.9. Black Rock Hill parking area (3,195 feet)

You usually can only see Black Rock Hill (on the right side of the view) when the leaves are off the trees. The rock gets its dark color from hornblende, a mixture of a number of minerals.

Mile 80.5. Glenwood Horse Trail and FSR 190 (N 37°29.572 W 79°32.969).
See BRP mile 71. See Map 14, Chapter 3.

Mile 81.9. Headforemost parking area (2,861 feet)

Local lore provides two stories for the origin of the name. One states that the mountain drops off steeply—headforemost—into the valley. The other says that if you were to fall while hiking on the mountain, you would go down headforemost.

Flat Top is the towering mountain to the right.

Trails of the Peaks of Otter Area, Blue Ridge Parkway Miles 83.1–86

Archaeological evidence suggests the Peaks of Otter area was used as a hunting and camping ground more than 8,000 years ago. Closer to our time, the Algonquian, Cherokee, Iroquois, and Sioux visited the area in search of its abundant and diverse wildlife. Buffalo, elk, and deer once roamed these mountains in numbers large enough to establish well worn and easily followed pathways across the ridgelines.

Settlers began to move in sometime after the Revolutionary War; around 1830 the first inn was established. By 1860 the Peaks of Otter was a popular resort for flatlanders wishing to enjoy the beauty of the mountains and seeking respite from hot summer temperatures. By the time the park service acquired the property in the 1930s, more than 20 families lived on the mountainsides and in the valleys bounded by the three Peaks of Otter—Sharp Top, Flat Top, and Harkening Hill.

The trails here are diverse and interesting enough to keep you occupied for quite some time. One drops quickly and steeply into a small gorge to arrive at a series of cascading waterfalls. Another gradually climbs to the 4,001-foot summit of Flat Top, the tallest of the three peaks. Other trails wind through open meadows and old, overgrown orchards and into a forest that is now reclaiming former farmlands. In addition to a moderately easy self-guided nature walk, the most famous excursion of the peaks area is a strenuous climb that leads to the summit of Sharp Top, which affords commanding views of the surrounding countryside.

This area can be enjoyed year-round. Spring arrives with hummingbirds, warblers, and woodpeckers seeking sustenance from the reawakening natural world. Wildflowers such as mayapple, bloodroot, and foam flower emerge from the slowly warming soil. In summer, an early evening's stroll may be rewarded with a sighting of an opossum beginning its nightly foray or a quickly moving bobcat dashing into the underbrush.

The changing leaf colors of the hickory, birch, oak, and maple brighten the hillsides around Abbot Lake and announce the coming cooler weather. In winter, the Peaks of Otter Lodge, with its picture-windowed sunroom, is a pleasant place to sip a cup of coffee and warm yourself after tracking a gray fox along one of the area's snow-covered pathways.

Peaks of Otter has a park service visitor center (with small bookstore), picnic area, campground, camp store, gift shop, and the Peaks of Otter Lodge. A special tour bus to near the summit of Sharp Top operates during the heaviest tourist months.

Mile 83.1. Fallingwater Cascades Trail [BRP 21] (2,557 feet)
(N 37°28.390 W 79°34.852) Map 8

> Length: 1.6 miles, circuit
> Difficulty: moderate

This is a true year-round trail, each season offering its own rewards. Snow melt and spring rains swell the amount of water rushing over the falls as the sound echoes within the narrow gorge. Tunnels of mountain laurel and rhododendron (in full bloom) provide a welcomed coolness

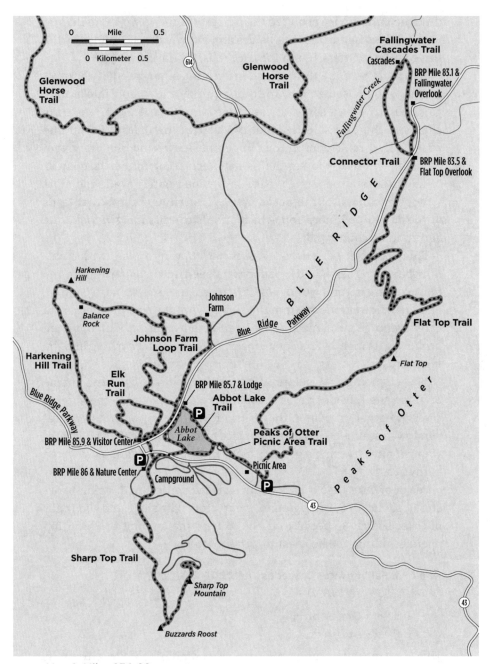

Map 8. Miles 83.1–86

and relief from summer heat, while the intense colors of changing leaves on the surrounding mountainsides are an eye-pleasing sight in the fall. The stillness and isolation of winter is accented by snow-covered branches and 30-foot icicles growing on the rocks of the cascades.

In conjunction with the Flat Top Trail [BRP 22], the Fallingwater Cascades Trail was named a National Recreation Trail in 1982.

The loss and gain in elevation classify this hike as a moderate one.

.0 As you leave the parking lot, turn right, descending through tunnels of rhododendron and mountain laurel.

.1 Come to a bench with views of the nearby mountainsides. Descend steeply on stone steps, but in 100 feet level off onto a rough and rocky pathway. In spring and periods of heavy rain, the sounds of crashing water will soon be heard.

.3 Cross hemlock-lined Fallingwater Creek on a footbridge, and arrive at the beginning of the cascades.

.4 Drop steeply on natural stone steps and come to a bench. A few feet farther is another bench; switchback to the left. To the left is a good view of the cascading waters; turn to the right to continue on the loop trail.

.5 To the left is an even better view of the cascades—also a large, inviting pool near the base of the falls. Continue on the loop trail.

.6 Cross the creek. Enjoy the feeling of isolation here, for most people turn back once they have reached the bottom of the cascades. Begin the climb back to the BRP and in a few feet come to a bench overlooking the steep, narrow confines of the creek gorge.

.9 A rock slide opens up additional views through the vegetation.

1.1 The trail to the right leads to the Flat Top parking area (200 feet) and the Flat Top Trail [BRP 22]. Turn left and continue to ascend.

1.2 Pass by a maple tree gigantic in stature.

1.3 Reach the top of the knoll, where there is an old bench. Begin to descend.

1.6 Arrive back at the Fallingwater Cascades Overlook.

Mile 83.5. Flat Top Trail [BRP 22] (2,610 feet)

(N 37°28.099 W 79°34.837) Map 8

Length: 4.5 miles, one way; 9 miles, out-and-back
Difficulty: moderate

Along with the Fallingwater Cascades Trail [BRP 22], the Flat Top Trail was named a National Recreation Trail in 1982. The pathway follows the ridgeline of the mountain to the summit, gaining 1,500 feet of elevation along the way, before dropping to the Peaks of Otter picnic area. (A car shuttle can reach the picnic area by turning left onto VA RT 43 directly across from the Peaks of Otter Visitor Center—mile 85.9. Follow VA RT 43 for about half a mile to the picnic area entrance.)

Except for a few spots, most of the ascents and descents are gradual. The reward for doing the full length is the quiet and solitude you will experience compared with the mobs of people that you would encounter on the Sharp Top Trail [BRP 28] in the summer and fall. It is suggested that you pass up the Cross Rocks Trail at the 2.2-mile mark. It is a narrow and slippery path, and the views are basically the same as those obtained at the summit.

.0 Begin the ascent along the ridgeline.

.3 Cross through a gap.

.6 Come to a bench, switchback to the left, and wind around the hillside.

.9 Switchback to the right on a hillside covered with a profusion of ferns.

1.1 Begin to pass through mountain laurel and rhododendron. Here is a good wintertime view of the open fields of Johnson Farm on Harkening Hill. Through the trees, the summit of Flat Top can be seen, still almost 1,000 feet above you.

1.3 Switchback to the right in a rock field.

1.5 Arrive at a bench. The view here shows that you are already higher than many of the surrounding mountains. Continue to ascend with a series of switchbacks, but soon the trail becomes steeper and rockier.

2.1 Come to another bench.

2.2 Come to the intersection with Cross Rocks Trail (which is very steep and slippery). A rock outcropping at this intersection affords a good view of the Federal Aviation Administration installation on top of Apple Orchard Mountain to the north. Continue to the right.

2.7 Drop into a small gap, only to rise again and make the final climb among giant boulders.

2.85 Reach the 4,001-foot summit of Flat Top. Rock outcroppings give commanding views—the Piedmont to the east, Sharp Top to the south, and Harkening Hill, Chestnut Mountain, and Jennings Creek to the west. Begin the descent from the summit.

3.0 A pleasant open area has a good view of Sharp Top; continue to descend.

3.4 Cross over a ridgeline, switchback to the right, and continue on a now wider pathway.

3.6 Cross another ridgeline and descend rapidly. Abbot Lake is now visible through the vegetation.

4.0 Swing around to the southeast side of the mountain.

4.1 Enter a laurel thicket and begin a series of switchbacks.

4.5 Arrive at the Peaks of Otter picnic area parking lot. (The Peaks of Otter Lodge is .6 mile away via Peaks of Otter Picnic Area Trail [BRP 24] and Abbot Lake Loop Trail [BRP 23].)

Mile 85.7. Peaks of Otter Lodge (2,525 feet) (N 37°26.895 W 79°36.269)

Lodging, dining, restrooms, and gift shop. 804-542-5927 or 540-586-1081; www.peaksofotter.com.

♿ Mile 85.7. Abbot Lake Loop Trail [BRP 23] (2,525 feet) (N 37°26.895 W 79°36.269) Map 8

> *Length: 1 mile, circuit*
> *Difficulty: easy*

This is a pleasant stroll (also a good place to walk off a little bit of the delicious Sunday brunch served in the lodge restaurant). The trail goes completely around the lake, offering possible glimpses of snapping turtles and water snakes.

Sunrise and sunset are optimal times to do this walk, as the glow of the sun may be softly reflected by the lake. Not long after the turn of the twenty-first century, volunteers labored long and hard to turn the entire trail into a handicapped-accessible route, easily negotiated by someone in a wheelchair.

Abbot Lake below the Peaks of Otter can take on an ethereal look on a foggy day.

Brochures are available at the trailhead (or at kidsinparks.com) as the pathway has been designated one of the TRACK (Trails, Ridges, and Active Caring, Kids) trails along the Blue Ridge Parkway. The program is sponsored by the BRP, the Blue Ridge Parkway Foundation, and other organizations that hope to encourage more children to experience nature firsthand by taking walks in the woods. There are plans to expand the program, so be on the lookout for other trails along the parkway to be designated TRACK routes.

.0 Begin at the steps descending from the front of the restaurant; turn right, toward the BRP. Soon the pavement ends.

.1 The trail to the right leads to the Harkening Hill [BRP 27] and Johnson Farm [BRP 26] trails and the visitor center. Bear left, cross the creek, and walk next to the water's edge. Tree stumps show recent beaver activity. Hawks and buzzards are often spotted soaring overhead.

.3 Cross the inlet stream on a wooden footbridge and make a slight ascent into the woods.

.55 The trail coming in from the right leads to the Peaks of Otter campground.

.6 As you begin to cross the dam, note there is a bench on a little knoll from which to enjoy the view.

.7 Trail intersection. (A right turn onto Peaks of Otter Picnic Area Trail [BRP 25; see below] will lead to Polly Woods Ordinary,

Peaks of Otter picnic area, and the Flat Top Trail [BRP 23].)
Bear left onto the pavement to return to the lodge.

.8 Cross a small inlet on a footbridge and go around the point
on the lake. The benches there provide a fine view of Sharp
Top directly across the lake.

1.0 Arrive back at the lodge.

Mile 85.7. Peaks of Otter Picnic Area Trail [BRP 24] (2,525 feet)
(N 37°26.895 W 79°36.269) (Abbot Lake to Flat Top Trailhead in Picnic Area)
Map 8

> Length: .35 mile, one way—add another .3 mile if you are walking
> down from the restaurant via the Abbot Lake Loop Trail; .7 mile,
> out-and-back—add another .7 mile if you are walking from the
> restaurant and back via the Abbot Lake Loop Trail
> Difficulty: easy

This short trail is most often used by those who wish to walk from the
restaurant and lodge to the Flat Top Trail. Along the way is the Polly
Woods Ordinary, a travelers' inn from the 1800s.

.0 Having followed the Abbot Lake Loop Trail from the lodge,
begin at the dam and soon reach Polly Woods Ordinary.
Pass the cabin, go down steps, and follow the road.

.2 Enter the woods directly across from the restrooms.

.3 Emerge from the trees. Pass by Big Spring, which has been
running for at least 400 years.

.35 Reach the parking lot and the Flat Top Trailhead [BRP 22].

Mile 85.9. Peaks of Otter Visitor Center (2,550 feet)

Natural and human history displays and ranger office, restrooms, water,
and gift shop.

Mile 85.9. Elk Run Self-Guiding Trail [BRP 25]
(N 37°26.734 W 79°36.589) Map 8

> Length: .8 mile, circuit
> Difficulty: moderately easy
> Recommended

Signs identify plants and animals of the forest and explain their inter-
dependence. The pathway is moderately easy, especially if done in the
direction described—this allows you to ascend rather gradually and to
descend on the only short, steep section of the trail.

Like all the self-guided trails on the BRP, this walk will give you an increased awareness and understanding of your surroundings on some of the other trails.

.0   Begin in the breezeway of the visitor center, and in 10 feet bear left at the intersection.

.05 Cross and then parallel a creek; ascend gradually.

.1   Cross the creek and come to a bench.

.15 Turn right onto an old road, but be alert because the trail turns off the road, to the right, in 150 feet.

.2   Arrive at a bench among a jumble of rocks; ascend the hillside.

.4   Come to another bench and cross the creek; continue the ascent.

.5   Arrive at a bench on top of the ridge. The trail bears to the left and begins a rapid descent.

.7   At an old cemetery is another bench. Abbot Lake can be seen through the vegetation.

.8   Arrive back at the visitor center.

Mile 85.9. Johnson Farm Loop Trail [BRP 26]

(N 37°26.734 W 79°36.589) Map 8

Length: 2.1 miles, circuit
Difficulty: moderate
Highly recommended

The Johnson Farm Loop Trail (a TRACK Trail; see page 76) is one of the most fun excursions to be taken on the BRP. In addition to a pleasant walk through a mixed hardwood forest of the Southern Appalachian Mountains, there is the reward of visiting the Johnson Farm. The farm was occupied from 1854 to the mid-1940s and was part of a larger community whose members both farmed and served the needs of tourists who visited the Peaks area long before the parkway was constructed. The park service has done an excellent job of restoring the land and the buildings and furnishing the farmhouse as it would have appeared around 1930.

A great variety of living history demonstrations are presented on a regular basis (check with the visitor center for times and dates). The audience is usually invited to join in these activities. Among other things, you may find yourself planting or harvesting a garden, stirring some simmering apple butter, or making a patchwork quilt. This trip back

You may be the only person to visit the Johnson Farm on a winter day.

into time provides insight into the recent human culture and history of the mountains you are exploring while on the BRP.

(The Johnson Farm Loop and Harkening Hill [BRP 27] trails make use of the same pathway near the end of this walk.)

.0 Begin at the north end of the visitor center parking lot; walk on the pathway toward the Peaks of Otter Lodge.

.1 At the top of a small rise, note the maple tree that is riddled with yellow-bellied-sapsucker holes. (A number of trees nearby have also been visited by the woodpeckers.)

.25 Come to a couple of trail intersections. Go past the first trail to the left—you will return from the Johnson Farm on this pathway. Take the second trail to the left (the one to the right leads .1 mile to the Peaks of Otter Lodge). Cross a creek and come into an open field that has an excellent view of the rock formations on Flat Top Mountain. Continue on a pathway through the field.

.5 Cross a creek, leave the field, and slab a hillside through the woods.

.7   Ascend in a gully between two ridgelines, then switchback to the right onto the hillside.

.8   Turn left onto a dirt road—avoid using the unauthorized trail that continues straight ahead.

.9   Come to the Johnson Farm site—barn, house, other buildings, and gardens. Be sure to take advantage of the hard work of the park service and volunteers who have helped to restore and interpret the farm. Join in some of the living history demonstrations that are presented. Swing around the farmhouse and garden and ascend the hillside.

1.0   Come to a bench overlooking the farm; enter the woods.

1.25   Arrive at an intersection. (The visitor center may be reached in 2.6 miles by turning right and following the Harkening Hill Trail [BRP 27].) The Johnson Farm Loop Trail bears left and descends.

1.35   Enter the first mountain laurel thicket on this trail.

1.45   Cross over a large-bouldered stream.

1.6   Cross a small side stream.

1.8   Arrive back at the trail intersections you passed earlier. The visitor center is .3 mile to the right; the Peaks of Otter Lodge is .1 mile to the left.

Mile 85.9. Harkening Hill Trail [BRP 27] (N 37°26.734 W 79°36.589) Map 8

Length: 3.3 miles, circuit
Difficulty: moderately strenuous
Recommended

The Harkening Hill Trail, with its short sections of steep ascents and descents, offers yet another chance to become aware of the human and natural history of the Blue Ridge Mountains. The Harkening Hill area was used as farmland until the 1940s, as evidenced by the old fruit trees and open meadows (now kept cleared by the park service).

The hardwood trees in the wooded areas are young, showing that much of Harkening Hill was open farmland not too long ago; they show, too, that nature can, more or less, return an area to its original state once left alone.

(The Harkening Hill and Johnson Farm Loop [BRP 26] trails make use of the same pathway near the end of this walk.)

.0   Begin in the breezeway of the visitor center and turn left to the amphitheater. Quickly ascend a series of switchbacks through a deciduous forest of poplar, dogwood, and oak.

.5   Reach the top of a spur ridge—the site of an old orchard.

.75   Attain the summit of a minor knob; there is a limited view from the rocks to the left. Descend to a gap on a narrow ridgeline, and resume the ascent on a gentler grade.

1.0   There should be plentiful blackberries and raspberries in season here!

1.1   Note the large boulder perched on two smaller rocks.

1.2   Begin to ascend steeply; wind around the mountainside.

1.6   Ascend wooden steps between two giant boulders; walk the ridgeline, where the mountainside drops off steeply to the left.

1.8   Attain the summit of Harkening Hill—3,364 feet. There are limited views to the northwest. The rocks make a nice lunch spot and a place to enjoy the antics of the scampering chipmunks. Begin the descent.

1.9   A 300-foot side trail leads to Balance Rock, a large boulder balanced on a much smaller one.

2.1   Pass through a high, possibly overgrowing, meadow.

2.4   Come to an old road; follow it for only 200 feet before turning right.

2.6   A trail intersection. (To the left is the Johnson Farm Loop Trail [BRP 26], which leads to the Johnson Farm [.25 mile] and the visitor center [.9 mile beyond the farm].) The Harkening Hill Trail continues to the right—a wide pathway through azalea and mountain laurel.

2.75   Cross a water run.

2.9   Cross a small side creek.

3.1   A trail intersection. (To the left is the beginning of the Johnson Farm Loop Trail [BRP 26]; the other pathway leads to the Peaks of Otter Lodge [.1 mile].) Turn right to continue on the Harkening Hill Trail.

3.3   Return to the visitor center.

Mile 86. Peaks of Otter campground (2,875 feet)

Camp store, restrooms, water, bus station for bus to summit of Sharp Top, and picnic area. VA RT 43 with access to Bedford (full services), home to the National D-Day Memorial. The small town lost more men per capita during the World War II invasion of Normandy than any other locale in America.

Mile 86. Sharp Top Trail [BRP 28] (N 37°26.571 W 79°36.556) Map 8

> *Length: 3 miles, out-and-back*
> *Difficulty: strenuous*
> *Recommended*

The Sharp Top Trail, despite its ascent of 1,400 feet in only 1.5 miles, has been one of the most popular recreation trails in the country since the nineteenth century. Thousands of people continue to make this pilgrimage every year.

The sweat and strain of the ascent is compensated by mountain laurel, azaleas, chipmunks, and especially the views from the bare-rocked summit. The Piedmont lies to the east, while the Allegheny Mountains rise to the west. Most impressive, however, are the long views to the north and south of the BRP snaking its way along the backbone of the Blue Ridge Mountains.

You may want to take this walk in early spring or late fall in order to avoid the hordes of people making use of the trail during the usual tourist season. (During the season a tourist bus is operated that will deliver you to within .3 mile of the summit, allowing you to be lazy if you wish to get the view without really putting forth any effort. However, you miss the exercise and joy of reaching the mountaintop under your own power. Check at the camp store, visitor center, or Peaks of Otter Lodge for rates, times, and dates of the bus.)

.0 Begin at the Sharp Top parking lot, close to the camp store. Climb steps and begin the ascent.

.1 The trail becomes paved for a short distance.

.2 Cross the bus road.

.3 Walk through the first mountain laurel on this trail.

.5 Cross a rock field in a draw. In a few hundred feet ascend steeply on rock steps.

.75 Ascend steps set in a rock facing and switchback to the left. There is a good view to the southwest.

1.2 Come onto the ridgeline and reach a trail intersection. (A side trail to the right leads, in about .4 mile, to Buzzard's Roost for a grandstand view to the east, south, and west.) To continue to Sharp Top, turn left and ascend.

1.3 Climb steps so steep that the park service has provided handrails.

1.45 Cross side trails to the bus loading area.

1.5 Attain the summit of Sharp Top with its superb 360-degree view! To the east is the Piedmont and the town of Bedford; to the west is Harkening Hill and Harveys Knob, with the James River Valley just beyond. Wheat's Valley, Flat Top Mountain, and Thunder Ridge are to the north; the rocks of Buzzard's Roost are to the south; and beautiful Abbot Lake is shimmering almost 1,600 feet directly below. Retrace steps.

Mile 89.1. Powell's Gap (1,916 feet) (N 37°28.308 W 79°38.515)

VA RT 618 and access to U.S. Forest Service's North Creek campground.

Mile 89.4. Upper Goose Creek parking area (1,925 feet)

Goose Creek Valley is directly below the overlook.

Mile 90. Porter's Mountain Overlook (2,101 feet)

There is a view into Goose Creek Valley and across to Porter's Mountain when the leaves are off the trees.

Mile 90.9. Bear Wallow Gap (2,258 feet)

It is said that bears used to "wallow" in a wet area in this gap to cool off and cover themselves with mud to keep insects at bay during the summer. VA RT 695 to Montvale and VA RT 43 to Buchanan (full services).

Mile 90.9. Appalachian Trail (N 37°29.114 W 79°40.112). See Chapter 3.

Mile 90.9. Glenwood Horse Trail (N 37°30.899 W 79°39.993).
See BRP mile 71. See Map 15, Chapter 3.

Accessed a short distance down VA RT 43.

Mile 91.8. Mills Gap parking area (2,432 feet)

A sweeping view of the James River Valley. Picnic table.

Mile 91.8. Appalachian Trail (N 37°28.776 W 79°40.978). See Chapter 3.

Mile 92.1. Purgatory Mountain parking area (2,415 feet)

Supposedly the carriage road that went near this area was so rough that passengers felt as if they had been sentenced to Purgatory.

Mile 92.5. Sharp Top parking area (2,339 feet)

One of the best places to get a photograph of the bulk of Sharp Top, one of the Peaks of Otter.

Mile 92.5. Appalachian Trail (N 37°28.477 W 79°41.529). See Chapter 3.

Mile 93.1. Bobblets Gap Overlook (2,148 feet)

Another view of Sharp Top. Next to the overlook is the cemetery of the Bobblet family that lived in the area in the early 1900s.

Mile 93.1. Glenwood Horse Trail. See BRP mile 71. See Map 15, Chapter 3.

Mile 93.1. Appalachian Trail (N 37°28.042 W 79°41.946). See Chapter 3.

Mile 95.2. Pine Tree Overlook (2,490 feet)

A sweeping view of Goose Creek Valley and the mountains beyond.

Mile 95.3. Harveys Knob Overlook (2,490 feet)

The soaring vista of the wide valley just north of Roanoke has Harveys Knob to the right in the view.

Mile 95.3. Appalachian Trail (N 37°26.729 W 79°43.599). See Chapter 3.

Mile 95.9. Montvale Overlook (2,441 feet)

The original route of the Appalachian Trail passed through the hamlet visible below the overlook.

Mile 95.9. Appalachian Trail (N 37°26.467 W 79°44.060). See Chapter 3.

Mile 95.9. Spec Mine Trail [FS 28] (N 37°26.467 W 79°44.060).
See Map 15, Chapter 3.

> *Length: 2.9 miles, one way; 5.8 miles, out-and-back*
> *Difficulty: moderately strenuous (out-and-back), moderate*
>   *(one way with car shuttle)*

The blue-blazed Spec Mine Trail drops from the crest of the Blue Ridge Mountains to the floor of Back Creek Valley. Most of the time, it travels either narrow ridgelines or deeply wooded mountainsides, providing an excellent feeling of isolation. Except for the first few hundred feet, this trail is on Jefferson National Forest land, meaning camping is allowed. The best spot to leave your automobile is at the Montvale Overlook, about 200 feet north of the trailhead.

If you hike the trail in the direction described, the walk will be a gradual descent of the mountain. However, to return you must regain nearly 1,400 feet in less than 3 miles, making the hike a moderately strenuous one.

A car shuttle could be arranged by driving north on the BRP to Bear Wallow Gap at mile 90.9. Take VA RT 43 to Buchanan, go south on US RT 11, turn left onto VA RT 640 for 4.5 miles, and make another left onto VA RT 645. In .5 mile arrive at the Spec Mine Trailhead directly across the road from a pond. The trail sign is often obscured by overgrown vegetation, so be on the lookout for the pond on the left.

.0   Begin at the Montvale Overlook at mile 95.9, walk south for 200 feet, and cross the parkway to reach the signed Spec Mine Trailhead. Drop down a narrow ridgeline.

.1   Passing through mountain laurel, slab to the left of a high knob. There are good views back to the BRP.

.4   With galax and running cedar lining the pathway, swing around to the west side of a knob.

.6   Cross a spur ridge and continue to descend.

1.1   Come onto a ridgeline and ascend a knob; head in a westerly direction following the ups and downs of the narrow ridgeline.

1.5   Cross through a rock outcropping to move from the left to the right side of the ridgeline. Descend more steeply.

1.7   Switchback to the right, leave the ridgeline, and walk on a hillside.

1.9   A small field on the left is a possible good campsite (no water); come onto an old road.

2.0   Cross FSR 634.

▶ An adventurous and somewhat strenuous circuit hike may be accomplished by following the Spec Mine Trail to this point, turning right onto FSR 634 (a part of the Glenwood Horse Trail) for about 3 miles to arrive at the Hammond Hollow Trail [FS 27]. Turn right onto this pathway and ascend rather quickly, gaining about 1,000 feet in approximately 2 miles. Intersect the Appalachian Trail, turn right, and follow the AT as it parallels the BRP for 3 miles to return to the Montvale Overlook. (Camping is permitted along FSR 634 and the Spec Mine and Hammond Hollow Trails.) Full length of this circuit hike is almost 11 miles.

Proceed straight ahead to continue on the Spec Mine Trail.

2.2   Cross an old road, but continue straight.

2.3   Swing to the right and avoid the faint trail to the left.

2.6   Cross a small water run and walk beside an overgrown field. The trail may be faint but soon becomes an obvious old road-bed again. The forest here is being overtaken by vines.

2.9   Arrive at VA RT 645.

Mile 96.2. Iron Mine Hollow parking area north (2,364 feet)

More sweeping views of the Great Valley.

Mile 96.4. Iron Mine Hollow parking area south (2,372 feet)

The area is named for the mines that proliferated in the late 1800s.

Mile 97. Taylors Mountain Overlook (2,340 feet)

Taylors Mountain is to the left in the view, with Porters Mountain to the right.

Mile 97. Appalachian Trail (N 37°25.883 W 79°44.960). See Chapter 3.

Mile 97.7. Black Horse Gap (2,402 feet)

Site of an old carriage road that once stretched from the flat lands of Virginia to the mountains of what would later become West Virginia.

Mile 97.7. Appalachian Trail (N 37°25.478 W 79°45.443). See Chapter 3.

Mile 99.6. The Great Valley Overlook (2,493 feet)

One more panoramic view of the Great Valley. Picnic table.

Mile 100.9. The Quarry Parking Overlook (2,170 feet)

A part of the view takes in the quarry that has been in operation since the early 1900s, removing dolomite, a rock that started out as sediment on the floor of an ocean that existed here around 500 million years ago.

Mile 101.5. Curry Gap (1,985 feet)

FSR 191, with access to US RT 460.

Mile 105.8. US RT 460

Access to Roanoke (9 miles) and Bedford (21 miles).

Mile 106.9. N&W Railroad Overlook (1,160 feet)

Norfolk and Western Railroad played a significant role in the development of the city of Roanoke. Its successor, Norfolk Southern, is still an economic engine for the area.

Mile 107. Coyner Mountain Overlook (1,150 feet)

Obscured by trees, Coyner Mountain is barely visible to the left from the overlook.

Mile 107.6. Glade Creek

Mile 109.8. Read Mountain Overlook (1,165 feet)

Rising like a bunion in Roanoke Valley, Read Mountain is named for David Read, a settler of the mid-1840s. If you are looking for a change from hiking along the BRP, you should be aware that local residents worked hard to preserve the mountain, and its upper portion is now the Read Mountain Preserve, containing an excellent hiking trail.

Mile 110.6. Stewarts Knob Overlook (1,275 feet)

At one time, this was the first overlook (driving southward on the BRP) that provided a good view of the city of Roanoke. It has now been so long since the overlook has been maintained that a somewhat obscured view is only available when the leaves are off the trees. Hopefully, this will be remedied sometime in the future.

Please Note: As this book went to press, a public comment period had ended concerning the construction and/or closure of a number of trails on or connecting to parkway property from BRP mile 110.6 to mile 126.2. Depending on the decisions that are reached, you may find a number of new trails within this area. As you read the trail descriptions between these miles, you will be alerted as to what trails are being planned and a short description of their routes. However, since decisions had not yet been reached, you may find things are different from what is described. Consult BRP personnel for the latest information.

Mile 110.6. Stewarts Knob Trail [BRP 29] (N 37°17.837 W 79°52.300) Map 9

Length: .075 mile, one way; .15 mile, out-and-back
Difficulty: easy leg stretcher

The short Stewarts Knob Trail leads to a point that at one time had a good view of downtown Roanoke. Sadly, the view is now obscured by ever-growing trees and vegetation. It would take a concerted effort to return—and keep—this viewpoint to its former glory. However, the trail does provide access to the northern end of the Roanoke Valley Horse Trail and Roanoke's Wolf Creek Greenway (see the next entry below).

The Stewarts Knob Trail begins at the north end of the parking area and makes a short rise through dogwood trees and poison ivy. In less than a minute it levels out. Continue level for another minute and then drop slightly to the former viewpoint. Look for persimmons in the fall. The Roanoke Valley Horse Trail [BRP 30] continues from the viewpoint.

Please Note: As this book went to press, there was the possibility that a new loop trail would be constructed from the Stewarts Knob Overlook. It would continue uphill at the point where the Stewarts Knob Trail begins to level out, soon make a left, and rise onto the hill to a loop trail intersection. Continuing uphill, it would eventually turn to descend and return to the loop trail intersection and the overlook.

Roanoke Valley Horse Trail, Blue Ridge Parkway
Miles 110.6–121.4

The impetus for the Roanoke Valley Horse Trail was provided by equestrians of the area. Forced in by encroaching developments, the trail is almost always within shouting distance of the BRP. Small portions offer a bit of isolation, but every section comes into close contact with housing developments, paved roadways, and private property.

The route is maintained by volunteers. Some portions may be well used, while others can be overgrown and possibly hard to follow. Be prepared, especially on the heavily traveled parts, for muddy, churned-up trails peppered with horse droppings. The overgrown portions may require you to negotiate pathways choked by weeds and briers.

The horse trail parallels the BRP on miles 110.6–121.4. However, one section has yet to be built; its completion remains stalled by the logistical problems of providing a horse crossing over the Roanoke River and a loading and unloading area on BRP property. Therefore, the trail does not exist on miles 114.7–116.4.

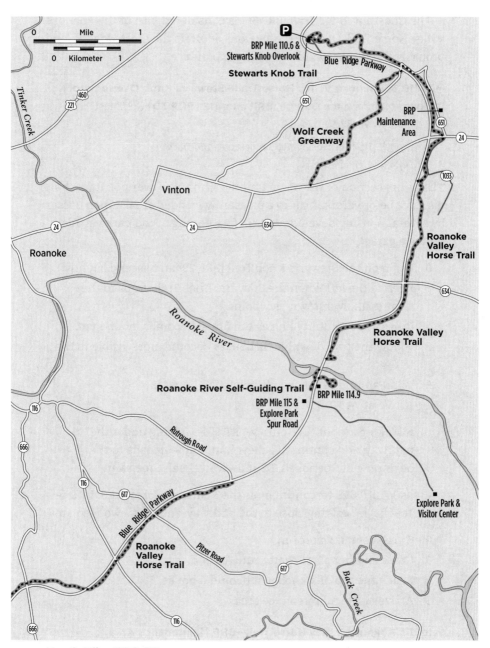

P

BRP Mile 110.6 &
Stewarts Knob Overlook

Stewarts Knob Trail

Blue Ridge Parkway

Tinker Creek

460
221

651

**Wolf Creek
Greenway**

BRP
Maintenance
Area

651

24

1033

Vinton

24

24

634

**Roanoke
Valley
Horse Trail**

Roanoke

634

Roanoke River

**Roanoke Valley
Horse Trail**

Roanoke River Self-Guiding Trail

BRP Mile 114.9

BRP Mile 115 &
Explore Park
Spur Road

116

666

116

Rutrough Road

617

Blue Ridge Parkway

Explore Park &
Visitor Center

**Roanoke
Valley
Horse Trail**

Pitzer Road

617

666

116

Back Creek

0   Mile   1

0   Kilometer   1

Map 9. Miles 110.6–118

The Chestnut Ridge Trail [BRP 36] is considered part of the Roanoke Valley Horse Trail. Of all of the sections, it offers the most wooded, and probably the most rewarding, hiking experience.

Mile 110.6. Roanoke Valley Horse Trail—Stewarts Knob Overlook to Parkway Maintenance Garage, BRP mile 112 [BRP 30] (1,275 feet) (N 37°17.837 W 79°52.300) Map 9

> *Length: 1.5 miles, one way; 3 miles, out-and-back*
> *Difficulty: moderate*

The initial section of the horse trail rises from the overlook for a short distance before dropping into a pleasantly wooded area. It then passes by several housing developments before ending at the parkway maintenance garage.

.0   Begin on the Stewarts Knob Trail [BRP 29] and ascend slightly.

.05 Keep to the left when the Stewarts Knob Trail drops to the right to an overgrown viewpoint.

.2   Cross under a utility line as the forest becomes more open.

.3   Follow the trail downhill as houses become more visible to the left.

.6   Wind around in the woods below the houses.

1.1 Arrive at VA RT 651.

> ▶ Making a right turn onto VA RT 651, walking under the parkway, and continuing a few hundred feet leads to the beginning of Roanoke's 2.2-mile Wolf Creek Greenway.

Cross VA RT 651 to continue on the Roanoke Horse Trail. In a few more feet begin walking close to the parkway, entering a wooded area.

1.2 Cross a small water run.

1.3 Cross another small water run. Ascend.

1.4 Reach the top of a knob just behind a house.

1.5 Arrive at the maintenance area.

Mile 112. Roanoke Valley Horse Trail—BRP Maintenance Area to Roanoke River, BRP mile 114.7 [BRP 31] (N 37°17.294 W 79°51.092) Map 9

> *Length: 3.6 miles, one way; 7.2 miles, out-and-back*
> *Difficulty: moderate*

The Wolf Creek Greenway parallels its namesake stream through a concrete culvert.

The first third of this part of the horse trail is either a road walk or a hike right next to houses. The second third is a pleasant walk, sometimes through open areas and sometimes in wooded areas. The final third is in a forest of hardwood and mountain laurel as the land drops to the Roanoke River.

.0   Walk through the woods in front of the BRP maintenance area.

.3   In a corner of a field, bear left to come to a BRP entrance access road. Follow the road downhill to VA RT 24 and follow it to the east.

.35   Use caution crossing VA RT 24 and follow VA RT 1033 (Chestnut Mountain Road—N 37°17.046 W 79°51.008) for 100 feet. Be alert! Turn right onto the trail entering the woods. Remain in the woods.

.6   Walk between the parkway and Chestnut Mountain Road.

.8   Pass by the gravesites of Abram and Allie Baker. Make a series of ascents and descents in the woods next to several houses.

1.0   Veer away from the houses.

1.2   Cross a small water run and switchback to the left. Be alert! Do not continue to go straight; switchback to the right and begin a series of switchbacks to the top of a knob. The trail is now in pleasantly open woods.

1.4 Be alert! At the park border, do not follow the boundary line downhill. Rise slightly uphill to walk just below a few houses.

1.5 Descend to cross a small water run, and move away from the houses.

1.7 Pass to the left of a small tree farm plot and turn right to descend. Be alert! Look for the trail to go to the left under the power lines. (Do not go downhill with the power lines.) The trail may be obscure here as it slowly descends to the BRP.

2.1 Parallel the BRP as houses become visible again.

2.3 Cross VA RT 634 (Hardy Drive) and ascend on Hammond Drive.

2.6 Be alert! Turn right into the woods following a utility line right-of-way.

2.7 Be alert! Veer away from the utility lines and enjoy the rich aroma of a cattle pasture.

3.2 Enter the woods on a wide, soft, and pleasant pathway. Mountain laurel lines the trail.

3.4 The route narrows as it begins to descend.

3.6 The trail ends underneath the Roanoke River Bridge. You must scramble uphill to reach the parkway. (The Roanoke Valley Horse Trail picks up again at BRP mile 116.4. See Chapter 4.)

   Please Note: As this book went to press, there was the possibility that a new trail would be constructed connecting the horse trail underneath the Roanoke River Bridge to the proposed Vinton Business Center Greenway a short distance back to the north at BRP mile 114.

Mile 112.2. VA RT 24

Food, gas, and lodging located just off the BRP. Access to Roanoke (5 miles), Vinton (2 miles), and Stewartsville (4 miles).

Mile 112.9. Roanoke Basin Overlook (1,250 feet)

Unless this overlook has been recently maintained, trees will block the view.

Mile 114.7. Roanoke River Bridge

3.
The Appalachian Trail

From Springer Mountain in Georgia, the Appalachian Trail follows the crest of the Appalachian Mountains through 14 states and covers more than 2,100 miles on its way to the summit of Katahdin in Maine's Baxter State Park. Every year, hardy souls complete the full length in 4 to 6 months, but the majority of people use the trail for much shorter periods of time—a few hours, a day, a weekend, or possibly a week. Trailside shelters, plenty of easy access points, an extensive network of side trails, and ideal campsites on the George Washington and Jefferson National Forest lands are what draw many of these hikers to the AT along the BRP.

Virginia contains more than 500 miles of the AT, about one-quarter of its total distance. Of that, a little more than 100 miles parallel the BRP from Rockfish Gap (mile 0) to Black Horse Gap (mile 97.7), where the trail swings to the west and leaves the main crest of the Blue Ridge Mountains. Construction of the parkway on the original route of the AT south of Black Horse Gap necessitated a major relocation in the 1940s and 1950s. Before that, the trail had continued in the direction the BRP now follows—crossing Rocky Knob and the Pinnacles of Dan before entering North Carolina near Galax, Virginia.

The AT is the result of one man's vision and many people's hard work. Benton McKaye foresaw the growth of population in the eastern United States. He also recognized the human need to be able to step back from civilization for a while to become refreshed and renewed by the peace and beauty of the natural world. His 1921 proposal for an extended footpath in the Appalachian Mountains resulted in volunteers building the first few miles of the AT in New York in 1922. Fifteen years later, the final link in the AT was completed on a ridgetop in central Maine. Volunteers (and some federal and state employees) continue to relocate, build, and maintain America's premier National Scenic Trail.

If you want to spend some energetic but rewarding days filled with the camaraderie of the trail, contact one of the local clubs and join them on a workhike to maintain a section of the AT along the BRP.

Maintains the AT on BRP miles 0–13.6:

Old Dominion Appalachian Trail Club
P.O. Box 25283
Richmond, VA 23260
www.odatc.net

Maintains the AT on BRP miles 13.6–27.2:

Tidewater Appalachian Trail Club
P.O. Box 8246
Norfolk, VA 23503
www.tidewateratc.com

Maintains the AT on BRP miles 27.2–97.7:

Natural Bridge Appalachian Trail Club
P.O. Box 3012
Lynchburg, VA 24503
www.nbatc.com

Maintains the section of the AT south of BRP mile 97.7:

Roanoke Appalachian Trail Club
P.O. Box 12282
Roanoke, VA 24024
www.ratc.org

All distances are measured as a one-way hike, and descriptions are arranged in a north-to-south direction. The AT is well marked and usually well maintained. If you desire more information, consult the *Appalachian Trail Guide to Central Virginia*. This and other AT guidebooks and additional information about the trail are available from

The Appalachian Trail Conservancy
P.O. Box 807
Harpers Ferry, WV 25425
304-535-6331
www.appalachiantrail.org

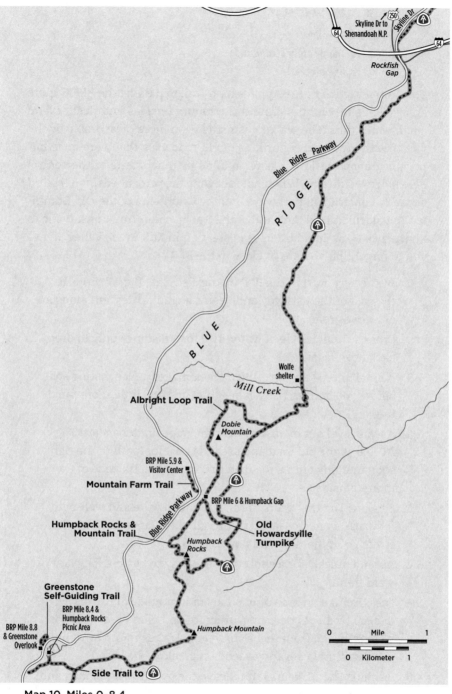

Map 10. Miles 0–8.4

Mile 0 (N 38°01.864 W 78°51.470) Map 10

> *Length: 7.85 miles*
> *Difficulty: moderately strenuous*
> *Shelter: mile point 4.8*

This initial section of the Appalachian Trail to parallel the BRP is quite enjoyable as it contours around the mountainsides and past several small water runs. The walking is made even more pleasurable by the fact that the route uses portions of old roadways that were once important transportation links for numerous inhabitants of the central Blue Ridge Mountains. When not following these roadbeds, you'll be on superbly constructed pathways built by volunteers of the Old Dominion Appalachian Trail Club and of the Appalachian Trail Conservancy's Konnarock Crew. In addition, the isolation in Mill Creek Valley allows you to forget that you are so close to the BRP.

.0 At the very start of the BRP in Rockfish Gap, the AT drops to the east of the parkway and begins a gradual descent along an old woods road.

.5 Cross a small trickle of water; rise for a distance only to drop back down again.

.9 A small moss- and fern-lined creek makes a nice resting spot before you start to rise again—this time at a little more rapid rate.

1.3 As you level out in an area of large grapevines, be alert! The AT leaves the old road and ascends on a footpath to the right, soon merging onto a roadbed to continue its traverse of the mountainside.

1.6 Be alert! The trail veers to the left onto a wide and well-built footpath, soon crossing a creek valley and ascending to a long stretch of minor ups and downs.

3.2 Ascend quickly for a short distance only to begin a long downward trend.

3.8 Pass through an area of previous mountain farm use (as evidenced by an old decaying structure and piles of stones that were removed from the earth to enable the ground to be put to agricultural use) and ascend on an old woods road.

4.0 Be alert! The AT bears left to leave the overgrown roadbed and begin its long switchbacked descent into Mill Creek Valley.

4.8 Arrive at uniquely built Wolfe shelter and its distinctive privy. Enjoy the peace and solitude of this small and isolated mountain valley before crossing Mill Creek and rising via a multitude of switchbacks.

5.7 Come to a good view of Rockfish Valley, Rockfish Gap, and mountains in the southern part of Shenandoah National Park.

6.3 Be alert! The Albright Loop Trail [BRP 2] comes in from the right to join with the AT.

6.7 A side trail to the left goes .2 mile to the Glass Hollow Overlook, a worthwhile short excursion if you have the time and energy.

7.6 You could continue straight along the AT into the next section described below, but to return to the BRP, make a right onto the Old Howardsville Turnpike [BRP 3] and ascend.

7.85 Arrive at the Humpback Gap parking area. Northward for .2 mile on the BRP would lead to the Humpback Rocks Visitor Center (water and restrooms) and Mountain Farm Trail [BRP 1].

Mile 6 (N 37°58.112 W 78°53.793) Map 10

> Length: 5.8 miles (plus the additional .3-mile side trail to the Humpback Rocks picnic area; plus an additional .6 mile if you take the optional side trip to Humpback Rocks)
> Difficulty: strenuous

Views to the west from Humpback Rocks on the optional side trip make this a nice walk in the evening, while the eastward views on Humpback Mountain might lure you for a sunrise hike. Abundant springtime trillium, evidence of former inhabitants, remote ridgeline walking, and possible deer sightings are additional attractions. The hike is strenuous due to the climb up to Humpback Rocks.

Camping is not permitted on this section.

.0 Begin by following the route of the Old Howardsville Turnpike [BRP 3] that descends from the middle of the Humpback Gap parking area.

.25 Turn right along the white-blazed route of the AT, continuing to follow the route of the Old Howardsville Turnpike. Notice how well constructed the rock cribbing is that shores up the roadbed, a testament to the skills of those who built this road by hand centuries ago.

.8 Be alert! The unmaintained Old Howardsville Turnpike continues to descend eastward to the left; bear right and ascend along the white-blazed AT.

1.7 Pass Bear Spring on the right of the trail.

2.5 Pass another spring to the left of the trail.

3.2 The blue-blazed trail to the right leads .3 mile to Humpback Rocks and grand views of the Back Creek Valley and Pine Ridge. Continue left to stay on the AT.

4.2 Attain the summit of Humpback Mountain. Rock outcroppings allow views of Rockfish Gap and Shenandoah National Park to the north, Shenandoah Valley to the west, and Rockfish Valley to the east. Begin to descend.

5.2 The view to the south is of Wintergreen Resort.

5.8 Take the blue-blazed trail (same as [BRP 3] in Chapter 2) to the right for .3 mile to arrive at the Humpback Rocks picnic area (BRP mile 8.4).

Mile 8.4 (N 37°56.718 W 78°55.588) Map 11

Length: 1.5 miles, plus .3 mile on the approach trail
Difficulty: moderate

After ascending the .3-mile approach trail, this AT section is almost all downhill. Perhaps its most significant feature is at the end of the section—a delicious, cool drink from Dripping Rock Spring.

Camping is not permitted on this section.

.0 At the far end of the Humpback Rocks picnic area parking lot, follow the blue-blazed trail uphill (marked with an AT symbol—[BRP 3] in Chapter 2).

.3 Trail intersection. Turn right onto the AT and descend, passing by Laurel Springs (unreliable) and ascending to come close to the Wintergreen Resort.

.6 A rock outcrop provides a view to the west. Because this can be a precarious crossing in inclement weather, there is a blue-blazed side trail going behind the outcrop to provide safe passage.

1.3 The trail to the left goes into Wintergreen Resort; continue right on the AT.

1.5 Arrive at Dripping Rock Spring parking area (BRP mile 9.6).

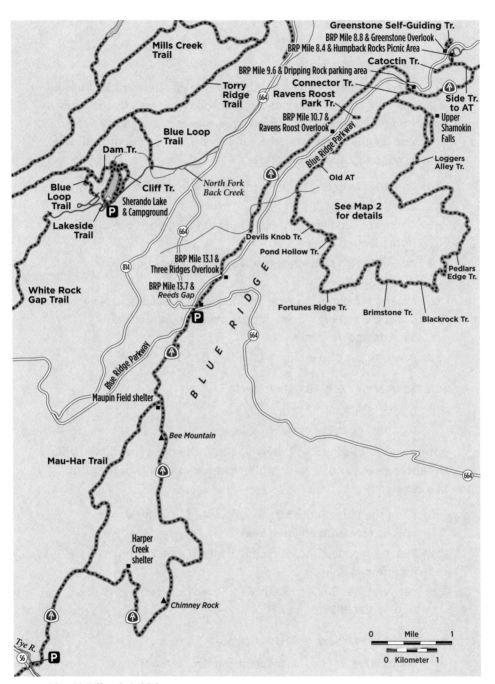

Mills Creek Trail

Greenstone Self-Guiding Tr.

BRP Mile 8.8 & Greenstone Overlook

BRP Mile 8.4 & Humpback Rocks Picnic Area

Catoctin Tr.

BRP Mile 9.6 & Dripping Rock parking area

Torry Ridge Trail

Connector Tr.

Ravens Roost Park Tr.

Side Tr. to AT

Upper Shamokin Falls

BRP Mile 10.7 & Ravens Roost Overlook

Blue Loop Trail

Dam Tr.

Loggers Alley Tr.

Blue Ridge Parkway

Old AT

Blue Loop Trail

Cliff Tr.

North Fork Back Creek

See Map 2 for details

Sherando Lake & Campground

Lakeside Trail

Devils Knob Tr.

Pond Hollow Tr.

White Rock Gap Trail

BRP Mile 13.1 & Three Ridges Overlook

BRP Mile 13.7 & Reeds Gap

Pedlars Edge Tr.

Fortunes Ridge Tr.

Brimstone Tr.

Blackrock Tr.

BLUE RIDGE

Blue Ridge Parkway

Maupin Field shelter

Bee Mountain

Mau-Har Trail

Harper Creek shelter

Chimney Rock

Tye R.

0   Mile   1

0   Kilometer   1

Map 11. Miles 8.4–27.2

Mile 9.6 (N 37°56.478 W 78°56.184) Map 11

> *Length: 4.3 miles*
> *Difficulty: moderate*

This short excursion is worthwhile because of the abundant spring wildflowers, a steeply plunging stream, and two views. One is along a grassy ridge, and the other is from a prominent outcropping.

Except for the areas near the road crossings, camping is allowed anywhere along this section of the AT.

.0 From the Dripping Rock Spring parking area, cross the BRP and descend.

.5 There are good views of Shenandoah Valley and Torry Ridge from an open ledge.

1.2 A .1-mile side trail leads to a westward view from a rock outcropping.

2.0 Cross a bubbling, gurgling, rushing stream making its way down the steeply sloping mountainside; continue with ascents and descents.

4.3 Arrive at the Three Ridges Overlook (BRP mile 13.1).

Mile 13.1 (N 37°54.422 W 78°58.749) Map 11

> *Length: .5 mile*
> *Difficulty: moderately easy*

Spring and fall flowers will draw you into the open meadows, while the short ascent and descent will help awaken your legs after driving in a car all day.

.0 From the Three Ridges Overlook, ascend into the woods and emerge onto an open field.

.2 Reach a wooded knoll; descend through a park service–maintained field.

.5 Arrive at VA RT 664 in Reids Gap. Three hundred feet to the right is the BRP (mile 13.7).

Mile 13.7 (N 37°54.090 W 78°59.131) Maps 11 & 12

> *Length: 47 miles (does not include any of the side trails)*
> *Difficulty: strenuous*
> *Shelters: mile points 1.6, 7.7, 15.2, 22.2, 32.4, and 38*
> *Highly recommended*

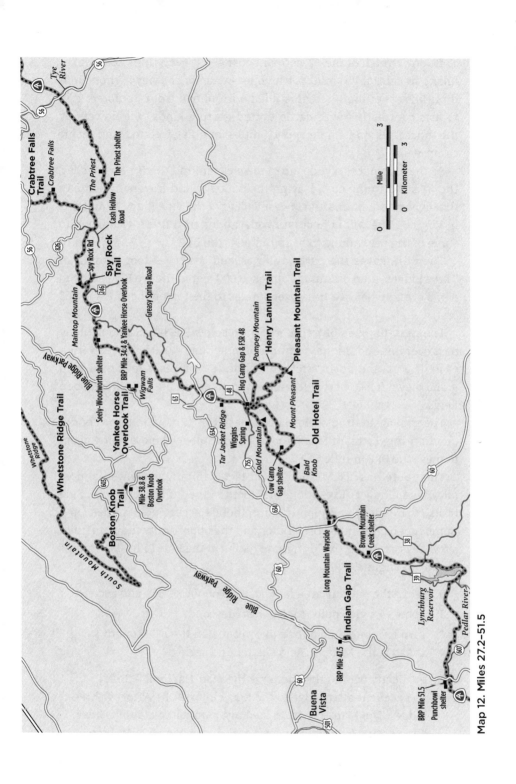

Map 12. Miles 27.2–51.5

This long stretch of the AT contains just about everything that makes hiking in central Virginia worthwhile—magnificent views, rhododendron-lined mountain streams filled with native trout, remote virgin forests contrasting with cattle-dotted grazing lands, wildflowers by the thousands, and ample opportunities for quiet, isolated, and scenic campsites.

As the BRP makes a wide arc to the west around the Tye River Valley, the AT stays to the east, leaving the parkway and traversing some of the highest mountains and lowest valleys of the Blue Ridge Mountains in Virginia. The wildly fluctuating elevations turn these 47 miles into some of the best hiking to be found near the BRP.

The trail leaves the parkway to ascend the 3,970-foot summit of Three Ridges, then plummets almost 3,000 feet to the Tye River, only to climb even higher in a little over 4 miles to the top of The Priest (4,063 feet).

The next 18 miles of trail never drop below 3,200 feet and actually pass over three additional summits of more than 4,000 feet in elevation each. The up-and-down effort this altitude requires is rewarded with grand views from short side trails, rock outcroppings, and wide, open fields.

The trail again drops below 1,000 feet—this time to follow a rhododendron-lined stream to a stand of virgin timber—before rising again to meet the BRP at mile 51.5.

This route has six AT shelters; in fact, camping is allowed almost anywhere along it. (Exceptions are noted in the trail description.) Side trails (also noted) and plentiful automobile access points open up a number of circuit-hike possibilities and the opportunity to spend quite a few days camping, exploring, and hiking in the Blue Ridge Mountains of central Virginia.

.0   Leave the parking area in Reids Gap on VA RT 664 and ascend.

.8   Come to a viewpoint to the west; descend.

1.6 Turn left onto an old road to continue on the AT. Straight
     ahead is the Maupin Field shelter and spring.

     ▶ Directly behind the shelter is the Mau-Har Trail [FS 303],
     an excellent alternative to the long climb of the AT over Three
     Ridges. The Mau-Har drops steadily, paralleling Maupin Creek
     and passing by numerous waterfalls—one over 40 feet high.
     This 3-mile side trail rejoins the AT at the 8.2-mile point,
     .8 mile south of Harpers Creek shelter.

1.7 Leave the roadway and turn left onto a pathway going uphill to begin a long, steady climb.

2.0 Arrive at the summit of Bee Mountain; descend slightly only to rise again.

3.6 The rock outcropping to the right provides a view of The Priest.

4.2 Attain the highest point on Three Ridges and begin to descend via switchbacks.

5.7 Pass Chimney Rocks.

6.2 Arrive at another view of The Priest.

7.7 Come onto an old road and turn left. (Harpers Creek shelter and water are .1 mile to the right.)

8.7 At the intersection with the Mau-Har Trail [FS 303], bear left.

▶ A right turn onto Mau-Har will lead back to the Maupin Field shelter in 3 miles.

10.7 Cross the Tye River on a cable-suspension bridge and arrive at VA RT 56. The BRP (mile 27.2) is 11.5 miles to the right on VA RT 56. Cross the paved road to continue on the AT, and begin the 4-mile, switchbacked climb to the summit of The Priest.

13.1 A rock outcropping overlooks the Tye River Valley.

14.9 The wooded summit of The Priest offers no views, but .2 mile beyond, a short side trail leads to a panorama of Pinnacle Ridge to the west and Three Ridges to the north. Descend.

15.2 Trail intersection. One-tenth mile to the left is The Priest shelter and spring. Bear right to continue on the AT, where camping is prohibited for the next .3 mile.

16.0 Come to VA RT 826, a dirt road passable by automobile. The road descends .5 mile to the forest service's Crabtree Falls Trail before continuing on about another 4 miles to VA RT 56 near Montebello.

▶ The 3-mile Crabtree Falls Trail [FS 526] descends along Crabtree Creek passing by five major falls areas and numerous smaller cascades before arriving at VA RT 56 a few miles east of Montebello.

Continue on the AT by crossing VA RT 826 and ascending into the woods.

16.5 Reach the top of the ascent and descend.

16.9 Cross Cash Hollow Road (impassable by car) and gradually ascend for the next 1.5 miles.

18.3 Views of Little Priest, The Friar, High Peak of Tobacco Row, and The Cardinal are obtained from Cash Hollow Rock.

19.1 Attain the 4,040-foot top of Maintop Mountain, where there are no views due to its wooded summit.

19.4 Trail intersection.

▶ The side trail to the left goes .1 mile to Spy Rock for a 360-degree view unequaled anywhere else in the area. Maintop Mountain is due north, while the whole Religious Range—The Priest, Little Priest, The Friar, Little Friar, and The Cardinal are visible to the northeast, east, and south. Whetstone Ridge and Fork Mountain are to the west. Don't pass up the chance to enjoy this wonderful vista.

19.9 Cross Spy Rock Road (may appear on older maps and in references as Fish Hatchery Road). (VA RT 56 near Montebello is 1.5 miles to the right on Spy Rock Road.) Ascend.

20.7 Ascending through hemlocks, reach the highest point on the ridgeline. Unfortunately, the trees are under attack from the hemlock woolly adelgid. First appearing on the West Coast in the 1920s, the insects had minimal effect on western hemlocks, but by the 1950s, eastern hemlock trees began to suffer. Apparently having no resistance to the insects, which suck the sap from the base of the trees' needles, eastern hemlocks have been dying at an alarming rate. Many of the trees may be dead by the time you hike here.

22.2 The trail to the left goes to the Seely-Woodworth shelter and spring in .1 mile. Bear right to continue on the AT.

25.0 A rock outcropping affords a view of The Priest.

26.0 Cross Greasy Spring Road.

26.5 Cross FSR 246.

27.7 Arrive at FSR 63, an automobile access point. (To the right, via FSR 63 and VA RT 634, is US RT 60 [7 miles], about 3 miles east of the BRP [mile 45.6] in Humphrey Gap.) Cross FSR 63 to continue on the AT.

28.5 Continue to ascend in an open field as a better vista unfolds with every step you take.

29.0 Arrive at the summit of Tar Jacket Ridge. Gaze northward to marvel at what you have traversed so far—Elk Pond Mountain, Maintop Mountain, and The Priest. Turn 180 degrees to see where you are going—over Cold Mountain and Bald Knob. Descend on an old road.

30.0 Come into Hog Camp Gap. (FSR 48 is passable by automobile and goes to Wiggins Spring and a good campsite .5 mile to the right. The spring is a true joy, as it bubbles forth gallons of cool, clear water every hour. US RT 60 is less than 4 miles beyond Wiggins Spring via VA RT 755 and VA RT 634.)

▶ One-half mile to the left in Hog Camp Gap is a nice diversion—the 5.5-mile Henry Lanum Trail [FS 702]. It just misses the summit of Pompey Mountain but does lead to a .4-mile side trail [FS 701] to the top of Mount Pleasant for good views of the surrounding countryside. A spring and campsite are located about midway on the loop.

Cross FSR 48 and begin the ascent of Cold Mountain to continue on the AT from Hog Camp Gap. Watch the blazes closely as the AT follows a maze of dirt roads and trails.

31.2 Arrive at the 4,022-foot summit of Cold Mountain. Enjoy this final 360-degree grandstand view. Tar Jacket Ridge and Elk Pond Mountain are almost due north, while the Religious Range is to the northeast. Your route over Bald Mountain lies to the south. Camping is prohibited in this open area. Descend.

32.4 Come into Cow Camp Gap and cross a roadbed. The Cow Camp Gap shelter and spring are .6 mile to the left along this old road, which is the Old Hotel Trail.

▶ The Old Hotel continues for 2.25 miles from the shelter to end at FSR 48, just a few hundred feet from the trailhead for the Henry Lanum Trail. Along the route is the spot where a former landowner, a Dr. Richeson, had a dwelling to which he would frequently invite guests. It eventually came to be known as "The Hotel" (and thus the name for the trail). Foundations of the building are still there but are hard to find.

Cold Mountain's open ridgeline provides a 360-degree vista.

33.5 Attain the wooded summit of Bald Knob (4,049 feet) and begin a long, gradual descent—eventually dropping below 3,000 feet for the first time in more than 18 miles.

36.2 Come into the Long Mountain Wayside picnic area on US RT 60 (4 miles east of BRP mile 45.6). Cross the highway, bear right, and descend via switchbacks.

37.2 Cross and begin to parallel Brown Mountain Creek, passing by old foundations and other remnants of former settlements.

38.0 Arrive at the Brown Mountain Creek shelter and spring. Cross the creek on a footbridge.

40.0 Cross FSR 38 (passable by automobile), which leads, to the left, to US RT 60 at Long Mountain Wayside (3.5 miles).

40.4 Cross Swamping Camp Creek.

42.0 A view of Lynchburg Reservoir and dam.

42.9 Cross the Pedlar River on a well-constructed bridge, step across FSR 39, and ascend.

43.4 Pass through a 4.5-acre virgin forest.

43.7 Cross a dirt road. Continue with several small ups and downs.

46.7 Cross VA RT 607.

47.0 Arrive at the parking area on the parkway at BRP mile 51.5.

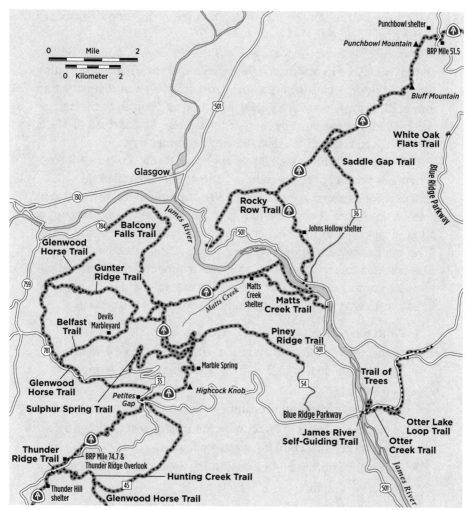

Map 13. Miles 51.5–74.7

Mile 51.5 (N 37°40.428 W 79°20.074) Map 13

> *Length: 21 miles (does not include any side trails)*
> *Difficulty: strenuous*
> *Shelters: mile points .4, 9.2, and 13.2*

The AT again swings away from the BRP, this time to the west. Rising to 3,372-foot Bluff Mountain, the trail then follows a narrow, rocky ridgeline to impressive views overlooking the James River Water Gap. Thousands of years of erosion have allowed Virginia's longest river to carve its way through the Blue Ridge Mountains as it flows eastward to the Chesapeake Bay.

Water seems to be the focal point of this AT segment. Johns Hollow shelter is located in a wide, flat valley created by a stream descending the steep slopes of Little Rocky Row. Crossing the James River, the trail enters the James River Face Wilderness Area and comes to the narrow confines of a gorge built by Matts Creek. Large pools, close to Matts Creek shelter, are hard to resist on warm summer days.

The trail then climbs steadily to Highcock Knob (3,073 feet) before arriving at the end of the section in Petites Gap (BRP mile 71).

Except for the area around US RT 501, the trail along the southern side of the James River, and BRP land near Petites Gap, camping is allowed throughout this section. Three side trails north of the James River offer circuit-hike opportunities. In fact, the James River Face Wilderness Area has a network of trails interconnecting with the AT, allowing a number of extended backpacking excursions, described below. Road access is at the beginning, middle, and end of the section.

.0 From the parking area at mile 51.5, cross the BRP and ascend.

.4 Come onto an old road and turn left. The road to the right descends 1,000 feet to the Punchbowl shelter and spring next to a small pond.

.6 Leave the roadbed and continue to ascend on a worn pathway.

1.0 Attain the summit of Punchbowl Mountain, descend slightly, but soon resume climbing via switchbacks.

2.0 Attain the summit of Bluff Mountain; descend.

2.5 Pass a viewpoint.

3.6 Trail intersection.

▶ The blue-blazed Salt Log Gap Trail [FS 511] to the right descends 4.5 miles through Belle Cove Valley to reach US RT 501 a couple of miles north of Glasgow.

Bear left to continue on the AT.

4.6 Trail intersection.

▶ Blue-blazed Saddle Gap Trail [FS 703] drops 2.5 miles to FSR 36 about 3 miles north of US RT 501.

Bear right and ascend out of the gap to continue on the AT.

6.1 Reach the high point on the ridgeline and descend, only to begin another climb.

7.0 A short path to the left leads to Fullers Rocks. The impressive view is of the James River cutting through the Blue Ridge Mountains and of the steep mountainsides south of the river in the James River Face Wilderness Area.

7.2 Trail intersection.

> ▶ To the right, blue-blazed Rocky Row Trail [FS 512] goes down almost 3 miles to US RT 501, about 2.5 miles west of where the AT crosses US RT 501 at mile 11.1.

To continue on the AT, make a hard left. Descend steeply, sometimes on switchbacks, sometimes not. Also, cross several dirt roads.

9.2 Johns Hollow shelter and spring are just to the left of the AT. Soon, cross FSR 36 and other dirt roads. Watch closely for the blazes.

11.0 Cross US RT 501 (BRP mile 63.7 is 3 miles to the left; Glasgow is almost 3 miles to the right). Cross under railroad tracks just a few hundred feet later.

11.1 The dedicated efforts of Bill Foot, a deceased member of the Natural Bridge Appalachian Trail Club, enable you to enjoy and cross the James River on a 625-foot bridge free of any road traffic.

11.2 Swing right to follow the AT just above the river's southern shore.

12.4 The trail bears away from the river to begin an ascent along Matts Creek.

13.1 The blue-blazed Matts Creek Trail comes in from the left; continue to the right along the white-blazed AT.

13.2 Pass by the Matts Creek shelter. The water supply is from the stream, so be sure to treat before using. Cross the creek on a footbridge.

13.9 Come to a series of views overlooking the James River.

16.0 Reach a ridgeline and trail intersection. The AT bears to the left and ascends.

> ▶ The Balcony Falls Trail [FS 7], a portion of which some maps and guidebooks identify as an extension of the Sulphur Spring

Trail, bears right. It gradually descends for 5.5 miles, passing a couple of views of the James River, to reach VA RT 782. You can reach this trailhead in an automobile by following FSR 35 (which becomes VA RT 781) from Petites Gap (BRP mile 71) for 3 miles to VA RT 759. (Along the way, the road passes trailheads for the Sulphur Spring Trail [FS 7; same as Balcony Falls Trail] 1 mile from the BRP, and the Belfast Creek Trail [FS 9] 2 miles from the BRP.) Turn right onto VA RT 759 and follow it for 3 miles to VA RT 782. (About 1.5 miles from the junction of VA RT 781 and VA RT 759 is the Gunter Ridge Trailhead [FS 8] .3 mile beyond the Glenwood Iron Furnace.) A right turn onto VA RT 782 for another 1.5 miles will bring you to the Balcony Falls Trailhead [FS 7].

16.5 Trail intersection. The AT makes a hard left and continues to ascend.

▶ The Belfast Creek Trail [FS 9] goes right for .4 mile to an intersection with the Gunter Ridge Trail [FS 8], then bears left for 1.5 miles to Devils Marbleyard, a large area of giant boulders. It then descends Belfast Creek for another mile to VA RT 781. (See trailhead directions in the mile point 16 description above.) The Gunter Ridge Trail [FS 8] bears right from the intersection and uses switchbacks through a profuse growth of mountain laurel to reach VA RT 781 in 4.5 miles. (These trailhead directions may also be found in the mile point 16 description above.)

18.3 Trail intersection. Cross to continue to gradually ascend on the AT.

▶ To the left, the Sulphur Spring Trail [FS 7] descends 2 miles to the AT and Balcony Falls Trail [FS 7] intersection (mile point 16). To the right, the Sulphur Spring Trail passes the Piney Ridge Trail [FS 2] in 1.5 miles and continues to follow the old road another 2.5 miles to Sulphur Spring and FSR 35. (See the mile point 16 description above for trailhead directions.)

The Piney Ridge Trail [FS 2] bears left from the Sulphur Spring Trail to gradually descend the ridgeline for 3.5 miles to FSR 54. This trailhead may be reached by leaving the BRP at mile 63.7, following US RT 501 west for .5 mile, and turning left onto FSR 54. The trail begins about a half mile up this road.

18.8 Marble Spring campsite. The spring is .1 mile to the right. Continue on the AT with ascents, steeply at times.

19.8 Attain Highcock Knob (no views) and descend quickly.

21.0 Arrive at Petites Gap and FSR 35. The BRP (mile 71) is less than 500 feet to the left.

Mile 71 (N 37°33.564 W 79°29.429) Map 13

Length: 3.4 miles
Difficulty: strenuous

Passing through the Thunder Ridge Wilderness Area, the AT climbs more than 1,300 feet in less than 2 miles. Late spring wildflowers are especially plentiful on the ascent. A second climb is rewarded with a view of the James River and the distant Allegheny Mountains to the west.

Except in the areas around Petites Gap and the Thunder Ridge Overlook, camping is permitted along this entire section.

.0 Cross FSR 35 in Petites Gap (.1 mile west of BRP) and ascend on an old road into the Thunder Ridge Wilderness Area.

.4 Be alert! The trail turns left from the old road onto a footpath.

1.0 Pass a view to the right.

2.0 Arrive at the summit of Thunder Ridge (no views). Descend, only to rise again.

3.3 Trail intersection. To the left is the Thunder Ridge Overlook parking lot (BRP mile 74.7). Bear right and come to the view overlooking the Great Valley and Allegheny Mountains. Continue beyond the view and, in .1 mile, leave the AT to reach the parking lot via a side trail to the left.

Mile 74.7 (N 37°32.385 W 79°29.425) Map 14

Length: 1.7 miles
Difficulty: moderately easy
Shelter: mile point 1.4

This short segment is most notable for the easy access it provides to the Thunder Hill shelter and accompanying spring. Columbine and trillium line the pathway in May and June.

Camping is allowed on the entire section except in the areas around the Thunder Ridge Overlook and the BRP crossings. Hunting Creek Trail [FS 3] also provides a few isolated campsites.

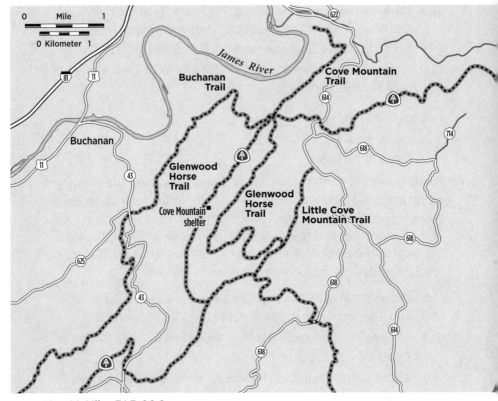

Map 14. Miles 74.7–90.9

.0   Park at the Thunder Ridge Overlook, take the approach trail to the AT, and turn left.

.3   Cross the BRP (mile 74.9).

.4   Trail intersection.

> ▶ Blue-blazed Hunting Creek Trail [FS 3] descends, by way of switchbacks and rhododendron tunnels, for 2 miles to FSR 45. (See Chapter 2, mile 74.7, for a detailed description of this trail and directions to the trailhead on FSR 45.)

To continue on the AT, bear right on a gently ascending pathway.

1.4   Come to the Thunder Hill shelter and spring.

1.7   Arrive at the BRP (mile 76.3).

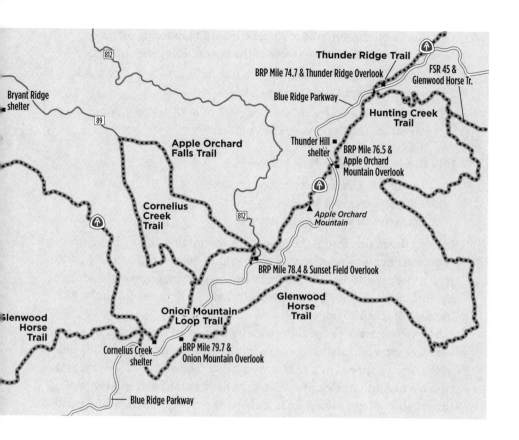

Mile 76.3 (N 37°31.312 W 79°30.238) Map 14

Length: 2.6 miles
Difficulty: moderately strenuous

A superb relocation by volunteers of the Natural Bridge Appalachian Trail Club and the Appalachian Trail Conservancy's Konnarock Crew permits the AT to cross the top of Apple Orchard Mountain as it once did in the 1930s. Camping is prohibited near the BRP road crossings and on the summit of the mountain.

.0 Park at the Apple Orchard Overlook (BRP mile 76.5) and walk back to the AT crossing at mile 76.3. Turn left onto the AT in a level area, but soon begin to ascend.

.6 Rock steps enable you to pass under The Guillotine, a most interesting rock formation.

.9   Rocks on the summit of Apple Orchard Mountain permit a more than 250-degree view of the surrounding mountains.

2.3   Come to FSR 812, and in less than .1 mile, turn left onto a side trail to Sunset Field Overlook.

2.6   Arrive at Sunset Field Overlook (BRP mile 78.4) and a grand view into the Great Valley of Virginia.

Mile 78.4 (N 37°30.442 W 79°31.441) Map 14

> *Length: 18 miles (does not include side trails)*
> *Difficulty: strenuous*
> *Shelters: mile points 2.9, 7.8, and 14.8*

Leaving the main crest of the Blue Ridge Mountains, the AT heads west to cross a couple of relatively level ridgelines before losing nearly 2,000 feet to descend to VA RT 714. From this road it makes more than ten ascents and descents (one of over 1,000 feet) before rejoining the BRP in Bear Wallow Gap (mile 90.9).

Springtime travelers of this challenging part of the AT will be compensated by a profuse array of blooming wildflowers. Mayapple is one of the first to appear in late March, quickly followed by bloodroot and trillium in April. Azalea and wild geranium burst forth in May, while rhododendron and mountain laurel line the trail in late May and early June.

A 7.5-mile circuit, via the Apple Orchard Falls [FS 17] and Cornelius Creek [FS 18] trails, offers a chance to view the falls, do some isolated ridgeline walking, and find plenty of flat campsites. Additional side trails present other options.

Except for areas near the road crossings, camping is permitted throughout the section and on the side trails.

.0   Begin at the Sunset Field Overlook and descend on the Apple Orchard Falls Trail.

.2   Trail intersection; turn left to continue on the AT.

> ▶ The Apple Orchard Falls Trail [FS 17] goes straight ahead for 1 mile to the falls and 3.4 miles more to FSR 59 and the intersection with the Cornelius Creek Trail [FS 18]. (See Chapter 2, mile 78.4, for a detailed description and trailhead directions.)

.9   Reach the ridgeline and descend.

1.4   Trail intersection; the AT bears to the left.

▶ The Cornelius Creek Trail to the right traverses Backbone Ridge and Cornelius Creek for 3 miles to arrive at FSR 59 and an intersection with the Apple Orchard Falls Trail.

2.9   Trail intersection; bear right to continue on the AT.

▶ The short blue-blazed trail to the left goes to the Cornelius Creek shelter and water. (The BRP [mile 80.4] may be reached by following the unblazed trail behind the shelter for .1 mile to a dirt road. Turn left on the road to reach the BRP in 1,000 feet.)

4.0   Come to a view of the Federal Aviation Administration installation atop Apple Orchard Mountain. Continue with minor ups and downs on the ridgeline. Eventually begin a long descent.

7.5   Follow a dirt road to the right. Be alert! In less than .1 mile the trail turns to the left and descends along a creek.

7.7   The blue-blazed trail to the left goes .5 mile to VA RT 714. Keep to the right on the AT.

7.8   Pass by the Bryant Ridge shelter and cross Hamps Branch, the shelter's water source.

9.4   The blue-blazed trail to the left goes .8 mile to VA RT 714. Keep to the right on the AT.

10.0 Reach the ridgeline and continue with very minor ups and downs. However, eventually begin a long descent with occasional views.

11.6 Come onto VA RT 614, turn right, cross the bridge, and in less than 500 feet turn left uphill into the woods.

▶ This point may be reached by driving VA RT 619 from the BRP in Powell Gap (mile 89.1) to the intersection with VA RT 614. Turn left and stay on VA RT 614 to pass by the Little Cove Mountain Trailhead and, .9 mile beyond that, arrive at the AT crossing. Little Cove Mountain Trail [FS 25] ascends for nearly 3 miles to join the AT at mile point 15.8 (below).

13.0 Trail intersection; the AT bears to the left and begins a long series of ups and downs on the ridgeline.

▶ The Cove Mountain Trail [FS 23] drops to the right 2 miles to reach VA RT 622 about .2 mile from VA RT 614 in Arcadia. One-tenth of a mile down the Cove Mountain Trail, the Buchanan

Hikers always look forward to a rest break at Appalachian Trail shelters, such as the one on Cove Mountain.

Trail [FS 24] bears left and descends for 3 miles, via trail and dirt roads, to reach VA RT 43 about 1 mile south of Buchanan.

14.8 A short side trail to the left goes to Cove Mountain shelter (water not readily available).

16.1 Fork in the trail.

▶ The Little Cove Mountain Trail [FS 25] turns to the left to reach VA RT 614 in about 3 miles.

Bear right to continue on the AT.

18.0 Arrive at VA RT 43. The BRP (mile 90.9) is less than 500 feet to the left.

Mile 90.9 (N 37°29.114 W 79°40.112) Map 15

>Length: 1.8 miles
>Difficulty: moderate

From the parking area on VA RT 43, walk downhill and cross the road within .1 mile to reenter the woods and ascend. For the next 1.7 miles the AT meanders through a hardwood forest. Changing leaf colors make this an exceptionally pretty walk in the fall. The section ends at the Mills Gap Overlook (BRP mile 91.8).

Except for the areas near road crossings, camping is permitted along this section.

Mile 91.8 (N 37°28.776 W 79°40.978) Map 15

>Length: .7 mile
>Difficulty: easy

After crossing the BRP at Mills Gap Overlook, the AT stays almost in sight of the parkway with little variation in elevation. The section ends at the Sharp Top Overlook (BRP mile 92.5).

Camping is not permitted on this section.

Mile 92.5 (N 37°28.477 W 79°41.529) Map 15

>Length: .6 mile
>Difficulty: easy

Crossing the BRP from the Sharp Top Overlook, the AT stays close to the parkway and experiences almost no change in elevation. FSR 4008 is reached in .6 mile. Follow the old road to the left to arrive at the Bobblets Gap Overlook (BRP mile 93.1).

Camping is prohibited on the entire section.

Mile 93.1 (N 37°28.042 W 79°41.946) Map 15

>Length: 2.4 miles (does not include side trails)
>Difficulty: moderate
>Shelter: mile point .1

Continuing on the narrow, main crest of the Blue Ridge Mountains, the AT crosses a couple of wooded knobs and passes by Bobblets Gap shelter. Side trails present options for extended hikes and/or campsites.

Camping is prohibited on the AT here but is allowed on the side trails and along forest service roads.

.0   Follow the woods road to the right of Bobblets Gap Overlook. In 300 feet cross FSR 4008 and turn left onto the AT.

.1   The blue-blazed trail to the right leads 1,000 feet to the Bobblets Gap shelter and spring.

.9   Trail intersection.

> ▶ Blue-blazed Hammond Hollow Trail [FS 27] to the right descends about 2 miles to FSR 634. Combining the Hammond Hollow Trail with FSR 634, FSR 4008, and/or the Spec Mine Trail [FS 28] (BRP mile 96) makes for a couple of nice circuit hikes.

Bear left to continue on the AT.

2.1   Come onto a woods road.

2.4   Cross the BRP (mile 95.3) and come to the Harvey's Knob Overlook.

Mile 95.3 (N 37°26.729 W 79°43.599) Map 15

Length: .7 mile
Difficulty: moderate

The AT leaves Harvey's Knob Overlook (good views of Flat Top and Sharp Top), ascends a small knob, and descends to the Montvale Overlook at BRP mile 95.9.

Camping is not permitted on this section.

Mile 95.9 (N 37°37.26.467 W 79°44.060) Map 15

Length: 1 mile
Difficulty: moderate

The AT ascends from the Montvale Overlook, passes over a ridgeline, and quickly descends to cross the BRP at Taylor's Mountain Overlook (BRP mile 97).

> ▶ The Spec Mine Trail [FS 28] leaves the BRP 200 feet south of the Montvale Overlook. (A detailed description and trailhead information may be found in Chapter 2, mile 95.9.) This trail may be combined with FSR 634, FSR 186, the AT, and/or the Hammond Hollow Trail [FS 27] for two pleasant circuit hikes.

Camping is permitted along the side trails and the forest service roads, but not on the AT.

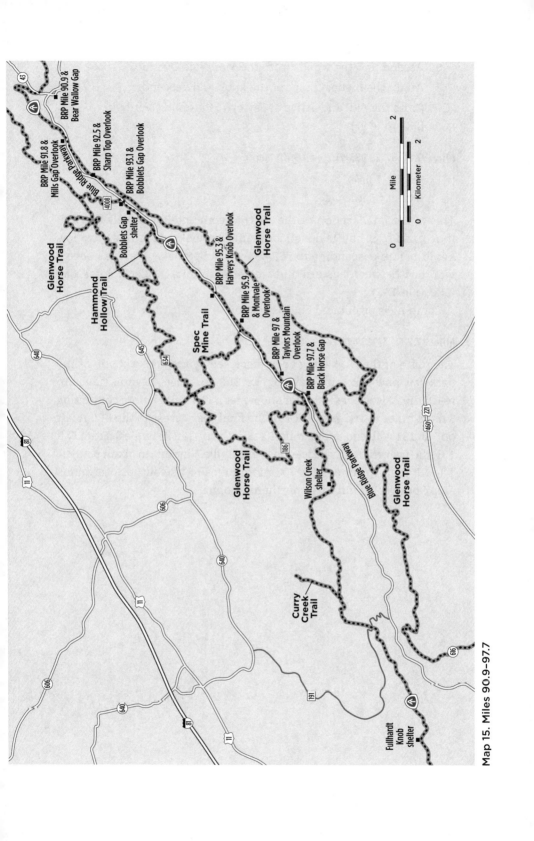

BRP Mile 90.9 &
Bear Wallow Gap

BRP Mile 91.8 &
Mills Gap Overlook

BRP Mile 92.5 &
Sharp Top Overlook

BRP Mile 93.1 &
Bobblets Gap Overlook

Blue Ridge Parkway

Glenwood
Horse Trail

Bobblets Gap
Shelter

Hammond
Hollow Trail

Glenwood
Horse Trail

BRP Mile 95.3 &
Harveys Knob Overlook

BRP Mile 95.9
& Montvale
Overlook

Glenwood
Horse Trail

Spec
Mine Trail

BRP Mile 97 &
Taylors Mountain
Overlook

BRP Mile 97.7 &
Black Horse Gap

Glenwood
Horse Trail

Wilson Creek
Shelter

Glenwood
Horse Trail

Blue Ridge Parkway

Curry
Creek
Trail

Fullhardt Knob
Shelter

Mile
Kilometer

Map 15. Miles 90.9–97.7

.0   Ascend into the woods from the Montvale Overlook.

.7   Attain the highest point of the knob and descend.

1.0   Cross the BRP and arrive at Taylor's Mountain Overlook (BRP mile 97).

Mile 97 (N 37°25.883 W 79°44.960) Map 15

Length: .7 mile
Difficulty: moderate

This is the final section of the AT that completely parallels the BRP. It ascends from the Taylor's Mountain Overlook and crosses two low knolls before descending to FSR 634 (an old roadway that was once a vital link between eastern and western Virginia) in Black Horse Gap (BRP mile 97.7).

Camping is prohibited on this section.

Mile 97.7 (N 37°25.478 W 79°45.443) Map 15

The route of the AT, having been displaced by the construction of the parkway, now takes its leave of the BRP. It crosses several ridges to reach the Wilson Creek shelter and water in 2.5 miles before continuing 3 more miles to arrive at FSR 191, the final easy access to the BRP. A left on FSR 191 will lead to BRP mile 101.5 in Curry Gap (1.1 miles). From FSR 191, the trail gradually descends to Troutville, Virginia, in about 6 miles. The AT then continues for 700 more miles to its southern terminus atop Springer Mountain in northern Georgia.

4.
The Roanoke River to Julian Price Memorial Park
Blue Ridge Parkway Miles 114.9–296.9

Just south of the Roanoke River the land takes a very marked and noticeable change. No longer steep and narrow, the Blue Ridge Mountains spread out onto a broad and rolling plateau. The parkway meanders through the bucolic scenery and farmlands of rural Virginia.
Open meadows, grazing cattle, and rows of rustling cornstalks line the
BRP.

Roanoke, a growing metropolis in the Great Valley of Virginia, dominates many of the views along the northern portion of this section.
Suburban developments are surprisingly close to the parkway in many
places. Private land, not national forests, lines both sides of the BRP.
When Virginia deeded land for the parkway, it reserved the right for
more road crossings than North Carolina did, and this is one of the
reasons why you will see more private land and development along
this portion of the parkway.

Less public land and fewer trails mean there are not as many opportunities for extended overnight hikes as in the previous section. However, Rocky Knob Recreation Area and Doughton Park have systems of
interconnecting trails leading to isolated backcountry campsites on
BRP land.

Trails may be fewer in number per mile of BRP in this section, but
you are compensated by their quality. Pathways are no longer confined
to the single, narrow ridgeline and steep hillsides. Many (BRP miles
169 and 238.5) wander over high, open meadows. These grazing lands
provide 360-degree views, and the gently rolling fields make for easy
walking. Other trails (BRP miles 217.6 and 241) take advantage of dramatic views provided by rocky bluffs that drop steeply to the east.

As stated, human impact is more prevalent on this portion of the
BRP. Moses H. Cone built more than 25 miles of carriage roads (BRP mile
294) on his estate, which is now a part of the parkway's property. What

had been intended as a retreat for employees of a private company has now become the Julian Price Memorial Park (BRP mile 295.9), complete with a campground and three superb hiking paths. Rugged trails (BRP miles 167.1 and 243.7) drop into isolated valleys to pass by decaying remnants of former homesteads. Shorter trails (BRP miles 154.5 and 176.2) lead to reconstructed mountain homes and communities. Still others (BRP miles 116.4 and 294) come into contact with the backyards of present-day housing developments.

Mile 114.9. Roanoke River Self-Guiding Trail [BRP 32] (960 feet)
(N 37°15.151 W 79°52.328). See Map 9, Chapter 2.

> Length: .6 mile, out-and-back (not including the two side trails, each
> .2 mile, out-and-back)
> Difficulty: moderate (the first side trail is strenuous; the second, easy)

There are actually three different routes contained in this one trail. The main route is a self-guided nature trail with signs identifying particularly interesting spots and plants along the way. The short side trails lead to the bank of the Roanoke River and out to a point overlooking the slow-moving waters of the stream.

Please Note: As this book went to press, there was the possibility that a new trail would be constructed from this overlook and parallel the parkway southward (with a side trail to Explore Park (BRP mile 115) to connect with the Roanoke Valley Horse Trail [BRP 33] at BRP mile 116.4.

.0 Begin at the parking lot and descend gradually.

.1 A side trail drops rather steeply to the rocks along the river, giving access to a reportedly good fishing spot below the hydroelectric generating plant. To continue on the self-guiding trail, go straight, cross under the BRP, and arrive at another side trail to the left. This is an easy, gradually descending walk that leads to a view of the river. Bear to the right to continue on the self-guiding trail. The terrain here drops steeply down the sides of the Roanoke River canyon wall, but the pathway remains wide and well constructed.

.2 Come to a bench allowing you to rest in the coolness of the forest. In a few feet begin a loop trail by turning right, ascending slightly, and coming to another bench. Note the sharp contrast between the many evergreens on one side of the trail and the dominant deciduous trees on the other.

.3 Begin to loop back by swinging to the left and going down a few steps. A few more feet leads to a bench with good winter-time views of the river canyon.

.4 Return to the beginning of the loop trail. The parking lot is .2 mile from here.

Mile 115

At mile 115 is a 1.5-mile spur road that is built on a former landfill with three overlooks providing views of the reclaimed land and Pine Mountain. At the end of the road is the Blue Ridge Parkway Visitor Center (restrooms and water) and Virginia's Explore Park (N 37°14.296 W 79°51.099), a once-operating historical park that has become sort of stuck in time itself. During the late twentieth century, the park opened with a reconstructed nineteenth-century community, eighteenth-century settler's cabin, and seventeenth-century Native American settlement. In addition, there were interpretive programs, fishing, kayaking, mountain biking, equipment rentals, special events, a fine-dining restaurant, Blue Ridge Parkway and Virginia's Explore Park visitor centers, and multiple trails in woodlands and along the Roanoke River. Some of the pathways were for mountain bikers only, while other routes were designated exclusively for foot travel.

Unfortunately, the park was unable to sustain itself and closed for a period of time. Thanks to the efforts of local mountain bikers and other outdoors enthusiasts, the park has reopened to hikers and bikers approximately 10 miles of trails coursing through the 1,110 acres. In an effort to appeal to as many as people as possible, trails are constructed for beginning, intermediate, and expert mountain bikers. Some of the trails pass a number of the still-standing reconstructed buildings. One of the easiest hiking routes is the .65-mile (circuit) Society of American Foresters Trail. A brochure available at the trailhead is keyed to numbered stops along the route. Describing an upland environment, the text discusses natural and planted forest regeneration, small stream ecology, plant communities, and climax forests.

As this book went to press, there was a campground and no fee to use the trails, but since the park's fate is still undecided, you would be wise to stop at the Blue Ridge Parkway Visitor Center (540-427-1800; open daily 9–5, May–October) to check on current conditions and regulations. More information about the park may be found at www.explore park.org.

Mile 116.4. Roanoke Valley Horse Trail [BRP 33] (N 37°14.388 W 79°53.139).
See Map 9, Chapter 2.

> *Length: 2 miles, one way*
> *Difficulty: moderate*

Alternating between woods and fields, this section of the horse trail is almost never out of sight of one house or another. Its trailhead is not directly accessible from the parkway, so to reach it, take the Mill Mountain Parkway at mile 120.5, continue past the picnic area and Mill Mountain Park, and proceed down the mountain on the Fishburn Parkway, which becomes Walnut Avenue. Bear right onto Ivy St., make a right onto Riverland Road in .1 mile, and turn left onto Rutrough Road in another 1.3 miles. Go under the parkway in an additional 1.5 miles and stop at the first dirt road.

.0 Ascend the road, which is actually a driveway to a private home.

.2 Leave the dirt road to the right and follow a woods road next to a house.

.6 Enter an open field.

.7 Begin to follow graveled VA RT 712.

.9 Cross VA RT 616; walk beside a driveway.

1.1 In an open field, walk next to the BRP. You are almost walking in someone's backyard. Ascend and descend through honey-suckle.

1.5 Cross VA RT 116 (Jae Valley Road) and walk in the open field.

1.7 Reenter the woods for a short time, and then come back out into the open.

1.8 Cross two creeks. Ascend via switchbacks in the woods.

1.9 Reach the top of a pine-covered knob next to a horse pasture; descend.

2.0 Arrive at BRP mile 118 (no parking or pull-off area).

Mile 118. Roanoke Valley Horse Trail [BRP 34]
(N 37°13.570 W 79°54.576) Map 16

> *Length: 4.5 miles, one way*
> *Difficulty: moderate*

This is by far the most wooded section of the horse trail to parallel the parkway. There are a number of pleasant spots along the route—possibly the most notable being a wooded stretch within sight of the small hamlet of Gum Spring. The trail comes back to the BRP in a couple of places, allowing you to decide on the length of your walk.

Also, this final section of the horse trail provides access to the Chestnut Ridge Trail [BRP 35], considered a part of the Roanoke Valley Horse Trail.

.0 At BRP mile 118, ascend into the woods on the western side of the parkway.

.2 Negotiate a set of switchbacks, cross a creek, and ascend.

.4 Attain the top of the knob.

.5 Almost touch the BRP, but abruptly swing away into a bottomland trail of honeysuckle, briers, mud, and muck.

.6 Ascend behind a subdivision.

.8 Cross paved VA RT 666 (Bandy Road); enter a pine forest next to the BRP. Soon you must be sure to avoid the path to the right, which goes into the subdivision.

1.0 Walk in another bottomland of muck, mud, and briers. Ascend through even more muck.

1.1 Turn left onto a wide pathway at the top of a knob.

1.2 In an open field of briers and weeds ascend next to the BRP.

1.3 Begin to descend into an overgrown forest.

1.5 Cross paved VA RT 668 (Yellow Mountain Road). Ascend, for a short distance, on a brier-covered rocky trail. Come almost to the parkway and descend.

1.7 Near the corner of a parking lot, turn left and ascend to walk the hillside above the little settlement of Gum Spring. Continue via a series of ups and downs, enjoying the shade of the woods.

2.9 Be alert! Do not take the road that goes uphill to the parkway. Continue on a smaller pathway.

3.1 Walk below the Gum Spring Overlook. (This overlook is at mile .1 on the Mill Mountain Parkway, which is connected to the parkway at BRP mile 120.5.)

3.15 Cross Mill Mountain Parkway and ascend into the woods.

3.25 Intersection. The trail to the right is a short connector pathway to the Chestnut Ridge Trail [BRP 35], considered a part of the Roanoke Valley Horse Trail. Bear left uphill to continue to follow the main route.

3.9 Cross the parkway (BRP mile 120.7, no parking or pull-off area), and begin to descend. The sounds of the rock crusher at the Rockydale Quarries will become very evident.

4.0 Avoid the cross trails and switchback to the BRP. Walk along a fence next to the parkway.

4.3 Swing to the left of an open field and next to a house and garden.

4.5 Arrive at VA RT 766 (Stable Road) and the end of the Roanoke Valley Horse Trail.

Mile 120.35. Roanoke Mountain Loop Road

The 4-mile loop road has 7 overlooks that, as you rise to the top of the mountain, provide increasingly expansive views of the Roanoke Valley and surrounding mountains.

Mile 120.35. Roanoke Mountain Summit Trail [BRP 35]

(N 37°12.658 W 79°56.157) Map 16

Length: .3 mile, circuit
Difficulty: moderately easy

Follow the narrow, winding side road off of the BRP (a 4-mile loop) to reach this pathway. The parking lots near the summit offer commanding views of the Roanoke Valley to the west and Back Creek Valley to the east. This is also a popular area for watching the sunset.

The loop trail leads to the top of Roanoke Mountain. The view from the summit is limited, but the rewards of this walk are worth it. It leads to the highest point of the mountain, where you can enjoy intimate contact with a mountaintop environment of evergreens, mountain laurels, and rock formations.

.0 Begin at the far end of the parking lot and immediately descend a set of stone steps with wooden handrails. In about 200 feet begin an ascent on more stone steps.

.1 Arrive at the summit of Roanoke Mountain, which offers good wintertime views; continue forward with a gradual descent while slabbing around the top of the mountain through mountain laurel.

.3 With a deep bear wallow on the right, begin a quick ascent of less than 300 feet to the parking lot.

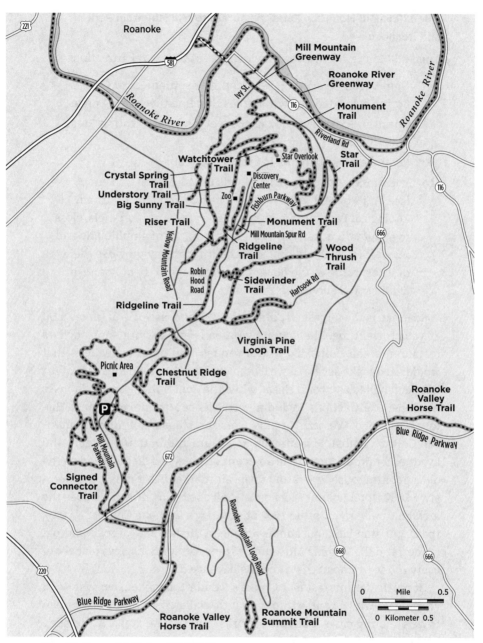

Map 16. Roanoke (miles 118–121.4)

Mile 120.5. Mill Mountain Parkway; access to Mill Mountain Park and Roanoke

The Mill Mountain Parkway provides access to several attractions:

.1 Gum Spring Overlook (1,440 feet). The settlement of Gum Spring is located below the trees that line the parking area.

1.1 Chestnut Ridge Overlook (1,460 feet) and the Chestnut Ridge Trail [BRP 36].

1.3 Roanoke Mountain picnic area (1,455 feet).

2.5 End of BRP jurisdiction. Left leads to Mill Mountain Park (see Trails of Mill Mountain Park below) and Mill Mountain Zoological Park (with more than 50 species of mammals, close to 40 birds, 3 dozen reptiles, and a number of amphibians and invertebrates). Right on J. B. Fishburn Parkway provides the quickest route to the downtown area of the city of Roanoke (2 miles; full services).

Roanoke is the largest city along the BRP and, as such, deserves a bit of your travel time. The downtown area is awash with sophisticated restaurants, museums, lively arts venues, and other attractions that would easily take several days to explore. The Taubman Museum of Art has been hailed as "world class," while the Center in the Square houses a number of attractions, including the Science Museum of Virginia, History Museum of Western Virginia, Harrison Museum of African American Culture, Pinball Museum, an aquarium and butterfly garden, and live theater productions. The adjacent farmers' market is billed as the oldest continuously operating open-air market in Virginia. The Tudor-style 1882 Hotel Roanoke sits on a knoll above downtown, as does the architecturally rich Gothic 1902 St. Andrew's Catholic Church. Nearby, the O. Winston Link Museum is an ode to the famous railroad photographer, and the Virginia Museum of Transportation displays just about every mode of transit that humans have used.

Of particular interest is Roanoke's wonderfully extensive system of greenways, which course throughout the valley, connecting downtown to neighboring cities, outlying suburbs, and natural areas. As detailed below (see BRP mile 120.5, Trails of Mill Mountain Park), two of those pathways start at Mill Mountain Park just off the parkway and descend into the city. From there, the Roanoke River Greenway provides a route along the river, giving access to the 3-mile Lick Run Greenway through a couple of city parks and alongside a stream known for its variety of birdlife and terminating at the Valley View Mall. The 1.25-mile Tinker Creek Greenway parallels the stream made famous in Annie Dillard's *Pilgrim at Tinker Creek.* The 2.2-mile Wolf Green Greenway passes an old grain silo overgrown by vegetation and is accessible from the Roanoke Valley Horse Trail [BRP 30] near Blue Ridge Parkway mile 110.6. Numerous other greenways have been completed in recent years, and more are in the building or planning stages.

Mile 120.5. Chestnut Ridge Trail [BRP 36] (1,460 feet)
(N 37°13.726 W 79°57.035) Map 16

> *Length: 5.3 miles, circuit*
> *Difficulty: moderate*

Part of the Roanoke Valley Horse Trail, the Chestnut Ridge Trail basically encircles the Roanoke Mountain picnic area. Leave the BRP at mile 120.5 and follow Mill Mountain Parkway for 1.1 miles to the Chestnut Ridge Overlook. (The picnic area is about .2 mile past the overlook.) The pathway, lined with galax, mountain laurel, and rhododendron, is wide and well graded for most of the way.

The trail crosses Mill Mountain Parkway twice and passes by quite a number of short side trails to the picnic area, so this walk can be as long or short as you wish. The last 1.5 miles are not as well maintained or quite as scenic as the rest of the hike. Also, you may be sharing the path with horseback riders—be careful where you step.

This is a recommended early morning or early evening hike for those who wish to escape the hustle and bustle of a picnic area.

.0 Begin at the Chestnut Ridge Overlook. Immediately come to a trail junction. One-tenth mile to the left is the Roanoke Mountain picnic area. Bear right and descend slightly through dogwood and maple. In less than 200 feet come to the red-blazed Chestnut Ridge Trail and turn left onto a wide pathway with little change in elevation. You'll find good wintertime views of the small community of Gum Spring here.

.15 Round a spur ridge and begin a series of small ascents and descents.

.6 With Mill Mountain Parkway less than 100 yards to the left, switchback to the right and descend.

.8 Switchback to the left and continue to descend.

1.0 Cross a culvert and begin an almost unnoticeable rise in elevation.

1.4 Round another spur ridge and descend.

1.5 A side trail to the right goes about 100 feet to VA RT 669. Keep left, ascend a short distance, and come to Mill Mountain Parkway. Along the road it is .4 mile left to the Roanoke Mountain picnic area and .6 mile to Chestnut Ridge Overlook. To continue on the Chestnut Ridge Trail, cross the road and reenter the woods. In a few feet a trail leading to VA RT 669 comes in from the right. (*Please Note:* As this book went to press, there was the possibility that a new trail would be constructed connecting the Chestnut Ridge Trail to those of Mill Mountain Park.) Bear left and begin to rise gradually.

1.6 Cross under a small utility line. Continue the gradual ascent on a forest floor that is conspicuously free of much undergrowth.

1.9 Cross under and parallel the utility line for 100 feet. The pungent smell of galax permeates the air.

2.1 To the left is a picnic table. The trail now begins a long swing around the picnic area. In a few hundred feet, cross a trail that, to the left, leads to the picnic area. Soon, cross a spur ridge and another short trail to the picnic area. Begin a descent and, at the switchback, veer away from the picnic area.

2.3 Avoid the unauthorized trail to the right; switchback to the left on a more gradual descent.

2.5 Descend steeply to cross a gully. You may be close to the picnic area, but this spot offers quiet solitude.

2.7 Make a hard left and follow the trail into a narrow gully between two small ridgelines. Rise gradually.

2.9 Switchback to the right (straight ahead leads to the picnic area). Ascend and follow an old roadbed.

3.1 Switchback to the left (there is another side trail to the picnic area).

3.2 Reach the top of a spur ridge. The picnic area is immediately to the left.

3.5 Note the many mine and quarry diggings next to the trail. The pathway here makes use of an old narrow gauge railroad bed. These railroads used to lace the Blue Ridge Mountains, bringing the area's rich natural resources out to mills and processing plants.

3.6 A trail to the left leads .2 mile to the picnic area.

3.8 Begin to ascend; many dogwood trees line the trail. Soon there are open views across a trailer park to the Rockydale Quarry and surrounding mountains. The character of the trail changes markedly. It becomes narrower and sometimes overgrown with thorns, briers, and poison ivy. Descend.

4.1 Descend steeply.

4.3 Cross under some large utility lines. The trail may be indistinct, but continue straight and reenter the woods.

4.4 Cross the utility lines and then parallel them for 200 feet before descending to the left into the woods.

4.5 Come to VA RT 672. Directly across the road is a short spur trail to a main portion of the Roanoke Valley Horse Trail [BRP 33]. To continue on the Chestnut Ridge Trail, turn left onto VA RT 672, cross under Mill Mountain Parkway, and reenter the woods to the left. The trail is almost in the backyards of some Gum Spring homes.

4.6 Pass under utility lines as the pathway becomes wider and finally regains a sense of isolation. Begin to climb as you enter the deeper woods.

5.3 Return to the starting point of the trail; the Chestnut Ridge Overlook is 150 feet to the left.

Trails of Mill Mountain Park, Blue Ridge Parkway
Mile 120.5 Map 16

Mill Mountain Park is located on its namesake mountain where the Mill Mountain Parkway splits in two (2.5 miles from the BRP) to become the Mill Mountain Spur Road and the J. B. Fishburn Parkway (which descends into Roanoke). The combination of history, unique natural features, amenities, and proximity to the city make the Mill Mountain trails exceptional. With the foundation of an old watchtower, stairs that lead to nowhere, an old toll booth, and what remains of an old car left behind from a teenage practical joke, the mountain is full of sights to take in. In addition to the approximately 10 miles of trails, the park has more to offer. The Roanoke Star, the world's largest neon star, is the most popular destination on the mountain, with the Star Overlook and its grandstand view of the city. The Rockledge Overlook gives you a great place to picnic and is close to a playground designed to match the natural environment. There is also a wildflower garden and the small Mill Mountain Zoological Park. The Discovery Center (N 37°14.999 W 79°56.114), open year-round with exhibits that include a working beehive, native reptiles, and more, can provide more information.

Star Trail (N 37°15.030 W 79°55.932) Map 16

Length: 1.6 miles, one way; 3.2 miles, out-and-back
Difficulty: moderate
Accessed from Riverland Road and the Star Trail parking lot

The first official trail of Mill Mountain Park, the Star Trail has an elevation change of almost 900 feet. Halfway down the mountain is a deep forest full of the sounds of wood thrushes and pileated woodpeckers.

Big Sunny Trail Map 16

Length: .7 mile, one way; 1.4 miles, out-and-back
Difficulty: moderate
Accessed from Prospect Road, Riser Trail, or Robin Hood Road

Along this wide, old dirt road is the shell of a very old car that now rests sideways on a tree.

Crystal Spring Trail Map 16

Length: .6 mile, one way; 1.2 miles, out-and-back
Difficulty: easy
Accessed from Woodcliff Road and Ivy Street

A flat trail, perfect for parents with small children. It stays along the bottom of the mountain but provides a good feeling of being in the middle of the woods.

Monument Trail Map 16

Length: 1.5 miles, one way; 3 miles, out-and-back
Difficulty: moderate
Accessed from Prospect Road and J. B. Fishburn Parkway

Be prepared to run into mountain bikers, as the trail's easy grade and proximity to Roanoke makes it very popular. Traversing a large portion of the mountain, it is lined by interesting rock outcroppings and large, old-growth oak trees.

The Roanoke Star atop Mill Mountain is the world's largest neon star.

Ridgeline Trail Map 16

Length: 1.3 miles, one way: 2.6 miles out-and-back
Difficulty: moderate
Accessed from Yellow Mountain Road, Discovery Center, and the
  Riser Trail

This trail follows along the Mill Mountain Parkway from the Blue Ridge Parkway to the Discovery Center. When hiked in that direction, the trail will climb with a moderate to more difficult slope. Keep your eye out for the sole American Holly tree right next to the trail.

Understory Trail Map 16

Length: .4 mile, one way; .8 mile out-and-back
Difficulty: moderate
Accessed from the Ridgeline Trail and the Mill Mountain Greenway

The rocky (in places) Understory Trail traverses the western side of Mill Mountain with little change in elevation just below the summit. Passing by the remains of the Mill Mountain Tramway (in use during the early part of the last century), it is a connector trail between the Ridgeline Trail and Mill Mountain Greenway.

Riser Trail Map 16

Length: .3 mile, one way; .6 mile, out-and-back
Difficulty: moderate
Accessed from the Big Sunny Trail and Ridgeline Trail

With a steep slope and one switchback, the route is a connector between the Big Sunny and Ridgeline Trails.

Virginia Pine Loop Trail Map 16

Length: 1.5 miles, circuit
Difficulty: moderate
Accessed from Hartsook Road or the Wood Thrush Trail.

Provides residents of the small Garden City community access to the rest of the trails on Mill Mountain.

Watchtower Trail Map 16

Length: .2 mile, one way; .4 mile, out-and-back
Difficulty: easy
Accessed from the Mill Mountain Greenway (Prospect Road) and the
  Star Overlook

Provides access from the Star Overlook to the Mill Mountain Greenway. It is a short descent from the neon star with beautifully handbuilt stone steps that blend well with the original historic retaining wall.

Mill Mountain Greenway Map 16

> *Length: 3.5 miles, one way; 7 miles, out-and-back*
> *Difficulty: moderate*
> *Accessed from the Discovery Center and the Watchtower Trail*

This is a part of the extensive system of greenways throughout the Roanoke Valley and will connect you with some of those other routes. Starting high atop Mill Mountain, it follows the original roadway down the mountain, connects with city streets, and ends at Elmwood Park in downtown Roanoke.

Wood Thrush Trail Map 16

> *Length: 1.6 miles, one way; 3.2 miles, out-and-back*
> *Difficulty: moderate*
> *Accessed from the Star Trail at Riverland Road and the Mill Mountain*
>   *Spur Road*

Meandering along the bottom of the mountain, the trail has two stream crossings with handbuilt bridges and only minor changes in elevation. Be on the lookout for the flock of turkeys that has made its home here for decades.

Sidewinder Trail Map 16

> *Length: .5 mile one way; 1 mile out-and-back*
> *Difficulty: moderate*
> *Accessed from Mill Mountain Parkway and Wood Thrush Trail*

The heavily switchbacked (that's how it received its name) Sidewinder Trail gradually descends from the Mill Mountain Parkway to the Wood Thrush Trail.

Mile 121.4. US RT 220

Full services located just off the BRP. Access to Roanoke (5 miles) and Rocky Mount (21 miles).

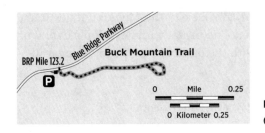

Map 17. Buck Mountain Trail (mile 123.2)

Mile 123.2. Buck Mountain Trail [BRP 37] (1,465 feet)

(N 37°11.812 W 79°58.955) Map 17

Length: 1 mile, out-and-back
Difficulty: moderately strenuous

The Buck Mountain Trail climbs steadily to obtain—if the vista has been recently maintained—good views of the mountains surrounding the southern Roanoke Valley. Because of its close proximity to the city, the area receives an inordinate amount of use and abuse. There are quite a number of unauthorized pathways. Please stay on the trail to help preserve the beauty of this place.

Please Note: As this book went to press, there was the possibility that a new trail would be constructed across the parkway from the overlook and go southward to connect with a proposed Roanoke Valley greenway a short distance south of BRP mile 124.

.0 Follow blacktop for the first 200 feet. There is a great diversity of deciduous trees on the mountainside, and they put on a very vibrant and colorful display in the fall. The well-used pathway, with concrete and wood water bars, makes a series of short, quick rises interspersed with some level spots.

.3 Come to a bench overlooking Fort Lewis Mountain. From here the trail becomes steeper and rockier.

.5 At the summit of the knob turn left, where you will find a bench and (depending on recent maintenance) views of the Roanoke Valley. McAfee Knob and Tinker Mountain dominate the distant skyline. Continue around the small loop trail to look down on the BRP and Rockydale Quarry. Retrace steps.

Mile 126.2. Masons Knob Overlook (1,425 feet)

Masons Knob, named for mid-1700s settler John Mason, rises to an elevation of 3,153 feet.

Mile 128.7. Metz Run Overlook (1,875 feet)

Named for the stream that makes a nice cascade as it flows underneath the bridge just south of the overlook.

Mile 129.3. Poages Mill Overlook (2,132 feet)

A limited view of the southern end of the Roanoke Valley.

Mile 129.6. Roanoke Valley Overlook (2,125 feet)

Another view of the southern end of the Roanoke Valley. A plaque provides a quick overview of the city's history.

Mile 129.9. Lost Mountain Overlook (2,205 feet)

Straight across the valley from the parkway, Lost Mountain reaches an elevation of 2,160 feet, about 40 feet lower than the overlook.

Mile 132.9. Slings Gap Overlook (2,860 feet)

The ridgeline closest to the overlook is the dividing line between Roanoke County and Franklin County. The valley between this ridgeline and the next one to the east contains the North Fork of the Blackwater River, which flows eastward into Smith Mountain Lake. The word "Slings" is believed to be a derivation of Schilling, the name of a resident who once lived nearby.

Mile 133.6. Bull Run Knob Overlook (2,885 feet)

Trees may obscure much of the view, but reaching a height of 3,202 feet, Bull Run Knob is visible rising above them.

Mile 134.9. Poor Mountain Overlook (2,970 feet)

Some sources say the mountain is called poor because of the lack of nutrients in its soil. Other references state it was named for a Major Poore, who served with Andrew Lewis during the French and Indian War. Today, the Poor Mountain Natural Area Preserve protects the world's largest population of piratebush.

Mile 135.9. US RT 221

Food and gas located close to the BRP. Access to Roanoke (19 miles). Also access to VA RT 602.

Mile 136. Adney Gap (2,690 feet)

The area was probably named for Thomas Adney, who was forcibly put onto a boat in England and dropped off in Charleston, South Carolina in 1760. After making his way to Franklin County, Virginia, he taught school, surveyed land, and operated a hemp beating mill. In the 1930s, the Appalachian Trail followed Adney Gap Road for almost a mile from the gap to US RT 221 at Bent Mountain. At the time, hikers could obtain accommodations at the Bent Mountain Post Office.

Mile 138.6. Sweet Annie Hollow (2,889 feet)

Local lore holds that the Annie who lived in this area gained a reputation of sweetly entertaining (for a price) soldiers during the Revolutionary War.

Mile 139. Cahas Knob Overlook (3,015 feet)

Cahas Knob is the prominent peak rising to an elevation of 3,560 feet, the highest point of Franklin County.

Mile 143. BRP Pine Spur maintenance facilities

Mile 143.9. Devils Backbone Overlook (2,708 feet)

Devils Backbone is the ridge to the right. Directly in front of the overlook is Blackwater Valley. Cahas Knob rises in the distance to the left.

Mile 144.8. Pine Spur Overlook (2,709 feet)

Named for the abundance of white pine at the overlook and in the nearby forest. The view is much the same as that from Devils Backbone Overlook, with Grassy Hill to the right, close to the town of Rocky Mount.

Mile 145.3. VA RT 610

Mile 145.7. VA RT 791

Mile 146.4. VA RT 642

Mile 148.1. VA RT 641

Mile 148.4. VA RT 663

Mile 149.1. VA RT 640

The two-room (originally one-room) Kelley Schoolhouse operated from 1877 to 1939, when it became a store. It closed in the 1980s. As this book went to press, various groups were hoping to restore it.

Mile 150.5. VA RT 639 and VA RT 221

Access to Roanoke.

Mile 150.9. VA RT 681 and VA RT 640

Mile 152. VA RT 888

Mile 153.6. VA RT 993

Mile 154.1. Smart View Overlook (2,564 feet)

An open view of the Pigg River Valley to the east. The red, orange, and yellow of the dogwood, maple, oak, and hickory leaves near the overlook make this a colorful place to be in autumn.

Mile 154.1 Access Trail to Smart View Loop Trail [BRP 38] (2,605 feet)
(N 36°56.019 W 80°11.100) Map 18

A short, easy trail only .1 mile in length passes from the openness of the Smart View Overlook (with a view of the Pigg River Valley) through the forest to connect with the Smart View Loop Trail [BRP 39] at the .4-mile point in that trail's description.

Mile 154.5 Smart View Picnic Area

The picnic area has several loops with tables, restrooms, and the Trails family cabin, occupied from the 1890s to about 1925, when it was converted into a barn.

Mile 154.5. Smart View Loop Trail [BRP 39] (2,560 feet)
(N 36°55.673 W 80°11.383) Map 18

> Length: 3 miles, circuit
> Difficulty: easy to moderate

A fern-lined pathway, open meadows, abundant wildflowers, an old mountain cabin, and superb views are awaiting those who walk the Smart View Loop Trail. Large, stately oaks testify that this area was once open farmland that gave the trees the room needed to grow to such magnificent proportions.

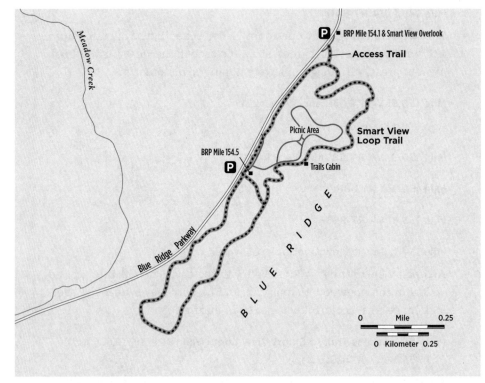

Map 18. Mile 154–154.5

.0 Begin at the fence in the parking lot outside the picnic area. Cross through the fence stile and walk in an open meadow.

.1 Arrive at a bench and enter the woods.

.2 The side trail to the right leads to the picnic area.

.4 Come to another bench. The Access Trail to Smart View Loop Trail [BRP 38] to the left leads, in a few hundred feet, to the Smart View Overlook at BRP mile 154.1. Bear right and descend on a fern-lined pathway.

.5 Switchback under utility lines and cross the creek on a log footbridge. The trail continues to descend into a hollow.

.6 Begin to ascend through a rhododendron thicket.

.7 Ascend steeply on rock steps and come to a bench. The wild-flowers are especially plentiful here.

1.0 A water fountain and restrooms are to the right; continue straight.

1.1 The trail to the right goes to the picnic area; bear left and descend.

1.2 Arrive at a cabin built by the Trails family in the 1890s. You'll also find a bench and a splendid view of the flatlands of the Piedmont to the east.

1.3 Cross a small creek on a stone bridge and switchback to the left to ascend a knob. (The parking lot at the beginning of the trail may be reached by following the path to the right.) Some older books or resource materials may identify the rest of this hike as the Rennet Bag Trail. At one time, cheese was made by curdling the milk in rennet, which is one of the stomachs of a cow.

1.5 Come to a bench with another good view of the Piedmont.

1.9 Begin to descend through an evergreen forest.

2.1 Switchback to the right.

2.6 Another bench—this one in the cool shade of a deep forest.

3.0 The trail to the right will take you back to the picnic area. Turn left and arrive at the starting point.

Mile 155.3. VA RT 793

BRP Smart View maintenance facilities. Access to Endicott (4 miles) and VA RT 680.

Mile 156.3 VA RT 635

Mile 157.6. Shortt's Knob Overlook (2,806 feet)

Barely visible through the trees, 2,907-foot Shortt's Knob is named for Amos Shortt, who lived near its base.

Mile 158.9. VA RT 637

Access to Floyd.

Mile 159.3. VA RT 860

Access to Floyd, Endicott, and Ferrum (13 miles; full services). With the Blue Ridge Farm Museum, Heritage Archive, Institute, Folklife Festival (held in October), and other special events and classes, Ferrum College is a major resource and attraction concerning life, past and present, in the Blue Ridge Mountains.

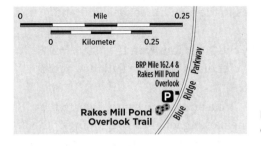

Map 19. Rakes Mill Pond Overlook Trail (mile 162.4)

Mile 161.3. VA RT 615

Mile 162.1. VA RT 711

Mile 162.4. Rakes Mill Pond Overlook Trail [BRP 40] (2,475 feet)
(N 36°51.940 W 80°17.092) Map 19

> Length: .1 mile, out-and-back
> Difficulty: easy leg stretcher

This short walk will bring you down stone steps to a pleasant view of a mill dam built in the early 1800s and a rhododendron-lined pond and stream. A very pleasant and peaceful spot, with possible signs of beaver activity.

Mile 162.9. VA RT 710

Mile 163.2. VA RT 797

Mile 163.5. VA RT 709

Mile 165.3. Tuggle Gap and VA RT 8 (2,752 feet)

Full services located close to the BRP. Access to Floyd (6 miles; full services). In the 1960s and 1970s, Floyd County experienced a back-to-the-land movement that attracted individuals interested in a bohemian or alternative lifestyle. At first there was a friction between the new residents and the established population, but as time went on and the town of Floyd gained a reputation as a quality artists' and musicians' colony, an amicable truce was reached. Today the town attracts a wealth of tourists to its galleries, restaurants, and music venues.

Seats don't get much use when the mountain and bluegrass music starts up at the Floyd Country Store each Friday, Saturday, and Sunday. It seems that just about everyone—from old geezers to dreadlocked young adults to grade-schoolers—can't resist jumping up to do some clogging or buck dancing. This is an old-time music experience not to be missed. In addition to sponsoring music events, the nearby Jacksonville Center for the Arts showcases the local talent in a number of media. The entire town comes alive during a series of festivals throughout the year, including those dedicated to harvest time, international music, wine, food, and more.

Trails of the Rocky Knob and Rock Castle Gorge Area, Blue Ridge Parkway Miles 167.1–169

Rock Castle Gorge, contained in the 4,500-acre Rocky Knob Recreation Area, is a significant feature of the Blue Ridge. Millions of years of stream erosion have carved a deep, narrow, and impressive valley. Views from the BRP and the upper portions of the Rock Castle Gorge [BRP 41] and Black Ridge [BRP 44] Trails can be quite breathtaking. The gorge's terrain drops steeply, almost vertically in some places, with a high point of 3,572 feet on Rocky Knob to a low of 1,700 feet at Rock Castle Creek.

This great difference in elevation and the moist environment of the gorge help create one of the most botanically diverse areas of the parkway and a haven for ferns. It also allows you to experience two seasons in just one walk. By mid-March, bloodroot may be blooming near the creek, while winter snows could still be falling on Rocky Knob and Grassy Knoll. If the fall weather is a bit too chilly, camp in the gorge to prolong summer's warmer temperatures.

Until the 1920s, a complex mountain community existed within the confines of this rugged topography. Farmers scratched out a living, while the rushing waters of Rock Castle Creek powered a thriving industry of sawmills and gristmills. In its heyday, more than 70 families lived in the area. Reminders of those days will be encountered along the trails.

The recreation area contains a small park service visitor center, campground (3,050 feet), picnic grounds, and backcountry camping (1,790 feet). As this book went to press, part of the trail system was to be named a TRACK Trail (kidsinparks.com), designed to encourage kids outdoors.

Mile 167.1. Rock Castle Gorge Trail [BRP 41] (3,020 feet)

(N 36°49.893 W 80°20.681) Map 20

> *Length: 10.6 miles, circuit*
> *Difficulty: strenuous*
> *Highly recommended*

Rock Castle Gorge Trail was named a National Recreation Trail in 1984 because of its geographical and historical significance. Backcountry camping is allowed (one of only three such places on BRP land) on a site next to Rock Castle Creek—about 3.5 miles from the beginning of the trail. Required permits (free) can be obtained at the ranger station (mile 167; 540-745-9661) or the campground office. Vehicle access to within .25 mile of the campsite is possible by leaving the BRP at mile 165.3 to follow VA RT 8 to the east. In 6 miles turn right onto VA RT 605, and in a little more than .5 mile arrive at a gated fire road. The campsite is .25 mile up the fire road.

High open meadows, precipitous views, tumbling cascades, historical sites, and free backcountry camping make this a hike you shouldn't miss. Trout fishing is also said to be good on both Rock Castle and Little Rock Castle Creeks.

The full length of this hike should not be undertaken lightly. Steep and narrow descents and arduous ascents definitely classify Rock Castle Gorge Trail as strenuous.

.0   At the entrance to the Rocky Knob campground, cross the BRP and pass through the fence stile. Turn left and descend through open meadow.

.1   Arrive at a bench, enter the woods, and cross a fence.

.3   Switchback and cross a rhododendron-lined water run (actually the headwaters of Little Rock Castle Creek). Soon turn left and cross a damp area on a log bridge; the trail descends gradually through a pleasant hardwood forest.

.5   Come to another bench. In a couple of hundred feet begin a gradual ascent of an old road.

.8   Switchback to the right on the old road.

.9   There is a bench here at the ridgeline. Begin to descend.

1.1   Arrive at a bench overlooking an area that was obviously settled at one time. Look around and perhaps discover the foundation of a decayed cabin or the remains of an old orchard. Cross the creek on a log bridge as the trail begins a gradual climb.

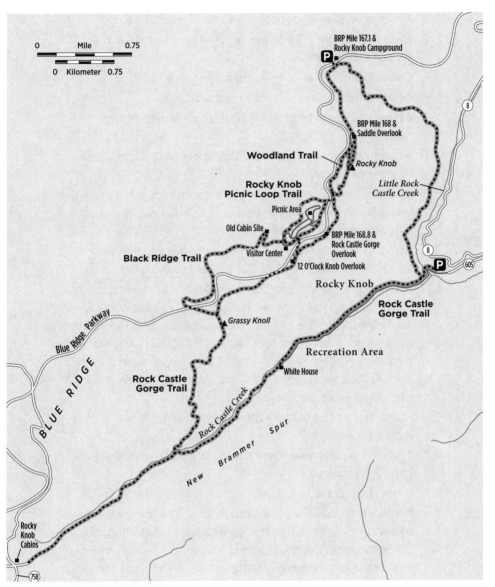

Map 20. Miles 167–174.1

1.5 Another bench sitting atop another ridgeline. Descend.

1.6 Even though the hillside has become very steep, the trail remains well built.

1.8 Come to a bench at the start of a steep descent.

1.9 Another bench; continue to descend steeply.

2.3 Arrive at a bench in a draw. The descent becomes more relaxed.

2.5 At another bench begin to parallel Little Rock Castle Creek in an open valley.

2.7 The inviting pools will make you want to cool your feet in the creek. You'll also find yet another bench. Soon cross a small side stream on a log bridge.

3.0 Arrive at the fire road and turn right to continue on Rock Castle Gorge Trail. VA RT 605 is 250 feet to the left.

3.25 Arrive at the backcountry camping area, site of a former Civilian Conservation Corps camp. From 1937 to 1942, corps workers helped build the BRP and structures contained within the Rocky Knob Recreation Area (and many other places along the parkway). All that remains of the CCC camp are old foundations, but benches, fire grates, and pit toilets are available for the modern-day camper.

3.4 A bench next to the creek affords a cool place to rest during hot summer days.

3.7 The road swings away from the creek and follows along the base of a mountain.

4.2 Cross the creek on a bridge.

4.5 Arrive at the White House, built in 1916. The former residence of a well-to-do citizen of the Rock Castle community, this property is still in private hands—be sure to treat it with respect so that others may continue to enjoy this portion of the Rock Castle Gorge Trail. The road continues up the creek as the valley begins to narrow.

4.7 Cross the creek on a bridge.

4.8 Recross the creek, which descends a number of 1- and 2-foot waterfalls. Ascend steeply through rhododendron.

5.1 The road is now high above the creek, which has a series of beautiful waterfalls rushing through moss- and lichen-covered boulders.

5.3 Arrive at a bench overlooking the creek gorge.

5.4 Level out for a short distance as you pass by a vertical rock facing that turns into a 100-foot waterfall during spring rains.

5.6 Be alert! The trail leaves the road to the right, drops down, passes a bench, and crosses Rock Castle Creek on a bridge. (The road continues to the left for more than a mile to end next to the Rocky Knob Cabins on VA RT 758. *Please Note:* As this book went to press, the cabins were closed. It is unclear if they will ever reopen. Contact BRP Main Office for up-to-date information.)

5.7 Pass by an old house site.

5.8 Come to a bench and soon cross through a jumble of boulders known as Bare Rocks. While the small caves and holes are tempting to inspect and explore, please be aware that many animals—including copperheads and rattlesnakes—may make their homes here.

6.2 Continue the ascent through rhododendron tunnels. Soon ascend more steeply.

6.4 The creek to the right tumbles down a lovely series of cascades.

6.5 Cross the creek and continue with a more gradual ascent through mountain laurel and rhododendron.

6.6 Begin an ascent on a series of short switchbacks.

6.8 Come to a bench in a gap where the trail levels out for a short distance.

7.0 Arrive at a bench overlooking a rhododendron-surrounded water run. Soon cross over a fence and enter a cattle-grazing area.

7.1 Come onto Grassy Knoll and follow arrowed posts through the pastureland.

7.3 Just before entering the woods, you'll find a bench amid the bucolic surroundings.

7.5 Cross a fence and walk under some microwave towers.

7.6 Emerge onto the open meadows and reap the rewards for all of your hard huffing and puffing climbing out of Rock Castle Gorge. The high, open pastures afford grand 360-degree views, and the gently sloping land makes for easy and relaxing walking. Bear right and descend along the fence line. (The gravel road to the left is part of the Black Ridge Trail [BRP 44], which joins the Rock Castle Gorge Trail at this point.)

7.7 Uplifted stones make some interesting formations. The views seem to get better with every step you take. This area is very reminiscent of the Bald Mountains along the North Carolina/ Tennessee border.

8.0 Cross a fence and enter the woods as the descent quickens.

8.2 Arrive at a bench with limited views into Rock Castle Gorge. Come out of the woods and onto open meadows for more superb views.

8.3 Enter some woods to ascend around a knob.

8.5 Do not follow the red boundary markers at the top of the knob. Continue straight ahead and descend for another great view.

8.7 The Black Ridge Trail [BRP 44] turns left and goes uphill through the field to arrive at the small Rocky Knob Visitor Center in .1 mile. (Water and sanitary facilities are available nearby.) Bear right to continue on the Rock Castle Gorge Trail and come to another view into the gorge.

8.8 Begin a series of small ups and downs through mountain laurel.

9.0 Pass by the Rock Castle Gorge Overlook (BRP mile 168.7).

9.1 Reenter the woods and make a short, steep ascent.

9.2 Ascend on rock steps and walk on a narrow, precipitous trail for a short distance.

9.3 Pass by a side trail to the left that leads to the picnic area in .25 mile. Begin the ascent of Rocky Knob.

9.4 Two trail options here. The trail straight ahead goes to the Saddle Overlook in about .5 mile of fairly level walking, making it possible to bypass the climb to the top of Rocky Knob. Rock Castle Gorge Trail bears to the right, switching back through mountain laurel, and goes to the knob and then down to the Saddle Overlook. The rest of this trail description follows that route.

9.7 Attain the ridgeline, which has limited views; follow it next to a steep drop-off.

9.8 Arrive at the summit of Rocky Knob, the highest point of the Rock Castle Gorge Trail. An old shelter, where Earl Shaffer, the first Appalachian Trail thru-hiker (1948) spent the night when this route was a part of the AT, allows good views into the gorge. Bear right and descend steeply. (The trail to the left simply goes down to the optional pathway to the Saddle Overlook.)

10.0 The trail coming in from the left is the optional pathway. (Taking it would lead back to the picnic area in .6 mile.) Bear right and pass by the Saddle Overlook (BRP mile 168). Ascend into the woods.

10.2 Cross over the top of a knob.

10.3 Pass through a fence stile and come into an open pasture for the final stretch of great views. Follow vehicle tracks for a few hundred feet and then veer left onto a pathway. Pass by fenced-in box springs and follow arrowed posts through the field. Go through a small, old orchard.

10.5 Begin to closely parallel the BRP.

10.6 Cross through the fence stile to the left to arrive back at the Rocky Knob campground.

Mile 168. Saddle Overlook and access to Rock Castle Gorge Trail
[BRP 41] (3,380 feet)

A great place to watch the annual hawk migration in the fall. Heated air from sun-warmed cliffs and rock outcroppings couples with warm air rising from the lowlands to create forceful drafts, or thermals, that the hawks use to soar upward. In addition, by gliding near the crest of the ridges, they are able to take advantage of the winds that strike the Blue Ridge Mountains where air currents are forced across the mountain crests, providing more uplift.

Sometimes as early as mid-August, ospreys, American kestrels, and a few bald eagles begin the procession southward. The migration begins in earnest in the middle of September as broad-winged hawks take to the skies. Peak daily sightings of a thousand or more are not uncommon. In the early weeks of October, peregrine falcons join the movement, while later in the month, one of the smallest hawks, the sharp-shinned, becomes the dominant migrant. Joining the procession at this time are the larger but fewer Cooper's hawks. Making use of the cold winds of November, red-tailed hawks, northern harriers, and red-shouldered hawks zip by leafless trees. Soaring over a Blue Ridge Parkway that could be covered by December snows, northern goshawks and golden eagles bring the migratory season to a close.

Mile 168.8. Rock Castle Gorge Overlook (3,195 feet)

Access to the Rock Castle Gorge Trail [BRP 41].

Mile 169. Rocky Knob picnic area and visitor center (3,155 feet)

Visitor center, small gift shop, restrooms, and water fountains.

Mile 169. Rocky Knob Picnic Loop Trail [BRP 42]
(N 36°48.698 W 80°21.004) Map 20

> *Length: 1.3 miles, circuit*
> *Difficulty: moderately easy*

This trail is an enjoyable diversion from the picnic area, which, during the summer months and on holidays, may be overflowing with visitors. The path stays within shouting distance of the picnic area, yet as it passes through a hardwood-, rhododendron-, and hemlock-crowded forest, it allows the walker to become detached from civilization for a while.

.0   Begin at the trail sign to the left and behind the Rocky Knob Visitor Center.

.05 The trail to the left is the Black Ridge Trail [BRP 44], which leads to the Rock Castle Gorge Trail [BRP 41]. Bear right to continue on the Rocky Knob Picnic Loop Trail and descend through a pleasant hardwood forest.

.2   The trail to the left is another part of the Black Ridge Trail; stay to the right to continue on the Picnic Loop Trail.

.3   With a nice feeling of isolation, the trail descends through a towering forest, which is made all the more appealing in late spring when the abundant rhododendron are in full bloom.

.5   Cross a small water run and begin a series of small ups and downs through rhododendron tunnels.

.7   Emerge from the rhododendron into open forest and ascend; the trail to the right goes back to the picnic area.

.8   Switchback to the right, avoiding the unauthorized trail that continues straight ahead.

.9   The trail to the left [BRP 43] leads to Rocky Knob and the Saddle Overlook. Bear right and come into the picnic area, where there are a number of confusing side trails. Pass by a large picnic shelter, walk through the parking lot, reenter the woods, and ascend.

1.3 Arrive back at the visitor center.

Mile 169. Woodland Trail [BRP 43] (N 36°48.789 W 80°20.842) Map 20

Length: .8 mile, one way; 1.6 miles, out-and-back
Difficulty: easy

This is a short, easy connector trail between the Rocky Knob picnic area and the Saddle Overlook (BRP mile 168). It offers nothing particularly exciting, but it does open up a number of options to connect with the other trails in the Rocky Knob Recreation Area.

The trailhead may be reached by driving into the picnic area to the second restroom building (beyond the picnic shelter).

.0 Ascend gradually.

.2 Cross the BRP and ascend into the woods.

.25 Meet Rock Castle Gorge Trail [BRP 41]; turn to the left.

.3 The Rock Castle Gorge Trail switches back to the right to begin its ascent of Rocky Knob. Continue straight on the well-built Woodland Trail, passing through mountain laurel and paralleling the BRP.

.7 The trail to the right makes a steep ascent to the summit of Rocky Knob. Bear to the left and rejoin the Rock Castle Gorge Trail. Bear left again.

.8 Arrive at the Saddle Overlook for a good view into Rock Castle Gorge.

Mile 169. Black Ridge Trail [BRP 44] (N 36°48.698 W 80°21.004) Map 20

Length: 3 miles, circuit
Difficulty: moderate
Highly recommended

Bucolic mountain farms, rhododendron and mountain laurel thickets, and relaxing walking in high, open meadows make the walker feel on top of the world. If time restraints prohibit you from walking the full trail, at least take the time to enjoy the views along the open pastures (from mile point 1.6 to the end of the trail), which are reminiscent of the Bald Mountains on the North Carolina/Tennessee border.

.0 Begin to the left and behind the Rocky Knob Visitor Center.

.05 The trail to the left leads to the 12 O'Clock Knob Overlook and Rock Castle Gorge Trail [BRP 41]. (You will return via the latter.) Bear to the right.

.2 The trail to the right is the Picnic Loop Trail [BRP 42]. Bear to the left and continue to descend on the Black Ridge Trail.

.3 Turn right to follow a utility line right-of-way.

.4 At an old cabin site turn left, cross a creek, and ascend on an old, fern-lined woods road.

.7 The road is beside open meadows—enjoy the farmland views to the west.

1.0 Swing away from the fields and continue the ascent, now through mountain laurel and rhododendron.

1.1 Level out and parallel the BRP; soon begin to ascend gradually.

1.5 Be alert! Turn left from the road, cross a fence, and enter open fields.

1.6 Cross the BRP; pass through a fence; ascend in a cow pasture on the gravel road.

1.8 At the top of the ridge, make a hard left (to the right is the Rock Castle Gorge Trail [BRP 41]), and follow the fence line down the open meadow.

1.9 Gradually descend and pass by an interesting rock formation. This stretch of the trail is absolutely superb. The walking is gently sloping downhill, the views are 360 degrees, and the constant winds will cool you down even on the hottest day. Walking and hiking just doesn't get much better than this.

2.2 Cross a fence and enter the woods, descending a little more quickly.

2.5 Arrive at a bench with limited views into Rock Castle Gorge. Soon come back to open meadows with better views.

2.6 Reenter woods and ascend around a knob.

2.7 Do not follow the red-paint boundary markers at the top of the knob. Continue straight and descend for one final grand view.

2.9 The Rock Castle Gorge Trail [BRP 41] continues straight ahead. Turn left through an open field, cross the BRP, ascend some stone steps, and come back to the original intersection. Turn right.

3.0 Arrive at the Rocky Knob Visitor Center.

Mile 169.1. 12 O'Clock Knob Overlook (3,210 feet)

Turkey sightings have been frequently reported at and near the overlook, especially early in the morning or late in the afternoon.

Mile 170.4. VA RT 720

Mile 171.3. VA RT 720

Mile 171.7. VA RT 726

Mile 174. Rock Castle Gap and VA RT 799 (2,970 feet)

Access to Willis and Hubbards Mill.

Mile 174.1. VA RT 758

Access to Rocky Knob Cabins and Meadows of Dan. *Please Note:* As this book went to press, the cabins, built by the Civilian Conservation Corps in the 1930s, were closed. At this time, it is unknown if they will ever reopen. Contact BRP Main Office for up-to-date information.

Mile 174.2. VA RT 758 and VA RT 778

Mile 174.7. VA RT 778

Mile 175.9. VA RT 603

Mile 176.2. Mabry Mill (2,853 feet)

Coffee shop, gift shop, restrooms, and water.

Mile 176.2. Mountain Industry Trail (Mabry Mill) [BRP 45]
(N 36°45.004 W 80°24.322) Map 21

> *Length: .4 mile, circuit*
> *Difficulty: easy*
> *Highly recommended*

E. B. Mabry operated a gristmill and blacksmith shop on this site from 1910 to 1935. The park service has restored the mill and added structures and exhibits that highlight the more colorful elements of rural Blue Ridge Mountain life of the early 1900s. Various displays, devices, and live demonstrations on gristmilling, blacksmithing, and other preindustrial mountain crafts bring these nostalgic bygone days back to life.

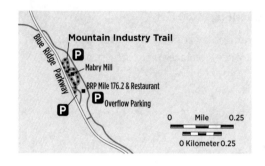

Map 21. Mountain Industry Trail (mile 176.2)

During the fall, parking (and walking space) is often minimal, as large crowds arrive to watch the annual apple butter– and sorghum molasses–making demonstrations. (Check with the visitor center at Rocky Knob for times and dates of all demonstrations.)

This walk is highly recommended. The information learned will enhance future hikes. As this book went to press, plans were to name the trail a TRACK Trail (kidsinparks.com), designed to encourage kids outdoors.

Also, be on the lookout for turtles, ducks, and other aquatic life in and around the pond. Mabry Mill may be the most photographed scene on the entire BRP. The best time to photograph the mill is probably early evening, when the glow of the setting sun is reflected in the pond.

.0 Begin north of the restaurant, enjoy the view of the mill across the pond, and in a couple of hundred feet bear left at the intersection and cross the flume that brings water to power the mill. Come to the mill and visit with the miller (during tourist season). Continue on the paved pathway.

.1 Pass by millstones, a lumber-drying rack, a log cart, a bark mill for obtaining tannin, and Matthews Cabin.

.15 Study the whiskey still and sorghum-making display.

.2 Turn left and walk through the shed of the blacksmith shop, where you can discover what an important role the blacksmith played in the daily life of mountain communities. A soap-making display is next.

.25 Rest on a bench overlooking the rustic Mabry Mill site.

.3 Cross over the flume, go down some steps, and cross the creek.

.4 Arrive back at the parking lot.

Mabry Mill is believed to be the parkway's most photographed location.

Mile 176.3. VA RT 603

Mile 177.7. Meadows of Dan and US RT 58 (2,964 feet)

Full services located just off the BRP. Access to Stuart (16 miles) and Hillsville (21 miles).

Mile 178.8. VA RT 744

Mile 179.2. Round Meadow Overlook

There is now no meadow here, but the lush forest beside the parking area is colorful in the fall.

Mile 179.2. Round Meadow Creek Trail [BRP 46] (2,800 feet)
(N 36°42.990 W 80°25.377) Map 22

> *Length: .4 mile, circuit*
> *Difficulty: moderately easy*

The narrow gorge of Round Meadow Creek is a wonderful spot on hot summer afternoons; you can actually feel the temperature drop as you descend. Cool hemlock groves, a gurgling stream, flowering rhododendron, and towering pines are this trail's attractions.

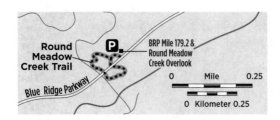

Map 22. Round Meadow Creek Trail (mile 179.2)

.0 Begin the trail by descending through a grand display of rhododendron.

.1 Reach the creek, which is lined with hemlock and rhododendron. Turn left, walking along the stream and under the BRP.

.2 Be alert! The trail leaves the old road and ascends to the left through lofty evergreens.

.4 Cross under the BRP and arrive back at the Round Meadow Overlook.

Mile 179.4. Round Meadow Creek (2,800 feet)

Mile 180.1. VA RT 600

Mile 180.5. VA RT 634

Mountain crafts and antiques located close to the BRP.

Mile 183.4. Pinnacles of Dan Gap (2,875 feet)

When the Appalachian Trail was being scouted in the early 1900s, trailblazers marked a route over Pinnacles of Dan (not visible from the parkway) as a joke, thinking the mountain's nearly straight up and down slopes to be so tough that it would be rejected. Myron Avery, who was instrumental in establishing the AT's full length from Georgia to Maine, thought it so spectacular that he made it the official route, although at first the summit was reached by a .3-mile side trail. The hike immediately became a favorite of many hikers.

Mile 183.9. VA RT 614

Access to Mount Airy, North Carolina.

Mile 186.7. VA RT 631

Access to Laurel Fork.

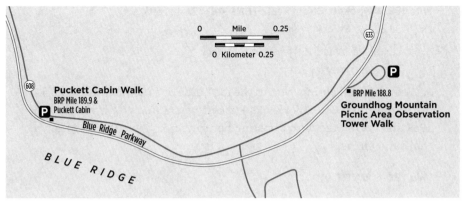

Map 23. Groundhog Mountain (mile 188.8)

Mile 187.7. VA RT 639

Mile 188.8. Groundhog Mountain Picnic Area Observation Tower Walk
[BRP 47] (3,025 feet) (N 36°38.724 W 80°31.721) Map 23

Length: less than 400 feet, out-and-back
Difficulty: easy leg stretcher

A short walk of less than 1 minute leads to the tower for a commanding view of the quartzite peak of Pilot Mountain, the Dan River Valley, and surrounding scenery. A great payoff for so little effort!

The picnic area, with restrooms and water, is surrounded by fences displaying different construction styles.

Mile 189.1. Pilot Mountain Overlook (2,950 feet)

If this vista has been recently maintained, the solitary peak you see in the view is Pilot Mountain, whose summit slopes are composed of quartzite. The mineral resists erosion, so the top of the mountain has an odd look. Pilot Mountain State Park has trails along the mountain's terrain.

Mile 189.2. VA RT 608

Food, gas, and lodging located close to the BRP.

Mile 189.9. Puckett Cabin Walk [BRP 48] (2,848 feet)
(N 36°38.581 W 80°32.812) Map 23

> *Length: less than 150 feet, out-and-back*
> *Difficulty: easy leg stretcher*

A 30-second walk brings you to the log home of a member of the Puckett Family. Mrs. Orleans Hawks Puckett was a midwife from 1865 to 1939 and is credited with assisting her rural neighbors in more than a thousand births.

Mile 190.6. VA RT 910

Mile 191.4. VA RT 608

Mile 192.3. VA RT 648

Mile 193.7. VA RT 691 (2,675 feet)

Food and gas located just off the BRP. Access to Hillsville, Virginia, and Mount Airy, North Carolina.

Mile 194.7. VA RT 608

Mile 198.4. VA RT 685 with access to VA RT 608

Mile 198.9. VA RT 608

Mile 199.1. VA RT 608

The route of the Appalachian Trail used to run along this road.

Mile 199.4. Fancy Gap. US RT 52 (2,925 feet)

BRP maintenance facilities and full services located close to the BRP. Access to Hillsville, Virginia, and Mount Airy, North Carolina (14 miles). Mount Airy was the boyhood home of Andy Griffith and served as the model for his television show's town of Mayberry. Mount Airy has embraced the legend in a big way, and visitors can eat at Snappy Lunch, get a haircut at Floyd's City Barber Shop, stop in at a motel room dedicated to Aunt Bee, see the Old Courthouse Jail with its re-created scene of Mayberry's sheriff's office, and tour Griffith's childhood home.

Mile 199.9. VA RT 778

Mile 202.2. VA RT 608

Mile 202.8. Granite Quarry Overlook (3,015 feet)

The view includes Hanging Rock and Pilot Mountain. A plaque describes Mount Airy granite.

Mile 203.9. Piedmont Overlook (2,900 feet)

The rolling terrain of the Piedmont recedes to the east.

Mile 204.8. VA RT 700

Mile 206.3. VA RT 608 with access to VA RT 620, VA RT 97, and VA RT 775

Mile 207.7. VA RT 608

Mile 209.3. Parsons Gap, VA RT 715, and access to Galax

Mile 209.8. VA RT 716

Mile 211.1. VA RT 612 and access to Galax

Trails of the Blue Ridge Music Center, Blue Ridge Parkway Mile 213

Constructed soon after the turn of the twenty-first century, the Blue Ridge Music Center (usually open late April through October) (N 36°34.433 W 80°50.967) celebrates the rich tradition of music found in the Appalachian and Blue Ridge Mountains. Within the modern 17,000-square-foot structure is a visitor center, gift shop, and museum exhibit titled *The Roots of American Music*. Be sure to spend some time here tracing the history of this music through contemporary (and near-contemporary) local artists, back to the creation of the music generations ago by early settlers who arrived here from Europe and West Africa. Special concerts by nationally and internationally known artists are scheduled on a regular basis, with some concerts presented in the adjacent amphitheater. It's always a pleasure to stop here, because there is almost always some kind of music—from a solitary lap dulcimer player to a full group of bluegrass musicians—being presented just about any time the center is open. Also located on the approximately 2,000 acres are the interconnected High Meadow [BRP 49] and Fisher Peak [BRP 50] Trails.

Free concerts are a prime attraction of the Blue Ridge Music Center.

More information may be obtained from

Blue Ridge Music Center
700 Foothills Road
Galax, VA 24333
276-236-5309
www.blueridgemusiccenter.org

Mile 213. High Meadow Trail [BRP 49] (2,622 feet)
(N 36°34.433 W 80°50.967) Map 24

Length: 1.4 miles, one way; 2.8 miles, out-and-back
Difficulty: moderately easy

The High Meadow Trail lives up to its name. It starts in a forest where members of the heath family make up much of the undergrowth. The pathway then traverses the upper edge of a meadow whose open space enables you to gaze across the countryside and to enjoy a great expanse of sky, hopefully beautifully blue with large white, puffy clouds floating by on the day you decide to walk it. Other highlights include crossings of Chestnut Creek, streamside summer and fall flowers, an interesting rock formation, and the opportunity to extend the hike by taking the Fisher Peak Trail [BRP 50].

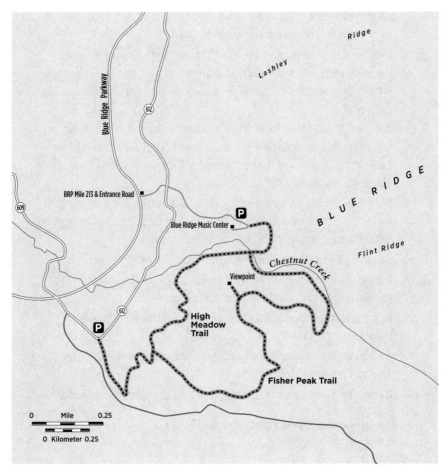

Map 24. Mile 213

High Meadow Trail is one of the parkway's TRACK Trails, designed to help children become more comfortable in the outdoors. Brochures should be available at the trailhead (or at kidsinparks.com).

This description is written as if you were going to hike the trail from the Blue Ridge Music Center. However, be aware that the road for the center is gated when the center is closed for the season or at 5:00 p.m. during the months the center is open to the public. If you are going to be out later than 5:00 p.m., start the hike from its other end located on Foothills Road (VA RT 612). To reach that trailhead, turn right onto Foothills Road (VA RT 612) just a short distance after turning off the parkway at mile 213 and follow it to a parking area on the right in .4 mile.

.0   At the handicapped area of the Blue Ridge Music Center parking area, descend the service road.

.06 Descend the steps and bear left, crossing the rhododendron-lined stream. Pass through the meadow and enter the woods where an abundance of fallen pine needles soften the pathway.

.35 Be alert! The Fisher Peak Trail comes in from the left. Keep to the right to continue on the combined High Meadow/Fisher Peak Trail. If you are lucky, a tune will come wafting across the air from the music center.

.5   Benches under an interesting rock face make for a nice place to take a break and listen to the sounds of the forest mingling with those coming from the music center.

.6   Break out into the meadow and enjoy the open space.

.7   Just after crossing a wet area on footbridges, bear left and ascend into the woods via switchbacks.

.9   Return to the edge of the meadow for 300 feet before going back into the woods.

1.0 Be alert! The Fisher Peak Trail goes off to the left. Bear right and gradually descend.

1.4 Cross the road to arrive at the parking area on Foothills Road.

Mile 213. Fisher Peak Trail [BRP 50] (2,618 feet)
(N 36°34.063 W 80°51.503) Map 24

Length: 3.3 miles, circuit
Difficulty: moderate

Interconnected with the High Meadow Trail [BRP 49], the Fisher (sometimes referred to as Fishers) Peak Trail provides additional miles of hiking close to the Blue Ridge Music Center. The trail's lower elevations are within a mixed forest of hardwoods and evergreens. The latter gradually fade away as the route gains elevation into a woodlands full of rhododendron and azalea growing below oak, maple, and poplar trees. The highlight is the view onto the music center. See the introduction of the High Meadow Trail for directions to the trailhead located on Foothills Road (VA RT 612).

Historical Note: Before being displaced by the construction of the parkway, the original route of the Appalachian Trail crossed over Fisher Peak's terrain.

Vast expanses of sky are visible from the open fields of the High Meadow Trail.

.0   Cross Foothills Road and ascend in the meadow on an old road.

.2   Leave the meadow and enter the woods.

.25 Be alert! The trail bears left off the woods road into a forest with an understory of mountain laurel and galax. Soon descend a spur ridge and cross a small water run.

.5   Be alert! Bear right at the loop trail intersection and ascend on an old woods road paralleling a small stream. (You will return via the route to the left.)

.7   Walk under utility lines for a few hundred feet before leaving them by bearing left to stay on the trail.

.9   Within a plot of planted pines, cross over a spur ridge and descend on long switchbacks to soon rise out of a rhododendron-thick hollow.

1.5 With an abundance of rhododendron and mountain laurel on a high point on the ridge, bear left onto a side trail to arrive at a bench with a view of the music center. On one of my visits here I felt transported back in time: I closed my eyes and listened to music rising up from the lower elevation. I imagined that I was a traveler returning after a long trip through the mountains and the music was the first welcoming sound I heard as I was nearing home. After enjoying the view, return to the main trail and turn left.

1.6 Begin a downward trend. The sound of Chestnut Creek becomes louder as you descend.

2.2 Be alert! The High Meadow Trail to the right goes .35 mile to the music center. Stay to the left to continue on the combined Fisher Peak/High Meadow Trail.

2.4 Benches below a rock formation.

2.5 Begin walking along the upper edge of an open meadow.

2.6 The trail swings to the left and rises on switchbacks to reenter the woods.

2.8 The route returns to the meadow for just a few hundred feet.

2.9 Be alert! Having returned to the original intersection of the hike, you need to bear right to retrace your steps.

3.3 Return to the parking area.

Mile 213.3. VA RT 612

Mile 215.3. VA RT 799

Mile 215.8. VA RT 89

Access to Galax, Virginia (7 miles; full services). Galax is home to the world-famous Old Fiddler's Convention, first held in 1935 and now taking place in early August. If you can't make it at that time, the town's Rex Theater comes alive with bluegrass music every Friday night as the Blue Ridge Backroads show is broadcast live on 98.1 FM.

Mile 216.9

Virginia–North Carolina state line.

Mile 217.3. NC RT 18

Access to Sparta (15 miles) and Mount Airy (22 miles).

Trails of the Cumberland Knob Recreation Area, Blue Ridge Parkway Mile 217.5

Construction of the BRP began in this area on September 11, 1935, and the Cumberland Knob Recreation Area, the parkway's first recreation area, was built in 1936 by the Civilian Conservation Corps. A common theory is that the area received its name from William Augustus, the duke of Cumberland and son of King George III. The duke was commander of the British forces in their victory against the army of Bonnie Prince Charlie in the Battle of Culloden in April 1746.

The 1,000-acre recreation area, at an elevation of 2,740–2,860 feet, has a picnic grounds and restroom facilities. The picnic area is often full on sunny summer weekends and holidays.

Mile 217.5. Gully Creek Trail [BRP 51] (N 36°33.235 W 80°54.445) Map 25

Length: 2.5 miles, circuit
Difficulty: moderately strenuous
Recommended

The small, bubbling cascades of Gully Creek lead you into a cool, narrow canyon lined with abundant ferns, pungent galax, and extensive mountain laurel and rhododendron thickets. Although it begins and ends at the Cumberland Knob picnic area, the trail travels quite some distance and, at its farthest point, gives the impression that not many people bother to walk its full length. Therefore, Gully Creek is a recommended outing for those who wish to enjoy the serenity of quiet sur-

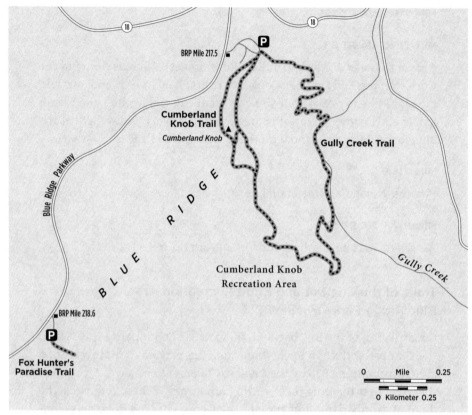

Map 25. Miles 217.5–218.6

roundings and lightly traveled pathways. However, be forewarned—the climb out of the Gully Creek canyon makes this a moderately strenuous excursion.

.0 Begin behind and to the left of the comfort station. Descend rather quickly.

.2 Begin a series of switchbacks through mountain laurel and rhododendron.

.4 Cross a small water run.

.5 Switchback and parallel the creek.

.8 Come to a small set of cascades as the unmistakable smell of galax fills the air. Cross the creek.

.9 The creek makes some nice, small waterfalls in this area. For the next .3 mile cross the creek at least seven more times.

1.2   Begin the ascent on fern-lined switchbacks.

1.4   Reenter thick stands of rhododendron and mountain laurel.

2.2   Cumberland Knob Trail [BRP 52], to the left, leads .2 mile to Cumberland Knob and .4 mile to the picnic area. Bear right to remain on the Gully Creek Trail.

2.4   The trail to the left is another portion of the Cumberland Knob Trail. Come into the picnic area.

2.5   Arrive back at the comfort center parking area.

Mile 217.5. Cumberland Knob Trail [BRP 52]
(N 36°33.235 W 80°54.445) Map 25

Length: .6 mile, circuit
Difficulty: easy leg stretcher

This nice, extended leg stretcher affords a chance to escape the crowds and noise of the picnic area. Wildflowers seem to be everywhere. So does poison ivy. A shelter and open area on top of the knob may provide a quieter place for a picnic.

The Cumberland Knob Trail makes use of a short section of the Gully Creek Trail [BRP 51].

.0   Follow the trail to the right of the restrooms, passing several interpretive signs and a small cemetery.

.1   Enter the woods, where the smell of galax becomes immediately apparent. Flame azalea and rhododendron blossoms line the trail in the spring. Be on the lookout for blueberries in late summer and early fall.

.3   Arrive at the shelter and a somewhat obstructed view. A connector trail to the Gulley Creek Trail [BRP 51] bears right. Swing left around the shelter and descend to continue on the Cumberland Knob Trail. The azalea is particularly thick here.

.4   Just before entering the field, swing around to the right, staying on the edge of the woods. Beware! That wonderful garden of lush green leaves next to the pathway is actually a profuse array of poison ivy.

.5   Trail intersection. The Gulley Creek Trail is to the right. Turn left to continue on the Cumberland Knob Trail, and in a few feet come onto a paved pathway next to the field.

.6   Arrive back at the restrooms.

Mile 218.6. High Piney Spur Overlook (2,805 feet)

A grandstand view of North Carolina's Piedmont.

Mile 218.6. Fox Hunter's Paradise Trail [BRP 53]
(N 36°32.420 W 80°55.132) Map 25

> *Length: .1 mile, out-and-back*
> *Difficulty: easy*

A paved pathway that emanates from the upper parking lot goes through a mountaintop forest to a grand view overlooking a valley and the flatter Piedmont lands to the east. Fox hunters used to sit on this spur ridge listening to the baying of their hounds echoing off the surrounding mountainsides.

Mile 220.4. NC RT 1460

Mile 220.5. NC RT 1461

Mile 221.8. NC RT 1461

Mile 221.8 Saddle Mountain Trail (N 36°33.125 W 80°56.423) Map 26

> *Length: 2.9 miles, circuit*
> *Difficulty: moderately strenuous*

A number of parcels of land adjacent to the BRP were purchased shortly after the turn of the twenty-first century as preservation measures. Some are now owned by organizations and others by the state of North Carolina; additional ones have been donated to the National Park Service. Three of those tracts—at Miles 221.8, 324.7, and 325.9—were protected with large donations from Fred and Alice Stanback, and trails on each of those properties —designated as Stanback Trails—opened in 2013.

Accessed from Mile 221.8, the Saddle Mountain Trail, a moderately strenuous circuit trail (with a bit of an out-and-back) of 2.9 miles, ascends through the more than 500 acres of the Mitchell River Game Lands to the summits of Saddle Mountain and the Horn of Saddle Mountain. At Mile 221.8, exit the BRP eastward on Saddle Mountain Church Road and, almost immediately, turn right onto Mountain Lake Road. In 300 more feet, make a left onto a graveled game-lands road and continue for .5 mile to a gate and the trailhead parking area.

Beyond the gate, the trail continues on the gravel road for .5 mile to the loop trail intersection. Bearing right, the hike begins to climb,

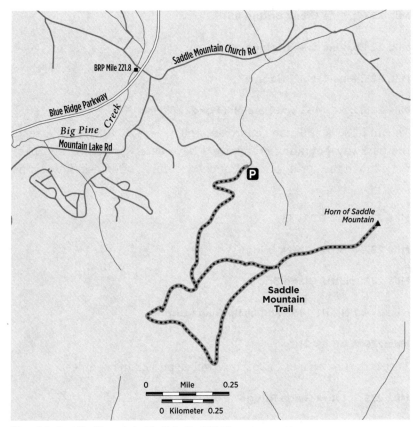

Map 26. Saddle Mountain Trail (mile 221.8)

sometimes steeply, to cross Saddle Mountain's summit before turning onto the side trail to the Horn of Saddle Mountain at 1.7 miles. Returning to the loop trail, the hike descends back to the gravel road that returns hikers to the parking area at 2.9 miles.

Please Note: Luxuriant growths of vegetation can overtake much of the pathway during the warmer months. It may be best to undertake this hike after the vegetation has died back in the fall.

Mile 222.8. Pine Creek Bridge #1

Mile 223.1. Pine Creek Bridge #2 and NC RT 1486

Mile 223.8. Pine Creek Bridge #3

Mile 224.1. Pine Creek Bridge #4

Mile 224.2. Pine Creek Bridge #5

Mile 224.8. Pine Creek Bridge #6

Mile 225. Pine Creek Bridge #7

Mile 225.3. NC 1463 and Hare Mill Pond (2,591 feet)

The mid-1800s mill stood approximately where NC RT 1463 intersects the parkway. Migrating mergansers have been spotted on and near the pond in the spring and fall, and wood ducks often nest here in the summer.

Mile 226.3. NC RT 1433

Mile 227.4. Brush Creek Bridge

Mile 228.1. Little Glade Bridge

Mile 229.2 NC RT 1468 and Little Glade Bridge

Mile 229.7. US RT 21

Access to full services in Sparta (7 miles) and Elkin (21 miles).

Mile 229.9. Little Glade Bridge

Mile 230.1. Little Glade Mill Pond Overlook (2,709 feet)

In addition to the wildlife that may be seen on the Little Glade Mill Pond Trail [BRP 54], it may be possible, in summer, to observe a Louisiana waterthrush, hooded warbler, ovenbird, and dark-eyed junco from the comfort of your automobile.

Mile 230.1. Little Glade Mill Pond Trail [BRP 54]
(N 36°26.531 W 81°01.873) Map 27

> *Length: .2 mile, circuit*
> *Difficulty: easy*

An easy loop around the pond offers the possibility of glimpses of aquatic life—newts, snapping turtles, frogs, dragonflies, and a good variety of fish. Rhododendron lines the creek, and rose hips adorn bushes in the fall.

Several picnic tables overlook the pond.

Map 27. Little Glade Mill Pond Trail (mile 230.1)

Mile 230.5. Little Glade Bridge

Mile 230.9. NC RT 1108 and NC RT 1111

Access to Sparta.

Mile 231.5. NC RT 1109

Mile 231.8. NC RT 1110

Mile 231.9. Brush Creek Bridge

Mile 232.5. Stone Mountain Overlook (3,115 feet)

Stone Mountain's distinctive granite summit rises 600 feet from the surrounding land. Referred to as a "Yosemite-like dome" in a national outdoors publication and defined as a pluton by geologists, the mountain had its origins 400 million years ago as magma began cooling and crystallizing underground. About 200 million years later, the overlying layers of rocks began eroding, lessening weight upon the lower rock and permitting it to swell upward. Large pieces of it fractured and broke off, creating the dome seen today. The trails of Stone Mountain State Park traverse the geological marvel.

Mile 233.7. Bullhead Mountain Overlook (3,200 feet)

Bullhead Mountain is the lump of land visible through the low gap in the mountain ridgelines directly ahead. It may take a bit of imagination to see the "bull's head."

Mile 234. Deep Gap and NC RT 1115

Mile 235. Mahogany Rock Overlook (3,436 feet)

Virginia is to the right in the vista; North Carolina, to the left. This is also the midpoint of the parkway.

Mile 235.7. Devils Garden Overlook (3,428 feet)

The rocky Devils Garden is located at the low meeting point of the two ridgelines.

Mile 235.7. Mountains-to-Sea Trail (N 36°26.049 W 81°06.256).
See Chapter 1.

Having come westward from its origination on North Carolina's Outer Banks at the Atlantic Ocean, the Mountains-to-Sea Trail now begins to parallel and connect with the BRP in numerous places for more than 300 miles as it continues its journey to its western terminus atop Clingman's Dome in the Great Smoky Mountains National Park.

Mile 236.9. Air Bellows Gap Overlook (3,744 feet)

Named for a nearby gap whose shape funnels high winds through it, especially in winter.

Trails of Doughton Park, Blue Ridge Parkway
Miles 238.5–244.7

Doughton Park was originally known as "The Bluffs," called so for the precipitous cliffs overlooking Basin Cove. In 1951, the area was named in honor of Robert Lee Doughton, a North Carolina congressman and staunch supporter of the BRP.

Like the Rocky Knob Recreation Area and Rock Castle Gorge, the mountains, valleys, and hollows of Doughton Park were once home to a number of inhabitants. However, whereas Rock Castle Gorge supported several communities, the population here was much sparser. People were more isolated from one another. Martin Brinegar's family lived near the summits of the Blue Ridge, while Martin Caudill's numerous offspring were spread out on the upper reaches of Basin Creek. A few other families scratched out a living along the banks of Cove Creek. Cabins, old foundations, and other reminders of these tenacious people, who inhabited the area until the 1920s and 1930s, will be encountered on some of the trails in the park.

Doughton Park, at 5,700 acres (the parkway's largest recreation area), has more than 30 miles of pathways that traverse a variety of terrain and pass through several different vegetation zones. The gently undulating meadows make strolling rather easy while you enjoy stirring views of faraway peaks and nearby valleys. Rocky, rugged, and narrow ridgelines are natural pathways from the meadows into forests crowded with rhododendron and mountain laurel. The warmer environs of Basin and Cove Creeks are home to luxuriant ferns and carpets of running cedar. Often in the spring, these valley floors are bursting with flowers while the mountain summits of Doughton are still covered with snow.

Because the eastern edge of the park is bordered by the Thurmon Chatham Game Land, your chances of catching a glimpse of a deer, rabbit, squirrel, raccoon, fox, or maybe even a bobcat or bear are increased.

A primitive backcountry campsite that can only be reached by foot travel is located in the valley where Basin and Cove Creeks meet. Free camping permits may be obtained from the ranger station (49800 Blue Ridge Parkway, Laurel Springs, NC 28644; 336-372-8568) at BRP mile 245.4.

In addition to the primitive campsite, Doughton Park also contains a park service campground, coffee and gift shop, picnic area, and the Bluffs Lodge. *Please Note:* Bluffs Lodge and the coffee and gift shops were closed as this book went to press. Contact BRP Main Office for up-to-date information.

Quickest Route to NC RT 1730 and the Primitive Campsite

Drive south on the parkway from Doughton Park to BRP mile 248. Head east on NC RT 18 for 6 miles, turn left onto NC RT 1728 for 4 miles, and then make another left onto unpaved NC RT 1730. Watch carefully for a small parking area on the right, 3 miles beyond this intersection at a bridged stream (N 36°22.505 W 81°08.698). To the left is the end of the Grassy Gap Fire Road [BRP 62]. Walk 1.7 miles on this road to reach the campsite.

Mile 238.5 Brinegar Cabin Overlook and Mountains-to-Sea Trail (see Chapter 1) access (via Bluff Mountain Trail [BRP 57])

Mile 238.5. Brinegar Cabin Walk [BRP 55] (3,508 feet)
(N 36°25.129 W 81°08.762) Map 28

> *Length: .2 mile, out-and-back*
> *Difficulty: easy leg stretcher*

Brinegar Cabin.

Martin Brinegar built this log cabin in the 1880s. His family lived here until the 1930s, when the property was purchased by the park service. A short walk brings you to the cabin and down to a springhouse that once served as the "refrigerator" for the Brinegar family. Exhibits and special interpretive demonstrations are presented during the tourist season.

Mile 238.5. Cedar Ridge Trail [BRP 56] (N 36°25.129 W 81°08.762) Map 28

Length: 4.5 miles, one way; 9 miles, out-and-back
Difficulty: moderately strenuous from BRP to Grassy Gap Fire Road;
strenuous if hiked in the opposite direction

The Cedar Ridge Trail is a longer and possibly more enjoyable route into Basin Cove than the Bluff Ridge Trail [BRP 60]. Its pathway is certainly gentler, as it descends for more than 4 miles from the BRP to the Grassy Gap Fire Road at NC RT 1730 near Abshers, North Carolina.

Abundant spring flowers, such as cinquefoil and fire pink, make up for the relatively few scenic overlooks. The purple and pink flowers of rhododendron and mountain laurel accompany late May and early June hikers almost the entire distance of the trail.

.0   Ascend on the Bluff Mountain Trail [BRP 57] from the Brinegar Cabin parking lot. Soon enter a meadow of cinquefoil and wild strawberries.

.1   Reach the top of the rise and descend.

.2   Intersection. The Bluff Mountain Trail goes to the right. Turn left and pass through the fence stile to continue on the Cedar Ridge Trail.

.3   Enter a thick rhododendron tunnel.

.6   Begin a series of switchbacks.

1.1   Go out of and back into national park lands. Ascend slightly over a small knob and resume your descent.

1.4   Begin to walk right on top of the ridgeline, which has become narrower. Soon rock outcroppings to the right allow some limited views into the basin.

1.8   Ascend and then descend on switchbacks. There is another small rock outcropping on the right.

2.3   Ascend for 300 feet and then resume the descent, sometimes on switchbacks. Take note that as the rhododendron begins to fade, the forest floor becomes more open.

3.7   At a switchback, a slight break in the vegetation gives another limited view into the valley. The mountain laurel becomes much heavier.

3.9   Take note of the well-crafted stone wall along the pathway. The builders of this trail have ensured that it will be here for some time to come.

4.4   Fire pinks are quite abundant as you pass through a fence stile.

4.5   Arrive at the Grassy Gap Fire Road [BRP 62]. The parking area on NC RT 1730 is 300 feet to the left. (See p. 173 for directions to this parking area.)

Mile 238.5. Bluff Mountain Trail [BRP 57] (N 36°25.129 W 81°08.762) Map 28

Length: 7.5 miles, one way; 15 miles, out-and-back
Difficulty: moderate, with some long easy stretches
Highly recommended

A soft pathway of pine needles and grass. Open meadows with views to wave after wave of Blue Ridge Mountain summits. Towering pine

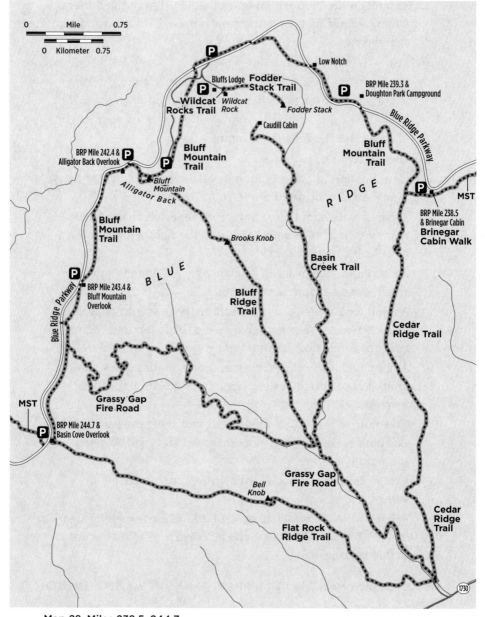

Map 28. Miles 238.5–244.7

groves contrasted with wind-stunted trees. Precipitous cliffs overlooking Caudill Cabin, nestled in the upper reaches of Basin Cove. All of these turn Bluff Mountain Trail into some of the best walking to be found along the BRP. In other words, do not miss this one!

The full length of the trail parallels the parkway and comes into contact with a number of parking areas. With a car shuttle you can make this walk as long or as short as you wish. The picnic area and campground provide water and restrooms.

The eastbound Mountains-to-Sea Trail (see Chapter 1) goes northward from the parking lot, while the westbound portion follows the full route of the Bluff Mountain Trail.

.0 Begin at the trail sign in the Brinegar Cabin parking lot and ascend.

.1 Good view back onto Brinegar Cabin and the valleys below. Continue through the small field and descend.

.2 Trail intersection. The pathway to the left is the Cedar Ridge Trail [BRP 56]. Bear right to continue on the Bluff Mountain Trail.

.4 Slab to the left of a knob. (Follow the trail and not the roadway.) The pathway widens as you enter open fields with good views of the surrounding mountains.

.7 Cross through a fence stile, enter an old pine grove, and continue with gradual ups and downs.

1.1 Slab to the left of a knob and ascend into the RV portion of the campground. (Water is available here.) Cross the parking lots and bear to the right, leaving the RV campground.

1.3 Cross the BRP and ascend.

1.4 Come to a trail-map poster in the main part of the campground. Walk just below the campground road and descend gradually past several campsites. (Water and restrooms are available in the campground.)

1.7 Leave the campground and continue to descend through a hardwood forest and rhododendron tunnels.

1.9 Cross the parkway in Low Notch (BRP mile 239.9), where there is a view of mountain summits stretching as far as you can see. Ascend through a heavy forest.

2.0 Cross through a fence stile.

2.1 Ascend into an open field and walk along the fence line, passing by a livestock loading pen.

2.3   Cross through a fence stile and continue to ascend.

2.4   Pass by an overlook parking lot, enjoying the views from the open meadows.

2.5   Top the knoll and begin to descend.

2.6   Cross the BRP and walk along the fence.

2.7   Arrive at the Doughton Park Coffee Shop, BRP mile 241.1. (*Please Note*: The coffee shop was closed as this book went to press. Contact BRP Main Office for up-to-date information.) The trail continues at the far end of the parking lot. Descend the steps and enter woods.

2.8   Diagonally cross the BRP to your left and ascend into woods and rhododendron. The trail here becomes a little indistinct, but cross the picnic area road, bear right (avoiding the trail that goes left to the Bluffs Lodge), and continue to ascend.

3.0   The views begin to open up as you climb and reach the top of a knob. Restrooms and water are to your right.

3.2   Pass through a fence stile and continue to enjoy the wonderful views, especially to the south and west. Make sure that you follow the trail and not the old roadway.

3.6   Reach the top of the knob for the best views yet. Begin to descend.

3.8   Pass through a fence stile and walk on the sidewalk next to the parking area.

4.0   Cross through another fence stile and ascend once again in the open field.

4.2   Intersection. The Bluff Ridge Trail [BRP 60] takes off to the left. Bear right to continue on the Bluff Mountain Trail.

4.3   Pass through another fence stile and walk along the edge of a rocky cliff. The view is truly breathtaking, with the BRP and steep mountain walls dropping into Cove Creek Valley directly below you. Descend first through wind-stunted evergreens and then on steep switchbacks in a dense forest.

4.5   Switchbacks begin to level out.

4.7   The Alligator Back Overlook (BRP mile 242.4) is on your right. Continue straight on the Bluff Mountain Trail and in a few feet come to a stone-walled overlook. The view here is into Cove Creek Basin. Continue to parallel the BRP.

4.9 The rocks to the right provide another viewpoint.

5.0 Walk directly below the BRP. Wildflowers, thorn bushes, and poison ivy are abundant. Look back to see the rugged Bluff Mountain ridgeline that you descended. Soon slab to the left of a knob, staying almost level in a pleasantly wooded area.

5.6 Cross a small water run in a draw and return to walking just below the BRP, where you will find good views from the open field.

5.8 Pass by the steps to the Bluff Mountain Overlook (BRP mile 243.4). Continue straight and go through a fence stile. The grassy pathway is made even softer by needles dropped from the lofty evergreens lining the trail.

6.0 Leave the evergreens behind and enter a hardwood forest.

6.3 Do not take the steep trail up to the old road! Instead, bear left and follow the pathway below the roadbed.

6.4 Cross Grassy Gap Fire Road [BRP 62] and continue through an open meadow.

6.6 Swing around the ridge and into the woods. There is very little elevation change from here to the end of the trail.

6.9 Open fields provide an opportunity to look out across Basin Cove. Soon slab to the right of a knob and enter woods on a pine needle–softened pathway.

7.4 Trail intersection. The Flat Rock Ridge Trail [BRP 63] goes off to the left. Bear right to continue on the Bluff Mountain Trail.

7.5 Pass through a fence stile and ascend the steps to the Basin Cove Overlook (BRP mile 244.7) for a grandstand view of Stone Mountain to the northeast. The westbound Mountains-to-Sea Trail crosses the BRP to continue its journey toward the Great Smokies.

Mile 239.3. Doughton Park campground (3,650 feet)

Mile 241. Doughton Park coffee shop (3,685 feet)

Small gift shop, restrooms, picnic area, and Bluffs Lodge. *Please Note:* The coffee and gift shops and Bluffs Lodge were closed as this book went to press. Contact BRP Main Office for up-to-date information.

Mile 241. Mountains-to-Sea Trail (N 36°26.042 W 81°10.647). See Chapter 1.

Mile 241. Fodder Stack Trail [BRP 58] (N 36°25.824 W 81°10.572) Map 28

Length: 1 mile, out-and-back
Difficulty: moderate

As it snakes its way to the rock jumbles of Fodder Stack, the trail is a narrow path passing by aspen trees and superb views of the sheer walls of Basin Cove. The views to the east are unobstructed; early risers can watch the day begin in peace and solitude. The trail's close proximity to the picnic area, lodge, and campground make it very popular at other times of the day.

.0   The trail begins at the far end of Bluff Lodge's upper parking area. Drop steeply; you'll get wonderful views into Basin Cove.

.07 Come to a bench with a vantage point of Caudill Cabin almost directly below.

.2   Arrive at another bench with equally breathtaking views.

.3   Begin to ascend, soon coming to yet another dramatic view from the rock outcropping to the right. Continue on a narrow ridgeline.

.4   Come to a bench with a view to the northwest. The trail levels out somewhat.

.5   Bear to the left and climb up on a rock-obstructed pathway as you begin to circle around Fodder Stack. (Do not take the dangerous, unauthorized trail that goes steeply downhill.) Soon arrive at a bench just below the summit. Retrace steps.

Mile 241. Wildcat Rocks Trail [BRP 59] (N 36°25.824 W 81°10.572) Map 28

Length: .1 mile, out-and-back (with a short loop at the farthest point)
Difficulty: easy
Recommended

This trail, recommended for its ease and impressive view, also begins at the far end of Bluff Lodge's upper parking lot. Bear to the right to begin. The trail extends to views overlooking Caudill Cabin and the expanse of Basin Cove. It then loops back to the parking lot via rhododendron tunnels and the lodge's manicured lawn.

Please Note: Do not attempt to reach the Caudill Cabin by hiking directly down the mountainside from Wildcat Rocks. The rough terrain is extremely hazardous, and the steep slopes are easily eroded by foot traffic. See the Basin Creek Trail [BRP 61] for access to the cabin.

Mile 241. Bluff Ridge Trail [BRP 60] (N 36°25.305 W 81°10.019) Map 28

Length: 2.8 miles, one way; 5.6 miles, out-and-back
Difficulty: moderately strenuous from BRP to Cove Creek; very strenuous
if hiking in the opposite direction

A steep journey, the Bluff Ridge Trail is the shortest route from the BRP to the backcountry campsite on Cove Creek. The trail offers excellent views near the parkway but soon enters heavy woods as it quickly drops 2,000 feet in less than 3 miles.

For easiest access to the trailhead, drive the picnic area road to its turnaround. Leave your car here and follow the trail markers uphill through the open field.

.0 Follow the trail markers from the parking area uphill through the open meadow.

.2 Trail intersection. The Bluff Mountain Trail [BRP 57] goes to the right. Enjoy the magnificent setting here before bearing left to continue on the Bluff Ridge Trail. Soon cross through a fence stile and come to a shelter with an outstanding view to the southeast of Cove Creek Valley and innumerable ridgelines of the Blue Ridge Mountains stretching off into the distance. A wonderful place to be for sunrise. Descend and cross through another fence stile.

.3 The rocks to the right afford a limited view into the upper reaches of Cove Creek Valley. Descend steeply.

.6 Come into a gap with a trail sign pointing the way. Ascend steeply through mountain laurel.

.9 Reach the top of the ascent and descend at a more moderate pace. Soon rise gradually.

1.2 Reach the top of another knoll; descend gradually on the narrower ridgeline. Soon, however, begin to climb again.

1.7 Attain the top of a knoll.

1.8 Reach the top of another knoll and descend steeply. Level out somewhat as you enter a mountain laurel thicket.

2.3 Turn to the left, onto a switchback.

2.6 Drop into a small gap, but continue with a steep descent following the backbone of the ridgeline on switchbacks.

2.8 Arrive at the backcountry campsite on Cove Creek. (Camping permits are available from the Doughton Park campground contact station or the ranger station near mile 245.4.) A right turn onto Grassy Gap Fire Road [BRP 62] will lead back to the parkway in 5 miles. To the left, just a few feet, is the beginning of Basin Creek Trail [BRP 61]. Following Grassy Gap Fire Road to the left will bring you to NC RT 1730 in 1.7 miles. (See p. 173 for auto access to NC RT 1730.)

Mile 241. Basin Creek Trail [BRP 61] Map 28

Length: 6.6 miles, out-and-back
Difficulty: moderately strenuous

Ascending the tumbling waters of Basin Creek, the trail passes by many artifacts and reminders that these mountain hollows were populated at one time. The numerous members of the Caudill family lived in and farmed the hidden reaches around Basin Creek. The main family cabin, located at the end of the trail, sits nestled between Fodder Stack and Bluff Ridge. The rural nature of the small community within this area demanded that the Caudills and their neighbors be willing to pitch in and help one another in times of need.

The Basin Creek Trail is reached only by hiking one of Doughton Park's other trails to the backcountry campsite on Cove Creek. It is listed here at BRP mile 241 because its quickest access from the parkway would be via the Bluff Ridge Trail [BRP 60]. However, the easiest access would be to walk 1.7 miles from the end of Grassy Gap Fire Road [BRP 62] at NC RT 1730. (See p. 173 for vehicle access to NC RT 1730.)

Basin Creek is also well known for some of the best native brook trout fishing in the area.

.0   Begin the trail next to the backcountry campsite, at the intersection of Grassy Gap Fire Road [BRP 62], Bluff Ridge Trail [BRP 60], and Basin Creek Trail [BRP 61].

.05   Walk through rhododendron on an old roadway. There are some inviting large pools in the creek next to you. Continue to ascend through hemlock.

.6   All that remains of this old cabin is the chimney.

.7   Cross Basin Creek where running cedar lines the trail. Soon come back to the old roadbed.

1.0   The creek makes a few pretty cascades—also, some pools that would be hard to resist on hot summer days.

1.1   Cross Basin Creek. You are now almost constantly passing through tunnels of rhododendron and mountain laurel.

1.2 Cross Basin Creek again, and then recross it near some small waterfalls. Ascend rather steeply for a short while.

1.3 Come to a limited view of a 30-foot waterfall and descend back to the creek.

1.4 Cross a creek and walk through a forest that obviously was pastureland at one time.

1.5 Cross another creek and continue to parallel Basin Creek on the old road.

1.8 Cross Basin Creek.

1.9 Pass by another chimney and cross the creek.

2.0 Cross the creek. Again ascend somewhat steeply and enter more former grazing lands. The old roadway more or less disappears. Continue with small ascents and descents.

2.2 Step over a side stream and pass by another cabin site. Cross Basin Creek.

2.4 Enjoy the 30-foot waterfall. Cross Basin Creek.

2.6 Cross Basin Creek again and ascend on a narrow path.

2.8 Cross the creek here and in 200 feet.

3.0 Cross Basin Creek for the final time. Ascend steeply, avoiding the old road and staying close to the creek.

3.3 Arrive at the restored Caudill Cabin. Fodder Stack, Wildcat Rocks, and Bluff Ridge are almost directly above you. Retrace steps.

Mile 242. Ice Rock

The reason for the name will be obvious during the colder months.

Mile 242.4. Alligator Back Overlook (3,388 feet)

The "alligator back" is the outcrop of gneiss close to the overlook. A metamorphic rock, gneiss is easy to recognize by its mineral grains that are arranged in a banded structure.

Mile 242.4. Mountains-to-Sea Trail (N 36°25.274 W 81°11.381). See Chapter 1.

Mile 243.4. Bluff Mountain Overlook and access to Bluff Mountain Trail [BRP 57] (3,334 feet)

Flat Rock Ridge is to the right in the view, with Bluff Mountain to the left.

Mile 243.7. Grassy Gap Fire Road [BRP 62] (3,218 feet)

(N 36°24.245 W 81°11.913) Map 28

> *Length: 6.5 miles, one way; 13 miles, out-and-back*
> *Difficulty: moderate*

By far the gentlest route into Basin Cove, the Grassy Gap Fire Road takes 6.5 miles to descend 1,800 feet from the BRP, pass by the backcountry campsite, and arrive at NC RT 1730 near Abshers, North Carolina. Being an old road, its wide pathway enables family and friends to walk side by side, allowing sociable conversation and mutual discoveries. Along the way are a couple of chances to explore the homesites of former inhabitants of the Basin Cove area. Also, the headwaters of Cove Creek, which the road parallels much of the way, are known to carry a large number of native brook trout.

For an easy half-day walk, arrange a car shuttle to meet you at NC RT 1730 (see p. 173 for directions).

.0 The trailhead for Grassy Gap Fire Road is not marked well. Be on the lookout for a gated road about .5 mile south of the Bluff Mountain Overlook (BRP mile 243.4). The overlook is the closest parking area to the Grassy Gap Fire Road. Begin the walk by passing through a fence stile.

.1 Cross the Bluff Mountain Trail [BRP 57] and go through a fence. Be sure to shut the gate behind you. Enter the woods and begin your long, gradual descent.

.4 Cross over a spur ridge and enter a rhododendron thicket.

.6 Emerge from the rhododendron and make a wide, arching switchback.

.9 Do not take the side road that comes in from the right.

1.0 In periods of wet weather there should be a small spring on the left.

1.2 The road cuts across the ridgeline and swings to the opposite side.

1.8 Now in a wider, flatter area, pass by some reminders of the former human inhabitants of this area. Explore a little and you may find rusted barrel hoops, old tools, and maybe the foundation of a now nonexistent cabin. Cross the creek on a stone and metal culvert.

2.2 Cross a well-constructed stone bridge and begin to closely parallel the creek.

2.4   Where another creek comes in from the left, arrive in an open valley littered with artifacts from the days when mountain people tried to make a living along these creeks.

2.6   Cross the creek as it descends in a series of small cascades. Rhododendron and hemlock ensure that the trail will be lined with green vegetation throughout the year.

2.8   Cross the creek and begin a gradual ascent.

3.4   Resume the gradual descent.

4.2   There is a nice wading pool here as Grassy Gap Fire Road once again crosses the creek.

4.4   A small wooden bridge precedes your arrival into the wide Basin Cove Valley.

4.8   Arrive at the intersections with Bluff Ridge [BRP 60] and Basin Creek [BRP 61] Trails. The primitive backcountry campsite is on your right along the banks of Cove Creek. (Free camping permits may be obtained from the Doughton Park campground contact station or the ranger station at BRP mile 245.4.) Cross Basin Creek and continue to follow Grassy Gap Fire Road.

4.9   Reach the top of a small rise and begin to gradually descend.

5.4   Cross a small side stream on a wooden bridge. The rhododendron, hemlock, ferns, and running cedar give this valley a lush, green look even in winter.

6.0   A stone wall lines the roadway where there is one final good view back upstream.

6.5   Arrive at the intersections with Cedar Ridge [BRP 56] and Flat Rock Ridge [BRP 63] Trails. A few feet beyond is the parking area on NC RT 1730.

Mile 244.7. Basin Cove Overlook and access to the southern end of Bluff Mountain Trail [BRP 57] (3,312 feet)

A view of Stone Mountain.

Mile 244.7. Mountains-to-Sea Trail (N 36°23.447 W 81°11.993). See Chapter 1.

Mile 244.7. Flat Rock Ridge Trail [BRP 63]
(N 36°23.447 W 81°11.993) Map 28

> *Length: 5 miles, one way; 10 miles, out-and-back*
> *Difficulty: moderately strenuous from BRP to Grassy Gap Fire Road;*
> *strenuous if hiking in the opposite direction*

The Flat Rock Ridge Trail is a more rugged, and therefore possibly a more rewarding, hike into Basin Cove than the Cedar Ridge Trail [BRP 56]. Worthwhile views into Basin Cove open up on soaring rock outcroppings as rhododendron and mountain laurel appear to line almost every inch of the trail. Be on the lookout for deer, turkey, and maybe even a black bear.

Although the narrow ridgeline that the pathway follows eventually descends into the valley, it seems to have more than its share of small knobs and knolls. The trail, of course, goes up and over almost every one of them. Switchbacks and excellent trail-building techniques (take note of the superbly constructed stone walls used to stabilize the trail) make these ups and downs a little easier to negotiate.

.0 From the Basin Cove Overlook, pass through a fence stile and descend.

.1 Trail intersection. The Bluff Mountain Trail [BRP 57] bears to the left. Turn right to follow the Flat Rock Ridge Trail, pass through another stile, and descend via switchbacks. The flame azalea is especially beautiful here.

.4 Gradually descend through rhododendron and mountain laurel.

.5 Reach the top of a rise and begin to descend through rhododendron tunnels that are almost unbelievably colorful in late May and early June.

.7 A break in the vegetation allows a view into Basin Cove. Descend on a series of switchbacks, taking note of the stone walls lining the pathway.

1.2 Come to the game land boundary. The ridgeline here is now quite narrow. Soon come into a gap and begin to ascend.

1.7 Reach the top of the rise, where a rock outcropping gives a limited view of Bluff and Cedar Ridges. In a few feet the view to the east gives you the feeling that you are high above any of the surrounding lands.

1.9 A grandstand view into Basin Cove! Continue to descend via switchbacks in rhododendron.

2.5 Come out of the rhododendron and onto a narrow ridgeline. The rhododendron has evidently come to the limit of its environment, as there is almost a definite line here—the rhododendron now disappears, and mountain laurel takes its place as the dominant understory in the forest.

2.8 Begin a gradual rise.

3.0 Resume the descent.

3.2 Be alert! The trail turns to the left and descends along the side of the mountain. Do not continue straight by following the game land boundary line.

3.4 Return to the ridgeline and the boundary markers.

3.5 Begin an ascent.

3.6 Resume descent.

3.8 Ascend again.

4.0 Descend.

4.4 Breaks in the vegetation reveal the fact that you are much, much lower than you were the last time you had a good view.

4.8 Cove Creek becomes audible below you.

5.0 Cross the creek and arrive at Grassy Gap Fire Road [BRP 62] and Cedar Ridge Trail [BRP 56]. Left on Grassy Gap Fire Road for 1.7 miles will lead to the primitive campsite and the intersections with Bluff Ridge [BRP 60] and Basin Creek [BRP 61] trails. The parking area on NC RT 1730 is just a few feet to the right. See p. 173 for vehicle access to this parking area.

Mile 245.5. Bluffs ranger office and BRP maintenance facilities

Mile 246.1. NC RT 1143, with access to NC RT 18

Mile 246.9. NC RT 1144

Mile 247.2. NC RT 1175 (Miller's Campground Road)

Mile 248. NC RT 18 (N 36°23.463 W 81°14.731)

Full services located close to the BRP. Access to Laurel Springs (2 miles) and North Wilkesboro (24 miles) and the Doughton Park backcountry campsite (see p. 173).

Mile 248.9. Laurel Fork Viaduct

Mile 249.3. NC RT 1613

Mile 250. NC RT 1615

Mile 250.8. NC RT 1616 and NC RT 1620

Mile 251.5. Alder Gap (3,047 feet)

Mile 252.4. NC RT 1619

Mile 252.8. Sheets Gap Overlook and NC RT 1568 (3,343 feet)
View of Yadkin Valley.

Mile 255.2. NC RT 1567 and NC RT 1622

Mile 256. NC RT 1624

Mile 256.5. NC RT 1628

Mile 256.9. NC RT 1628
Access to coffee shop, gift shop, and gas station.

Mile 257.7. NC RT 1628 and NC RT 1630

Mile 258.7. Old NC RT 16 and Sally Mae's on the Parkway
Restrooms, water, and Sally Mae's on the Parkway. In addition to many of the usual gift shop items, the trading post offers some interesting articles produced by a number of local artists, including toys, wood carvings, brooms, pottery, metalwork, and more. Even some of the food offerings—such as baked goods, hams, relishes, and jellies—are made in the region.

Mile 258.7. Mountains-to-Sea Trail (N 36°22.505 W 81°08.698). See Chapter 1.

Mile 259.2. NC RT 1632

Mile 259.8. NC RT 1634

Mile 260.3. Jumpinoff Rocks Overlook (3,165 feet)
The view of mountainous terrain to the east shows that the Blue Ridge Mountains, unlike they were north of Roanoke, are definitely not just one ridgeline wide here.

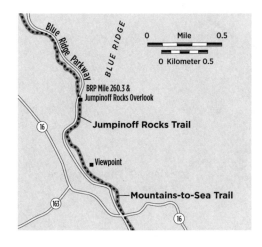

Map 29. Mile 260.3

Mile 260.3. Jumpinoff Rocks Trail [BRP 64]

(N 36°19.475 W 81°22.78) Map 29

> *Length: 1 mile, out-and-back*
> *Difficulty: easy*
> *Recommended*

Lined with galax, pepperbush, and trailing arbutus, this path offers a nice break from riding in an automobile. The viewpoint at the end of the walk is quiet and secluded from the parkway—a favorable location to enjoy a sunrise or have an afternoon snack.

.0   Begin by rising through rhododendron thickets.

.1   Come into a small gap where a break in the vegetation permits a view into the deep valley below.

.15   A bench on which to rest.

.25   Level off and then begin to descend through mountain laurel.

.3   Arrive at another bench.

.4   Galax becomes abundant and lines both sides of the trail.

.5   Arrive at the view looking out across the valley to prominent Stone Mountain in the distance. Retrace steps.

Mile 260.3. Mountains-to-Sea Trail (N 36°19.475 W 81°22.78). See Chapter 1.

Mile 261.2. Horse Gap and NC RT 16 (3,108 feet)

Access to West Jefferson (12 miles) and North Wilkesboro (22 miles).

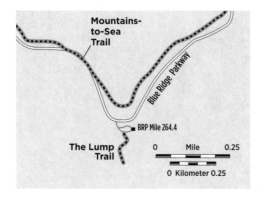

Map 30. The Lump Trail (mile 264.4)

Mile 262.2. Daniel Gap (3,170 feet)

Mile 264.4. The Lump Trail [BRP 65] (3,465 feet)
(N 36°16.558 W 81°22.748) Map 30

> *Length: .2–.3 mile (the trail is a field area)*
> *Difficulty: moderately easy*
> *Highly recommended*

There is no real trail here, but what an appropriate name for the area! This high, open meadow is just a large "lump" of land that ascends quickly from the parkway. There are excellent views from the top into Yadkin Valley and out across the multitude of ridges that rise to meet the horizon in all directions.

Walk through the fence and wander around on The Lump, enjoying the views and, in season, possibly a wild strawberry or two. This windswept knob might provide a cool yet sunny spot for a lazy summer afternoon of sunbathing.

A plaque at the parking area provides information about Tom Dula, made famous in the "Tom Dooley" folk song.

Mile 265.1. Calloway Gap and NC RT 1360 (3,439 feet)

Mile 266.8. Mount Jefferson Overlook (3,699 feet)

Originally known as Negro Mountain, the name was changed to Mount Jefferson when the nearby eponymous state park was created in the 1950s. One of the park's trails leads to the 4,515-foot summit for a grandstand view.

Mile 267.6. NC RT 1167

Mile 267.8. Betsey's Rock Falls Overlook (3,405 feet)

The narrow (very narrow in dry weather) waterfall is to the left in the view. Access to the Mountains-to-Sea Trail (see Chapter 1) is possible by walking the BRP southward to mile 268.

Mile 268. NC RT 1166

Mile 269.7. NC RT 1365

Mile 269.8. Phillips Gap and NC RT 1168 (3,221 feet).

Mile 270.2. Lewis Fork Overlook (3,290 feet)

The stream flows through the valley visible from the overlook.

Mile 270.2. Mountains-to-Sea Trail (N 36°19.475 W 81°22.78). See Chapter 1.

Trails of the E. B. Jeffress Park Area, Blue Ridge Parkway Miles 271.9–272.5

This small recreation area was named in honor of E. B. Jeffress, chairman of the North Carolina State Highway and Public Works Commission in 1933. In addition to being an enthusiastic supporter of the BRP project, he led the fight to keep the parkway from becoming a toll road.

The park contains picnic tables and restrooms.

Mile 271.9. Cascades Trail [BRP 66] (3,570 feet)
(N 36°14.724 W 81°27.469) Map 31

> Length: .9 mile, circuit
> Difficulty: moderate
> Recommended

The park service has placed signs along the Cascades Trail identifying much of the plant life to be found in the Blue Ridge Mountains. As with other signed, self-guiding trails, this short walk is recommended because it offers knowledge that will enrich your additional excursions along the BRP.

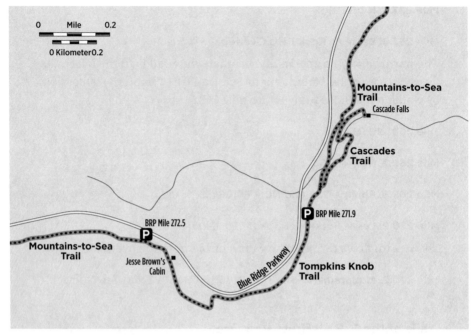

Map 31. Miles 271.9–272.5

Dropping quickly off the ridgeline, the pathway follows Falls Creek to the cascades. The rushing, roiling falls of 50 or 60 feet will be most impressive after a hard spring rain. Spring is also the time to enjoy an abundance of trillium and jack-in-the-pulpit near the falls.

The climb back up from the cascades gives this trail a moderate rating (and possibly moderately strenuous if you are a little out of shape).

The Mountains-to-Sea Trail (see Chapter 1) makes use of a portion of this pathway.

.0   Begin on the paved trail next to the restrooms.

.05   Bear to the right at the loop trail intersection and pass by several large Solomon's seal plants. Begin to descend.

.1   There is a bench next to bountiful flame azalea that put on a very colorful display here in mid- to late May. The cascades soon become audible as you quickly descend through mountain laurel and rhododendron.

.3   Cross Falls Creek on a log bridge and bear right at the loop trail junction.

.4 Arrive at the upper viewing platform at the top of the cascades.

.45 Come to the lower viewing platform, which brings you even closer to the rushing waters of the falls. Retrace your steps to return.

.5 Bear right at the loop trail junction and enjoy the attractive bell-shaped dog hobble flowers. Follow the small cascades of the creek upstream.

.6 Arrive at a bench under a birch tree.

.7 Another bench.

.9 Bear right at the loop trail intersection, and in a few feet return to the parking lot.

Mile 272.5. Tompkins Knob Trail [BRP 67] (3,657 feet)
(N 36°14.660 W 81°27.957) Map 31

> Length: .6 mile, one way; 1.2 miles, out-and-back
> Difficulty: easy

The Tompkins Knob Trail is a connector trail between the Tompkins Knob parking lot and the E. B. Jeffress Park picnic area. Along the way, this easy route passes by Jesse Brown's Cabin, occupied in the late 1800s. The trail also goes by the Cool Spring Baptist Church, a log structure noteworthy not only for its historical significance but also for its rib-pole roof construction.

The Mountains-to-Sea Trail makes use of the Tompkins Knob Trail.

.0 Descend on the trail from the northern end of the Tompkins Knob parking lot.

.1 Pass by Jesse Brown's Cabin, which was moved to this site sometime near the turn of the twentieth century to be closer to Cool Spring. In a few feet, go by the Cool Spring Baptist Church. The building itself was actually used only during inclement weather; most of the religious services were held outdoors. Continue past the church on a level trail and into an old orchard.

.2 Descend rather quickly.

.25 As the descent levels out a little, arrive at a bench in a hardwood forest. A few sassafras trees are scattered about, but Solomon's seal and mayapple are plentiful.

.35 Enter a stand of pine trees whose dropped needles help soften the pathway.

.5 Come to another bench.

.6 Arrive at the picnic area in E. B. Jeffress Park (BRP mile 271.9). Restrooms and water are just across the parking lot.

Mile 274.3. Elk Mountain Overlook (3,786 feet)

Panoramic view of the Yadkin Valley.

Mile 274.3. Mountains-to-Sea Trail (accessed just south of the overlook) (N 36°13.966 W 81°26.437). See Chapter 1.

Mile 276.4. Deep Gap (3,142 feet)

US RT 421 and access to Boone (12 miles) and North Wilkesboro (26 miles).

Mile 277.3. Stoney Fork Valley Overlook (3,405 feet)

Be watching for cerulean warblers darting about in the vegetation during the late spring and early summer months.

Mile 277.3. Mountains-to-Sea Trail (N 36°13.703 W 81°30.316). See Chapter 1.

Mile 277.9. Osborne Mountain View Overlook (3,500 feet)

You'll probably have to be here when the leaves are off the trees in order to appreciate the view.

Mile 277.9. Mountains-to-Sea Trail (N 36°13.475 W 81°30.767). See Chapter 1.

Mile 278.3. Carroll Gap Overlook (3,430 feet)

With mountain laurel in the foreground, the view looks onto tree farms and out to Deep Gap.

Mile 280.9. US RT 421 and US RT 221

Access to Deep Gap (4 miles) and Boone (7 miles; full services).

Mile 281.4. Grandview Overlook (3,240 feet)

Another wide vista of the Yadkin Valley.

Mile 281.4. Mountains-to-Sea Trail (accessed 100 yards south of the overlook) (N 36°13.657 W 81°33.9948). See Chapter 1.

Mile 285.1. Boone's Trace Overlook (3,155 feet)

The overlook's signboard provides background on Daniel Boone, who lived in the area. Lore proclaims that Boone passed near this spot on his way to Kentucky.

Mile 285.5. Bamboo Gap. Access road to Boone

Mile 286.4. Goshen Creek Bridge

Mile 288.1. Aho Gap. Public road crossing

Mile 289.5. Raven Rocks Overlook (3,834 feet)

Grandfather Mountain is in the far distance, while the white expanse of the Moses Cone Manor House can be discerned upon the slope of Flat Top Mountain.

Mile 289.5. Mountains-to-Sea Trail (N 36° 11.874 W 81°36.254). See Chapter 1.

Mile 289.8. Yadkin Valley Overlook (3,830 feet)

One more sweeping look into the Yadkin Valley.

Mile 290.4. Thunder Hill Overlook (3,776 feet)

Thunder Hill Overlook provides a far-reaching view onto the flatter lands of the Piedmont. It also becomes quite crowded on the Fourth of July, as it is possible to see the fireworks of at least three different localities from here.

Mile 290.4. Thunder Hill Trail [BRP 68] (N 36°08.173 W 81°38.598) Map 32

> *Length: less than .3 mile, out-and-back (to the apple trees)*
> *Difficulty: moderately easy*

Passing through a fence on the opposite side of the parkway from the overlook will take you on a pathway, a part of the Mountains-to-Sea Trail (see Chapter 1), that locals refer to as the Thunder Hill Trail. The route rises at a gradual rate in an open meadow for spectacular 360-degree views. The rocks at .1 mile make a good place to watch a sunrise, sunset, or the night sky. A few hundred feet beyond are a few old apple trees that still produce some fruit. Be watching for horned lark and dark-eyed junco in the meadow during summer.

Mile 290.4. Mountains-to-Sea Trail (N 36°08.173 W 81°38.598). See Chapter 1.

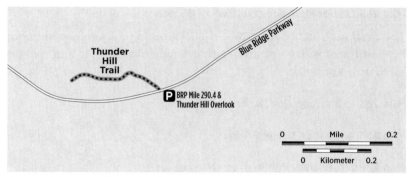

Map 32. Thunder Hill Trail (mile 290.4)

An easy walk with wide-open views, the Thunder Hill Trail is popular with residents of nearby Boone.

Mile 290.7. Green Hill Road

Mile 291.8. US RT 321, US RT 221, and Mountains-to-Sea Trail
(N 36°08.871 W 81°39.765). See Chapter 1.

Access to Boone (7 miles; full services) and Blowing Rock (2 miles; full services).

The influx of national chains has changed Boone, but its downtown area has retained much of the feel of when the town and Appalachian State University were smaller in size. Mom-and-pop establishments;

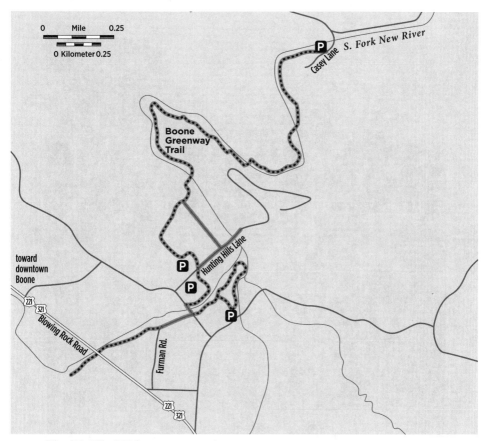

Map 33. Mile 291.8

natural, organic, and vegetarian restaurants; microbreweries; bakeries, delis, and coffee shops; and local art galleries still populate the downtown area, accommodating the thousands of college students and tourists who roam the streets, their different lifestyles juxtaposing and adding color to the scene. Outdoors activities have always been a focus of the town, and outfitters, such as Mast General Store and Footsloggers, still thrive after decades of being in business.

Although it misses downtown, the Boone Greenway Trail (see Map 33) passes by a historic ruin, has picnic shelters and interpretive signs, and follows the South Fork of the New River through open fields and some forests that feel amazingly isolated. Another stretch provides access to shopping and some nice restaurants. One of my favorite spots is the connector trail that encircles a created wetland that attracts a variety

Visitors of all ages and sizes utilize the Boone Greenway Trail.

of birdlife. Most of the route is relatively flat, making it a good outing for families, yet there is a system of side trails that provides more of a challenge if so desired. You could easily enjoy a long morning or afternoon walk of several miles if you were to walk the greenway's full length.

A town whose shops, restaurants, and lodgings definitely cater to travelers, Blowing Rock received its name from the nearby "Blowing Rock," a cliff above Johns River Gorge. Wind coming from the gorge goes by the rock with such force that it returns light objects thrown toward

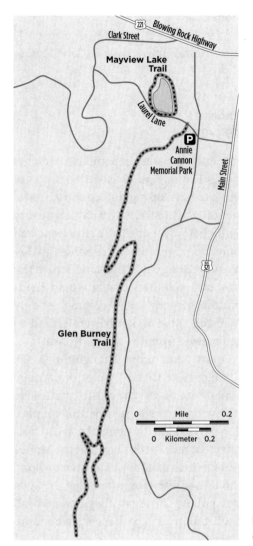

Map 34. Glen Burney Trail (mile 291.8)

the gorge. It's a commercially developed place, so there is a fee to visit. However, there are several free trails (Map 34) that emanate almost directly from town streets. The steep and strenuous 1.6 miles (3.2 miles, out-and-back) Glen Burney Trail passes by three waterfalls—the Cascades, Glen Burney Falls, and Glen Mary (some sources say Marie) Falls. For an easier stroll, head to the town's Broyhill Park and the route that encircles Mayview Lake. Annie Cannon Memorial Park has a pathway meandering through the gardens.

Mile 293.5. Moses H. Cone Overlook (3,888 feet)

There may be no view from the overlook if it has not been recently maintained, but it does mark the entrance into Moses H. Cone Memorial Park.

Trails of Moses H. Cone Memorial Park, Blue Ridge Parkway Miles 294–295.4

Around the turn of the twentieth century, having ensured his personal wealth as the "Denim King," Moses H. Cone purchased this property near Blowing Rock, North Carolina, to develop a grand country estate.

Moses and his wife, Bertha, not only appreciated the natural beauty of the mountains but sought to enrich its diversity. The Cones imported a variety of apple trees that would bloom profusely in spring and display their colorful fruit into November. The couple also landscaped the estate by creating lakes and extensive plantings of white pine, hemlock, sugar maple, and rhododendron. Meadows were created not only for sheep and cattle, but they and the apple orchards were placed so as to be pleasing to the eye when viewed from the Manor House.

For the walker and hiker, the most outstanding change the Cones made to the landscape was to build more than 25 miles of carriage trails that twist, wind, and meander into every part of the estate. Like Grassy Gap Fire Road [BRP 62], the wide carriage trails permit couples, families, and friends to walk abreast, making for more of a social outing. All of the trails are interconnected; most walks begin at the Manor House (4,000 feet). Numerous possibilities exist for extensive daylong hikes through the property without ever retracing your steps. Because these roads were built for horses pulling carriages, they rise and fall at gentle grades. The most difficult trail in this park receives no more than a moderate rating.

Some of the carriage roads are popular with the local population. Expect to share a part of your day with other walkers, picnickers, joggers, horseback riders, and in winter, cross-country skiers.

A craft shop is operated in the Manor House by the Southern Highland Handicraft Guild, and during the tourist months artisans demonstrate their skills on the front porch. There is also a park service information desk and bookstore. Recommended tours of the Manor House are held on a scheduled basis. Check at the information desk for dates and times.

Horseback riding is permitted along the carriage roads of the Moses H. Cone Memorial Park.

Mile 294. Rich Mountain Carriage Trail [BRP 69]

(N 36°08.970 W 81°41.594) Map 35

> *Length: 10.2 miles, out-and-back*
> *Difficulty: moderate*
> *Recommended*

The Rich Mountain Carriage Trail is one of only two trails that ascend instead of descend from the Manor House. On the way to the summit of Rich Mountain, for excellent views of the estate and surrounding countryside, the trail goes through open fields and into rhododendron-thick forests, circles by small Trout Lake and old building foundations, and passes other reminders that the Cones worked every part of their estate.

Rich Mountain Carriage Trail is one of the longest trails in the park and thus is one of the least used. This ensures a peaceful and relaxing walk.

Although the out-and-back length is 10.2 miles, there are a couple of options to make your walk a little shorter:

You could begin or end the walk where the trail intersects Flannery Fork Road .9 mile from the Manor House. Auto access to this point may be obtained by following the parkway south from the Manor House to BRP mile 294.6 in Sandy Flat Gap. Exit the parkway, turn right, go under the BRP, and bear right onto Flannery Fork Road. Be aware that you would have to be dropped off here, as there is not a parking area at the point where the Rich Mountain Carriage Trail crosses Flannery Fork Road.

A second option for shortening the walk to the summit of Rich Mountain is to make use of the Shulls Mill Road Extension [BRP 81] of the Rich Mountain Carriage Trail.

The Mountains-to-Sea Trail (see Chapter 1) uses a portion of the Rich Mountain Carriage Trail.

.0   From the parking area next to the Manor House, descend the steps leading to the Carriage Barn and turn left onto a gravel road.

.1   Cross under the BRP and arrive at an intersection. To the right is Flat Top Mountain Carriage Trail [BRP 70]. Bear left to continue on the Rich Mountain Carriage Trail and enter woods thick with magnolia trees.

.35 Switchback to the right.

.45 Switchback to the left.

.6   Switchback to the right.

.7   Cross a small stream on a culvert.

.9   Pass by a stock-loading pen and cross Flannery Fork Road. Continue to descend along the rhododendron-lined road. Trout Lake can be seen through the vegetation.

1.1 Come to the intersection with Trout Lake Trail [BRP 80]. Continue straight and begin to walk beside the lake.

1.3 Cross over the dam and outlet stream. Begin a gradual rise.

1.5 Trail intersection. The Trout Lake Trail is to the left. Make a hard right to continue on the Rich Mountain Carriage Trail.

1.7 Magnolias are plentiful along the trail.

2.3 Switchback to the left.

2.7 The field you are heading for can be seen through the vegetation.

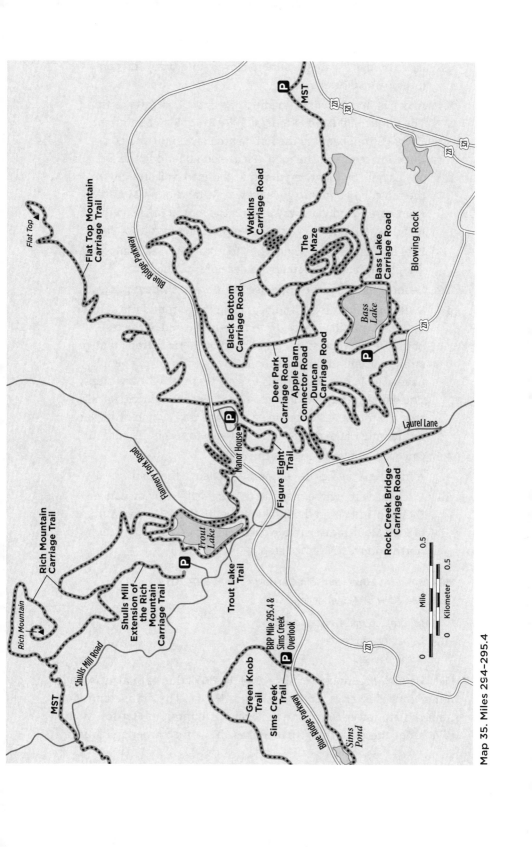

Map 35. Miles 294–295.4

2.8 Pass through a gate (be sure to close it after you) and come into open pastureland.

3.1 Arrive at another stock-loading pen and a trail intersection. The Shulls Mill Road Extension [BRP 81] of Rich Mountain Carriage Trail bears to the left. Switchback right and continue to ascend on the road. (Please do not add to the erosion of this field by following the unauthorized trail straight up the hillside.) There are good views of Grandfather Mountain from here. Wind your way around the mountain, leaving the meadow and entering a rhododendron and hardwood forest.

3.7 Pass by a fence stile where the Mountains-to-Sea Trail (see Chapter 1) leaves the road and descends to the left.

4.2 Reenter the meadow. Cone used this area as a deer park.

4.3 Switchback to the left and begin spiraling around the summit of the mountain. (Please, from here to the end of the trail, do not leave the road and follow the unauthorized trails that go straight uphill through the field. Lazy and uncaring people have established these trails to save themselves a few steps. The damage they are doing to this hillside is evident. Recall that the route was originally a carriage trail, which by its very nature must take this roundabout way to reach the summit.)

4.6 Once again, please stay on the road.

4.9 A final time, avoid the temptation to leave the road.

5.1 Circle back to where the road meets itself. Now you can leave the road and climb the final few feet to the 4,370-foot summit of Rich Mountain. Here are excellent views, especially to the north and west. Retrace steps.

Mile 294. Flat Top Mountain Carriage Trail [BRP 70]
(N 36°08.970 W 81°41.594) Map 35

> *Length: 5.6 miles, out-and-back*
> *Difficulty: moderate*
> *Recommended*

Like the Rich Mountain Carriage Trail [BRP 69], this path also ascends rather than descends from the Manor House. The grandstand view from the fire tower that Cone built on the summit of Flat Top Mountain is not the only thing that makes this a recommended journey.

Wildflowers line much of the trail through a deep maple forest, and broad pastures provide additional vistas. You can even visit Mr. and Mrs. Cone's final resting place to thank them for providing such pleasurable roadways to walk on.

.0   From the parking area next to the Manor House, descend the steps leading to the Carriage Barn and turn left onto a gravel road.

.1   Cross under the BRP and arrive at an intersection. The Rich Mountain Carriage Trail [BRP 69] goes left. Bear right to continue on the Flat Top Mountain Carriage Trail. Begin to ascend, with a field on one side of you supplying views of Grandfather Mountain, while the sugar maples and magnolias on the other side of the road provide some cool shade from the sun.

.2   Switchback to the right, entering woods. Soon switchback left, where, in May, white trillium fills the forest floor.

.7   Enter an open field.

.75   Make a left at the trail intersection onto a grassy road.

.9   Follow the grassy road around the gravesite of Moses and Bertha Cone, Mrs. Cone's sisters, and in later years, her constant companions, Sophie and Clementine Lindau.

1.0   Return to the intersection, turn left, and resume your ascent through the manicured pasture.

1.4   Just before reentering the woods, you will get a couple of good views of Grandfather Mountain and some views of the development in Blowing Rock, North Carolina. Begin a series of switchbacks in the forest, where wildflowers proliferate.

2.0   Make a quick zigzag where you can see part of the shopping mall in Blowing Rock. Continue ascending on switchbacks lined with mayapple, wild mustard, and chickweed.

2.55   Swing around the final switchback.

2.8   Ascend the fire tower to observe the surrounding scene: Grandfather Mountain to one side, Blowing Rock to the other and below, green fields, the Cones' gravesite, and the road you just walked. Retrace steps.

Mile 294. Watkins Carriage Road [BRP 71]

(N 36°08.970 W 81°41.594) Map 35

Length: 3.8 miles, one way; 7.6 miles, out-and-back
Difficulty: moderate

In springtime the Watkins Carriage Road will be the place for wild-flower lovers to walk. The carriage road switches back at least ten times on its descent from the Manor House to US RT 221 near Blowing Rock. Nature seems to have chosen a special, different wildflower to grow in the wide, flat area of each switchback. You can expect lousewort, wild geranium, violets, painted trillium, rhododendron, mountain laurel, and more.

The Watkins Carriage Road is also a part of the Mountains-to-Sea Trail (see Chapter 1).

.0 Go down the steps from the front porch of the Manor House and turn left onto paved Watkins Carriage Road, enjoying the views out across the Cone estate.

.1 The pavement ends. Cinquefoil, speedwell, white trillium, wild mustard, and wild strawberries line the road.

.2 Pass by an old springhouse and orchard.

.45 Enter the woods, where the wildflowers become even more prolific. The forest is carpeted with white trillium, touch-me-nots, buttercups, purple asters, Solomon's seal, iris, and chickweed.

.55 Intersection. The Deer Park Carriage Road [BRP 74] goes to the right. Bear left and continue to descend on the Watkins Carriage Road. Speedwell and other flowers persist in large numbers.

.9 Lousewort is the special flower of this switchback. Descend as rhododendron begins to close in on the road.

1.1 Wild geranium dominates a switchback to the right.

1.5 Switchback left amid a tract of lousewort.

1.8 This switchback to the right has three flowers in abundance—cinquefoil, wild strawberries, and violets.

2.3 Another switchback with dominant flowers—violets and white trillium.

2.4   Galax and painted trillium prosper on this switchback to the left.

2.5   Lousewort once again prevails.

2.6   One final switchback dominated by lousewort.

2.7   Intersection. To the right is the Black Bottom Carriage Road [BRP 72]. Bear left to continue on Watkins Carriage Road.

3.0   Walk next to a fence enclosing a field and pond.

3.2   The shopping mall in Blowing Rock is visible in the distance.

3.3   Enter a forest of hemlock and rhododendron.

3.8   Cross over a stream, pass through the gate, and arrive at the end of the Watkins Carriage Road. US RT 221 is .2 mile to the right via a dirt road.

Mile 294. Black Bottom Carriage Road [BRP 72]
(N 36°08.970 W 81°41.594) Map 35

Length: .5 mile, one way; 1 mile, out-and-back
Difficulty: easy

The Black Bottom Carriage Road is a short connector trail between Watkins Carriage Road [BRP 71] and the intersection of The Maze [BRP 75] and the Apple Barn Connector Road [BRP 76]. This means that you must first walk one of these roads in order to reach the Black Bottom Carriage Road. A little different from the other carriage roads, this one passes through a moist bottomland rich in ferns and mosses.

.0   At the intersection of Watkins [BRP 71] and Black Bottom [BRP 72] Carriage Roads (2.7 miles from the Manor House via the Watkins Carriage Road), bear right to begin walking the Black Bottom Carriage Road. At first you will descend, but soon begin a gradual rise next to a stream. This bottomland forest contains hardwoods, rhododendron, and galax.

.1   Cross the stream and swing to the left into a moist, mossy area of many small water runs.

.2   Cross the stream on a culvert, begin a steady rise, and enter a forest of pines.

.4   The pine trees start to thin out.

.5   Arrive at the junction with The Maze [BRP 75] to the left and the Apple Barn Connector Road [BRP 76] to the right.

Bass Lake in Moses H. Cone Memorial Park is popular for family outings.

Mile 294. Bass Lake Carriage Road [BRP 73]

(N 36°08.970 W 81°41.594) Map 35

> *Length: 1.7 miles, one way; 3.4 miles, out-and-back*
> *Difficulty: easy*
> *Recommended*

Moses Cone built two lakes on his estate, stocked them with bass and trout, and named them accordingly. The larger is Bass Lake, a focal point of the view from the Manor House porch.

Bass Lake Carriage Road is an easy, level route around the lake with good views back up to the Manor House. It begins where the Deer Park Carriage Road [BRP 74] and the Apple Barn Connector Road [BRP 76] intersect, quickly drops through a hardwood forest, and then encircles the lake. The road ends at a parking area on US RT 221 near the Blowing Rock Stables.

By vehicle, you may reach the parking area on US RT 221 by following the parkway south from the Manor House and exiting at BRP mile 294.6. Follow US RT 221 toward Blowing Rock. There is a large, signed parking area on the left soon after you pass Laurel Lane (which will be on your right). This is primarily used for horse trailers; the park service would prefer that you leave your car in the designated Bass Lake parking lot instead.

.0   From the intersection of the Deer Park Carriage Road [BRP 74] and the Apple Barn Connector Road [BRP 76], walk downhill on the Bass Lake Carriage Road.

.5   Arrive at the intersection with The Maze [BRP 75], which comes in from the left. (Straight ahead will keep you on the Bass Lake Carriage Road, but you would miss the walk around the lake.) Make a hard right and walk next to the lake on a road shaded by stately maple trees.

.6   Pass by the foundation of a former boathouse. Purple asters line the road.

.9   Cross an inlet stream. The Manor House is visible uphill.

1.0   Cross a second inlet stream.

1.1   Cross the third inlet stream.

1.2   Now at the most scenic spot on this walk, you're able to look all the way across the lake and uphill over the estate to the Manor House.

1.3   Intersection. A left would return you from whence you came. Make a right to finish the walk on the Bass Lake Carriage Trail.

1.45   Walk uphill through rhododendron and maple.

1.55   Intersection with the Duncan Carriage Road [BRP 77] coming in from the right. Bear left steeply uphill to continue on the Bass Lake Carriage Road.

1.7   Arrive at the parking area on US RT 221.

Mile 294. Deer Park Carriage Road [BRP 74]

(N 36°08.970 W 81°41.594) Map 35

> *Length: .7 mile, one way; 1.4 miles, out-and-back*
> *Difficulty: moderately easy*

With the large number of deer that are seen along the parkway today, it may be hard to believe that the population at the turn of the twentieth century was almost decimated. The local inhabitants' hunting dogs ran down and killed as many, if not more, deer than the inhabitants killed for meat. Loss of habitat due to farming and lumbering added to the pressures on the deer.

Moses Cone recognized what was happening to the deer in the Southern Appalachians and imported herds from farther north. He kept the herds in "deer parks" (hence, the name of this carriage road) on his estate in the hope that their numbers would grow and could then be released into the wild. Obviously, Cone's experiment, and the resiliency of the native deer, succeeded.

The Deer Park Carriage Road is a connector trail that descends from Watkins Carriage Road [BRP 71] to join with the Bass Lake Carriage Road [BRP 73]. It more or less follows the fenced-in boundary of the main pasture below the Manor House and is the quickest route from the house to Bass Lake.

.0   To begin this walk, just over half a mile from the Manor House, make a hard right at the intersection with the Watkins Carriage Road [BRP 71], which goes off to the left. Descend past Solomon's seal in a mixed forest of maple, magnolia, and poplar.

.2   Walk next to a fence where dwarf iris bloom.

.4   The rise is so slight as to be almost imperceptible.

.5   Resume the gradual descent through hemlocks.

.7   Arrive at an intersection and the end of the Deer Park Carriage Road. The Apple Barn Connector Road [BRP 76] goes off to the left while the Bass Lake Carriage Road [BRP 73] is to the right.

Mile 294. The Maze [BRP 75] (N 36°08.970 W 81°41.594) Map 35

Length: 2.3 miles, one way; 4.6 miles, out-and-back
Difficulty: moderate

You could not really become lost on this walk, but the road certainly does twist, turn, and almost double back on itself, making you wonder which direction you will be heading next. Most of the length of the road is in a deep forest whose dominant trees alternate among oaks, pine, and magnolias. Cone's talent for landscape architecture is evident in the way many of the stands of trees are arranged. The thick vegetation mutes much of the exterior sound, making this a quieter walk than some of the other carriage roads.

The Maze begins at the intersection of the Black Bottom Carriage Road [BRP 72] and the Apple Barn Connector Road [BRP 76] and ends at the intersection with Bass Lake Carriage Road [BRP 73], about .3 mile from the parking area on US RT 221. (See Bass Lake Carriage Road [BRP 73] description for directions to the parking area.)

.0   Walk uphill from the intersection of the Black Bottom Carriage Road [BRP 72] and the Apple Barn Connector Road [BRP 76].

.2   The Maze begins to wind around and is just a few feet below where you are now walking.

.3   Mighty white pines drop their needles on the road.

.5   Switchback to the left.

.6   Take a wide curve to the right among oak trees. Magnolias are also numerous.

.8   Come back into nice, neat rows of pines.

1.2   Squirrels seem to enjoy this particular spot where the road makes a switchback to the left.

1.5   Switchback to the right.

1.7   Your peace, isolation, and tranquility are broken. Come around a bend in the road and encounter a housing development that has been built right on the border of Moses H. Cone Memorial Park. Watch out for the dogs!

2.1   Finally leave the housing development behind.

2.3   Arrive at an intersection and the end of The Maze. Bass Lake is directly in front of you. A hard right will bring you to the Manor House via the Bass Lake [BRP 73] and Deer Park [BRP 74] Carriage Roads. A right will allow you to walk around the lake on the Bass Lake Carriage Road. A left turn will bring you to the parking area on US RT 221 in about .3 mile.

Mile 294. Apple Barn Connector Road [BRP 76]
(N 36°08.970 W 81°41.594) Map 35

> Length: .2 mile, one way; .4 mile, out-and-back
> Difficulty: easy

This is a short trail that connects the Black Bottom Carriage Road [BRP 72] and The Maze [BRP 75] with the Deer Park [BRP 74] and Bass Lake [BRP 73] Carriage Roads. Cone built apple barns to sort and house the harvest from his 30,000-tree orchards.

Mile 294. Duncan Carriage Road [BRP 77]
(N 36°08.970 W 81°41.594) Map 35

> *Length: 2.5 miles, one way; 5 miles, out-and-back*
> *Difficulty: moderate*

Cone's landscaping expertise is also evident on the Duncan Carriage Road. This route passes by stands of planted white pines and several apple orchards as it drops from the Manor House to the parking area on US RT 221.

.0 Go down the steps from the front porch of the Manor House and turn right, enjoying the view out across the estate.

.2 Enter woods and turn left onto a dirt road. (Straight ahead is just a service road.)

.5 Returning to the edge of the meadow, switchback to the right and walk under a venerable old magnolia tree.

.6 Switchback to the left.

.8 Arrive at an intersection. Rock Creek Bridge Carriage Road [BRP 78] is to the right. Bear left to continue on Duncan Carriage Road. Come back to the meadow, ascend slightly, and proceed beyond one of Cone's old apple orchards.

1.0 Resume the descent and stroll in a pine forest for a brief stretch.

1.2 Switchback left.

1.4 Return to the meadow for the final time and switchback right.

1.8 Cross over a stream on a culvert and switchback left.

2.35 Intersection. The Bass Lake Carriage Road [BRP 73] is to the left. Bear right and ascend to continue on Duncan Carriage Road.

2.5 Arrive at the parking area on US RT 221.

Mile 294. Rock Creek Bridge Carriage Road [BRP 78]
(N 36°08.970 W 81°41.594) Map 35

> *Length: 1.7 miles, one way; 3.4 miles, out-and-back*
> *Difficulty: moderately easy*

The Rock Creek Bridge Carriage Road has become, in the last several years, extremely popular with the horseback riders of the Blowing Rock area. If you don't mind a bit of mud, a few droppings, and sharing your walk with the horses, the road can be a pleasant enough venture. It begins at the .9-mile point on Duncan Carriage Road [BRP 77], crosses under US RT 221, and parallels that highway before making a loop around a heavily wooded knob. The trail ends on Laurel Lane.

You may gain vehicle access to the far trailhead by following the parkway south from the Manor House. Exit the BRP at mile 294.6 in Sandy Flat Gap and follow US RT 221 toward Blowing Rock. At the first right, turn onto Laurel Lane. The trailhead is across from the stables.

.0   Having followed the Duncan Carriage Road [BRP 77] .9 mile from the Manor House, turn right onto the Rock Creek Bridge Carriage Road and descend through the woods.

.5   Break out of the woods.

.6   Go under US RT 221 and ascend.

.7   Swing around a knob and continue to ascend.

.8   Switchback to the right and then to the left.

1.0   Turn right to walk the loop around a knob. Ascend where lousewort lines the road.

1.1   Bear right at the loop trail intersection. Amble in a deep woodland heavily populated by Solomon's seal. There is a limited view into the valley where the road swings around the knob.

1.4   Bear right at the loop trail intersection.

1.5   Return to the main road and descend in rhododendron.

1.7   Arrive at Laurel Lane.

Mile 294. Figure Eight Trail [BRP 79] (N 36°08.970 W 81°41.594) Map 35

Length: .5 mile, circuit
Difficulty: easy
Recommended

This self-guiding pathway is said to be the same one the Cones used for their daily morning walks. The park service keeps the almost level trail under white oak, red maple, and black cherry in excellent repair. Signs along the way provide information about the Cones, their estate, and the trailside plant life.

Besides being a short, pleasurable walk, this recommended trip offers a lot of background information that will enhance the rest of your walks on the estate.

.0   Go down the first flight of steps from the Manor House; turn right. Ascend gradually and begin the trail lined with chickweed, Solomon's seal, and violets. Soon turn left where the trail is bordered by rhododendron on one side and white trillium on the other.

.1   Enter a dense rhododendron thicket.

.2   Intersection. Make a hard right and begin the figure eight. Stay straight at the next two intersections.

.3   Having completed the figure eight, bear right and gradually descend, passing birch, oak, and sugar maple.

.5   Arrive back at the Manor House.

Mile 294.6. Sandy Flat Gap (3,828 feet)

US RT 221 and access to BRP maintenance facilities and Blowing Rock (2 miles). Also access to Shulls Mill Road and Flannery Fork Road.

Mile 294.6. Trout Lake Trail [BRP 80] (N 36°09.156 W 81°42.221) Map 35

Length: 1 mile, circuit
Difficulty: easy
Recommended

Since it is almost perfectly level and is exactly 1 mile, the Trout Lake Trail has become popular with the locals as a jogging track. The most outstanding feature is a hemlock-dominated cove forest. Such forests are quite rare along the BRP.

You can reach the Trout Lake Trailhead by following the BRP south from the Manor House. Exit the parkway at mile 294.6, double back underneath the BRP, and bear left onto Shulls Mill Road. You will pass two roads to the right that lead to the two parking lots for the Trout Lake Trail [BRP 80]. Take the second road and park as soon as possible.

.0   From the road between the two parking lots for the Trout Lake Trail, descend steeply toward the lake. In 100 feet arrive at the main trail, turn left, and walk among violets, rhododendron, and bluets.

.3   Intersection. The Rich Mountain Carriage Trail [BRP 69] goes left for 3.6 miles to the summit of Rich Mountain. Bear right to continue on the Trout Lake Trail. Descend into the magnificent and wonderful hemlock cove forest.

.5   Cross the dam and outlet streams. Continue to circle the lake.

.6   Intersection. The Rich Mountain Carriage Trail [BRP 69] goes 1.1 miles to the left to reach the Manor House. Bear right to progress on the Trout Lake Trail.

.7 Where violets become abundant you will lose sight of the lake.

.9 Come to the Trout Lake parking area road and turn right. Watch for jewelweed and speedwell.

1.0 Be alert! The trail turns to the right into the woods. In a couple of hundred feet take the trail uphill and arrive back at the point where you started this walk.

Mile 294.6. Shulls Mill Road Extension of the Rich Mountain Carriage Trail [BRP 81] (N 36°09.156 W 81°42.221) Map 35

Length: .5 mile, one way; 1 mile, out-and-back
Difficulty: moderate

This is a shortcut to the summit of Rich Mountain. Be forewarned, though, that like most shortcuts, the extension road ascends the mountain at a steeper grade than most of the other carriage roads. If the road were just a little bit longer, it would be rated a moderately strenuous hike.

You can reach the Shulls Mill Road Extension Trailhead by following the BRP south from the Manor House. Exit the parkway at mile 294.6, double back underneath the BRP, and bear left onto Shulls Mill Road. You will pass two roads to the right that lead to the two parking lots for the Trout Lake Trail [BRP 80]. Take the second road and park as soon as possible.

.0 Walk back toward the road you came in on and turn right onto the trail that ascends rather steeply.

.3 A small spring runs just below the road at a wide curve.

.5 Arrive at the junction with the Rich Mountain Carriage Trail [BRP 69]. A turn to the right will bring you to the Manor House in 3.1 miles. Make a left turn and you can ascend to the summit of Rich Mountain in 2 miles.

Mile 295.4. Sims Creek Trail [BRP 82] (3,609 feet)
(N 36°08.743 W 81°42.680) Map 35

Length: .2 mile, out-and-back
Difficulty: easy

Follow the pathway from the middle of the Sims Creek Overlook through a heavy growth of rhododendron. Arrive at the Green Knob Trail [BRP 83], which comes in from the left, and Sims Creek in .1 mile. Cross the creek on a footbridge and arrive at a bench and a surprisingly splendid little flower garden. Abundant butterflies flutter about, song-birds chirp cheerfully, and the sun brightens the banks of the creek. The variety of wildflowers is phenomenal—violets, white violets, jewelweed, jack-in-the-pulpit, wake robin trillium, Solomon's seal, wild mustard, and clusters of speedwell.

This is certainly a nice spot to take a break from riding in the car.

Mile 295.4 Sims Creek Overlook (3,609)

Provides access to the Green Knob Trail [BRP 83].

Trails of Julian Price Memorial Park, Blue Ridge Parkway Miles 295.9–297

As president of Jefferson Standard Life Insurance Company, Julian Price intended for this land to become a recreation spot for the company's employees. Upon his unexpected death in 1946, the company donated the land to the parkway as a public recreation area.

The 4,200-acre park has become one of the most popular areas of the BRP. The campground's close proximity to the populations of Boone, Blowing Rock, and Asheville, North Carolina, almost guarantees that it will stay full during the usual tourist months.

All four of the park's trails are recommended trips. One encircles the lake, where bass and bream are abundant; another goes into a bottomland forest of wildflowers and hardwoods. A third takes you to one of only three backcountry campsites on BRP property. The longest pathway passes through an ancient lake bed that is surrounded by caves once used for shelter by archaic Indians.

In addition to the campground, Julian Price Memorial Park also has a picnic area and offers boat rentals for those who wish to enjoy the lake to its fullest.

Mile 295.9. Sims Pond Overlook

The pond was named after Hamp Sims, a former resident of the area.

Mile 295.9. Green Knob Trail [BRP 83] (3,447 feet)
(N 36°08.540 W 81°43.198) Map 36

> *Length: 2 miles, circuit*
> *Difficulty: moderately strenuous*

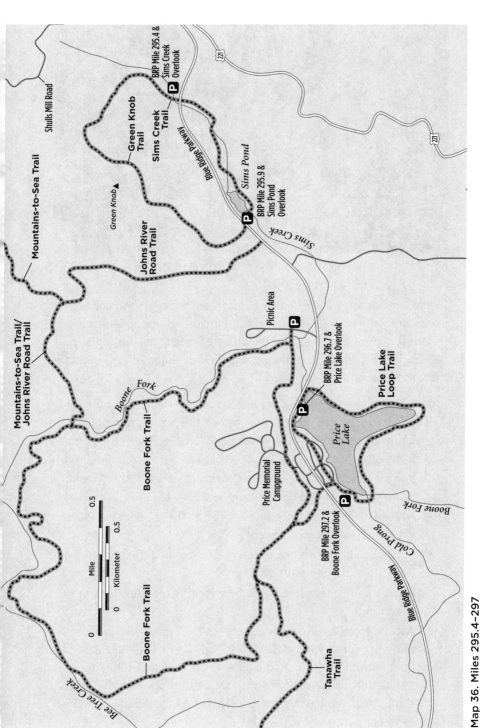

Map 36. Miles 295.4–297

Hikes on the Green Knob Trail begin at Sims Pond, frequented by anglers.

In just 2 miles you will be treated to many of the vegetation zones that occur along the BRP—lakeside, bottomland forest, rhododendron and mountain laurel thickets, small wildflower meadows, and open pasturelands. As a bonus, the rugged ridgeline of Grandfather Mountain may also be seen from the trail.

.0 Descend the steps from the Sims Pond Overlook. Cross the pond's outlet stream and walk beside the pond, a favorite haunt of zealous anglers. Rhododendron soon hides the pond from view.

.15 You are now beyond the pond. Cross and parallel Sims Creek through a moist and lush bottomland forest.

.3 At a man-made falls, begin to ascend as the creek descends via small pools and cascades.

.4 Arrive at a bench and cross the creek, enjoying the impressive showing of rhododendron.

.5 Cross a small side stream and be watching for a few jack-in-the-pulpits.

.6 Ascend to walk directly below the BRP's Sims Creek Viaduct and arrive at an intersection. The Sims Creek Trail [BRP 82] goes uphill for .1 mile to the Sims Creek Overlook (BRP mile 295.4). Bear left and cross Sims Creek to continue on the Green Knob Trail. Pass by a bench in a small field crowded with wildflowers.

.7   Cross the creek.

.8   Cross the creek and continue to ascend; birch trees dominate.

1.0   Pass through a fence stile and enter a verdant meadow. Continue to follow the obvious trail.

1.1   Arrive at a bench under a cool shade tree and amid a serene pastoral landscape. Continue to climb following trail post markers in the field.

1.2   Reenter the woods on an old road. Wild mustard makes up a large part of the undergrowth.

1.3   Come to another bench.

1.4   Bypass the very summit of Green Knob, but break out into the open just long enough to admire the rugged ridgeline of Grandfather Mountain in the distance. Cross through a fence stile, reenter the woods, and drop quickly.

1.5   Arrive at another bench, this one overlooking a field of wild strawberries. Descend steeply.

1.7   On this steep descent catch a glimpse of Price Lake with Grandfather Mountain as a backdrop.

1.8   Pass through a fence stile.

2.0   Cross through another fence stile, descend into a rhododendron thicket, and then diagonally cross the BRP to arrive back at the Sims Pond Overlook.

Mile 296. Johns River Road Trail [BRP 84] (3,449 feet)
(N 36°08.540 W 81°43.198) Map 36

> *Length: 1.75 miles, one way; 3.5 miles, out-and-back*
> *Difficulty: moderately easy*

Here's an official parkway trail that is a wonderful hike for those of you who are comfortable with hiking in the woods without any route markings to show the way. It may also be for you if you haven't ever done any hiking like this but wish to expand your woodlands experiences and hone route-finding skills. Actually, much of the way is on old woods roads, so most of the way is obvious—you just need to be alert at route intersections.

There is a very real possibility that you may not meet anyone else along the way. Because the beginning of the trail looks like the dozens of other gated dirt roads along the parkway, most people overlook it as a walking opportunity. Yet, there is much to recommend it. Small open fields provide a couple of nice views, rhododendron tunnels are fun to hike through (and full of flowers in late spring), and there are some nice wading pools at the end of the trail. Perhaps the nicest spot is the small valley about midway into the journey. Its solitude and feeling of isolation belie the fact that many homes dot Shulls Mill Road less than a mile away. The Mountains-to-Sea Trail (see Chapter 1) uses a portion of the route.

One other draw is the designated backcountry campsite (fire ring; no other amenities) at 1.6 miles. This is one of only three places where you can backcountry camp on parkway property along its full length, and it is necessary to obtain a permit. From mid-May until the end of October, permits must be obtained at Price Park Campground (mile 296.9; 828-963-5911). Off-season permits may be obtained at the Sandy Flats Ranger Office (5580 Shulls Mill Road—mile 294.6; 828-295-7591).

The closest safe parking area is the Sims Pond Overlook at mile 295.9.

.0   Walk southward from the Sims Pond Overlook for 600 feet and, at BRP mile marker 296, cross the parkway and ascend gradually on a gated woods road.

.25   Be alert! Stay left at the intersection and gradually descend. There are some great old oak trees growing in the meadow to the left, whose openness provides a view of Grandfather Mountain.

.5   Pass by a meadow with a picnic table before entering a deep woods. Fire pinks grow beside the route in June.

.9   The road becomes a trail where it becomes necessary to rock-hop a water run. Take a moment to enjoy the quiet and solitude of the narrow valley that bears the evidence of the work of beavers. Ascend into rhododendron tunnels.

1.1   The Mountains-to-Sea Trail comes down the bank from the right to join your route. Continue left and ascend on an old woods road, where the rhododendron tunnels are even more impressive.

1.3   Be alert! Do not take the route to the right; keep to the left to stay on the Johns River Road Trail, soon passing through ever deeper and more lush rhododendron tunnels.

1.6   Pass by the designated campsite and descend quickly, now on a narrow trail and not a woods road.

1.7   Be alert! It looks like the trail splits in two when you come to a small level spot. Keep to the left. (To the right is actually the course of a small water run.)

1.75 The Johns River Road Trail comes to an end as it arrives at Boone Fork, whose pools make for some nice wading on hot summer days. Cross the superbly constructed footbridge if you wish to join up with the Boone Fork Trail [BRP 85] located above the far bank.

Mile 296.5. Boone Fork Trail [BRP 85] (N 36°08.372 W 81°43.631) Map 36

Length: 4.9 miles, circuit
Difficulty: moderately strenuous
Highly recommended

Thanks to the extensive acreage of Julian Price Memorial Park, the Boone Fork Trail is one of those rare BRP trails that may wander quite some distance from the parkway yet remain within parkway boundaries.

This route has so much to enjoy that you should probably allow more than the 2 to 3 hours needed to walk it without taking any breaks. Bring a lunch and a book and relax. Soaking up your surroundings here, you can savor one of the most pleasurable trails the parkway has to offer. Two major streams are paralleled, allowing ample opportunity to investigate this environment. Beavers have built dams on Boone Fork in the past, and their activity may be evident along much of the stream. Wade through one of the cool pools and luxuriate in the warmth of the summer sun as you take a break on one of the large, flat rocks in midstream.

Bloodroot hails the arrival of spring around the second week of April. Mountain laurel and rhododendron bloom along Bee Tree Creek in May or June. Rock outcroppings make interesting formations that invite further explorations. Open meadows sit almost in the shadow of Grandfather Mountain.

The Mountains-to-Sea Trail (see Chapter 1) uses a portion of the Boone Fork Trail. In addition, brochures are available at the trailhead (or at kidsinparks.com) as the first mile of the Boone Fork Trail has been designated one of the TRACK (Trails, Ridges, and Active Caring, Kids) trails along the Blue Ridge Parkway. This program is designed to encourage more children to take walks in the woods.

.0   Cross the bridge behind the restrooms in the picnic area and in 200 feet turn right onto the loop trail. Parallel Boone Fork (named for a nephew of Daniel Boone), passing picnic tables and a water fountain.

.1   The flat land and bog here are believed to be the site of an ancient lake. Silt deposited by streams filled the lake bed, resulting in a rich soil that supports a wide diversity of plant life, including wild mustard, cinquefoil, and wild strawberries. In season enjoy a few blackberries, which also grow well here. Caves in the cliffs surrounding the lake served as shelter for archaic Indians.

.3   Enter the woods and possibly observe the first signs of beaver activity on this trail.

.5   Cross the creek on a footbridge.

.6   Pass next to a large overhanging boulder.

.9   The flat rocks at this small waterfall might entice you to take a short sunbath.

1.0   A solidly built footbridge, constructed by volunteers, crosses the stream to the right. You want to continue to the left to stay on the Boone Fork Trail, which is now a part of the Mountains-to-Sea Trail. Across the bridge, the Mountains-to-Sea Trail continues on its way eastward to Rich Mountain and Moses H. Cone Memorial Park. Johns River Road Trail [BRP 84] is also on the stream's far bank.

1.1   Ascend slightly to an old railroad grade. Note that the creek is much larger and moving more rapidly than when you started your walk.

1.3   Begin walking in heavy rhododendron growth as the creek drops even farther below you, making enough noise now to sound like a river.

1.5   The eroded trail to the right leads a short distance to Hebron Falls, a popular local destination for wading and picnicking.

1.7   Climb the wooden stepladder between two large boulders. Be alert! Three hundred feet after the ladder the trail makes an abrupt hard right (do not continue straight) and descends back down to the banks of Boone Fork. Turn left and follow the creek downstream next to a number of waterfalls.

1.9 Cross a small side stream on stepping stones.

2.0 Cross a footbridge and descend wooden steps before ascending other steps to begin walking along a railroad grade.

2.1 The trail becomes somewhat rough and makes several short ups and downs before gradually descending to the railroad grade.

2.3 Cross the creek, turn left, and ascend, following the water upstream.

2.5 Cross the creek on a bridge, recross it in 100 feet, and cross again in 150 feet. This isolated creek valley appears to be a favorite spot of numerous songbirds. Stop and listen to the melodies for a little while. As you ascend, you will cross the creek eight more times in the next .4 mile, sometimes on a footbridge, sometimes on stepping stones.

3.1 Step over the creek, which by this time is not much more than a trickle of water. Walk in a forest of birch so extensive that you would almost think you were in New England. Soon recross the creek three more times.

3.4 Passing by some overhanging rocks, the trail bears to the left to ascend into a meadow dotted by blackberry bushes.

3.5 Make a hard left and reenter the woods.

3.6 Break out into an open meadow and follow the faint path and road straight ahead.

3.7 Come to a utility line and descend to the left onto an old road through a forest of giant evergreens.

3.8 Intersection. Bear left as the Tanawha Trail (see Chapter 5) comes in from the right and shares the same pathway with the Boone Fork Trail for a short distance. Go through a fence stile and walk in a dense rhododendron tunnel.

4.0 Intersection. The Tanawha Trail turns to the right. Bear left to continue on Boone Fork Trail. Dwarf iris, chickweed, and wild geranium compete for growing space on the forest floor.

4.1 The trail to the right is a short connector to the campground. Bear left, cross the campground road, and walk by restrooms and water fountains on a paved trail.

4.3 Cross the campground road again and continue on an unpaved pathway.

4.5 Follow the trail behind the campground contact station (BRP mile 296.9) and make a couple of minor ups and downs.

4.6 Pass by Loops E and F of the campground. Continue to follow the trail and enter a growth of rhododendron.

4.7 Pass by the trail that leads from the campground to Price Lake.

4.9 Come into an open field and soon arrive back at the restrooms and picnic area.

Mile 296.7. Price Lake Overlook (3,393 feet)

One of the best views of the lake's expansive waters. Also a place to watch for belted kingfishers, Acadian flycatchers, and barn swallows, with the possibility of seeing loons, geese, ducks, and maybe even a sandpiper or two.

Mile 296.9. Price Memorial Park campground (3,440 feet)

Mile 297.2. Price Lake Loop Trail [BRP 86] (3,400 feet)
(N 36°08.142 W 81°44.305) Map 36

> *Length: 2.5 miles, circuit*
> *Difficulty: moderately easy*
> *Recommended*

The Price Lake Loop Trail is the perfect path for an early morning or early evening stroll.

Dull gray fog curling upward from the lake turns a brilliant pink as the morning sun rises in the east. Be watching for the darting flights of bats when they dive in search of one last insect before retiring for the day. Water snakes begin to wriggle toward open areas to warm themselves in the sun, and turtles may be seen breaking the surface of the lake. Songbirds are especially active around the lake in the early morning hours.

The long shadows of early evening help to hide the homes of muskrats and bog turtles. Birch leaves rustle in the cool breezes. Walking along the far side of the lake, across the water you can see the warm evening campfires beginning to flicker throughout the campground.

♿ The first .7 mile (and possibly more if a grant has been approved by time you walk here) of the trail is fully handicapped accessible and leads to an accessible fishing dock. In addition, brochures at the trailhead (or at kidsinparks.com) are keyed to the pathway's first mile, which has been designated as one of the BRP's TRACK Trails, designed to encourage children to become more enthusiastic in communing with nature. (The lake is the site of the TRACK Trail program's first water trail, and brochures are also available for it.)

.0   At the southern end of the Boone Fork Overlook, turn left onto a trail bordered with rhododendron. (Boone Fork Overlook is reached by driving onto the road for the amphitheater.)

.2   Cross Cold Prong on a footbridge. The smooth, slow-moving water of the stream reflects the sunlight and overhanging rhododendron. Walk through a bottomland forest.

.3   Cross wide Boone Fork on a footbridge. Pass by a bench and enter a small birch forest.

.4   Walk out to the water's edge for your first good view of Price Lake. An especially beautiful sunrise spot.

.5   Continue walking next to the water and arrive at a bench where a number of painted trillium bloom.

.6   Reenter the woods and swing away from the lake. Songbirds appear to enjoy this locality, as the volume of their music is greater here than at other areas around the lake.

.7   Cross a small water run.

1.0   Pass over a creek on a footbridge and come to a bench. Ascend slightly for just a short distance.

1.2   Come to another bench.

1.4   Pass by a giant boulder that has trees growing on top of it. The trees have wrapped their roots around the rock, extending themselves into the soil.

1.7   Come onto the BRP and walk over the bridge with a view across Price Lake.

1.1   Walk along the Price Lake Overlook (mile 296.7) and enter a rhododendron tunnel at the southern end of the overlook. Make several small ups and downs.

2.1   Come into the campground and begin to follow a paved pathway. In a few hundred feet pass by a restroom and Loop A of the campground.

2.4   In a field of Solomon's seal, wild geranium, and mayapple, leave the campground. In a few feet come to an intersection.

The trail to the right goes to other sections of the campground and is a connector trail to the Tanawha Trail (see Chapter 5). Bear left and walk through the amphitheater to continue on the Price Lake Loop Trail.

2.5 Return to the Boone Fork Overlook.

5.
The Tanawha Trail

Just as the Linn Cove Viaduct is considered a monumental engineering and design achievement, so too must the Tanawha Trail. Constructed at a cost of almost three-quarters of a million dollars, the pathway uses innovative and extravagant trail-building techniques. Not content to use the usual log footbridges, the Tanawha Trail crosses some streams on high, arching structures of wood and steel whose lines blend in with the natural surroundings. Boardwalks, some close to 200 feet long, facilitate traversing boulder-strewn hillsides while protecting delicate environments from trampling footsteps. Wooden staircases wind around stone outcroppings, enabling the trail to pass through areas that would have been too rugged to cross had traditional trail-building techniques been employed.

The word "Tanawha" means "fabulous eagle" or "hawk." Long before European settlers arrived, the Cherokee Indians used the word to describe what is now known as Grandfather Mountain. In fact, more than half the length of the Tanawha Trail is on the southeastern slope of this 5,946-foot summit, the highest of the Blue Ridge Mountains. One of the oldest in the world, Grandfather Mountain contains a myriad of scenic locations to investigate and appreciate. Quartzite outcroppings line cascading streams. Sunlight, filtered through the opulent forest canopy, highlights giant fern fronds and soft beds of moss. One moment you could be walking in dark rhododendron tunnels typical of the Southern Appalachians. Just a short time later the trail will bring you into a spruce, hemlock, and birch forest more reminiscent of the mountains of Maine and New Hampshire. Rock fields and blueberry gardens provide open spots from which you can enjoy soaring vistas.

Once the side of Grandfather Mountain is traversed, the Tanawha Trail drops into a deep, mature forest. But just before it ends, it ascends to the bucolic serenity of man-made meadows. Bountiful and colorful wildflowers burst forth from the open fields in both the spring and the fall.

A couple of points along the Tanawha Trail provide access to the trails on Grandfather Mountain. These trails are on state park property, and for more information see the section *Trails of Grandfather Mountain* in Chapter 6. Please be aware that pets are not permitted on the Tanawha Trail.

The Mountains-to-Sea Trail (see Chapter 1) follows the route of the Tanawha Trail.

Please note: In a departure from the way the rest of this guidebook is arranged, the Tanawha Trail is described from its southern to its northern BRP mile point. There are two reasons for this. The park service inventory of BRP trails officially lists the Tanawha Trail as beginning at the Beacon Heights parking area (BRP mile 305.2) and ending in Julian Price Memorial Park (BRP miles 297.2). In addition, the walking is generally easier if you hike the Tanawha Trail from south to north.

Also, please keep in mind that the following descriptions include the short access trails going to and from the parking areas and overlooks. Most people just walk a section or two of the Tanawha Trail, and the information on access trails is provided so that they may know exactly how long a section is. If you were to walk the complete Tanawha Trail without going to any of these parking areas or overlooks, its full length would be about 13.5 miles, .8 mile shorter than if you were to add together the full lengths of all the sections.

Mile 305.2. Tanawha Trail (from Beacon Heights Parking Area to Stack Rock Parking Area at BRP Mile 304.8) (4,218 feet)
(N 36°05.035 W 81°49.812) Map 37

> *Length: .9 mile, one way; 1.8 miles, out-and-back*
> *Difficulty: moderate*

The beginning section of the Tanawha Trail drops from Beacon Heights to cross US RT 221 and then ascends to the southeastern flank of Grandfather Mountain. There are only limited views along the way, but wildflower lovers will be delighted to know that this short stretch possesses more than its fair share of colorful blossoms.

The route across rugged ground—boulder fields and several small stream crossings—is a good introduction not only to the Tanawha Trail but also to the flora and the terrain you'll encounter if, once you complete this short section, you continue to follow the trail across the southeastern-facing slopes of Grandfather Mountain.

.0 From the Beacon Heights parking area, cross the paved service road, bear left, and ascend, on trail, into the woods. Beginning sometime in April, the pathway is lined with the

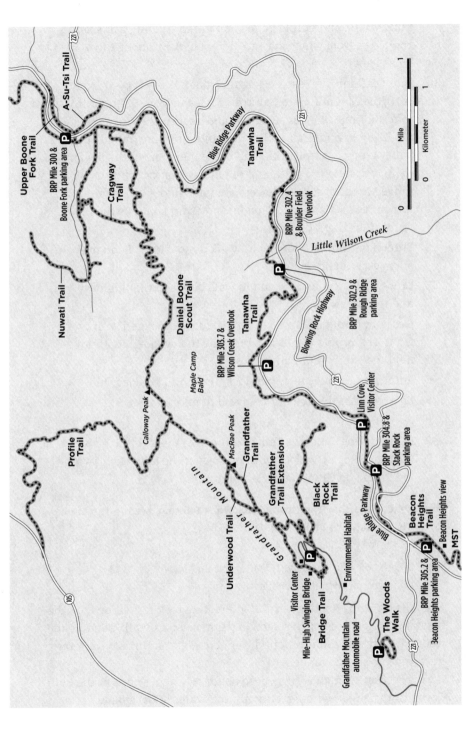

Map 37. Miles 305.2–302.9

pink, white, and purple petals of painted trillium, galax, and rhododendron, which start to bloom, in turn, about 2 to 4 weeks apart.

.07 Intersection. The Beacon Heights Trail [BRP 91] is to the right. Also, the Mountains-to-Sea Trail comes in from the right to join the Tanawha Trail. Bear left and descend. Spring hikers are likely to notice a number of painted trillium and lily of the valley along the trail. Although these members of the lily family may most often be thought of in association with the Blue Ridge Mountains, both flowers are known to grow as far west and north as Manitoba, Canada, and as far south as the mountains of northern Georgia.

.2 Enter a bottomland forest and walk almost level. Soon make a short ascent and descent.

.35 Cross US RT 221 and ascend to walk between that highway and the parkway.

.5 Descend through an area of large boulders covered with rock tripe. In a couple hundred feet, come to a wooden footbridge next to a stone foundation of the BRP.

.6 Enter a small but pretty hemlock forest and boulder field.

.75 Emerge from the boulder field and hemlock forest.

.8 Ascend steps.

.9 Bear left (the Tanawha Trail continues to the right) to arrive at the Stack Rock Overlook with its view of the Mile-High Swinging Bridge on Grandfather Mountain.

Mile 304.8. Tanawha Trail (from Stack Rock Parking Area to the Linn Cove Visitor Center at Mile 304.4) (4,286 feet)
(N 36°05.319 W 81°49.343) Map 37

Length: .65 mile, one way; 1.3 miles, out-and-back
Difficulty: moderately strenuous

The falls on Stack Rock Creek and interesting rock formations are the outstanding features of this section. Human handiwork, such as the wooden staircase winding around giant boulders, is almost as interesting as nature's own wonders.

This section—which is rugged, so be forewarned!—ends at the Linn Cove Visitor Center, where restrooms and water are available.

.0 Begin at the Stack Rock Parking Area and in 100 feet bear left. (The Tanawha Trail also goes right for .9 mile to the Beacon Heights parking area at BRP mile 305.2.) Descend through an area where galax is the dominant ground cover.

.15 Cross a small water run and ascend a wooden staircase winding around the giant rock formation. There are limited views to the east. Continue with short, steep ups and downs.

.3 Cross Stack Rock Creek with its beautiful falls and cascades. Ascend steeply on forty-nine stone and wooden steps. This is rugged country of giant rock outcroppings and boulders. In fact, the trail even passes through a narrow cleft in one of the rocks.

.35 Cross a small water run and continue with short, steep ups and downs in rhododendron.

.5 Break out of the rhododendron and into a hardwood forest.

.65 Arrive at the Linn Cove Visitor Center.

Mile 304.4. Tanawha Trail (from Linn Cove Visitor Center to Wilson Creek Overlook at BRP Mile 303.7) (4,315 feet)
(N 36°05.444 W 81°48.843) Map 37

Length: 1.35 miles, one way; 2.7 miles, out-and-back
Difficulty: moderately strenuous
&. *Handicap access: first .15 mile*

The first .15 mile of this section is paved and leads to a point directly below the Linn Cove Viaduct. There you can closely examine the preset segmented concrete construction of the viaduct that makes it such an engineering marvel.

After the viaduct, the trail, now unpaved, ascends steeply through large boulder fields to level off, somewhat, in a beech and birch forest.

.0 Follow the paved trail from the north end of the parking lot.

.15 Come to the point where you are standing directly below the viaduct. Continue on unpaved pathway. The trail now ascends quite steeply, and in a couple hundred feet you will be level with the floor of the viaduct. Continue ascending and walk through a tunnel created by leaning boulders. Do not enter a second tunnel; rather, bear to the right of it, ascend on stone steps, and continue to weave around additional boulders.

The wheelchair-accessible portion of the Tanawha Trail brings visitors below the Linn Cove Viaduct.

.4 Cross Linn Cove Branch on a wooden footbridge.

.5 Intersection. The trail to the right leads, in 60 feet, to a view over the viaduct and out to the mountains in the east. Continue on the main pathway, which is edged by galax, painted trillium, and rhododendron.

.7 Descend steeply only to reascend steeply. Repeat this pattern a number of times.

1.0 Cross a small water run.

1.25 Intersection. (The Tanawha Trail continues to the left.) Bear right to descend to the Wilson Creek Overlook. Walk under the BRP, bear right again, and ascend.

1.35 Arrive at the Wilson Creek Overlook.

Mile 303.7. Tanawha Trail (from Wilson Creek Overlook to Rough Ridge Parking Area at BRP Mile 302.9) (4,357 feet)

(N 36°06.035 W 81°48.528) Map 37

Length: 1.45 miles, one way; 2.9 miles, out-and-back
Difficulty: moderately strenuous

Without a doubt this is the most spectacular section of the Tanawha Trail. Blueberry fields and heath balds open up 360-degree views unequaled anywhere else along the trail.

Once again, the builders of this trail have done some pretty amazing work. In order to protect the fragile environment yet provide access to this area, a 200-foot-long elevated boardwalk crosses the landscape. Looking down onto the Linn Cove Viaduct from the boardwalk, you will soon recognize the similarity in design philosophies of the two structures.

.0   Descend the steps from the Wilson Creek Overlook, turn left under the BRP, and ascend. (Avoid the unauthorized trail that goes off to the right, back under the BRP.)

.1   Join the Tanawha Trail and bear right. (The Tanawha Trail also goes left for 1.25 miles to the Linn Cove Visitor Center.) Immediately cross Wilson Creek on a footbridge. The trail is lined with bluets and chickweed before it enters a stand of rhododendron.

.2   Descend around large rock outcroppings.

.3   Ascend steeply to pass large boulders.

.6   Pass through a field of fringed phacelia.

.8   Cross a spur ridge covered with lily of the valley.

.9   Arrive at an open rock outcropping for exciting 360-degree views. The ridgeline of Grandfather Mountain looms above, and the peaks and ridges to the south rise up from the parkway. The flatter lands of North Carolina are visible to the east. The boardwalk trail may be seen on the mountainside below you. Descend.

1.2   Come onto the boardwalk and continue to enjoy the open views. Mountain laurel and rhododendron in bloom in early spring add to the delights of this spot. Cross over the boardwalk and descend into the woods.

1.4   Use an arching footbridge to cross over the waters of a fork of Little Wilson Creek, which cascade over a flat, tilting rock facing.

Come to an intersection and bear right to descend to the Rough Ridge parking area. (The Tanawha Trail continues to the left.)

1.45 Arrive at the Rough Ridge parking area.

Mile 302.9. Tanawha Trail (from Rough Ridge Parking Area to Boulder Field Overlook at BRP Mile 302.4) (4,292 feet) (N 36°05.818 W 81°47.838) Map 37

> *Length: .8 mile, one way; 1.6 miles, out-and-back*
> *Difficulty: moderate*

The Tanawha Trail—what better way to experience the great diversity of Grandfather Mountain? The previous section meandered onto a rhododendron-covered landscape typical of the mountains of North Carolina. This short portion of the trail will seem to transport you several hundred miles to the north. The pathway enters a New England–type forest of hemlock, spruce, oak, and birch.

.0 Ascend the steps on the north end of the Rough Ridge parking area.

.05 Intersection. Turn right. (The Tanawha Trail also goes left for 1.4 miles to the Wilson Creek Overlook.) Ascend and watch for red squirrels, which inhabit Grandfather Mountain in significant numbers.

.2 Cross the water run that descends on a large, flat, sloping rock facing. Descend.

.3 Walk level for about 200 feet and then begin a series of small ups and downs.

.7 Intersection. Bear right to descend to the Boulder Field Overlook. (The Tanawha Trail continues to the left.)

.8 Arrive at Boulder Field Overlook.

Mile 302.4. Tanawha Trail (from Boulder Field Overlook to Boone Fork Parking Area at BRP Mile 300) (4,355 feet) (N 36°05.882 W 81°47.239) Maps 37 & 38

> *Length: 3.2 miles, one way; 6.4 miles, out-and-back*
> *Difficulty: moderate*

Still closely paralleling the BRP, this long section of the Tanawha Trail begins in a deep forest, with much of the pathway passing through rhododendron and mountain laurel tunnels. Be prepared for a change of scenery once the trail breaks out of this understory of dense vegetation. The forest floor becomes a jumble of rocks and boulders draped by large fronds of ferns and carpeted with soft, thick moss.

This section of the Tanawha Trail also provides access to some of the trails in the Grandfather Mountain State Park. (For more information, see the section *Trails of Grandfather Mountain* in Chapter 6.)

.0   Ascend the trail at the southern end of the overlook.

.1   Intersection. Turn right. (The Tanawha Trail also goes left to reach the Rough Ridge parking area in .7 mile.) Descend for a short distance.

.2   Ascend, passing by wake robin trillium.

.3   Level out for a short distance and then begin a series of short ups and downs.

.7   A break in vegetation allows a limited view to the east. False hellebore and lily of the valley line the trail. In fact, these two plants continue to grow close to the pathway for the rest of its length. Descend steadily.

.8   This area almost feels like a rain forest as you enter a stand of towering hardwoods and go by moss- and lily-covered rocks.

1.2   Cross a small water run.

1.5   Cross a second stream on a footbridge. The bluets are especially vibrant as you round a spur ridge.

1.8   Continue through a fairly open forest with slight ups and downs.

2.2   Among rhododendron, birch, and galax, cross over a ridgeline and descend.

2.4   Cross the stream and ascend.

2.6   Intersection. The Grandfather Mountain State Park's Daniel Boone Scout Trail comes in from the left to join with the Tanawha Trail for a short distance. Keep to the right to continue on the Tanawha Trail.

2.8   Intersection. The Grandfather Mountain State Park's Nuwati Trail comes in from the left. Keep right and descend to continue on the Tanawha Trail.

3.1   Intersection. Keep left where the A-Su-Tsi Trail [BRP 90] bears right to go under the BRP and descend to a parking area on US RT 221 in .4 mile. Just after the intersection, cross over the very pretty falls of Boone Fork on a formidable footbridge and arrive at another intersection. Bear right to descend to the Boone Fork parking area. (The Tanawha Trail continues to the left.) When arriving at one last intersection in a few more feet, keep to the left. (The Upper Boone Fork Trail [BRP 82] goes right and parallels Boone Fork for .55 mile to arrive at the Calloway Peak Overlook.)

3.2 Boone Fork parking area.

Mile 300. Tanawha Trail (from Boone Fork Parking Area to Cold Prong Pond Parking Area at BRP Mile 299) (3,900 feet) (N 36°07.198 W 81°46.893) Map 38

Length: 2 miles, one way; 4 miles, out-and-back
Difficulty: moderate
Recommended

Having traversed the length of Grandfather Mountain, the Tanawha Trail is no longer confined to staying within a few hundred yards of the parkway. This section veers quite a distance away from the BRP, resulting in a welcome respite from automobile noise and an opportunity to enjoy the serenity of a lush, green, mature hardwood forest. Rhododendron and mountain laurel tunnels increase the sensation of seclusion.

This walk is recommended if you are in search of a little peace and quiet. It is one of the few isolated spots you can reach with such little effort.

.0 Ascend from the southern end of the Boone Fork parking area. Arrive at an intersection in just a short distance. Bear to the right. (The Upper Boone Fork Trail [BRP 89] descends to the left and parallels Boone Fork for .55 mile to arrive at the Calloway Peak Overlook, BRP mile 299.7.)

.1 Intersection. Turn to the right and ascend. (The Tanawha Trail also goes to the left and arrives at the Boulder Field Overlook in 3.1 miles.)

.2 Come onto an old railroad grade lined with Solomon's seal. Descend gradually.

.3 Cross a small water run. Dwarf iris is abundant in early spring.

.5 The old railroad grade ends. Ascend.

.7 Cross over a ridgeline and continue to ascend through rhododendron tunnels.

.8 Arrive at the high point and begin to descend in a more open forest. Wildflowers are everywhere! Look for Solomon's seal,

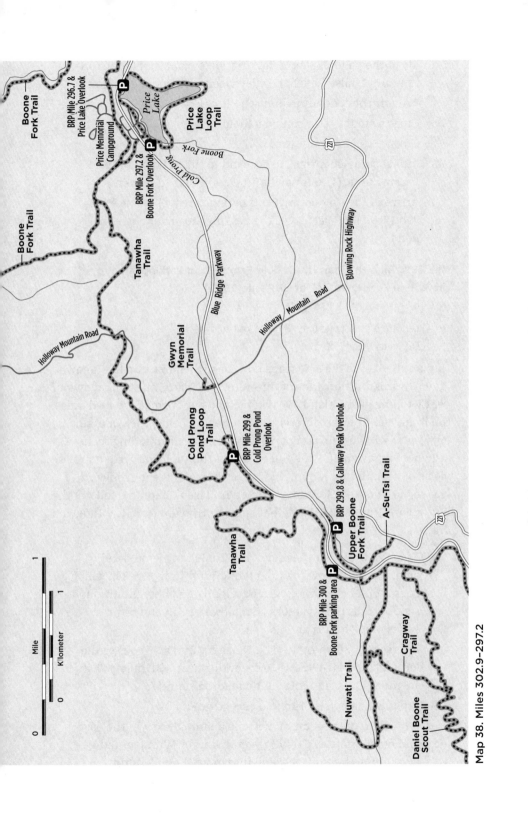

Map 38. Miles 302.9–297.2

lily of the valley, galax, dwarf iris, violets, mayapple, jack-in-the-pulpit, false hellebore, chickweed, and painted trillium.

1.1 Reenter rhododendron and switchback to the right.

1.5 Cross a small water run on a footbridge.

1.7 Cross a second water run.

1.8 Intersection. Bear right to descend to the Cold Prong Pond parking area. (The Tanawha Trail continues to the left.)

2.0 Arrive at the Cold Prong Pond parking area. The Cold Prong Pond Trail [BRP 88] leaves the parking area to encircle the pond.

Mile 299. Tanawha Trail (from Cold Prong Pond Parking Area to the Boone Fork Overlook at BRP Mile 297.2) (3,580 feet)
(N 36°07.735 W 81°46.188) Map 38

Length: 4 miles, one way; 8 miles, out-and-back
Difficulty: moderate

Human changes to the landscape now make their mark on the Tanawha Trail. On this portion the mature forest yields to open meadows of gently rolling pastureland. Weaving in and out of small wooded areas, the route enters three different stock-grazing fields. Each contains its own set of wildflowers and perspective on the surrounding scenery.

To help you visualize the full length of the Tanawha Trail, there are views of Grandfather Mountain from a couple of the meadows.

A segment of the Mountains-to-Sea Trail (see Chapter 1) follows the Boone Fork Trail [BRP 85] where it splits northward from the Tanawha Trail.

.0 Take the trail near the end of the Cold Prong Pond parking area. (Do not follow the Cold Prong Pond Trail [BRP 88], which goes around the pond.) Ascend slightly and descend through rhododendron. Soon cross a small water run and begin a series of slight ups and downs.

.2 Intersection. Turn right. (The Tanawha Trail also goes to the left and arrives at Boone Fork parking area, BRP mile 300, in 1.8 miles.) Descend into rhododendron tunnels.

.3 Cross a small water run and ascend gradually.

.6 A break in the vegetation permits a limited view to the east and of a portion of Grandfather Mountain. With painted trillium lining the trail, descend into more rhododendron.

A number of gracefully arching footbridges cross several water runs along the Tanawha Trail.

.8 A more open area in the woods allows bluets, wild mustard, violets, and cinquefoil to spread out across the forest floor.

1.0 Switchback to the right.

1.1 Pass through a fence stile and follow trail posts through the field, enjoying the open views. Soon come onto an old roadway.

1.25 Enter a small wooded area.

1.4 Be alert! As you are about to enter a field, the trail makes a hard turn to the left, staying on the edge of the woods. It leaves the forest in 250 feet to ascend into the meadow. In early spring you can admire the cinquefoil, violets, and buttercups; enjoy some wild strawberries later in the summer.

1.6 Enter a wooded area.

1.7 Ascend in a patch of mayapple, staying just below the summit of a knob.

1.8 Enter another meadow and soon pass through a fence stile. Catch a good view of Grandfather Mountain before descending.

2.2 Pass through a fence stile and a parking area and cross Halloway Mountain Road. (The BRP, mile 298.6, is about 1 mile to the right.) Pass through another fence stile and follow trail posts as they ascend the pasture.

2.3   Pass through a fence stile, turn right, and come onto a dirt road that enters the woods.

2.5   Pass under utility lines.

2.6   Be alert! The trail leaves the roadway to the left on a path lined with rhododendron and painted trillium.

2.7   Pass through yet another fence stile and follow the descending dirt road, not the one that ascends into the meadow. Go through a rhododendron tunnel and begin to follow trail posts, bearing to the left in an open meadow. This spot is peacefully secluded, good for soaking up a bit of sun. Soon you must be alert! Just before coming to a dip between two pastures, the trail makes a sudden, almost unapparent switchback to the right and descends to where the trail becomes apparent once again.

3.1   Cross a small water run. Enter the woods and walk along a fence line, soon crossing another small stream. Ascend.

3.3   Intersection. The Boone Fork Trail [BRP 85] comes in from the left to run concurrently with the Tanawha Trail for a short distance. At this point, the Mountains-to-Sea Trail (see Chapter 1) begins following the Boone Fork Trail to the left. Bear right to continue on the Tanawha Trail, pass through a fence stile, and enter a wide and dark rhododendron tunnel.

3.4   Intersection. The Boone Fork Trail [BRP 85] goes to the left. Bear right to continue on the Tanawha Trail.

3.5   Intersection. Pass by a connector trail to the Boone Fork Trail and bear right to continue on the Tanawha Trail.

3.7   The Julian Price Memorial Park campground is visible to your left. Come into a bottomland covered with Solomon's seal, mayapple, chickweed, and wild geranium. There are many small pathways going left to the campground. Stay on the main trail.

3.8   Arrive at campground site 46. The campground entrance is a few hundred feet to your left on the paved roadway. Continue on the short trail to the right that takes you across the BRP.

4.0   Come into parking area for the amphitheater and Boone Fork Overlook (N 36°08.142 W 81°44.305), BRP mile 297.2.

6.
Julian Price Memorial Park to US Route 441
Blue Ridge Parkway Miles 297–469.1

Leaving the gentle highland plateau of the central Blue Ridge Mountains, the parkway continues southward onto a landscape increasingly more elevated and rugged. No longer are there large rolling meadows such as those in Doughton Park. The topography is now inappropriate for farming or for establishing working estates like Moses H. Cone did. Instead, there is the spiny, rocky, mile-high ridgeline of Grandfather Mountain and the narrow, vertical confines of Linville Gorge. Six-thousand-foot summits become commonplace in the Black Mountains. Near its southern terminus the parkway takes its leave of the main crest of the Blue Ridge and traverses a hodgepodge of steep slopes and high pinnacles created by a series of cross ranges.

Due to the increasing altitude, the farther south you go on the BRP, the farther north you appear to be. Between 4,000 and 5,000 feet, the forest takes on the countenance of a hardwood forest common in New England. Beech, white birch, and similar trees begin to grow along the BRP in increasing numbers. Near the 6,000-foot level, parkway travelers enter a spruce-fir forest—an environment more like Canada than the southern United States.

Pisgah National Forest surrounds a major portion of this section of the BRP. It has a large network of pathways that intersect many of the parkway's trails to create an almost limitless array of overnight backpacking experiences. A couple of forest service trails (BRP miles 351.9 and 359.8) provide excellent spots for establishing base camps. From these you could spend days on additional walks and explorations. (Backcountry camping is permitted almost anywhere in the national forest.)

This large expanse of public land furnishes many trails that are free of, or have minimum signs of, any human impact. Views (BRP mile 422.4) are unobstructed by housing developments, roadways, or even relay towers. Hidden coves (BRP miles 359.8 and 407.6) give the impression that you may be one of the first people ever to walk through them.

Do remember, though, that the forest service and other nonparkway trails in this section may not be as regularly maintained as the BRP trails.

Other parkway trails descend to permit intimate contact with rushing waterfalls (BRP miles 316.4, 339.5, and 418.8) or ascend for stunning views from prominent points (BRP miles 407.6, 422.4, and 451.2). Self-guiding trails (BRP miles 308.2 and 431) provide interesting details to add to your enjoyment and knowledge of the parkway's natural surroundings. Balds, a unique Southern Appalachian phenomenon and natural mystery, may be observed and investigated firsthand (BRP miles 364.2 and 364.6).

Reminders of history will also be encountered while walking the trails of this section of the BRP. George W. Vanderbilt's 125,000-acre estate once encompassed much of what is now Pisgah National Forest. The over-16-mile Shut-In Trail (BRP miles 393.7 to 407.6) was originally constructed by Vanderbilt as a route from the Manor House in Asheville to his Buck Spring Hunting Lodge near Mount Pisgah. Devastating fires swept over many of these mountainsides in the first half of the twentieth century, and their effect on the land is still evident today (BRP mile 418.8). The Linville area (BRP mile 316.4) was named for a man and his son who were murdered by Indians in the 1700s, while Mount Pisgah's (mile 407.6) name is linked with a story as old as the Bible.

Mile 298.6. Holloway Mountain Road and access to US RT 221

Mile 298.6. Gwyn Memorial Trail [BRP 87] (N 36°07.885 W 81°45.735). See Map 38, Chapter 5.

There is not a true trail here, but a small glade where you could make a circuit walk of less than .1 mile while enjoying the beauty of a little water rivulet, bushes, and trees. A small bench (quite deteriorated the last time I was here) lets you take a rest from the miles of driving and hiking you have done along the parkway. In 1933, Rufus Lenoir Gwyn (1877–1963) was appointed to the North Carolina Committee on the Federal Parkway, which was tasked with deciding the BRP's route through the state.

This quiet respite is reached by exiting the parkway at mile 298.6, turning left onto NC RT 105, and immediately pulling into the small parking area on the left.

Mile 299. Cold Prong Pond Loop Trail [BRP 88] (3,580 feet)

(N 36°07.735 W 81°46.188). See Map 38, Chapter 5.

> *Length: .3 mile, circuit*
> *Difficulty: easy leg stretcher*

Strawberries! That word describes this short, level loop around Cold Prong Pond. The area next to the trail and the small meadow around the pond are carpeted by the strawberries' white blossoms in late spring. The succulent little berries become edible a few weeks later.

Strawberries are not, however, the only reason to leave your automobile and take this leg stretcher. Other wildflowers, such as cinquefoil and violets, line the pathway. Turtles may be spotted sunning themselves on small logs or other floating debris in the pond. Water snakes glide across the surface, creating ripples that glisten in the sun.

Activity around the pond slows as the cooler weather approaches, but you can enjoy the softly muted earth tones of the underbrush as it nears the end of its life cycle. Watch for a raccoon emerging from the woods in search of an early evening meal.

.0   Follow a pathway of rhododendron, wild mustard, and violets from the north end of the overlook. (Do not follow an access trail to the Tanawha Trail [see Chapter 5] that also leaves from the overlook.)

.05 Bear right at the loop trail intersection.

.15 Swing around the pond and start looking for a few of the wild strawberries.

.2   Veer away from the pond and follow trail posts through a small field. Wild strawberries are everywhere!

.3   Return to the loop trail intersection, bear right, and arrive back at the Cold Prong Pond parking area.

Mile 299.7. View of Calloway Peak (3,798 feet)

Calloway Peak is the highest point on Grandfather Mountain (and, thus, the highest point of the Blue Ridge Mountains).

Mile 299.8. Upper Boone Fork Trail [BRP 89] (3,900 feet)

(N 36°07.281 W 81°46.631). See Map 38, Chapter 5.

> *Length: .55 mile, one way; 1.1 miles, out-and-back*
> *Difficulty: moderately easy*

This may be the perfect place to let your restless children escape the car for a while and work off some excess energy. The path is only .55 mile long and ends at the very next parking area (BRP mile 300). The kids will enjoy watching the stream descend in small cascades as they climb up and over boulders lying about on the forest floor. Just before ending, the trail passes through one of the most easily reached stands of birch along the parkway.

.0 Descend from the Calloway Peak Overlook on a rhododendron-lined path and almost immediately turn left.

.1 Cross a small side stream.

.2 Walk right next to Boone Fork as it descends in small ripples and spills. Rhododendron opens up as you progress into a boulder-strewn landscape. Ascend along the stream.

.35 The trail swings to the right, away from the stream, and enters a wonderful stand of birch.

.4 Cross under the BRP.

.5 Intersection. Bear right to descend to the Upper Boone Fork parking area. The path to the left is an access trail to the Tanawha Trail (see Chapter 5).

.55 Arrive at Upper Boone Fork parking area.

Mile 299.9 A-Su-Tsi Trail [BRP 90]. See Map 38, Chapter 5.

Length: .4 mile, one way; .8 mile, out-and-back
Difficulty: moderately easy

The A-Su-Tsi Trail is not actually accessible from the parkway; BRP mile 299.9 is merely the point at which it passes under the BRP. The trailhead is reached by leaving the parkway at BRP mile 298.6, driving southward on Holloway Mountain Road, turning right onto US RT 221, and going just short of 2 miles to the parking area (N 36°06.919 W 81°46.638) on the right.

A-Su-Tsi translates from Cherokee as "to bridge"—a good description, since the trail provides a connection from US RT 221 to the Tanawha Trail and the pathways of Grandfather Mountain State Park. This is most significant during the winter months, when the A-Su-Tsi Trail provides the only access to these trails on the eastern side of Grandfather Mountain when the parkway is closed due to snowfall or other weather conditions.

.0 Gradually ascend along an old woods road lined by rhododendron and ferns.

.15 Gradually descend.

.3 Huge boulders add interest to Boone Fork as it descends the mountain. Pass under the parkway, where the route gradually ascends as a rough and rocky trail that may be overgrown.

.4 Arrive at the Tanawha Trail. To the right it is .1 mile to the Boone Fork parking area (BRP mile 300); to the left in less than .5 mile are Grandfather Mountain State Park's Nuwati and Daniel Boone Scout Trails. Also to the left is the parkway's Boulder Field Overlook in 3.1 miles.

Mile 300.6. Green Mountain Overlook (4,135 feet)

Green Mountain may be seen when the leaves are off the trees.

Mile 301.8. Pilot Ridge Overlook (4,400 feet)

Wide, expansive view.

Mile 302.1. View of Wilson Creek Valley (4,356 feet)

Much of what is seen in the wide view eastward is within the boundaries of Pisgah National Forest.

Mile 302.4. Boulder Field Overlook (4,355 feet)

The view across the parkway takes in Grandfather Mountain and Beacon Heights.

Mile 302.4. Access to the Tanawha Trail. See Chapter 5.

Mile 302.9. Rough Ridge parking area (4,292 feet)

If you have good eyesight, you may be able to identify the towns of Lenoir and Hickory. It's said that Charlotte can also be seen on clear days—extremely clear days (and with extremely good eyesight).

Mile 302.9. Access to the Tanawha Trail. See Chapter 5.

Mile 303.7. Wilson Creek Overlook (4,357 feet)

Wilson Creek is one of North Carolina's few designated Wild and Scenic Rivers.

Mile 303.7. Access to Tanawha Trail. See Chapter 5.

Mile 303.9. Yonahlossee Overlook (4,412 feet)

Traffic on US RT 221 can be heard from the overlook. When first constructed in the late 1800s, the road was known as the Yonahlossee Trail.

Mile 304.4. Linn Cove Visitor Center (4,315 feet)

Restrooms, water, and gift shop.

Mile 304.4. Access to the Tanawha Trail. See Chapter 5.

♿ The first .15 mile has handicap access.

Mile 304.8. Stack Rock parking area (4,286 feet)

There is a view of Grandfather Mountain's Mile-High Swinging Bridge.

Mile 304.8. Access to the Tanawha Trail. See Chapter 5.

Mile 305.1. US RT 221 and access to Blowing Rock and the Grandfather Mountain Entrance Station and trails

Trails of Grandfather Mountain, Blue Ridge Parkway Mile 305.1

Rising almost 2,000 feet above the BRP, the 5,946-foot summit of Grandfather Mountain is the highest point of the Blue Ridge Mountains. On clear days, when visibility is not obscured by haze, peaks almost 100 miles away may be seen from its rugged, quartzite ridgeline.

Hikers of Grandfather Mountain's trails will experience almost every type of environment to be encountered in the Blue Ridge. Birch forests, along with stands of hemlock and spruce, cover the moist lower slopes. Rhododendron thickets and blueberry patches thrive on many places around the mountain. Rushing streams start in the evergreen Canadian Forest zone on the ridge and tumble past caves whose entrances may be adorned with verdant growths of mosses and ferns. Rock outcroppings provide outstanding vistas, while dense jungles of hardwood almost prevent sunshine from reaching abundant wildflowers growing on the forest floor.

At one time you had to pay a fee to hike all of the trails. Not long after the death of the foresighted Hugh Morton, who saved the mountain from the encroachments of the modern world by turning the mountain

A rising pathway leads to the network of trails on Grandfather Mountain.

into a private nature preserve, the Morton family sold more than 2,400 acres of the undeveloped part of it to North Carolina, which established it as a state park in 2009. Under the auspices of the Grandfather Mountain Stewardship Foundation, the family continues to operate the developed part of the mountain (visitor fee required; www.grandfather. com), which is one of North Carolina's most popular tourist attractions, with its Mile-High Swinging Bridge (&) that entices thousands of visitors to cross it each year. Somewhat like a mini-zoo, the environmental habitat houses deer, black bears, cougars, golden and bald eagles, and otters. Picnic tables and scenic turnouts along the road, reminiscent of New Hampshire's Mount Washington Road, provide a chance to enjoy the landscape as you ascend. A visitor center, snack bar, souvenir shop, restaurant, museum, restrooms, and trailheads are located along the road. The Grandfather Mountain Roadway's entrance station (N 36°05.088 W 81°50.781) is on US RT 221, about a mile west of BRP at mile 305.1. You will have to pay the entrance fee if you wish to begin a hike from any of the trailheads located along the road. More information may be obtained from Grandfather Mountain, P.O. Box 129, Linville, NC 28646, 800-468-7325; https://grandfather.com.

However, you will not have to pay the fee if you begin your hike from one of the two state park trailheads. The Daniel Boone Scout Trail provides access from the BRP on the eastern side of the mountain; the

Profile Trail is the way to access the trail system from the western side. See the descriptions below for directions to these two access points. Camping is permitted only in designated areas. More information may be obtained from

> Grandfather Mountain State Park
> Highway 105 S Suite #6
> Banner Elk, NC 28604
> 828-963-9522
> www.ncparks.gov

Grandfather Trail. See Map 37, Chapter 5.

> *Length: 2.4 miles, one way; 4.8 miles, out-and-back*
> *Difficulty: very strenuous*
> *Markings: blue blazes*

This National Recreation Trail is probably the most spectacular excursion to be taken on Grandfather Mountain. It runs from the trailhead at the Black Rock parking area on the Grandfather Mountain Roadway to ascend and cross the alpine summit ridge. It connects with the Profile Trail a short distance before it terminates atop the highest point on the mountain, Calloway Peak, which is also a terminus for the Daniel Boone Scout Trail. Do not underestimate the Grandfather Trail's difficulty; at times you will use ladders or cables to scale steep, rocky cliffs!

Grandfather Trail Extension. See Map 37, Chapter 5.

> *Length: .6 mile, one way; 1.2 miles, out-and-back*
> *Difficulty: moderate*
> *Markings: red blazes*

As a connector trail, this pathway permits you to start a hike at the Trails parking area on the Grandfather Mountain Roadway and ascend to meet the Grandfather Trail at a point .3 mile from its beginning at the Black Rock parking area.

Underwood Trail. See Map 37, Chapter 5.

> *Length: .5 mile, one way; 1 mile, out-and-back*
> *Difficulty: strenuous*
> *Markings: yellow blazes*

Leaves the Grandfather Trail .5 mile from the Swinging Bridge trailhead on the Grandfather Mountain Roadway and rejoins it just past MacRae Peak. Provides easier passage than the more strenuous route of the

Grandfather Trail and is an alternative to that trail's exposure during high winds, thunderstorms, or other inclement weather.

Black Rock Trail. See Map 37, Chapter 5.

> *Length: 2 miles, out-and-back*
> *Difficulty: moderate*
> *Markings: yellow blazes*

Drops gradually from a parking area on the road that goes to the visitor center and Swinging Bridge. Somewhat rocky. Ends in a small loop providing views to the east overlooking portions of the Tanawha Trail and the BRP.

Bridge Trail. See Map 37, Chapter 5.

> *Length: .4 mile, one way; .8 mile, out-and-back*
> *Difficulty: moderately strenuous*
> *Markings: none*

Starts across the road from the Black Rock parking area on the Grandfather Mountain Roadway and ascends through a spruce-fir forest to go under the Mile-High Swinging Bridge and end at the visitor center.

The Woods Walk. See Map 37, Chapter 5.

> *Length: .4 mile, circuit*
> *Difficulty: easy*
> *Markings: none*

A loop along the mountain's lower slopes near the picnic area on the Grandfather Mountain Roadway. The self-guided nature trail, with interpretive signs, is an easy introduction to the natural world of the area. More than 60 wildflowers have been identified along its short route.

Profile Trail (N 36°07.157 W 81°49.990). See Map 37, Chapter 5.

> *Length: 3.8 miles, one way; 7.6 miles, out-and-back*
> *Difficulty: lower section is moderate; upper section becomes*
>   *moderately strenuous*
> *Markings: none*

Ascends from a parking area located off NC RT 105 (.2 mile north of the intersection of NC RT 184 with NC RT 105) and passes almost directly below the Grandfather profile on its way to end at the Grandfather Trail. It can be used as a route to Calloway Peak but requires you to use a portion of the strenuous Grandfather Trail to reach the summit.

Daniel Boone Scout Trail. See Map 37, Chapter 5.

> *Length: 3 miles, one way; 6 miles, out-and-back*
> *Difficulty: strenuous*
> *Markings: white blazes*

A National Recreation Trail, this pathway is most easily reached by taking the access trail from the Boone Fork parking area (BRP mile 300) to—and then turning left onto—the Tanawha Trail (see Chapter 5), passing by the Nuwati Trail, and arriving at the Daniel Boone Scout Trail in .6 mile from the parking area. (For another access route— .8 mile in length—turn left onto the Tanawha Trail after ascending on the A-Su-Tsi Trail [BRP 90] from the parking area on US RT 221.) From the Tanawha Trail, the Daniel Boone Scout Trail climbs an evergreen-covered ridge to end at Calloway Peak (5,946 feet above sea level), where it connects with the Grandfather Trail.

Nuwati Trail. See Map 37, Chapter 5.

> *Length: 1.4 miles, one way; 2.8 miles, out-and-back*
> *Difficulty: moderate*
> *Markings: blue blazes*

Begins at an intersection on the Tanawha Trail (see Chapter 5), about .4 mile from the Boone Fork parking area (BRP mile 300). Rocky, but fairly gentle. Ends at a view of Boone Fork Bowl, an isolated valley that some believe to have been glacially carved (although glaciers did not reach this far south during the last Ice Age).

Cragway Trail. See Map 37, Chapter 5.

> *Length: 1 mile, one way; 2 miles, out-and-back*
> *Difficulty: strenuous*
> *Markings: orange blazes*

A connector trail that covers the steep, rocky, and open landscape between the Nuwati Trail and the Daniel Boone Scout Trail. The easiest way to traverse this rugged route would be to ascend on the Daniel Boone Scout Trail and descend on the Cragway Trail, enjoying the views.

Mile 305.2. Beacon Heights parking area (4,218 feet)

Nice view of the profile of Grandfather Mountain from the parking area.

Mile 305.2. Access to the Tanawha Trail. See Chapter 5.

Mile 305.2. Beacon Heights Trail [BRP 91] (N 36°035.235 W 81°49.812).
See Map 37, Chapter 5.

Length: .7 mile, out-and-back
Difficulty: moderate

Ascend this extended leg stretcher to the 4,200-foot quartzite summit of Beacon Heights for the best views available of the landscape the BRP will pass through as you drive southward. Ridge after ridge rises toward the horizon, each a little higher than its predecessor as the mountains become progressively taller the farther south you gaze. From a second viewpoint, the ridgeline of Grandfather Mountain is visible.

The Mountains-to-Sea Trail (see Chapter 1) makes use of the Beacon Heights Trail for a short distance.

.0   From the southern end of the Beacon Heights parking area, cross, diagonally to the left, a paved service road. Ascend on a path marked for the Tanawha Trail. Galax, rhododendron, and trillium line the trail.

.05 Intersection. The Tanawha Trail (see Chapter 5) and the Mountains-to-Sea Trail (see Chapter 1) descend to the left. Bear right to continue on the Beacon Heights Trail.

.1   Pass by a bench.

.2   The Mountains-to-Sea Trail goes off to the right; bear left.

.3   Come to a bench at an intersection. Bear right for 100 feet to come onto a flat rock outcropping. Excellent views to the south and a wonderful spot to be for sunrise. Return to the intersection and bear right.

.35 Arrive at another flat rock overlook. This time enjoy a vista of Grandfather Mountain. Retrace steps.

Mile 305.2. Mountains-to-Sea Trail (N 36°035.235 W 81°49.812).
See Chapter 1.

Mile 306.6. Grandfather Mountain Overlook (4,063 feet).
Another view of Grandfather Mountain.

Mile 307.4. Grandmother parking area (4,063 feet)
No view, but the parking area is built on the western edge of Grandmother Mountain, whose ridgeline comes close to Grandfather Mountain.

Mile 307.6. Little Bald Overlook (4,015 feet)

A view into Linville Valley.

Mile 307.9

NC RT 1511 descends east from the parkway into the Wilson Creek Area of Pisgah National Forest. More than a dozen trails in this section of the national forest provide ample opportunity for exploration and overnight camping. Additional information on the Wilson Creek Area may be obtained by contacting

Grandfather Ranger District, USFS
109 Lawing Dr.
Nebo, NC 28761
828-652-2144
www.fs.fed.us

Mile 308.2. Flat Rock Parking Overlook

The wooded overlook provides access to the Flat Rock Self-Guiding Loop Trail [BRP 62].

Mile 308.2. Flat Rock Self-Guiding Loop Trail [BRP 92] (3,987 feet)
(N 36°02.935 W 81°51.381) Map 39

Length: .7 mile, circuit
Difficulty: moderately easy
Highly recommended

Signs along the trail identify and describe much of the plant life in the Blue Ridge Mountains. Take your time to walk this one; the detailed information will enrich your knowledge of the parkway environment.

The signs, however, are not the only highlights of the Flat Rock Self-Guiding Loop Trail. Flat Rock, a quartzite outcropping on the western side of Grandfather Mountain, permits a stirring outlook of Linville Valley and of Roan Mountain and other 5,000- to 6,000-foot summits far to the west in Cherokee National Forest.

.0   Begin at the trail sign in the center of the Flat Rock parking area.

.05 Bear left at the loop trail intersection. In a few feet is a sign supplying information about chestnut and oak.

.1   A sign about the American chestnut. The pathway is lined by Solomon's seal and wood anemones.

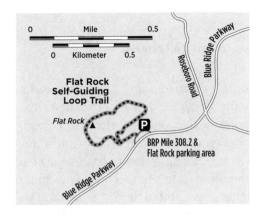

Map 39. Flat Rock Self-Guiding
Loop Trail (mile 308.2)

.2   Signs concerning mountain winterberry and galax. In a few feet pass by a bench and signs describing cucumber (magnolia) trees and withe rod. Begin walking on a path of smooth rock.

.25   Come onto Flat Rock, an outcropping laced with white quartzite. Swing around the rock for grand views of Black, Yellow, Hawk, Big Yellow, and Roan Mountains. Below is a large rock quarry in Linville Valley. Follow the trail arrows painted on the rock.

.3   Come to another view. This one is of Hump Mountain and the Blue Ridge Mountains to the south. Grandfather Mountain looms far above you. Begin a gradual descent.

.35   Pass by a sign identifying rhododendron, and in a few feet come to other signs about hobblebush, viburnum, red maple, and striped maple.

.55   Signs concerning Fraser magnolia and white oak.

.65   Bear left at the loop trail intersection.

.7   Return to the Flat Rock parking area.

Mile 310. Lost Cove Cliffs Overlook (3,812 feet)

A signpost at the overlook discusses the Brown Mountain lights, a phenomenon with early accounts from the 1700s that still occurs and whose origin is still a mystery. Stop at the overlook at night and you may get to form your own opinion after you see the twinkling below you.

Mile 310.3. NC RT 1519

Mile 311.2. NC RT 1518

**Mile 312.2. NC RT 181 and access to Pineola (2 miles)
and Morganton (32 miles)**

Leaving the parkway and turning eastward onto NC 181 will lead to some of the trails of the Linville Gorge Wilderness. The more than 2,000-foot gorge is a truly spectacular place that attracts scores of hikers. Visitors are especially drawn to the eastern and western rims (see mile 317.5 for the western rim trails), where soaring peaks and rock outcrops have grandstand views into the gorge and out to the west onto North Carolina's higher peaks and to the flatter lands of the Piedmont to the east. The gorge walls are so precipitous (and therefore less visited) that much of the area has never been logged. Trails wind through magnificent stands of old-growth forests of hickory, oak, maple, hemlock, and more. Hawks, vultures, and falcons are often seen riding thermals above the gorge, while the forest is home to the white-breasted nuthatch, scarlet tanager, pileated woodpecker, cedar wax-wing, and others. Also be aware that the rough and rocky terrain has a healthy population of rattlesnakes and copperheads.

Many of the trails terminate at the Linville River, where you must ford the stream if you wish to connect with the trail along the river or those on the western gorge wall. Please use caution when fording the river, and remember that the Linville Gorge is a wilderness area, with possibly few signs other than at trailheads. Be well prepared for very rugged terrain, little-maintained trails, and the vagaries of the weather.

A permit with a limit of two nights is required for camping on Friday, Saturday, and Sunday evenings and holidays from May 1 through October 31. Permits are issued from the forest service office by mail or in person. Day use permits are not required. For permits contact

Grandfather Ranger District
109 East Lawing Drive
Nebo, NC 2876
828-652-2144
www.fs.fed.us

Driving eastward from the parkway on NC 181 will lead to the Old Gingercake Road/NC RT 1264, which bears right to the Brushy Ridge Trail [FS 232]. A little farther along, Gingercake Acres Road/NC RT 181 turns off to the right and soon become FSR 210 to lead to the trailhead for Devil's Hole [FS 244] and Jonas Ridge [FS 245] Trails. Continue along

FSR 210 for the parking area for Hawksbill Trail [FS 248] and one for Spence Ridge [FS 233] and Little Table Rock [FS 236] Trails. Continue on FSR 210 to make a right onto FSR 210B and follow it to the parking area for the Table Rock Summit Trail [FS 242]. This is also the beginning of the Shortoff Mountain Trail [FS 235], which provides access to the Cambric Branch Trail [FS 234].

Brushy Ridge Trail [FS 232] Map 40

Length: 4.2 miles, out-and-back
Difficulty: moderate

The first mile of the Brushy Ridge Trail is along an almost level old roadbed, with possible good campsites. Beyond that, the trail descends quickly to an overlook of the river, with great views of the gorge, Hawksbill Mountain, and Table Rock Mountain along the way.

Devil's Hole Trail [FS 244] Map 40

Length: 1.5 miles, one way; 3 miles, out-and-back
Difficulty: moderate

The trail has a short rise from the trailhead parking area but then descends more than 1,100 feet through one of the Southern Appalachians' dense and diverse cove forests. Near the end, it crosses a small stream, rises to the top of a cliff, and then makes the final descent to the river. Hikers often ford the river to connect with the Linville Gorge Trail [FS 231].

Jonas Ridge Trail [FS 245] Map 40

Length: 5 miles, out-and-back
Difficulty: moderately strenuous

Starting with a steep climb to the open summit of Sitting Bear Mountain, the trail runs along the ridgeline close to the lip of the gorge before terminating at Gingercake Mountain. Like the Brushy Ridge Trail, it offers good views of the gorge and Hawksbill and Table Rock Mountains.

Hawksbill Trail [FS 248] Map 40

Length: 1.4 miles, out-and-back
Difficulty: moderate

Because it is so short and terminates at one of the area's most prominent peaks with wonderful views, the Hawksbill Trail is often crowded with people, even in the middle of the week. The first and last por-

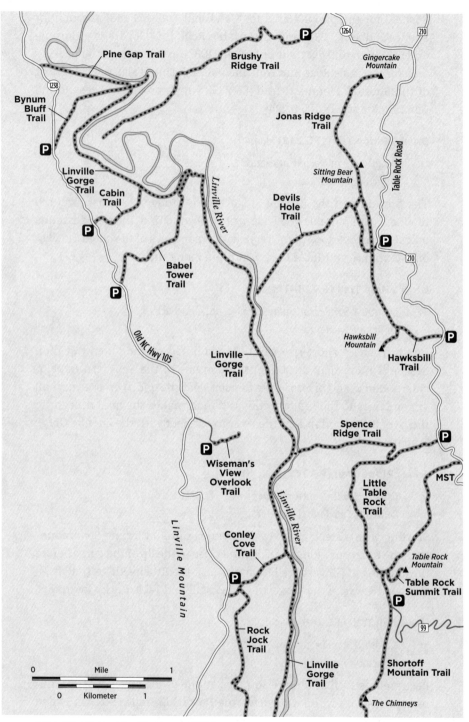

Map 40. Upper Linville Gorge Wilderness

tions of the pathway are steep and rocky, but you'll be rewarded with views even more spectacular than those already mentioned on the Brushy Ridge [FS 232] and Jonas Ridge [FS 245] Trails. A short distance before the summit is a side trail that connects with the Devil's Hole Trail [FS 244].

Spence Ridge Trail [FS 233] Map 40

Length: 1.75 miles, one way; 3.5 miles, out-and-back
Difficulty: moderately strenuous

Spence Ridge Trail is the most popular pathway into the gorge on the eastern side for two reasons. First, it starts out as an old level road for the initial .5 mile, passes by the Little Table Rock Trail [FS 236], and then descends at a rather moderate pace (when compared with other gorge trails) to the Linville River. Second, there is a footbridge, the only one in the wilderness, across the river, so you can access the Linville Gorge Trail [FS 231] without getting your feet wet. (Always check with the forest service beforehand to make sure this bridge has not been washed out.)

Little Table Rock Trail [FS 236] Map 40

Length: 1.6 miles, one way; 3.2 miles, out-and-back (both include the
distance needed to hike on the Spence Ridge Trail [FS 233])
Difficulty: moderate

The Little Table Rock Trail is one of the area's least-used routes. It branches off the Spence Ridge Trail [FS 233] about .4 mile from that pathway's parking area and makes several ups and downs to reach a campsite on Little Table Rock. From there it continues another .1 mile to end at a junction with the Table Rock Summit Trail [FS 242].

Table Rock Summit Trail [FS 242] Map 40

Length: 2.4 miles, out-and-back
Difficulty: strenuous

Table Rock has one of the most distinctive profiles in the Southern Appalachians, looking pretty much as its name describes it. The summit is a popular destination for hikers, while the rough and rocky sides of the mountain are a haven for rock climbers. Do not miss this one. The trail is a part of the Mountains-to-Sea Trail (see Chapter 1). Ascend from the trailhead parking area, pass by the Little Table Rock Trail [FS 236]

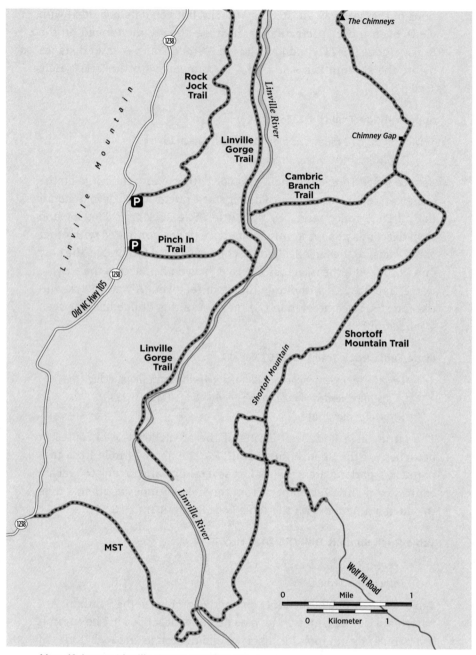

Map 41. Lower Linville Gorge Wilderness

coming in from the left, don't follow the MST when it bears off to the left, and arrive at the mountaintop for a sweeping 360-degree view.

Shortoff Mountain Trail [FS 235] Maps 40 & 41

Length: 8 miles, one way; 16 miles, out-and-back
Difficulty: moderate, if done in the direction described; moderately
strenuous if done in the opposite direction

Another popular route, the Shortoff Mountain Trail, which includes a portion of the Mountains-to-Sea Trail (see Chapter 1), runs along the eastern rim of the gorge, providing superb views and a number of small campsites. In less than a mile, it goes by The Chimneys, an area with interesting rock formations, and passes the Cambric Branch Trail [FS 234] at about the 2.1-mile mark. Home to peregrine falcons, the open cliffs of Shortoff Mountain, which provide views into the gorge, are reached about 5 miles into the trip. With the Mountains-to-Sea Trail staying to the right, the Shortoff Mountain Trail bears left and descends, with views of Lake James, via switchbacks to Wolf Pit Road off NC 126.

Cambric Branch Trail [FS 234] Map 41

Length: 3.4 miles, one way; 6.8 miles, out-and-back (both include the
distance needed to hike on the Shortoff Mountain Trail [FS 235])
Difficulty: strenuous

Quite primitive, and not used nearly as often as the other trails, the Cambric Branch Trail branches off the Shortoff Mountain Trail at 2.1 miles from that route's trailhead and drops quickly for 1,500 feet to end at the Linville River. Note that some sources list this as the Chimbric Ridge Trail, while others call it Cambric Ridge Trail.

Mile 312.9. Clark Road

Mile 313.2. Rose Road

Mile 314.6. Shuffler Road

Mile 315.5. Camp Creek Overlook

Rhododendron and mountain laurel are part of the understory in the forest that borders the overlook.

Mile 315.5. Camp Creek Trail [BRP 93] (3,442 feet)

(N 35°58.827 W 81°55.375) Map 42

> Length: .12 mile, out-and-back
> Difficulty: easy leg stretcher

The Camp Creek Trail, a short leg stretcher, descends steeply from the middle of the overlook in a corridor of mountain laurel and rhododendron. It soon arrives at a favorite local fishing spot on Camp Creek. The stream was named for the Camp brothers who logged the area in the early 1900s. Cool air rising from the rippling waters and deep shade provided by the lush vegetation might, on a hot summer day, cause you to linger longer than you had intended.

Trails and Visitor Center of the Linville Falls Recreation Area, Blue Ridge Parkway Miles 316.4–316.5

The Linville River and Falls receive their name from William Linville. In 1766, while on a hunting trip in the area, he and his son were attacked and killed by Indians. A 16-year-old companion lived to tell the world of the bloody incident.

Having wound its way through the Linville Valley, the river, like the James River far to the north in Virginia, has carved its way through the main ridge of the Blue Ridge Mountains to become an easterly flowing stream. The falls make an impressive 90-foot drop to enter the 12-mile-long Linville Gorge.

The gorge is a favorite spot for both amateur and professional geologists. Millions of years ago, as the earth's crustal plates were colliding, large slabs of land slid under other large slabs. This action can clearly be seen on the steep walls of the gorge, for different layers of rock are piled on top of one another. Interestingly, the falls expose a layer of cranberry gneiss (a metamorphic rock) sitting atop a shelf of rock believed to be 500 million years younger.

Three of the recreation area's trails lead to overlooks of the river and falls. The area also contains an extensive variety of plant life. One of the overlooks has six types of heath growing nearby. Two of those, the Carolina and catawba rhododendron, grow profusely on the precipitous walls of the gorge. Their many flowers, usually blooming about early May, dazzle spring visitors.

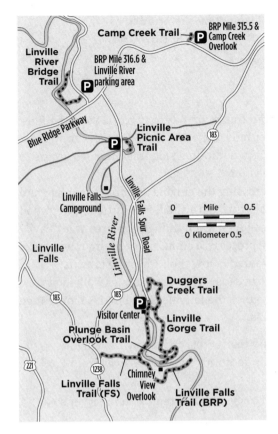

Map 42. Miles 315.5–316.5

Plants and water are also the focus of the recreation area's other trails. A short loop weaves over a moist forest floor to pass by the Duggers Creek Falls, and a leg stretcher descends to the banks of the Linville River.

Except for the Linville River Bridge Trail [BRP 99], all of the trails in the recreation area start from the parking area at the end of the Linville Falls Spur Road (BRP mile 316.4). Another exception is the short, .1-mile pathway, known as the Linville Picnic Area Trail [BRP 94] (Map 42), that emanates from the River Bend Overlook (located on the spur road, .4 mile from the BRP) and meanders pleasantly along the Linville River.

Land for the Linville Falls Recreation Area was donated by John D. Rockefeller Jr. The area contains a park service campground (3,197 feet), picnic area, small bookshop/visitor center, water, and restrooms.

Mile 316.4. Linville Falls Trail (sometimes referred to as Erwins View Trail) [BRP 95] (N 35°57.319 W 81°55.692) Map 42

Length: 2.1 miles, out-and-back
Difficulty: moderate
Recommended

Four side trails descend from this main pathway to views of the falls. The first overlooks the upper falls; the other three furnish varying perspectives on the lower falls. An additional side trail provides access to a forest service parking area on NC RT 1238.

The main trail begins by crossing the Linville River on a concrete and steel footbridge. It then passes through a small field dotted by dogwood trees before entering a dense forest. Even though this area was heavily logged before becoming BRP property, a small stand of virgin hemlocks still exists, and the trail is routed below their towering crowns.

This trail is recommended because it is a much easier walk for a view of the falls and gorge than either the Linville Gorge [BRP 96] or Plunge Basin Overlook [BRP 97] Trails.

.0 From the bookshop and restrooms, cross over the Linville River on an extravagant footbridge and walk away from the river.

.2 Pass through a field of dogwood. The rapids on the river soon become audible.

.3 A pleasant spot to look at a bend in the river.

.4 Intersection. The trail to the right ascends to a forest service parking area on NC RT 1238, which borders the Linville Gorge Wilderness (see BRP mile 317.5). Bear left to continue on the Linville Falls Trail. In 100 feet come to another intersection and turn left, descending along the trail bounded by a rail fence.

.5 Arrive at the view of the upper falls. The wide river is now channeled between a narrow cleft in the rock facing. The walls of the gorge are covered with mountain laurel and rhododendron. Retrace your steps and turn left at the intersection.

.6 Intersection. Bear left and ascend steadily into a majestic hemlock and hardwood forest.

.7 Pass by a bench.

Upper Linville Falls is reached by a hike of only .5 mile.

.8 Arrive at a high point and descend. Come to a rest shelter in 300 feet and bear to the left to the Chimney View Overlook.

.9 Come to the overlook and in 100 feet arrive at a second overlook. The scene spread out below you is well worth the walking you've done to reach it: The upper falls plunges 12 feet down the rock facing, while the lower falls drops more than 60 feet in a narrow channel. Rhododendron and mountain laurel appear to grow on every inch of the gorge. Retrace your steps back to the main trail.

1.0 Bear left at the intersection and ascend; the trail becomes a little steeper and rockier. Pass by a bench.

1.1 Arrive at a pleasant view out across the valley of the gorge. Take the side trail to another view of the falls—the most spectacular on the Linville Falls Trail. You are now high above the falls, with the peaks and ridges of the surrounding mountains soaring above you. Retrace your steps along the main route.

2.1 Arrive back at the bookshop, restrooms, and parking area.

Mile 316.4. Linville Gorge Trail [BRP 96] (N 35°57.319 W 81°55.692) Map 42

Length: 1.4 miles, out-and-back
Difficulty: moderately strenuous

A little rougher and not quite as heavily traveled as the Linville Falls Trail [BRP 95], the Linville Gorge Trail descends from the restrooms and parking area through attractive growths of rhododendron. It arrives at the Linville River's edge in the basin of the lower falls. Flat rocks near the bank invite you to take a break, enjoy the sunshine, and while away the day. The river itself will compel you to contemplate its power to carve such a deep channel through solid, hard rock.

.0   Ascend the steps to the left of the restrooms. Arrive at an intersection in 100 feet. The Duggers Creek Trail [BRP 98] goes off to the left. Bear right and ascend to continue on the Linville Gorge Trail.

.2   Cross a (usually) dry water run and descend very gradually.

.35   Intersection. The Plunge Basin Overlook Trail [BRP 97] is to the right. Bear left uphill through mountain laurel tunnels to continue on the Linville Gorge Trail. Soon, however, descend along a rock facing.

.5   Descend steeply on a staircase of 27 steps and switchback to the right. The rock facing you just came down is directly above you. The trail here is very steep, rough, and rocky.

.7   Arrive at the river's edge below the lower falls. Magnolia, rhododendron, and mountain laurel cling to the sides of the gorge. Retrace steps.

Mile 316.4. Plunge Basin Overlook Trail [BRP 97]
(N 35°57.319 W 81°55.692) Map 42

Length: .4 mile, out-and-back, plus .7 mile to access and return
from the trail
Difficulty: moderate

The Plunge Basin Overlook Trail is the shortest route you can take to view the lower falls. From this point you may readily observe how the river is gradually eroding the rock facing behind the falls.

To reach this trail, follow the Linville Gorge Trail [BRP 96] for .35 mile from the restrooms and parking area. Remember to include that distance when figuring how far you must really walk in order to reach the lower falls overlook.

.0   Bear right onto the beginning of the Plunge Basin Overlook Trail at its intersection with the Linville Gorge Trail.

.1   Pass by a bench, where the trail becomes a little steeper and follows a series of steps.

.2   Arrive at the overlook of the lower falls. Retrace steps.

Mile 316.4. Duggers Creek Trail [BRP 98] (N 35°57.319 W 81°55.692) Map 42

Length: .25 mile, one way; .5 mile, out-and-back
Difficulty: easy
Recommended

The Duggers Creek Trail is an interpretive trail of a different kind. The signs along the pathway do not identify plants and animals or provide historical information; instead, quotes by John Muir, Edwin Wayne Teal, and others help set a mood and instill an appreciation of the natural world.

The trail also enters a "mini Linville Gorge" lined with ferns and mosses as Duggers Creek drops from Jonas Ridge to the Linville River.

This easy trail is a most pleasant walk and, since lightly used, a good place to escape from the throngs that may be present on other routes.

.0   Ascend the steps to the left of the restrooms and parking area, and in 100 feet arrive at an intersection. The Linville Gorge Trail [BRP 96] is to the right. Bear left to walk on the Duggers Creek Trail.

.1   Be alert! Bear right slightly uphill and then bear left toward the pavement, but go uphill on the dirt pathway. Ascend through rhododendron tunnels. Soon you will cross Duggers Creek as it falls into a narrow ravine. Beyond the creek ascend steps lined by galax; almost immediately descend via switchbacks.

.25   Arrive at the far end of the parking area. The restrooms are just a few feet ahead, or you can retrace steps along the trail.

Mile 316.5. Linville River Bridge Trail [BRP 99] (3,250 feet) (N 35°58.466 W 81°56.146) Map 42

Length: .2 mile, out-and-back
Difficulty: easy leg stretcher

Dropping easily through rhododendron and giant hemlocks, this trail leads to the banks of the Linville River. At the end of the trail, you will be standing almost directly below one of the parkway's largest stone arch bridges; it crosses the river on 3 spans of 80 feet each. Though the waters of the river are wide and slow here, they will be rushing and plunging into the confines of the Linville Gorge just a few miles downstream.

Mile 317.5. US RT 221

A left turn onto US RT 221 (with services) and another left onto NC RT 183 will bring you to NC RT 1238 (Kistler Memorial Highway). This unpaved road is on the western edge of the Linville Gorge Wilderness, with access to a number of forest service trails into the wilderness. (See BRP mile 312.2 for details of the trails on the eastern side of the gorge and background information for the Linville Gorge Wilderness.) Also, about a mile along NC RT 1238 is the Linville Gorge Wilderness Cabin, where you may obtain maps and any required permits—if it is open (days and hours seem to vary greatly from year to year). At the very least, if your time is limited, take the drive and the short walk to the Wiseman's View Overlook Trail [FS 224].

From its intersection with NC RT 183, NC RT 1238 offers access to several trails:

Linville Falls Trail [no FS number], .1 mile along NC RT 1238. Map 42

> Length: .3 mile, one way; .6 mile, out-and-back
> Difficulty: moderately easy

The forest service's Linville Falls Trail is a moderately easy walk along a gradually descending woods road. It ends when it intersects with the BRP's Linville Falls Trail [BRP 95] at the .4-mile point on that route's description, giving access to the numerous overlooks of the falls.

Pine Gap Trail [no FS number], .9 mile along NC RT 1238. Map 40

> Length: .8 mile, one way; 1.6 miles, out-and-back
> Difficulty: moderate

With a moderately descending grade, the Pine Gap Trail is probably the most popular and easiest route into the gorge. It does become a bit more rugged at its lower end close to the Linville River, where it meets the Bynum Bluff Trail [FS 241] and the Linville Gorge Trail [FS 231].

Bynum Bluff Trail [FS 241], 1.4 miles along NC RT 1238. Map 40

> *Length: 1 mile, one way; 2 miles, out-and-back*
> *Difficulty: strenuous*

Although it starts out relatively mild for about 4. mile, the Bynum Bluff Trail then comes to a prominent point where it makes a rapid descent to the river and the intersection with the Pine Gap and Linville Gorge [FS 231] Trails.

Linville Gorge Trail [FS 231] Maps 40 & 41

> *Length: 11.5 miles, one way; 23 miles, out-and-back (be sure to add the*
> *distance of the trail/trails you take to reach the Linville Gorge Trail)*
> *Difficulty: strenuous*

The Linville Gorge Trail is the longest trail in the wilderness area, following the river for 11.5 miles. As such, it forms the basis for exploring not only the deepest reaches of the gorge, but also the route that will connect with the other trails to create circuit hikes of varying lengths.

From its northern end at the intersection of the Pine Gap and Bynum Bluff [FS 241] Trails, it is 1 mile to the Cabin Trail [FS 246], 2 miles to the Babel Tower Trail [FS 240], 3.4 miles to Devil's Hole Trail [FS 244], 4.5 miles to Spence Ridge Trail [FS 233], 5.5 miles to the Conley Cove Trail [FS 229], 8.7 miles to the Cambric Branch Trail [FS 234], and 9 miles to the Pinch In Trail [FS 228]. From the latter, it is 2.5 miles to the Linville Gorge Trail's terminus with private property; backtracking is necessary.

Do not underestimate the difficulty of hiking the Linville Gorge Trail. Although on maps the trail appears to stay close to the river, there are places with steep climbs that rise a few hundred feet above the stream and areas where boulders and downed trees must be negotiated.

Cabin Trail [FS 246], 2 miles along NC RT 1238. Map 40

> *Length: .8 mile, one way; 1.6 miles, out-and-back*
> *Difficulty: strenuous*

A rough route that descends close to 1,000 feet before coming to an end at the Linville Gorge Trail [FS 231].

Babel Tower Trail [FS 240], 2.7 miles along NC RT 1238. Map 40

> *Length: 1.25 miles, one way; 2.5 miles, out-and-back*
> *Difficulty: moderately strenuous*

The Babel Tower Trail is a moderately strenuous hike on a rough and rocky route that descends approximately 1,300 feet in a relatively short distance. It's a popular pathway, due in part to the Babel Tower, a 70-foot granite rock formation with cliffs that drop hundreds of feet to the river below. Nice views of the river and of Hawksbill and Table Rock Mountains.

Wiseman's View Overlook Trail [FS 224], 3.8 miles along NC RT 1238. Map 40

> *Length: less than .4 mile, out-and-back*
> *Difficulty: easy*

Here are absolutely stunning vistas that require very little effort (other than driving miles on dirt road) to reach. From the trailhead parking area, it is a few hundred feet to two stone overlooks situated on the very lip of the gorge. The wide, sweeping vista takes in the eastern rim's skyline—Hawksbill and Table Rock Mountains being the most distinctive points. Looking out to the east, it's possible to see the Blue Ridge Escarpment drop dramatically to the Piedmont. Directly below is the Linville River winding its way through the gorge. Be sure to investigate spots other than the developed overlooks, as you will discover additional vantage points.

Do not miss this place!

Conley Cove Trail [FS 229], 5.3 miles along NC RT 1238. Map 40

> *Length: 1.4 miles, one way; 2.8 miles, out-and-back*
> *Difficulty: moderate*

Because of its many switchbacks, the narrow Conley Cove Trail is one of the easier routes into the gorge. Passing by a cave and the intersection with the Rock Jock Trail [FS 247], it descends in a forest of oak, pine, and silverbell trees. Some nice campsites close to the river.

Rock Jock Trail [FS 247], 5.3 miles along NC RT 1238. Maps 40 & 41

> *Length: 4.3 miles, one way; 8.6 miles, out-and-back*
> *Difficulty: moderate*

Branching off the Conley Cove Trail [FS 229], the Rock Jock Trail follows the contour of the rim of the canyon. It should be a moderately easy hike, but downed trees and other maintenance issues may make it a rougher passage. These conditions may also make walking its full length from the northern parking area on the Kistler Memorial Road to

It's an easy roundtrip walk of less than half a mile to the spectacular vistas from the forest service's Wiseman's View Overlook.

where it emerges farther south onto the same road impossible. Therefore, be sure to check with authorities first. Great views, several waterfalls, and interesting rock formations.

Pinch In Trail [FS 228], 8.2 miles along NC RT 1238. Map 41

> *Length: 1.4 miles, one way; 2.8 miles, out-and-back*
> *Difficulty: strenuous*

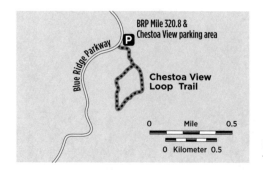

Map 43. Chestoa View Loop Trail (mile 320.8)

The Pinch In Trail is the southernmost trail providing access to the Linville Gorge Trail [FS 231]. Because of that, it is a somewhat popular route, but be aware that it loses more than 2,000 feet in less than 1.5 miles. There are, however, numerous good views along the way.

Mile 318.4. North Toe Valley Overlook

Think about this as you stand looking into the valley: The waters of the North Toe River eventually flow into the Gulf of Mexico.

Mile 319.8. Humpback Mountain Viaduct

Mile 320.8. Chestoa View Loop Trail [BRP 100] (4,090 feet)
(N 35°55.614 W 81°57.243) Map 43

> *Length: .8 mile, circuit*
> *Difficulty: easy*

On a ledge of Humpback Mountain, the Chestoa View Loop Trail ("chestoa" is a Cherokee word meaning rabbit) is an almost perfectly level path. It passes by vistas across the North Fork Catawba River Valley to the upper reaches of the Linville Gorge Wilderness and to higher peaks in the north. Hawks are often seen soaring and riding the warm updrafts rising from the valley.

There is no better place to begin a day than at one of the viewpoints, where you can watch the morning sunlight quietly spread across the valley and slowly brighten the distant ridgelines. Whorled loosestrife and Solomon's plume grow close to the parking area in the spring.

.0 Begin on the trail under oaks and hickory at the far end of the parking area. Go down the steps, turn right, go a few more feet, and take a left.

.05   Reach the first view of the valley. Table Rock Mountain is prominent to the north. Return to and descend very slightly on the graveled trail lined with chickweed and Solomon's seal.

.3   Bear to the left at the loop trail intersection.

.35   Arrive at an even better view—US RT 221 snakes its way into the valley, and high and lofty Grandfather Mountain forms a backdrop for the rest of the scenery. Continue to loop around the very edge of the rock ledge for additional views.

.6   Arrive back at the loop trail intersection and bear left.

.8   Return to the Chestoa View parking area.

Mile 323. Bear Den Overlook (3,359 feet)

The construction of the parkway overlook destroyed the rock formation that once served as a black bear home. Linville Mountain is directly across from the overlook, and the Black Mountains can be seen in the distance.

Mile 324.7. Bear Den Road

Mile 324.7. Little Table Rock Mountain Trail
(N 35°53.993 W 81°59.004) Map 44

> *Length: 4.2 miles circuit*
> *Difficulty: Moderately strenuous*

Little Table Rock Mountain is adjacent to the BRP (it shares nearly a mile along the parkway's border) and is another of the Stanback Trails (see mile 221.8 Saddle Mountain Trail for more information). Although the route can be steep at times and quite overgrown in some places (you may want to do this hike after the vegetation has died back in late fall and winter), the trail does rise to the 4,080-foot summit atop the Eastern Continental Divide for nicely rewarding views of the Little North Toe River Valley. It may also be possible to see Roan Mountain on clear days, while Linville Mountain can be seen when leaves are off the trees.

The trailhead is accessed by turning onto Bear Den Mountain Road (NC 1126) from BRP Mile 324.7. Go .1 mile to the stop sign, continue onto Humpback Mountain Road (NC 1128), and turn right onto gravel White Rock Road in .5 mile. Pay close attention, as you want to turn left at the next intersection (that may or may not be marked with a sign indicating access to NC Wildlife Resources Commission lands). Go past a couple of houses to the designated parking area.

Mile 325.9. Heffner Gap Overlook (3,057 feet)

The view takes in Honeycutt Mountain on the left and Whitenin' Spur on the right.

Mile 325.9. Overmountain Victory National Historic Trail (also known as the Rose Creek Trail) (N 35°52.682 W 81°59.448) Map 44

Length: 2.6 miles, out-and-back
Difficulty: moderate

A short distance from Heffner Gap Overlook is a brown and white Overmountain Victory National Historic Trailhead (OVNHT) marker. The route, which follows an old one-lane dirt road, goes 2.6 miles out-and-back through land administered as a game preserve (be aware hunting is permitted at certain times of the year) by the North Carolina Wildlife Resources Commission. The area traversed by the trail is heavily wooded, with long stretches of rhododendron thickets. A variety of wildlife has been spotted, including deer and black bear. The trail comes out at the McKinney Gap Road, which is very narrow and on a curve that does not have any room for parking.

The old roadway that the trail follows pre-dates extensive European settlement and is one of the few stretches left of the original route used by the Overmountain men in 1780. On September 29, 1780, several hundred horse-mounted patriot militia led by colonels Isaac Shelby and John Sevier traversed this route, heading toward the area of North Cove. The following day they continued over Dobson Knob and along Linville Gorge to join up with several hundred additional horse-mounted patriot militia led by Colonel William Campbell at the junction of the North Fork of the Catawba River and Paddy's Creek. Ultimately, these men, plus others who joined along the way, defeated Major Patrick Ferguson and his army of loyalists at Kings Mountain, South Carolina, on October 7, 1780. Historians say the battle helped lead to the colonies' victory over the British at Yorktown a year later.

The Overmountain Victory National Historic Trail travels through Virginia, Tennessee, North Carolina, and South Carolina for approximately 220 miles, retracing the route of the patriots. It actually has three designated routes. One is the true historic route (often inaccessible in places), a walking route (portions are still being built), and a

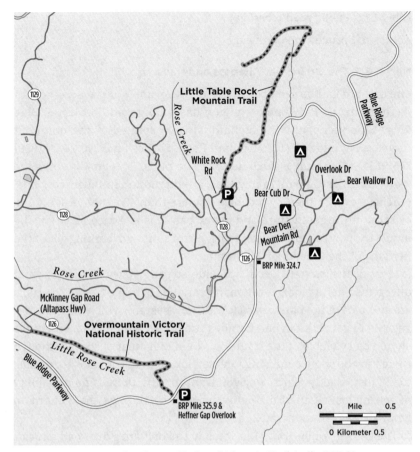

Map 44. Overmountain Victory National Historic Trail (mile 325.9)

route along public highways. See BRP miles 330.9 and 333.9 for other walkable sections of the trail.

Please note: As this book went to press, there were plans to build another walkable section of the OVNHT on the east side of Heffner Gap, but no date for its construction had been established. *Also note:* this is one of the Stanback Trails, constructed on land purchased, in part, with a large donation from Fred and Alice Stanback. See mile 221.8 for more information.

Mile 327.3. North Cove Overlook (2,815 feet)

Another view of Honeycutt Mountain, standing in front of Linville Mountain.

Mile 327.5. Public road crossing

Access to Spruce Pine (5 miles).

Mile 328.3. The Orchard at Altapass and trails. Map 45

The orchard can be seen below the parkway and may be accessed directly from the BRP. Apple growing has a long tradition in the Blue Ridge Mountains, and the orchard is now operated by the nonprofit Altapass Foundation (1025 Orchard Road, Spruce Pine, NC 28777, 828-765-9531; www.altapassorchard.org). The public is invited to hike the many trails, participate in hayrides, attend mountain music concerts, purchase or pick their own choice of more than 40 varieties of apples, or shop in the retail store and snack bar. This is a nice place for the family to spend an entire day hiking, picnicking, and learning about the heritage of the Blue Ridge Mountains.

Most of the orchard's trails provide soaring views to the east and offer a fascinating look at the many varieties of apple trees. (The trails are also part of the parkway's TRACK Trails system, which has been developed to get children and families connected with nature. Brochures should be available at the trailhead—or at kidsinparks.com.) Although there may be some confusing intersections where you may not be able to tell just exactly which way you want to turn, there is no possibility of getting lost as all of the pathways wander through the orchard on what are easy to moderate grades:

The easy 1.5-mile Trail #1 is actually the orchard's dirt road, providing access to the other trails and the orchard's retail store.

At a little more than 2 miles, the Loop Trail, Trail #2, is the longest. It is rated moderate as it descends into the woodlands at the lower reaches of the orchard before ascending back to Trail #1.

The Short-Cut Trail, Trail #3, connects to Trail #2 and wanders between the apple trees and open views obtained from a plot of planted blueberry bushes.

Appropriately named, the Delicious Trail, Trail #4, passes by numerous red and golden delicious apple trees along its .3 mile length.

Branching off Trail #2 near the northern lower edge of the orchard, the Virginia Beauty Trail, Trail #5, is a circuit route of .4 mile wandering by its namesake apple trees.

Also a circuit trail, the Transparent Trail, Trail #6, also branches off Trail #2 but at the more-southern upper edge of the orchard. Yellow Transparent (also known as Lodi) apples are primarily used to make applesauce.

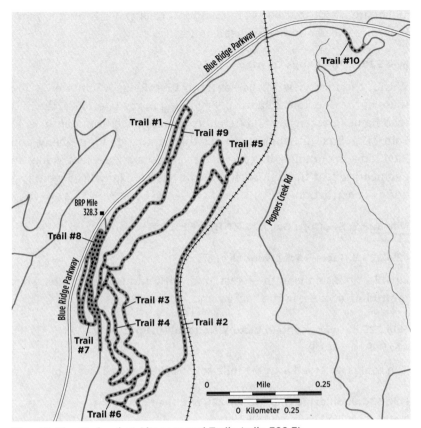

Map 45. The Orchard at Altapass and Trails (mile 328.3)

The short, .25 mile Butterfly Trail, Trail #7, loops around the Butterfly Garden (with a bench to rest and enjoy the view, flowers, and butterflies) at the upper edge of the orchard.

Located just below the BRP, Trail #8 is a circuit of .6 mile with views across most of the orchard.

Nearly flat, the York Trail, Trail #9, begins at the trailhead parking lot and, of course, goes by numerous apple trees before going slightly uphill through a gorgeous patch of jewelweed to end at the Orchard Road in .6 mile.

Located on the Orchard Road .7 mile north of the main trailhead parking, the Cemetery Trail is a .25 mile steep out-and-back pathway through a towering rhododendron tunnel to the grave of Charley McKinney (ca. 1780–ca. 1858). He was the area's first resident and fathered

48 children with four wives. In addition to his grave, I counted more than three dozen unmarked headstones.

Mile 328.6. The Loops Overlook (2,980 feet)

Within the nice view of the southern Blue Ridge Mountains is the route of the Clinchfield Railroad. Beginning in the late 1800s, the railroad hauled passengers and freight (primarily coal) from Kentucky to South Carolina. Although it crosses the Cumberland, Allegheny, and Blue Ridge Mountains, its route never exceeds a 2 percent grade, an engineering feat through such difficult terrain. Many lives were lost during construction.

Mile 329.5. Swafford Gap. NC RT 1113 (3,852 feet)

Mile 329.8. Table Rock Overlook (2,870 feet)

Linville Mountain is in the foreground, with unmistakable Table Rock protruding above it in the background.

Mile 329.8. Overmountain Victory National Historic Trail
(see BRP mile 330.9)

The trail is accessed about .1 mile south of Table Rock Overlook.

Mile 330.9. Gillespie Gap. NC RT 226 and the Museum of North Carolina Minerals (2,819 feet)

Museum of North Carolina Minerals, visitor center, small gift shop, restrooms, and water. Access to Spruce Pine (6 miles), Marion (14 miles), and NC RT 226A and Little Switzerland (3 miles).

The Museum of North Carolina Minerals (open year-round) was a small place with barely enough space to display its tiny and cramped exhibits when I first visited. However, a million-dollar renovation around the turn of the twenty-first century turned it into a larger and first-class museum with interactive displays. The mountains in the area contain some of the richest deposits of minerals and gems in America, and the museum includes samples of more than 300 varieties. It also documents the importance of the mining industry to the local economy (but very little about the environmental impact). Other exhibits will help you gain insight into the geological history along the parkway.

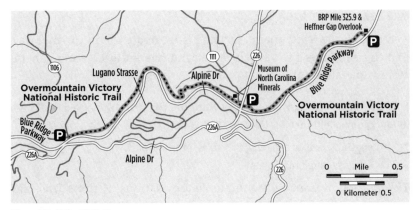

Map 46. Mile 330.9

Mile 330.9. Overmountain Victory National Historic Trail (see mile 325.9 for background information) (N 35°51.167 W 82°03.072) Map 46

> *Length: 1.3 miles, one way; 2.6 miles, out-and-back*
> *Difficulty: moderate*

An easy to moderate, walkable section of the Overmountain Victory National Historic Trail goes northward from NC RT 226 across from the Museum of North Carolina Minerals to about .1 mile south of the Table Rock Overlook (BRP mile 329). Paralleling the BRP on land that was the route that the Overmountain men took north after splitting their forces at Gillespie Gap, the pathway meanders through a mature hardwood forest with one of the nicest stands of tulip poplar trees found along the parkway. Deer, turkeys, and black rat snakes have been frequently seen.

Please note: Heavy understory vegetation growth may overtake the trail in summer. You may want to consider hiking it late in the year. Also note that there is another section of the Overmountain Victory National Historic Trail that may be accessed from the minerals museum. However, it is described from BRP mile 333.9 as the walking is easier from that point.

Mile 333.4. Little Switzerland Tunnel

The 542-foot tunnel, with a minimum height of 14 feet, 4 inches, is the first one visitors encounter in North Carolina as they head southward.

Mile 333.9. NC RT 226A

Access to Little Switzerland. Lodging is located close to the parkway, and the settlement of Little Switzerland has an interesting general store and restaurant.

Mile 333.9. Overmountain Victory National Historic Trail (see mile 325.9 for background information) (N 35°50.994 W 82°04.336). Map 44

> *Length: 1.9 miles one way; 3.8 miles, out-and-back*
> *Difficulty: moderately easy*

This portion of the Overmountain Victory National Historic Trail may be accessed by exiting the BRP at mile 333.9 and turning left (northward) onto NC 226 A. Continue 1.4 miles and make a left onto Leatherwood Road. The trailhead is on the dirt road on the right immediately after you go through the underpass of the BRP. The Overmountain Victory men's route was actually along what is now NC RT 226A, but because there is no room to build a trail near the road, the pathway is on parkway land.

Volunteers have done a nice job of constructing this trail with many switchbacks to ease negotiating the small changes in elevation. In addition, abundant wildflowers—such as yellow lady slipper, false Solomon's seal, black cohosh, mayapple, bee balm, and trillium—add to the beauty of the hike. (Stinging nettle can also be abundant in summer.)

Marked by white triangle blazing, the trail ascends the dirt road, but it soon veers onto a narrow footpath on a spur ridge of towering trees. Bird songs are plentiful here in the early morning. At about 1 mile, the route begins to descend through rhododendron to arrive at the North Carolina Minerals Museum parking lot at 1.9 miles. All in all, an enjoyable—and recommended—walk in the woods.

Mile 336.3. Gooch Gap and public road access

Mile 336.8. Wildacres Tunnel

The 330-foot tunnel (minimum height is 13 feet, 1 inch) is named for the nearby Wildacres Retreat, started in the 1920s by Thomas Dixon, whose book *The Clansman* was turned into one of the world's first feature movies, the controversial *Birth of a Nation*.

Mile 337.2. Deer Lick Gap Overlook (3,452 feet)

Linville Mountain is the ridgeline behind Wood Mountain directly across from the overlook.

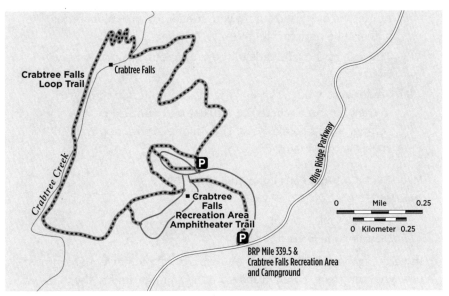

Map 47. Crabtree Falls Loop Trail (mile 339.5)

Mile 338.8. Three Knobs Overlook (3,880 feet)

The Black Mountains are seen in the distance.

Mile 339.5. Crabtree Falls Recreation Area Campground

Mile 339.5 Crabtree Falls Recreation Area Amphitheater Trail [BRP 101]
(N 35°48.770 W 82°08.607) Map 47

> *Length: .22 mile, one way; .44 mile, out-and-back*
> *Difficulty: easy leg stretcher*

Like so many other connector trails in the parkway's developed areas, this one is often overlooked. However, do not do so. It is a nice, easy leg stretcher with an abundance of wildflowers, especially in midsummer.

Also contained within the Crabtree Falls Recreation Area are the park service campground (3,760 feet) and a picnic area.

.0   Descend on the paved pathway where tulip poplars tower above and the understory is made up of small locust trees, rhododendron bushes, fire pinks, and black cohosh.

.05   The amphitheater is to the left; stay to the right and ascend gradually along the dirt route. This small plot of open space is crowded with milkweed and butterfly weed that attract numerous butterflies in midsummer. A few ripe blueberries will also be here for the picking.

.18   The trail to the left leads to the campground's Loop A. Stay right.

.22   Spiderwort, wild geranium, and hoary mountain mint grow in the open area where the trail comes to an end next to the campground's Loop B road. The Crabtree Falls Loop Trail [BRP 102] is across the road.

Mile 339.5. Crabtree Falls Loop Trail [BRP 102]
(N 35°48.928 W 82°08.732) Map 47

Length: 2.5 miles, circuit
Difficulty: strenuous

In early spring the abundance and variety of wildflowers are almost overwhelming as the trail drops from the campground to the falls—at 90 feet one of the best along the parkway. Be forewarned, however; the climb back up from the falls is strenuous.

.0   Descend from a parking area in the campground on a wide and graveled path. Watch for yellow lady slippers, dwarf iris, mayapple, buttercup, and false hellebore.

.15   Loop trail intersection; bear right.

.4   Pass by a bench and descend some steps. The falls soon become audible.

.5   Cross a water run on a wooden plank and descend 45 stone steps.

.7   Pass by another bench, continuing to descend on a switchback.

.9   Arrive at Crabtree Falls, which plunges down a rhododendron-, hemlock- and birch-lined rock facing. Walk the short side trail to stand just below the falls to experience the power and force of the falling water. Return to the main trail and cross the stream on a wooden bridge. Ascend on steps and then on switchbacks bordered by bloodroot, Solomon's seal, and ferns.

1.0   Pass by a bench and, in a few steps as you ascend on a switchback, be looking for a couple of jack-in-the pulpits. Ascend steeply below a rock facing.

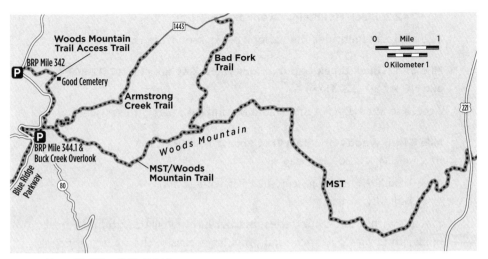

Map 48. Miles 342–344.1

1.1 Pass by another bench as the ascent becomes a little more gradual.

1.2 At a small waterfall in the creek, the pathway begins, once again, to ascend steeply.

1.3 Cross the stream on a wooden bridge and, in a few hundred feet, cross it again as the rhododendron-lined creek drops in pretty little cascades.

1.6 Reach the top of a ridgeline and descend for a few steps. Ascend and pass by a wonderful field of white trillium.

1.8 Cross the stream.

2.0 Bench.

2.1 Intersection. Loop B of the campground is to the right. Bear left, ascend, and then walk on a level trail through rhododendron tunnels.

2.4 Loop trail intersection. Bear right and ascend.

2.5 Arrive back at the parking area in the campground.

Mile 340.2. Crabtree Falls picnic area

Restrooms and water.

Mile 342.1. Victor Road

Mile 342.2. Black Mountains Overlook (3,892 feet)

The signpost identifies the various peaks seen from the overlook.

Mile 344.1. Buck Creek Gap Overlook (a parking area on NC RT 80) and NC RT 80 (3,373 feet)

Access to Micaville (14 miles) and Marion (14 miles; full services).

Mile 344.1. Woods Mountain Trail Access Trail [BRP 103]
(N 35°46.234 W 82°09.858) Map 48

> *Length: 2.1 miles, one way; 4.2 miles, out-and-back*
> *Difficulty: moderate*

Staying within BRP boundaries, but bordering Pisgah National Forest lands, an unpaved service road provides access to the forest service's primitive Woods Mountain Trail.

Even though it is just a dirt road, the Woods Mountain Trail Access Trail is, nonetheless, a worthwhile walk. Its ascents and descents are gradual and bordered by rhododendron, dogwood, and galax. The road passes through a plush hardwood forest, and the changing leaves make this a very colorful jaunt in the fall.

Although the road begins and ends at points on the BRP (miles 344.1 and 342), the route is only clearly marked to the point where the Mountains-to-Sea and Woods Mountain Trails go off to the right at .7 mile. If you are adventurous and feel comfortable walking a route that requires some navigation skills, the rest of the walk is just as rewarding and will provide you with a sense of accomplishment in completing it. You could be dropped off at one end and picked up at the other, refreshed by the natural world and ready to drive a few more miles along the parkway.

The Mountains-to-Sea Trail (see Chapter 1) follows portions of this route and the Woods Mountain Trail, from Buck Creek Gap to US RT 221 at the Woodlawn Rest Area.

.0 Exit the parkway at mile 344.1 and immediately park at the Buck Creek Overlook on NC RT 80. Follow the old, possibly very overgrown dirt road uphill and turn right to parallel the BRP on the Mountains-to-Sea Trail through a hardwood forest. (If the old road is too overgrown, you could just start the hike on the north side of the BRP overpass over NC RT 80.)

.3   Swing around a spur ridge as the road becomes lined with rhododendron. The pungent smell of galax assaults your sense of smell.

.5   The road levels out and then begins to gradually descend.

.7   Intersection.

▸ The Woods Mountain [FS 218] and Mountains-to-Sea Trails bear right and run together along the ridgeline of Woods Mountain, with the Mountains-to-Sea Trail crossing US RT 221 in 12 miles. Along the way, the route junctions with two other forest service trails—Armstrong Creek [FS 223] and Bad Fork [FS 227]. All of these trails are primitive and receive little maintenance. Camping is allowed anywhere along them.

Continue to the left if you are going to accomplish this entire hike.

.9   Swing around another spur ridge and continue to ascend. The BRP is almost directly below you.

1.3   Avoid the grassy woods road that comes in from the right.

1.4   Pass by a small radio relay antenna and in 200 feet avoid the dirt road to the right.

1.5   At the sight of the Good Cemetery, avoid another spur of the dirt road that comes in from the right. Descend gradually.

1.8   Reach a gap and ascend.

1.9   Level out and then ascend slightly to the parkway.

2.1   Arrive at BRP mile 342.

Mile 344.5. Twin Tunnel

The northernmost Twin Tunnel is 300 feet long and has a minimum height of 16 feet.

Mile 344.7. Twin Tunnel

This tunnel is a little longer at 401 feet but not as high, with a minimum height of 14 feet, 7 inches.

Mile 345.3. Singecat Ridge Overlook (3,406 feet)

Mackey Knob is to the right; Onion Mountain, to the left. You may be able to make out Lake Tahoma in the valley below—if the overlook's vegetation has recently been maintained.

Mile 345.3. Mountains-to-Sea Trail (N 35°45.384 W 82°10.596).
See Chapter 1.

Mile 347.2. Big Laurel Mountain Viaduct

Mile 347.6. Big Laurel Gap (4,048 feet)

FSR 482 and access to the Pisgah National Forest's Curtis Creek Campground.

Mile 347.9. Hewat Overlook (4,175 feet)

Spectacular view of the length of the Mount Mitchell and Black Mountains ridgeline.

Mile 348.8. Curtis Valley Overlook (4,460 feet)

The natural rock wall across from the overlook is topped by some good leaf colors in the fall.

Mile 349. Rough Ridge Tunnel

At 150 feet, this is the parkway's shortest tunnel. Minimum height is 13 feet, 9 inches.

Mile 349.2. Licklog Ridge Overlook (4,602 feet)

A grand panoramic vista that takes in Mackey Knob and Chestnut Mountain closest to the overlook, with the distinctive profiles of Hawksbill, Table Rock, and Grandfather Mountains identifiable in the distance. A great place to be for the sunrise and/or to watch the fog rise from the valleys to wrap around the many ridgelines receding to the far horizon.

Mile 349.9. Mount Mitchell Overlook (4,821 feet)

Another grand view of eastern America's tallest mountain.

Mile 350.4. Green Knob Overlook (4,761 feet)

The view is into the valley created by the Catawba River.

Mile 350.4. Lost Cove Ridge Trail (also known as Green Knob Trail)
[FS 182] (N 35°43.056 W 82°13.373) Maps 49 & 50

> *Length: 3.1 miles, one way; 6.2 miles, out-and-back*
> *Difficulty: moderate; moderately strenuous if hiked in the opposite*
> *   direction than the one described*

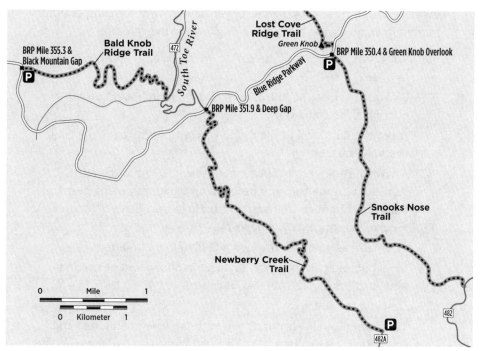

Map 49. Miles 350.4-355

The Lost Cove Trail, a forest service trail that begins on BRP property, rises for the first .5 mile from the parkway to the Green Knob Lookout for views of prominent Mount Mitchell and other peaks and ridges of the Black Mountain range. The trail then enters Pisgah National Forest to begin a long, gradual descent along an undulating ridgeline. (Once you leave BRP property at the lookout tower, camping is permitted anywhere along the trail. Good sites, however, are very limited.) The route passes through varying stands of evergreens and hardwoods, with Mount Mitchell visible much of the way. It ends at the forest service's Black Mountain campground on FSR 472.

The campground and far trailhead may be reached by automobile by driving south on the parkway from the Green Knob Overlook. Exit at BRP mile 351.9 in Deep Gap to follow unpaved FSR 472 as it drops along scenic South Toe River. The campground is 5 miles from the parkway. (Camping is also permitted along the forest service road.)

If you are staying in the forest service campground, the Lost Cove Ridge Trail would make a fine walk for the latter part of the day. Be dropped off to begin the hike a few hours before sunset, saunter down the ridge watching shadows grow longer, and arrive at the campground in time to enjoy dinner and an evening around the campfire.

.0   Walk northward along the parkway from the Green Knob Overlook.

.1   Diagonally cross the BRP and ascend via switchbacks on a possibly overgrown trail.

.4   Avoid the faint trail to the right and continue straight; the trail becomes steeper.

.5   Arrive on Green Knob. The lookout tower is just to the left. Bear right on the trail and descend on a pathway being over-taken by rhododendron and mountain laurel. Views of Mount Mitchell continue as you descend.

.6   Be careful as you pass through a field of loose boulders.

.75 Level out and pass by a few small spots that could be used for tent sites (no water available, of course).

.85 Descend steeply.

1.1 The descent mellows out as you enter an evergreen forest and proceed via switchbacks. Trail is lined with false hellebore.

1.2 Descend steeply for a short while only to level out a little later.

1.5 The trail makes a hard turn to the right and resumes the steep descent for .1 mile before leveling out in a lovely evergreen forest.

1.7 Ascend for the first time since leaving the lookout tower.

1.8 Reach the top of the rise and descend through rhododendron, enjoying the sweet and pungent odor of the galax covering the ground.

2.0 Descend steeply to reach a small gap and walk level for a short distance.

2.1 Rise steeply.

2.3 Reach the top of a rise where Mount Mitchell is clearly visible. Descend.

2.7 Level out and then descend gradually through rhododendron tunnels beneath towering evergreens.

2.8 The sound of the river is clearly audible.

3.0 Turn right and descend on long switchbacks.

3.1 Arrive at the forest service's Black Mountain campground.

Mile 350.4. Snooks Nose Trail [FS 211] (N 35°43.056 W 82°13.373) Map 49

> *Length: approximately 4 miles, one way; 8 miles, out-and-back*
> *Difficulty: strenuous*

As this trail does not receive regular maintenance, it may be hard to locate. Those who need a clearly defined pathway may want to forgo hiking it. Look to the east of the parkway and you'll eventually find an indication of the beginning of the route from the middle of the Green Knob Overlook. It descends a rugged ridgeline (with a few views) to FSR 482 at the edge of Curtis Creek Campground. Camping is prohibited on BRP property, but it is permitted on national forest land. Suitable sites are limited and may not be encountered until near the end of the trail.

The Curtis Creek campground is reached by automobile by driving north on the parkway. In Big Laurel Gap, BRP mile 347.6, turn right onto FSR 482 and descend several miles to the campground.

Mile 351.9. Deep Gap, FSR 472, and access to Black Mountain Campground (4,284 feet)

The forest service's Black Mountain Campground may be reached by exiting the BRP at mile 351.9 and following unpaved FSR 472 for 5 miles as it drops along scenic South Toe River. Camping is also permitted along the forest service road.

Mile 351.9. Newberry Creek Trail [FS 210]
(N 35°42.633 W 82°14.622) Map 49

> *Length: 2 miles, one way (plus an additional 1.5 miles on FSR 482A);*
>   *4 miles, out-and-back (if FSR 482A is not walked)*
> *Difficulty: moderate; moderately strenuous if hiked in the opposite*
>   *direction than the one described*
> *Recommended*

Another forest service pathway, the Newberry Creek Trail (sometimes referred to as the Deep Gap Trail) makes long, fairly gentle switchbacks to enter a bowl nestled between Chute Branch and Newberry Creek. Woodpeckers and other birds seem to be a little more numerous here than in many other parts of the national forest. Abundant at the beginning of the trail, ferns, mosses, and other plants of the understory become more lush as the route loses elevation. This trail is recommended because of the ease of walking (although you may have a hard time finding the beginning of the trail), beauty of the forest, and perception of isolation.

Once you are beyond BRP property, camping is permitted anywhere along the way. Several nice sites may be found near the end of the trail.

Automobile access to the far trailhead is obtained by driving north on the parkway to Big Laurel Gap, BRP mile 347.6. Descend east on FSR 482, go past the Forest Service's Curtis Creek campground, and turn right onto FSR 482A. This road ascends through the first tract of national forest land purchased under the Weeks Act on March 1, 1911. Arrive at a gate, which is locked. You will need to walk the final distance of approximately 1.5 miles to the trailhead.

.0   Directly across the BRP from FSR 472, begin to descend through a hardwood forest on a narrow pathway that may be unmarked and hard to find.

.2   Switchback to the left and listen for woodpeckers and song-birds, which appear to enjoy this portion of the forest. The trail is barely defined in some places.

.4   Switchback to the right among a number of dogwood trees, and just before coming to a water run, make a switchback to the left.

.5   Switchback right. The vegetation continues to grow lusher as you progress.

.6   Make three more switchbacks.

.8   Switchback right under a forest of poplar and maple.

1.1   Cross a good-sized water run and then pass over a spur ridge.

1.2   Begin walking through rhododendron and mountain laurel as galax becomes the dominant ground cover.

1.4   Switchback right and then left.

1.7   Cross another water run. The trailside vegetation has grown even lusher.

1.8   Walk next to a creek and by an old structure.

2.0   Cross the creek and come to FSR 482A. Follow the roadway for 1.5 miles to a gate and the parking area.

Mile 352.4. Bald Knob parking area (4,500 feet).
When the overlook has been maintained, there is a wide-ranging view of near or distant mountains and valleys.

Mile 354

It is near this point that the parkway leaves the Blue Ridge Mountains and begins a short traverse of the Black Mountains.

Mile 354.8. Toe River Gap (5,168 feet)

The area around the gap is a good place to possibly see Blackburnian warblers.

Mile 355. Bald Knob Ridge Trail [FS 186] (N 35°42.913 W 82°16.447) Map 49

> *Length: 2.8 miles, one way; 5.6 miles, out-and-back*
> *Difficulty: moderate*

Another forest service trail, this is an excellent walk into large and magnificent stands of virgin spruce and fir. The vegetation is so lush in this forest primeval that at times you could almost believe you were traipsing through a deep and dark rain forest. Hardwoods replace the evergreens once the trail begins to descend on long, gentle switchbacks to FSR 472.

Camping is allowed anywhere along this trail once you get past BRP property (about .2 mile into the walk). Several pleasant, grassy, and level spots would serve as favorable campsites.

You can reach the trail's end by automobile by following the BRP north from Black Mountain Gap to Deep Mountain Gap at BRP mile 351.9. Descend on FSR 472. The trailhead is just beyond a wide curve where the road crosses the South Toe River for the first time—just one mile from the BRP.

.0   Descend to the left from the parking area in Black Mountain Gap into an evergreen forest.

.1   The vegetation is already quite verdant and lush as the trail becomes level for a short distance.

.2   Descend.

.4   There are some good wintertime views to the right of the trail as the descent becomes more gradual. Also, several level grassy spots could make good tent sites.

.8   Enter a virgin forest.

1.1   Emerge from the virgin timber and enter a rhododendron tunnel.

1.3   Descend a little more rapidly.

1.5 Pass through more rhododendron tunnels; swing around the ridgeline. Descend via long switchbacks in a forest that becomes progressively more hardwoods than evergreens.

2.0 Follow the old road for a very short distance and then leave it.

2.4 Again follow an old road for just a very short distance. The tumbling waters of South Toe River become audible.

2.6 Turn right onto a wide old road.

2.8 Arrive at FSR 472.

Mile 355.3. Black Mountain Gap and Ridge Junction Overlook
(5,160 feet)

The view is of the Black Mountains descending into the South Toe River Valley.

Trails of Mount Mitchell State Park, Blue Ridge Parkway Mile 355.3

NC RT 128 ascends from the parkway to enter Mount Mitchell State Park. The park, designated as North Carolina's first state park in 1915 (primarily to preserve what was left of a magnificent virgin forest after rampant logging had destroyed most of it), offers a restaurant, museum, concession stand, and several hiking trails. The park's campground has only a few tent sites, so it is best to make reservations in advance on the Internet at www.reserveamerica.com or by calling 877-772-6762.

The highest point in the eastern United States, Mount Mitchell is the focal point of the Black Mountain range. The mountains are so named because the dark green spruce and fir covering the slopes appear almost black when viewed from a distance. The area is reminiscent of the alpine environment of Canada.

The trails of the state park emanate from Mount Mitchell's 6,684-foot summit (parking area: N 35°45.993 W 82°15.910). One follows the main crest of the Black Mountain range at more than 6,000 feet in elevation. It offers spectacular views of three intersecting mountain ranges—the Blue Ridge, Black, and Great Craggy Mountains. Other trails connect the park office with the restaurant and tent camping area and join with longer trails in the Pisgah National Forest.

Mount Mitchell's observation tower rises above the trees for views from the highest point east of the Mississippi River.

Backcountry camping is prohibited in the state park. However, as stated, park trails do connect with national forest trails where camping is permitted. Automobiles may be left overnight in the state park but must be registered.

More information about the state park may be obtained by contacting

Mount Mitchell State Park
2338 State Highway 128
Burnsville, NC 28714
828-675-4611
www.ncparks.gov

♿ **Summit Trail** Map 50

Length: .3 mile, out-and-back
Difficulty: easy

The paved pathway ascends from the upper parking lot to the mountain summit's observation tower, where, it is claimed, on clear days you can see more than 75 miles in all directions. Do not miss the chance to enjoy such a spectacular place while putting forth so little effort.

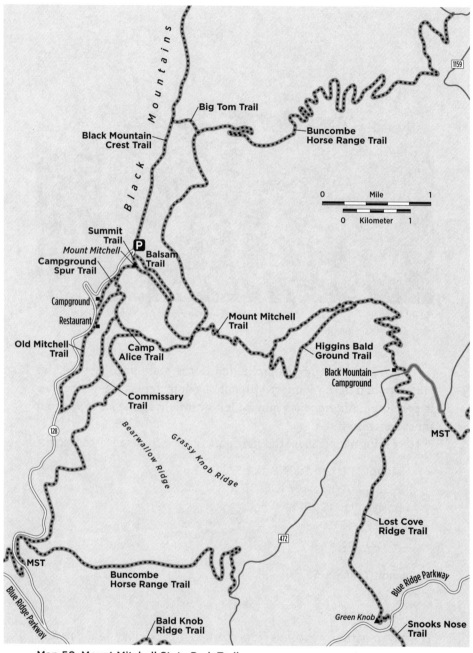

Map 50. Mount Mitchell State Park Trails

Balsam Trail Map 50

Length: .8 mile, circuit
Difficulty: moderately easy
Highly recommended

Here's a chance to become intimate with the mountain's Canada-like environment. Plaques placed along the rocky and rooty pathway provide information about the plants and animals that live here. Among the things you may learn: the little Michuax's saxifrage, whose name means "stone breaker," actually splits up large rocks, turning them into soil; the golden-crowned kinglet aids in the health of the forest by eating insects and their eggs from leaves and bark; and the Black Mountains are a spur ridge of the Blue Ridge Mountains and only about 15 miles long.

The Balsam Trail intersects the Mountains-to-Sea Trail (see Chapter 1).

Old Mitchell Trail Map 50

Length: 2 miles, one way; 4 miles, out-and-back
Difficulty: moderately strenuous

Passing by the restaurant and campground, and running along the ridge through the spruce and fir forest, the trail connects the park office with the Summit Trail. Good views of the summit and out across the neighboring ridgelines. The entire route is more than 6,000 feet above sea level.

Campground Spur Trail Map 50

Length: .4 mile, one way; .8 mile, out-and-back
Difficulty: moderate

This trail branches off the Old Mitchell Trail and connects the campground to the main park road.

Commissary Trail Map 50

Length: 1 mile, one way; 2 miles, out-and-back
Difficulty: moderately easy

Now a gravel park service road, the Commissary Trail follows the route of an old railroad grade from the park office to the Camp Alice Trail. Good views along the way, especially from the open fields on Bearwallow Ridge and Grassy Knob.

Camp Alice Trail Map 50

Length: .75 mile, one way; 1.5 miles, out-and-back
Difficulty: strenuous

Dropping steeply from its connection with the Old Mitchell Trail, the Camp Alice Trail passes through the high-altitude forest to the site of a logging camp that was active in the 1920s.

There are three forest service trails that connect with those of the state park. Intersecting other forest service trails, these routes provide miles and miles of pathways to explore the distinctive area around Mount Mitchell. A couple of them have designated campsites, while camping is permitted along any of them once you leave state park property.

More information about these trails may be obtained from

Appalachian Ranger District
632 Manor Road
Mars Hill, NC 28754
828-689-9694
www.fs.fed.us

The strenuous, 18-mile **Buncombe Horse Range Trail [FS 191]** (Map 50) (a part of the Mountains-to-Sea Trail) starts on lower elevations from NC RT 1159 near the forest service's Carolina Hemlocks Recreation Area on NC RT 80, rises close to 3,000 feet through open fields and into the spruce and fir forest near Mount Mitchell's main crest, and then descends to end on NC RT 42, a few miles west of BRP mile 351.9. Along the way it has connections with the forest service's Big Tom Gap Trail [FS 191A] (Map 50) (ascends steeply .4 mile to connect with Black Mountain Crest Trail [FS 179]) as well as the state park's Camp Alice Trail.

Almost 12 miles in length, the **Black Mountain Crest Trail [FS 179]** (Maps 50 & 51) is a strenuous but spectacular hike that traverses terrain across 12 summits with elevations above 6,000 feet. It starts from Mount Mitchell State Park's picnic area (and may be identified as the Deep Gap Trail here), crosses one summit after another, passes by the Big Tom Gap Trail [FS 191A] at 1.5 miles, and arrives at a designated campsite in Deep Gap at 4 miles, where the Colbert Ridge Trail [FS 178] (Map 51) goes right to NC RT 1158 near the Carolina Hemlocks Recreation Area on NC RT 80. At about 6 miles, the Woody Ridge Trail [FS 177] (Map 51) descends steeply to the right for a little more than 2 miles to a parking area near NC RT 1156. The Black Mountain Crest Trail begins a long descent on an old logging route at 7.5 miles and comes to an end on FSR 5578 a few miles south of Burnsville.

Perhaps the most popular trail descending from Mount Mitchell's summit is the strenuous 5.8-mile **Mount Mitchell Trail [FS 190]** (Map 50) (a part of the Mountains-to-Sea Trail; see Chapter 1). Branching off of the state park's Balsam Trail, it passes by the Camp Alice Shelter in 1.7 miles, meets the Buncombe Horse Range Trail [FS 191] at 1.8 miles, and has two junctions with Higgins Bald Ground Trail [FS 190A]. It ends at the forest service's Black Mountain Campground on FSR 472. Be aware that, although this is a great hike and much of it passes through virgin forest, you will experience almost 4,000 feet of elevation change.

Mile 358.5 (5,676.5 feet)

Highest point on the BRP north of Asheville.

Mile 359.8 Walker Knob Overlook (5,317 feet)

The overlook is located in Balsam Gap, the joining point of the Black Mountains and the Great Craggy Mountains. It's also the site of a railroad system that helped harvest timber from the area in the late 1800s and early 1900s.

Mile 359.8 Mountains-to-Sea Trail (N 35°44.904 W 82°20.029).
See Chapter 1.

Mile 359.8. Big Butt Trail [FS 161] (5,317 feet)
(N 35°44.904 W 82°20.029) Map 52

> Length: 6 miles, one way; 12 miles, out-and-back
> Difficulty: moderately strenuous

This pathway is one of the few forest service trails connecting to the parkway that has a number of spots that would be suitable campsites. One even has water available and would make a great place for a base camp. There are no other trails connecting with the Big Butt Trail, but do not let this deter you from exploring the area on your own. Just so you will know: A "butt" has nothing to do with the human body but, rather, is a term used to describe a prominent rise of land that drops off abruptly.

The trail descends through a variety of vegetations and terrains. The pathway stays on the ridgeline, but the ridge is at some points narrow, rocky, and steep and at others wide, lushly vegetated, and gently rolling. Large stands of evergreens, complete with a luxuriant understory

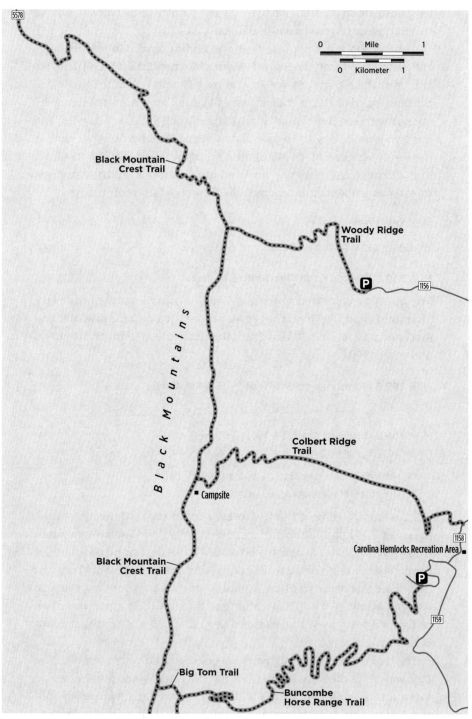

Map 51. Black Mountain Crest Trail

of ferns and moist mosses, evoke memories of rain forests in the Pacific Northwest. A diversity of hardwoods assures a colorful walk when leaves begin to change in the fall. Don't be surprised, in the spring, to meet a few locals carrying trowels and large sacks. They are gathering a delicious Southern Appalachian delicacy. Ramps grow profusely in large gardens along much of the length of this trail. You might even be tempted to try a few with your evening meal.

The trail ends on NC RT 197 in Cane River Gap. Reaching this far trailhead from the BRP involves quite a bit of driving. Head south on the parkway to Bee Tree Gap, BRP mile 367.6. Exit the BRP and descend on unpaved FSR 63 (usually closed from January 1 to April 1) through a lovely rhododendron and hemlock forest. The dirt road eventually becomes paved NC RT 2178. At the junction with NC RT 2173, turn left onto NC RT 2173 and arrive in the small hamlet of Barnardsville. Bear right onto paved NC RT 197 (which will eventually turn to dirt) for almost 10 miles to come to Cane River Gap. Be alert! There really is nothing here, except a wide pullout at the top of the rise, to identify the trailhead.

Please note: Land to the right of the trail (as viewed when walking in the direction described) is private property.

.0 Begin to the left in the BRP parking area on a pathway behind the trail sign. (Do not mistakenly follow the Mountains-to-Sea Trail [see Chapter 1] that ascends from the middle of the parking area.) Descend through red trillium, mayapple, and Solomon's seal.

.1 Enter an evergreen forest and come onto the ridgeline that you will be following the rest of the way.

.2 Pass by an old hunter's camp in rain forest–type lushness.

.3 Begin ascent to a knob.

.5 Reach the high point of the knob, which is covered by red trillium. Just beyond the knob, several spots would make nice campsites.

.7 Descend on a pathway being overtaken by briers.

.8 Low point in a gap. There are limited views to the right of the trail.

1.4 Having passed through a mossy, evergreen forest, rise and enter hardwoods.

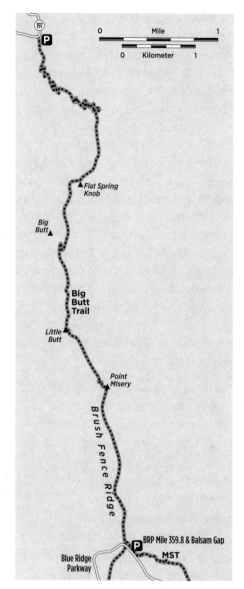

Map 52. Mile 359.8

1.5   At the top of the knob be sure to swing to the left on the blazed trail and not to the right on a faint pathway. Descend steeply via switchbacks. The red trillium is outrageously abundant.

1.8   The descent levels out somewhat.

2.1   Reach a gap where you might find a few level campsites. Ascend steeply on switchbacks along a rock facing of the knob. Be careful—the rock is slippery and dangerous in wet weather.

2.4 The open area on top of the knob permits a wonderful view of Mount Mitchell, the Black Mountain range, and Cane River Valley. Follow the up-and-down undulations of the narrowing ridgeline. There are occasional good views.

2.7 Ascend steeply on an overgrown, but still visible, path.

2.8 Swing to the left side of the ridge. Ramps are plentiful here. Views from the narrow ridge continue to get better as you ascend. Craggy Dome and the Pinnacle may be seen to the south. Heath is crowding in on the pathway.

3.0 Swing to the right of the ridge to miss the summit of Big Butt. Walk along a brier-infested trail and begin to descend.

3.2 Enter wide and rolling Flat Spring Gap with a spring to the right of the trail—a perfect spot to establish a base camp. Red trillium, mayapple, and ramps carpet the forest floor.

3.6 Reach another gap and other good campsites. Ascend and slab to the left of a knob on a pathway that, unless law enforcement action has been taken, is being used and abused by all-terrain vehicles.

3.8 Descend.

4.0 The ridgeline widens out, making a few more nice campsites. The trail is most definitely headed into its final descent.

4.2 The ridgeline narrows.

4.6 Be alert! The all-terrain vehicles have established a trail that cuts straight down the hill to the right. Look for your pathway to the left and descend on a long series of switchbacks.

5.0 Do not become confused by the maze of trails and faint roads. Continue down the ridgeline and rejoin the switchbacks.

5.6 A logging road is visible below. Violets and white violets appear.

5.8 The trail begins to follow a jeep road.

6.0 Arrive at Cane River Gap on NC RT 197.

Mile 361.2 Glassmine Falls Overlook (5,197 feet)
Glassmine Falls is visible from the overlook if you do not wish to walk the short Glassmine Falls Trail [BRP 104] that emanates from the parking area.

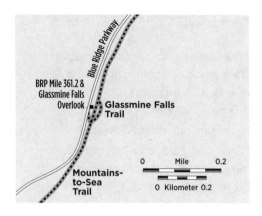

Map 53. Glassmine Falls Trail
(mile 361.2)

Mile 361.2. Glassmine Falls Trail [BRP 104] (5,197 feet)
(N 35°44.060 W 82°20.650) Map 53

> *Length: .1 mile, out-and-back*
> *Difficulty: easy leg stretcher*

A very short walk to a view of Glassmine Falls. The 200-foot falls drops quickly and steeply down the side of Horse Range Ridge. Exploiting an abundant local natural resource, a mica mine operated at the base of the falls in the early part of the twentieth century.

Mile 361.2. Mountains-to-Sea Trail (N 35°44.060 W 82°20.650).
See Chapter 1.

Mile 363.4. Greybeard Mountain Overlook (5,592 feet)

Greybeard is the summit directly across from the overlook.

Mile 363.6. Mountains-to-Sea Trail (N 35°42.656 W 82°21.848).
See Chapter 1.

Trails of the Craggy Gardens Recreation Area, Blue Ridge Parkway Miles 364.1–367.6

The Craggy Gardens are actually small grassy balds intermingled with large heath balds. They are the most easily accessed balds along the BRP. The scientific community still disagrees as to how and why balds exist. They are not above the tree line; many occur well below peaks adorned by spruce and fir. Research data has provided a number of theories attempting to explain this phenomenon, but unfortunately, information also exists to refute each one of these theories. David T. Catlin, in *A Naturalist's Blue Ridge Parkway*, discusses the varying theories.

Whatever the reason for the balds, Catawba rhododendron is the dominant plant in the Craggy Gardens. In mid-June, about a month after the rhododendron has bloomed in the lower elevations of the parkway, the gardens become ablaze with acre upon acre of the plant's pink and purple blossoms. If you are in the area in mid-June to early July, do not pass up the chance to enjoy this dazzling natural display that has delighted visitors from around the world.

One of the recreation area's trails ascends to the 5,840-foot Craggy Pinnacle for a view across the heath balds and out to the surrounding mountains. A self-guiding pathway winds in and among the voluminous rhododendron, and a forest service trail provides access to two tumbling waterfalls.

In addition to the trails, the Craggy Gardens Recreation Area contains a park service visitor center, gift shop, picnic area, and access to the Mountains-to-Sea Trail (see Chapter 1).

Mile 364.1. Craggy Pinnacle Trail [BRP 105] (5,640 feet)
(N 35°42.251 W 82°22.423) Map 54

> *Length: 1.2 miles, out-and-back*
> *Difficulty: moderate*

The Craggy Pinnacle Trail ascends in a true heath bald. Lining the trail are mountain laurel, rhododendron, blueberry, and mountain cranberry—all members of the heath family.

High winds and elevation can sometimes combine to make extraordinary conditions on the exposed summit. The valleys and lower ridgelines may be bathed in warm temperatures and sunshine, while the rhododendron and mountain laurel on the pinnacle are covered in a thick layer of rime ice.

This is also the trail to walk if you want to appreciate the full effect of the gardens in bloom in June and early July.

.0   Begin on the steps in the Craggy Dome Overlook and ascend through rhododendron.

.2   Arrive at an old box spring.

.3   Come to a bench with a grand view to the west. Intersection. Bear right and descend.

.4 Arrive at a view overlooking the visitor center and Craggy Flats. Retrace your steps.

.5 Bear right at the intersection and ascend.

.7 Arrive at the summit for an extensive 360-degree view of the Asheville Reservoir, Craggy Flats, Craggy Dome, Mount Mitchell, Big Butt, and Ogle Meadow. On a clear day you may even be able to see the mountains of Tennessee to the northeast. (Please do not go beyond the viewpoint so as to preserve the fragile environment.) Retrace your steps, staying to the right at the intersection.

1.2 Arrive back at the Craggy Dome Overlook.

Mile 364.4. Craggy Pinnacle Tunnel

The tunnel is 245 feet long; minimum height is 14 feet, 1 inch.

Mile 364.6. Craggy Gardens Visitor Center (5,497 feet)

Gift shop, restrooms, and water. With Craggy Pinnacle on one side of the parkway and Craggy Dome on the other, the long-ranging view westward has the Ivy River Valley below and the Bald Mountains on the North Carolina/Tennessee border in the far distance.

Mile 364.6. Craggy Gardens Self-Guiding Trail [BRP 106]
(N 35°41.967 W 82°22.801) Map 54

> Length: 1 mile, one way (including the Craggy Vista Trail [BRP 107]); 1.8
>   miles, out-and-back (excluding the Craggy Vista Trail on the way back)
> Difficulty: moderate

A pleasant walk from the visitor center to the picnic area, this self-guiding trail winds through rhododendron tunnels and ascends to an observation platform on Craggy Flats. It then descends to the picnic area. Signs identify plant life and discuss the different species of heath.

If you don't mind carrying your supplies, the two shelters (no tables) along the trail might be more desirable spots to enjoy your meal instead of the picnic area. The views are certainly better.

A segment of the Mountains-to-Sea Trail (see Chapter 1) makes use of the Craggy Gardens Self-Guiding Trail.

.0 Begin at the southern end of the visitor center parking area.

.05 Pass by a bench with a limited view. Ascend.

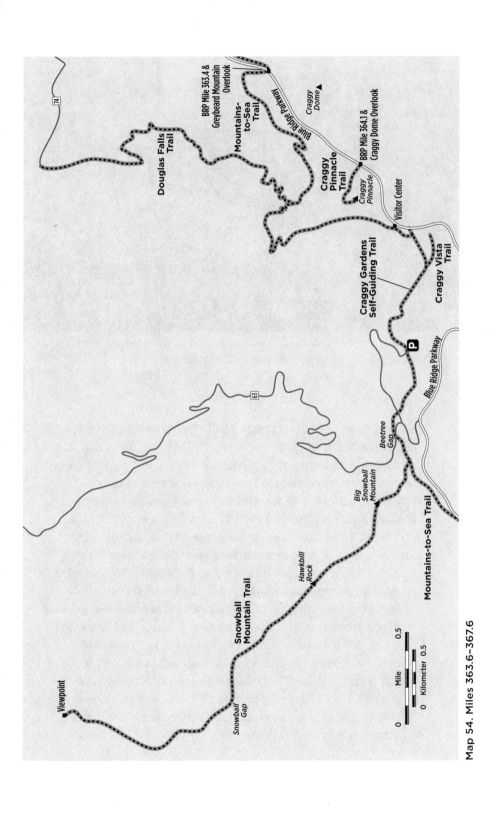

74

BRP Mile 363.4 &
Greybeard Mountain
Overlook

Mountains-
to-Sea
Trail

Douglas Falls
Trail

Blue Ridge Parkway

Craggy
Dome ▲

Craggy
Pinnacle
Trail

BRP Mile 364.1 &
Craggy Dome Overlook

Craggy
Pinnacle

Visitor Center

Craggy Gardens
Self-Guiding Trail

Craggy Vista
Trail

P

Blue Ridge Parkway

63

Beetree
Gap

Big
Snowball
Mountain

Mountains-to-Sea Trail

Hawkbill
Rock

Snowball
Mountain Trail

Viewpoint

Snowball
Gap

0   Mile   0.5

0   Kilometer 0.5

Map 54. Miles 363.6–367.6

At an elevation of more than a mile above sea level, the observation platform on Craggy Pinnacle overlooks the parkway winding below Craggy Gardens.

.1 Intersection.

▶ The 4-mile, strenuous Douglas Falls Trail [FS 162] (also known as the Halfway Trail) is to the right. (The Mountains-to-Sea Trail also follows this route for 1.2 miles before turning right to cross the parkway near Greybeard Mountain Overlook at mile 363.4). The forest service trail descends, steeply in places, to pass by Cascade Falls and Douglas Falls. The trail ends at a parking area on FSR 74. Be advised that most people who utilize this trail hike in from FSR 74 to Douglas Falls and then return the same way. The upper portion of the Douglas Falls Trail is less traveled, rough, and not as well maintained as the lower section.

Reaching the far trailhead on FSR 74 by automobile is rather involved. Drive south on the parkway and exit in Bee Tree Gap, BRP mile 367.6. Descend on dirt FSR 63, which at a lower elevation becomes paved NC RT 2178. Turn right on NC RT 2173, which becomes dirt FSR 74, and ascend to the trailhead. Allow at least 50 to 60 minutes of driving from the parkway to reach this point. (Be aware that both forest service roads are usually closed from January 1 to April 1.)

Stay to the left to continue on the combined Craggy Gardens Self-Guiding and Mountains-to-Sea Trails.

.15 Pass by a spring and another bench.

.3 Arrive in open Craggy Flats with excellent views of Craggy Pinnacle and Craggy Dome. Bear left through stunted rhododendron on the Craggy Vista Trail [BRP 107].

.4 Arrive at the observation platform for a vista to the southeast. Retrace your steps.

.5 Bear left at the intersection and go through the shelter and descend. The view to the east is quite wonderful. Descend.

.6 Enter woods.

.7 Pass by another shelter to the right. The descent becomes a little more gradual.

.8 Swing around the mountain for a different perspective on Craggy Pinnacle. Descend rapidly.

1.0 Pass by a bench and soon arrive in the picnic area, BRP mile 367.6 (N 35°41.985 W 82°23.459) (restrooms and water).

Mile 365.5. Craggy Flats Tunnel

The tunnel is 400 feet long; minimum height is 14 feet, 4 inches.

Mile 367.6. Bee Tree Gap (4,900 feet)

Craggy Gardens picnic area, restrooms, and water. This is also the southern trailhead for the Craggy Gardens Trail Self-Guiding Trail [BRP 106]. See mile 364.6.

Mile 367.6. Bear Pen Gap Trail [BRP 108]
(N 35°41.985 W 82°23.459) Map 54

The short Bear Pen Gap Trail, less than .2 mile in length, has been incorporated into the Mountains-to-Sea Trail (see Chapter 1), so there is no longer a sign identifying it as such. The route connects the Craggy Gardens picnic area to the Craggy Gardens Self-Guiding Trail [BRP 106].

Mile 367.6. Snowball Mountain Trail [FS 170]
(N 35°41.985 W 82°23.459) Map 54

> *Length: 7.5 miles, out-and-back*
> *Difficulty: moderate*

To reach the Snowball Mountain Trail, park in the Craggy Gardens picnic area and take the Mountains-to-Sea Trail (which has incorporated the parkway's Bear Pen Gap Trail [BRP 108] into its route) about .5 mile southward to cross the picnic area entrance road. Within a few hundred feet, turn right onto the (possibly) unmarked Snowball Mountain Trail. It's a steady but well-graded ascent of a little less than a mile to the summit of Big Snowball Mountain with a view of the Black Mountains. Beyond this is a short descent and ascent to the excellent view from Hawkbill Rock of the Great Craggy and Black Mountains to the northeast, and the Reems Creek drainage to the southwest. From this viewpoint, the trail continues on the undulating ridgeline with a drop into Snowball Gap before rising to the summit of Little Snowball Mountain, the site of a former fire tower (taken down and reassembled in the small Big Ivy community nearby). Little Snowball Mountain provides a spectacular 360-degree view.

Mile 367.6. Mountains-to-Sea Trail (N 35°41.985 W 82°23.459). See Chapter 1.

Mile 372.1. Lanes Pinnacle Overlook (3,890 feet)

Lanes Pinnacle is to the left in the view, with the upper elevations of the Great Craggy Mountains visible behind the ridgeline. The mountains on the far right are the Swannanoas.

Mile 373.8. Bull Creek Valley Overlook (3,483 feet)

Bull Creek Valley is below the overlook. A plaque tells the story of the last buffalo to be seen in the area.

Mile 374.4. Tanbark Ridge Tunnel

The tunnel is 780 feet long; minimum height is 14 feet, 1 inch.

Mile 374.45. Mountains-to-Sea Access Trail [BRP 109] (also known as the Rattlesnake Lodge Trail) (N 35°39.941 W 82°27.711) Map 55

Length: .8 mile, out-and-back
Difficulty: strenuous

The access trail ascends from a small parking area at the southern end of the Tanbark Ridge Tunnel. Rising steeply along a rhododendron-lined stream, it junctions with an old carriage road that serves as the route of the Mountains-to-Sea Trail (see Chapter 1) in this area. The pathway ends at the ruins of buildings that were the summer home of a prominent Asheville citizen near the turn of the twentieth century.

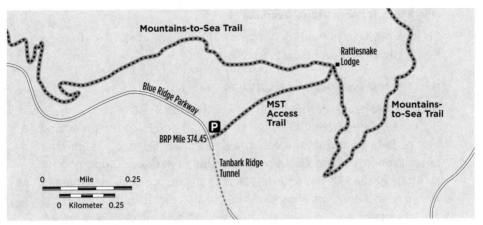

Map 55. MST Access Trail (mile 374.45)

.0 Begin at the small pull-off area at the southern end of Tanbark Ridge Tunnel and ascend steeply along the stream through rhododendron and mountain laurel.

.1 Level out a little and enjoy the small waterfalls of the creek.

.2 Cross a water run.

.25 Cross a larger stream.

.3 Wild geranium is prolific as the path becomes steeper.

.4 Arrive at the Mountains-to-Sea Trail and the ruins of a number of buildings. A little exploring here may turn up the spring that was the water source for Dr. Chase Ambler's early twentieth-century mountain retreat. He was an influential advocate for preserving the forests of the Southern Appalachians. A few iris grow in the area. Retrace steps.

Mile 375.2. Bull Gap (3,107 feet)

Mile 375.7. NC RT 694

Access to Weaverville (8 miles; full services and a thriving arts and crafts community).

Mile 375.7. Mountains-to-Sea Trail access (N 35°39.884 W 82°28.710).
See Chapter 1.

Mile 376.7. Tanbark Ridge Overlook (3,175 feet)

Swan Mountain is behind Tanbark Ridge. In the distance are High Swan, High Knob, and Lane Pinnacle.

Mile 377.4. Craven Gap and NC RT 694 (3,172 feet)

Access to Asheville (7 miles; full services) (see mile 388.8).

Please Note: As this book went to press, a public comment period had ended concerning the construction and/or closure of a number of trails and/or overlooks on or connecting to parkway property from about BRP mile 377.4 to mile 395. Depending on the decisions that are reached, you may find things on the ground, particularly concerning the Mountains-to-Sea Trail, different than described. Consult BRP personnel for the latest information.

Mile 377.4. Mountains-to-Sea Trail access (N 35°38.890 W 82°29.514).
See Chapter 1.

Mile 380. Haw Creek Valley Overlook (3,720 feet)

The wide panorama takes in the valley created by Haw Creek and looks westward toward the mountains of the North Carolina/Tennessee border.

Mile 380.4 Haw Creek Trail (N 35°36.872 W 82°29.543) Map 56

> *Length: .8 mile one way; 1.6 miles out-and-back*
> *Difficulty: easy when hiked in the direction described;*
>   *moderately easy in the other direction.*

The idea for the Haw Creek Trail (now a part of the city of Asheville's park system) was an initiative of volunteers of the Haw Creek neighborhood and the Carolina Mountain Club. The volunteers have wonderfully constructed the pathway, building in 13 switchbacks to make it easy to negotiate the route's 300-foot elevation change. Abundant wildflowers, such as false Solomon's seal, pea, rattlesnake plantain, and galax, along with mountain laurel and rhododendron bushes and a small grove of pines, add to the enjoyment of the short trail.

Closest parking on the parkway is .4 mile north at the Haw Creek Valley Overlook or about .1 mile south of the trail on an unofficial dirt pull off (where there is access to the MST; see Chapter 1). The far trailhead may be reached by exiting the BRP at Mile 382.4 and following US 70 (Tunnel Road) toward Asheville for 2.1 miles. Turn right onto New Haw

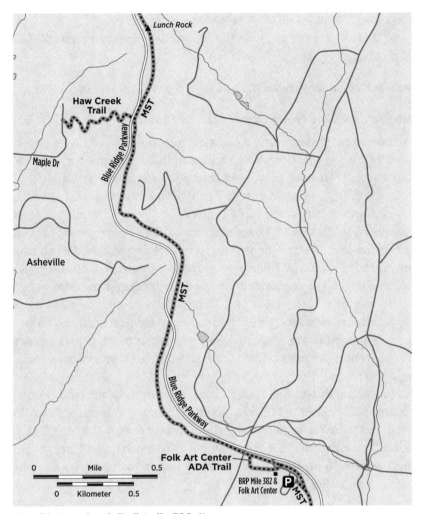

Map 56. Haw Creek Trail (mile 380.4)

Creek Road, continue 2 more miles to make a right onto Maple Road and reach the trailhead (N 35°36.791 W 82°29.837) in another .3 mile. Be aware there is barely room enough for two cars to get off the road and park at this spot.

.0   Descend from the parkway through a patch of false Solomon's seal.

.1   Rhododendron becomes a part of the understory.

.25   Mountain laurel is now the dominant understory plant.

.4 Pass through a grove of tall pines.

.8 Walk by Turk's cap lily as the trail comes to an end on Maple Road.

Mile 381. Mountains-to-Sea Trail (N 35°36.096 W 82°29.371). See Chapter 1.

Mile 382. Folk Art Center (2,230 feet) (N 35°35.535 W 82°28.859)

A massive native stone and wood structure, the Folk Art Center (operated by the Southern Highland Handicraft Guild, National Park Service, and Eastern National) provides a showplace for master artisans.

Even during a short visit to the center you might be able to watch a dull lump of clay being turned into a hand-formed drinking goblet unique in shape and style, see intricate patterns emerge as a weaver works her loom, or be delighted when nimble fingers transform bits of discarded cloth into a colorful and useful patchwork quilt. Dulcimer makers may fill the center with sweet sounds of old-time music.

The center features sales of the crafts, a museum, and a library of Appalachian literature. Live folk dancing, music concerts, and interpretive programs are presented on an irregular basis. A park service visitor center provides parkway information, a bookstore, restrooms, and water.

The Mountains-to-Sea Trail, running concurrently with the Folk Art Center ADA Trail [BRP 110], crosses the center's entrance road. Northward the pathway begins a long climb toward Craggy Gardens. To the south it parallels the BRP, descending to the French Broad River to connect with the Shut-In Trail. See Chapter 1 for more information on the Mountains-to-Sea Trail.

Mile 382. Mountains-to-Sea Trail to Lunch Rock
(N 35°35.535 W 82°28.859) Map 56

> *Length: 4.6 miles out-and-back*
> *Difficulty: moderate*

Beginning next to the Folk Art Center, this portion of the Mountains-to-Sea Trail's (See Chapter 1) proximity to Asheville, its moderate grade, and the nice view from the outing's high point has made this a popular day trip for the city's residents.

.0 Begin on the Folk Art Center ADA Trail [BRP 110] next to the information kiosk, soon coming to a loop trail intersection where the hike keeps to the right.

.17 Continue on the Mountains-to-Sea Trail when it veers off to the right, soon crossing a bridge over Riceville Road and passing by a side trail to the left.

1 Cross over the BRP.

1.9 The blue-blazed trail that ascends to the left leads to the parkway in just a few feet. (From there it would be possible to connect with the Haw Creek Trail [see mile 380.4] by crossing the BRP diagonally to the right.) Continue on the Mountains-to-Sea Trail as it begins to ascend a little more steeply.

2.3 Be alert! Take the side trail to the left to enjoy the view of Haw Creek Valley (and maybe Mount Pisgah in the distance) from Lunch Rock. Retrace your steps.

4.6 Return to the starting point.

♿ Mile 382. Folk Art Center ADA Trail [BRP 110]

(N 35°35.535 W 82°28.859) Map 57

Length: .4 mile, circuit
Difficulty: easy

The fully handicapped-accessible graveled pathway originates at the front of the Folk Art Center parking area. Along the way are interpretive exhibits of various trees that are often used for furniture making, carving, and other wood crafts.

.0 Walk from the Folk Art Center parking area, past the information kiosk, and onto the trail, which is also a part of the Mountains-to-Sea Trail. Going by the center, you can enjoy art objects displayed in the windows. Signs along the trail discuss various trees—red maple, tulip poplar, sassafras, American chestnut, sourwood, white oak, dogwood, pine, and others—found along the trail.

.1 Enter the woods and ascend gradually. Come to a loop trail intersection in 200 feet and keep to the right.

.17 The Mountains-to-Sea Trail veers off to the right. Stay on the main route, which soon becomes narrower.

.25 Intersection. The trail to the right goes to another portion of the Folk Art Center parking area. Stay to the left. Return to the loop trail intersection in another 100 feet and bear right.

.4 Return to the starting point.

Mile 382.3. BRP maintenance facilities and ranger office

Mile 382.4. US RT 70

Access to Asheville (5 miles; full services) (see mile 388.8) and Black Mountain (9 miles; full services with many art galleries and antiques stores).

Mile 383.5. Swannanoa River

Mile 384. Blue Ridge Parkway Destination Center (2,370 feet)

Opened in 2008, the $9.8 million Blue Ridge Parkway Destination Center (828-298-5330) is designed to be a "one-stop" place where visitors can learn, through a variety of exhibits and multimedia formats, about the entire length of the parkway, its natural and cultural history, many outdoors opportunities, and other attractions on or near the parkway. Other amenities within the environmentally friendly designed building, operated jointly by the U.S. National Park Service, the Blue Ridge Parkway, and the Blue Ridge National Heritage Area, are a 70-seat theater, visitor center, restrooms, free wi-fi, and bookstore and gift shop. This is a highly recommended stop.

Also within the same area is the headquarters of the BRP and the Destination Center Loop Trail [BRP 111].

Mile 384. Destination Center Loop Trail [BRP 111]
(N 35°33.893 W 82°29.218) Map 57

> *Length: 1.5 miles, circuit*
> *Difficulty: moderately easy*

In 2008, volunteers from the Carolina Mountain Club and FRIENDS of the Blue Ridge Parkway built a new trail from the Blue Ridge Destination Center to an existing section of the Mountains-to-Sea Trail (see Chapter 1), creating a loop hike. The route has become popular with the citizens of nearby Asheville and BRP employees, whose administrative offices are a scant few feet away. The Destination Center Loop Trail was the first parkway trail to be designated a TRACK trail for children. Brochures are available at the trailhead (or at kidsinpark.com).

The trailhead is located close to the far end of the BRP Destination Center parking lot at the bus and RV parking area.

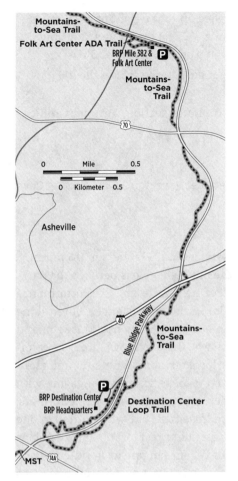

Map 57. Miles 382–384.7

.0 Enter the woods and bear right at the loop trail intersection, soon descending and passing by false Solomon's seal plants and faint trails going off to the right.

.15 Rise into an open area and descend into the woods.

.3 Rhododendron makes up the midstory, while English ivy covers much of the ground. Also watch out for copious growths of poison ivy (throughout the hike).

.4 Use caution crossing the BRP. Reenter the woods and ascend where traffic noise from nearby US RT 74 is very noticeable; the trail soon leads away from that highway.

.75 Attain the top of a small rise.

.9 A few houses are visible through the vegetation.

1.1 The Mountains-to-Sea Trail goes off to the right (it is 2.5 miles to the Folk Art Center, BRP mile 382, via that route). Continue left, pass under the parkway in a stone culvert, and rise.

1.2 Avoid the trail to the right that goes to the rear of the BRP Destination Center.

1.5 Having returned to the loop trail intersection, turn right and return to the starting point.

Mile 384.7. US RT 74

Access to Asheville (5 miles; full services) (see mile 388.8) and Bat Cave (17 miles).

Mile 388.8. US RT 25

Access to Asheville (5 miles; full services) and Henderson (16 miles).

The second-largest city along the BRP, Asheville is perhaps the parkway's most vibrant urban area, full of arts, crafts, and live performance venues. In the Park Place Education, Arts, and Science Center alone are the Asheville Art Museum, Colburn Earth Science Museum, and Diana Wortham Theatre. In many ways, the downtown area is a colorful venue itself. Groups of tourists, local residents, students, and alternative lifestyle types roam the streets, observing and engaging with musicians, impromptu drum circles, and other street art performers. National dining chains are well represented, but why patronize one when the city's more than 250 independent restaurants offer cuisines from low-cost home cooking and/or vegetarian fare to world-class gastronomical experiences? There are also about a dozen craft breweries and nearly a score of farmers' markets.

Walking opportunities abound within or in close proximity to the city. The half-mile trail in the 10-acre Botanical Gardens, with more than 600 plant species, provides a quick escape from the metropolitan bustle. Larger in size is the North Carolina Arboretum, whose 65 acres of cultivated gardens are traversed by 10 miles of pathways (Map 58). The trails closest to the Biltmore house showcase the beauty of the meticulously maintained gardens, while the routes on the west side of the estate wind around a small knob in a more natural woodlands.

An employee of Malaprop's (in my opinion one of the finest bookstores in the Blue Ridge) told me about the Asheville Urban Trail. It is a jaunt of a different kind. Its 1.7-mile length meanders along downtown streets, taking in 30 sites where various pieces of public art interpret the city's history. The outing begins at the Asheville Art Mu-

Richard Morris Hunt, the Biltmore House's architect, placed the gazebo at the head of Bass Pond so that guests could look across its expanse.

seum, where bronze turkeys and pigs evoke the city's earliest days when it was called Morristown. Of all the things trail planners could have chosen to commemorate one of Asheville's most celebrated residents, Thomas Wolfe, they chose bronze replicas of his size-13 shoes to place in front of "Old Kentucky Home," the boardinghouse operated by his mother. A bronze cane, top hat, and gloves recall the Grand Opera House of yesteryear; life-sized sculptures celebrate the Civic Center's performing arts activities; and a young boy on stilts represents Richard Sharp Smith, supervising architect of Biltmore House. Although many of the city's structures were built years before the trail was conceived, I couldn't help but notice the architecture of many of them, including the Art Deco designs of the 1928 City Building and the 1929 S&W Building.

Mile 388.8. Mountains-to-Sea Trail (N 35°31.241 W 82°31.616). See Chapter 1.

Mile 390.9. Dingle Creek

Mile 393.5. French Broad River

Mile 393.6. NC RT 191

Access to the North Carolina Arboretum and Asheville (full services) (see mile 388.8).

The Shut-In Trail, Blue Ridge Parkway Miles 393.6–407.6

Originally the Shut-In Trail, now a National Recreation Trail, stretched from George W. Vanderbilt's Biltmore Estate in Asheville to his Buck Spring Hunting Lodge near Mount Pisgah. Built in the last decade of the 1800s, the route fell into disrepair, and portions were destroyed by the establishment of the BRP. Volunteers helped reclaim old sections and build new paths to create the Shut-In Trail of today—running from the French Broad River to the Mount Pisgah Recreation Area.

One can easily envision a Vanderbilt hunting party ascending the mountains in noisy anticipation. The men, riding and leading horses laden with provisions, talk excitedly about the events of the next few days, while the dogs run ahead scaring up squirrels, chipmunks, and deer.

It is believed the trail's name comes from the copious rhododendron thickets that "shut-in" the trail, limiting vistas to just a few. As you hike the different portions of the trail, you will no doubt be able to contemplate the effort and toil the builders of this route expended as they had to cut, uproot, and hack their way through the tough, twisting rhododendron wood. Also take note of the rock wall foundations shoring up the steep sections of the trail. It took foresight to see the need for the walls and craftsmanship to ensure their durability.

A couple of side trails permit access to the forest service's system of trails in the Bent Creek Experimental Forest (see BRP mile 400.3). Also, the Shut-In Trail is a part of the Mountains-to-Sea Trail (see Chapter 1).

Along the Shut-In Trail's nearly 17-mile length, the elevation rises from 2,025 feet at the French Broad River to almost 5,000 feet at its southern terminus near Mount Pisgah. To make it a little easier on yourself, you might want to consider walking some sections of the trail in the opposite direction than described.

Mile 393.6. Shut-In Trail [BRP 112] (from near the French Broad River to Walnut Cove Overlook, BRP Mile 396.4) (2,020 feet)
(N 35°30.071 W 82°35.631) Map 58

> *Length: 3.1 miles, one way; 6.2 miles, out-and-back*
> *Difficulty: moderately strenuous*

For the initial ascent from near the French Broad River, the Shut-In Trail rises fairly gently on a system of old roadways. There are limited wintertime views of the river as you ascend. Also, the forest is a little more open on this section than on others; rhododendron thickets don't become numerous until you gain a bit more elevation.

The Shut-In Trail does not actually begin on the parkway. You can reach the trailhead by exiting the parkway at BRP mile 393.6. While still on the exit ramp, you will notice a very small parking area on the right side of the road. However, it may be wise not to leave your car here; continue on the exit ramp, turn right at the stoplight, and almost immediately turn left into the Bent Creek River and Picnic Park (N 35°30.078 W 82°35.609). Across the road from the park is a short (a few hundred feet) trail that will deliver you to the beginning of the Shut-In Trail.

.0 Begin to rise from the exit ramp road. The Mountains-to-Sea Trail (see Chapter 1) makes use of the Shut-In Trail, which it follows all the way to the Mount Pisgah area.

.2 Cross a small stream. Enter a mountain laurel tunnel.

.3 Emerge from the mountain laurel and ascend quickly.

.4 Come onto an old road with wintertime views of the French Broad River. Even though you are on a road, the ascent is still rather steep.

.7 Descend gradually.

1.0 Resume a gradual ascent in an open forest of poplar, maple, oak, and dogwood.

1.1 Turn left to join a different woods road and ascend gradually.

1.6 Bear left onto another old roadway and descend.

1.8 Turn left onto a dirt road and walk next to the BRP.

1.9 The trail leaves the road and ascends quickly.

2.0 Turn left onto yet another old woods road.

2.1 The road makes a switchback to the right and then one to the left. Ascend, and be cautious around the poison ivy growing in profusion along the road. Here are more wintertime views of the French Broad River.

2.5 Begin a gentle descent. The road here feels like an old country lane—vegetation on the forest floor is lush and green, and poplars line the wide roadway.

2.7 Reach a low point and gradually ascend.

2.8 Resume a gradual descent, watching out once again for the abundant poison ivy.

3.1 Arrive at the parkway and turn right to come to the Walnut Cove Overlook at mile 396.4.

Mile 393.8. French Broad Overlook (2,100 feet)

Flowing for 213 miles from its headwaters near Rosman, North Carolina, the river meets the Holston River at Knoxville, Tennessee, to form the Tennessee River.

Mile 396.4. Walnut Cove Overlook (2,915 feet)

The wide floor of the French Broad River Valley is below the overlook.

Mile 396.4. Shut-In Trail [BRP 113] (from Walnut Cove Overlook to Sleepy Gap Overlook, BRP 397.3) (N 35°28.480 W 82°36.886) Map 58

Length: 1.8 miles, one way; 3.6 miles, out-and-back
Difficulty: moderate

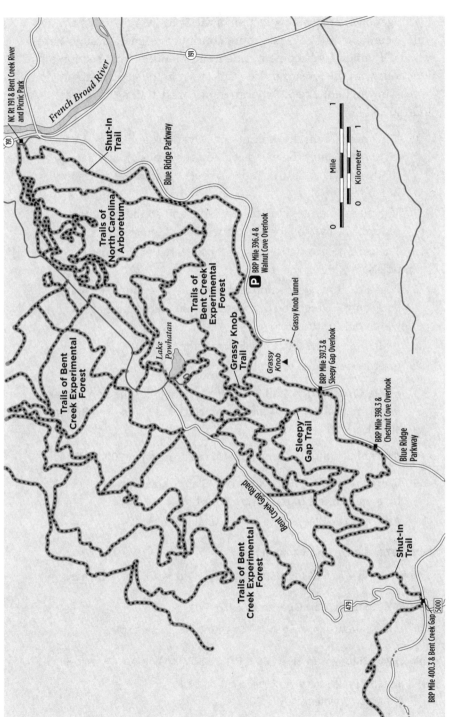

Map 58. Miles 393.6–400.3

No longer on old roads, this section of the Shut-In Trail makes a rather stiff ascent over a knob. The route continues to pass through hardwoods. Wildflowers become a little more plentiful. This section also junctions with the forest service's Grassy Knob Trail [FS 338] to provide access to the Bent Creek Experimental Forest trail system (see BRP mile 400.3).

.0   Walk north from the Walnut Cove Overlook and cross the BRP in 200 feet. Enter the woods behind the trail sign and ascend to the left. (The Shut-In Trail also goes right for 3.1 miles to BRP mile 393.6.)

.1   The mayapples are particularly large and abundant here. Ascend via switchbacks in a vine-choked forest.

.3   The ascent becomes almost level. Beware of voluminous poison ivy lining the trail.

.5   Reach the top of the knob and descend on a couple of switchbacks, after which the descent is rather steep. Once again watch out for the poison ivy.

.8   Walk next to the BRP for a short distance.

1.25   Intersection. Keep to the left.

▶ The Grassy Knob Trail [FS 338] descends into the Bent Creek Experimental Forest of the Pisgah National Forest (see BRP mile 400.3).

Cross a small water run (may be dry in summer) in 200 feet.

1.4   Cross an even smaller water run. Slab to the right of a knob through tunnels of mountain laurel.

1.8   Arrive at the Sleepy Gap Overlook at mile 397.3.

Mile 397.1. Grassy Knob Tunnel

The tunnel is 770 feet long; minimum height is 13 feet, 7 inches.

Mile 397.3. Sleepy Gap Overlook (2,930 feet)

The limited view is of ridgelines to the west. Picnic table.

Mile 397.3. Sleepy Gap Trail [FS 339] (N35°27.941 W 82°37.774) Map 58

Length: 1 mile, one way; 2 miles, out-and-back
Difficulty: strenuous

This forest service trail descends to the right steeply for 1 mile from the south end of the Sleepy Gap Overlook before intersecting with other trails in the Bent Creek Experimental Forest of Pisgah National Forest (see BRP mile 400.3).

Mile 397.3. Shut-In Trail [BRP 114] (from Sleepy Gap Overlook to Chestnut Cove Overlook, BRP mile 398.3) (N35°27.941 W 82°37.774)
Map 58

Length: .9 mile, one way; 1.8 miles, out-and-back
Difficulty: moderately strenuous

The hardwood trees seem to become even larger on this portion of the Shut-In Trail. Pay particular attention to the venerable old oaks growing on the summit of Grassy Knob. Be prepared for a couple of stiff ascents as the route traverses two high knobs.

.0 Ascend to the left from the southern end of the overlook on switchbacks through tunnels of mountain laurel. (The Shut-In Trail also goes northward from the overlook for 1.8 miles to the Walnut Cove Overlook, BRP mile 396.4.)

.3 Attain the top of a knob and descend gradually through more mountain laurel.

.45 Reach a gap; ascend steeply.

.6 Attain a high point. The forest is quite old here, and the trees have attained some very admirable dimensions. Descend somewhat steeply.

.8 Bear left.

.9 Arrive at the Chestnut Cove Overlook at mile 398.3.

Mile 398.3. Chestnut Cove Overlook (3,035 feet)

At one time, chestnuts were the predominant trees in the Southern Appalachians, making up to 25 percent of the woods in some areas. However, the chestnut blight, a fungal disease accidentally introduced into North America from Asia, removed the trees from the landscape by the end of the 1930s. The chestnut had played an important role in the daily life of mountain residents. In the fall they gathered the plentiful nuts, which provided a supplement to their diet and a source of cash when sold by the bushel. The tree's timber was used to build log homes and durable fences to keep livestock from roaming. Its bark, rich in tannin, was stripped and sold for the processing of hides. The roots and stumps of these fallen trees still produce sprouts that grow for a while before they become infested with fungus and die. The hope is that someday the sprouts will be able to resist the disease or that scientists will develop a strain that will not succumb to the blight.

Mile 398.3. Shut-In Trail [BRP 115] (from Chestnut Cove Overlook to Bent Creek Gap, BRP mile 400.3) (N 35°27.610 W 82°38.196) Map 58

Length: 2.8 miles, one way; 5.6 miles, out-and-back
Difficulty: strenuous

The Shut-In Trail now truly lives up to its name. Mountain laurel and rhododendron close in, forming tunnels and dark corridors for much of the way. The route moves the Shut-In Trail far away from the parkway, making one long descent into Chestnut Cove. This remoteness from automobile traffic and the shadowy caverns provided by the twisting rhododendron and mountain laurel branches instill a quiet and sense of isolation not possible on other stretches of the Shut-In Trail. However, there is a price to be paid for this retreat—be ready for a lengthy ascent out of the cove to return to the parkway.

.0 Cross the BRP from the Chestnut Cove Overlook, enter the woods, and turn left to descend away from the parkway. (The Shut-In Trail also goes right for .9 mile to arrive at the Sleepy Gap Overlook, BRP mile 397.3.)

.5 Cross a stream and follow an old roadbed for 250 feet before leaving it for a pathway to the left. Mountain laurel and rhododendron arc over the trail.

.7 Emerge from the heath tunnel and enter a hardwood forest of oak, maple, dogwood, and sassafras.

.9 Cross over a spur ridge and continue to descend.

1.1 Come onto a woods road and bear left.

1.4 Come into Chestnut Cove, cross the creek, and ascend for the first time since leaving the parkway. Rhododendron tunnels reappear.

1.6 As the old road begins to fade, look for a few jack-in-the-pulpits along the trail. Emerge from the rhododendron into a mixed hardwood forest.

1.8 Swing around a spur ridge and continue to ascend on a wide pathway.

2.0 Cross a small water run.

2.4 Cross another small creek and continue with the long ascent through hardwoods and mountain laurel tunnels.

2.8 Arrive at FSR 479 in Bent Tree Gap at mile 400.3. The BRP is just to your left.

Mile 399.1. Pine Mountain Tunnel

This is the longest tunnel on the BRP—1,434 feet. The minimum height is 14 feet, 2 inches.

Mile 399.7. Bad Fork Valley Overlook (3,350 feet)

A nice view of the Pisgah range with the dome of Mount Pisgah being the highest spot.

Mile 400.3. Bent Creek Gap (3,270 feet) (N 35°27.167 W 82°39.564)

Forest service roads in Bent Creek Gap provide access to trails in two different areas of Pisgah National Forest.

To the west, FSR 479 enters 5,500-acre Bent Creek Experimental Forest, established in 1925 to study, among other issues, how to keep forests sustainable. In addition to the Shut-In Trail, much of which passes through the area, the experimental forest has close to 30 miles of trails, many of them open to hikers, mountain bikers (who come here in droves from Asheville), and equestrians. Within the forest is the Lake Powhatan Recreation Area with a campground, swimming, and fishing.

More information about the experimental forest may be obtained from

> Bent Creek Experimental Forest
> 1577 Brevard Road
> Asheville, NC 28806
> 828-667-5261
> www.srs.fs.fed.us

To the east of the parkway, FSR 5000 descends to the North Mills River area. Several trails in this area are described below at miles 401.8 and 406.9. Information on other trails and a campground may be obtained from

> Pisgah Ranger District
> 1600 Pisgah Highway
> Pisgah Forest, NC 28768
> 828-877-3265
> www.fs.fed.us

Mile 400.3. Shut-In Trail [BRP 116] (from Bent Creek Gap to Beaver Dam Gap Overlook, BRP Mile 401.7) (N 35°27.167 W 82°39.564) Map 59

Length: 1.9 miles, one way; 3.8 miles, out-and-back
Difficulty: moderately strenuous

You'll finally get a view or two from this section of the Shut-In Trail. The path makes one long climb to the 4,064-foot summit of Ferrin Knob only to immediately make a steep descent back to the parkway.

.0 The trail ascends south from FSR 479 near the sign identifying the Bent Creek Experimental Forest. (The Shut-In Trail also goes north from the road for 2.8 miles to the Chestnut Cove Overlook, BRP mile 398.3.) Turn right onto an old road in 250 feet.

.5 Pass by a delicious-tasting spring, which unfortunately may not be running at the end of a long, dry summer season. Continue to ascend gradually.

.9 Make a switchback to the left.

1.3 Attain the summit of Ferrin Knob, where there used to be a fire tower. Enjoy the view to the northeast. Begin a steep descent through a beautiful display of mayapple.

1.5 Level out for a short distance in a wildflower-crowded gap. Then continue to descend gradually through abundant dogwood trees and swing to the right of a knob.

1.9 Arrive at Beaver Dam Gap Overlook at BRP mile 401.7.

Mile 400.9. Ferrin Knob Tunnel #1

It's 561 feet long with a minimum height of 14 feet, 2 inches.

Mile 401.1 Wash Creek Valley Overlook (3,435 feet)

The creek below the overlook can become a raging torrent in times of high rain. My father, raised in the mountains of West Virginia, called such rains "gully washers."

Mile 401.3. Ferrin Knob Tunnel #2

Its length is 421 feet; minimum height is 14 feet.

Mile 401.5. Ferrin Knob Tunnel #3

Just 375 feet long; minimum height is 13 feet, 9 inches.

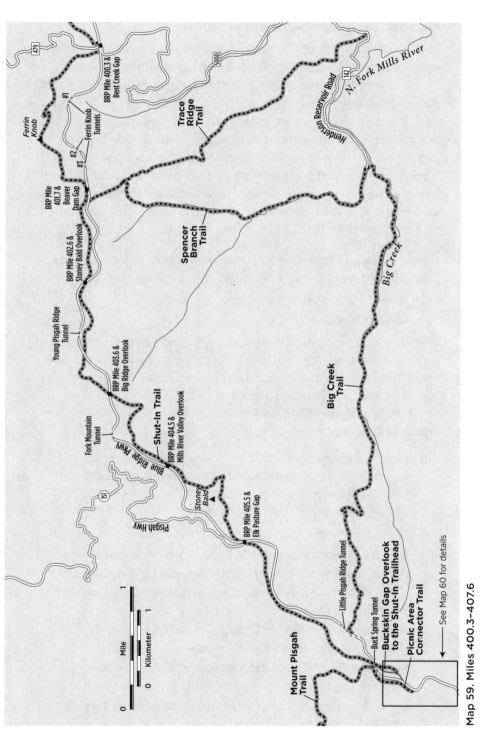

Map 59. Miles 400.3–407.6

Mile 401.7. Beaver Dam Gap Overlook (3,570 feet)

The only living genus of the family *Castoridae*, the beaver is found no-where else in the world but North America. Watching beavers build a dam or home is to really understand the phrase "busy as a beaver." Two adult beavers can bring a 3-inch sapling down in about 3 min-utes. When working on a dam, they will fell a tree (often 2 to 3 feet in diameter), trim off the branches in convenient sizes, and carry the logs with their teeth to the dam. Dam construction is adapted to local conditions—to lessen pressure from a fast-moving creek, the dam will be bowed upstream, and in times of high water, the beavers will open up temporary spillways. Working together, 2 beavers can construct a 12-foot-long, 2-foot-high dam with only 2 nights of labor.

Mile 401.7. Shut-In Trail [BRP 117] (from Beaver Dam Gap Overlook to Stoney Bald Overlook, BRP Mile 402.6) (N 35°27.235 W 82°40.806) Map 59

Length: .9 mile, one way; 1.8 miles, out-and-back
Difficulty: strenuous

Even though the trail stays close to the BRP for the entire length of the section, it definitely does not rise at the same easy grade as the park-way. Three times, in only .9 mile, the route will bring you quickly over a knob or ridge and then plummet downhill.

Take note of the excellent work the trail builders have done with rock cribbing to stabilize the steep hillsides.

.0   From the Beaver Dam Gap Overlook turn left onto the trail and begin an immediate ascent. (The Shut-In Trail also bears to the right for 1.9 miles to Bent Tree Gap Overlook, BRP mile 400.3.)

.15   Reach the top of a knob and promptly descend.

.2   In a gap covered in poison ivy, begin to rise once again.

.3   Attain the high point, but abruptly descend via switchbacks secured by rock walls. Looking down on the parkway, slab to the right of a knob.

.5   Arrive at the low point in a gap and ascend very steeply. Cancer root and violets line the pathway.

.7   Reach the ridgeline and descend on steep switchbacks. Buttercups and orchids are abundant on this hillside.

.9   Cross the parkway and arrive at Stoney Bald Overlook at BRP mile 402.6.

Mile 401.8. Trace Ridge Trail [FS 354] Map 59

The forest service's 3.1-mile, moderately strenuous Trace Ridge Trail is unmarked and unmaintained, but it is included here for those who enjoy such a challenge or are looking for a place to backcountry camp along the route once it leaves BRP property. Park at the Beaver Dam Overlook (BRP mile 401.7; N 35°27.235 W 82°40.806), walk southward on the parkway for about .1 mile, and look for the faint old woods road descending to the east. Following a ridgeline, the trail connects with numerous other forest service trails and terminates on FSR 142 in the North Mills River area of Pisgah National Forest.

Mile 402.6. Stoney Bald Overlook (3,570 feet)

The Astronomy Club of Asheville often uses this overlook to observe the heavens because of its isolation and lack of lights from civilization.

Mile 402.6. Shut-In Trail [BRP 118] (from Stoney Bald Overlook to Big Ridge Overlook, BRP Mile 403.6) (N 35°27.233 W 82°41.635) Map 59

Length: 1.2 miles, one way; 2.4 miles, out-and-back
Difficulty: moderately strenuous

Once again, there is nothing particularly spectacular about this section of the Shut-In Trail. It climbs several knobs through a hardwood forest before coming to an end at another overlook. The route does pass by a few wildflowers that have not been seen in any great numbers until now.

.0   Take a couple of steps down from the south end of the Stoney Bald Overlook, then immediately begin to ascend. (The Shut-In Trail also goes to the north by crossing the BRP, entering the woods, and traveling .9 mile to Beaver Dam Gap Overlook, BRP mile 401.7.)

.4   Reach the top of a knoll. Descend and slab around the left side of a small knoll.

.6   Begin a very rapid descent.

.7   Cross the BRP (no parking or pull-off area) and slab to the right of a knob. Pass a few jack-in-the-pulpits.

.9   Cross over a low ridge and descend. Rattlesnake plantain, bellwort, robin plantain, and trailing arbutus are all abundant.

1.2   Cross the parkway and arrive at Big Ridge Overlook at BRP mile 403.6.

Mile 403. Young Pisgah Tunnel

Minimum height is 14 feet, 6 inches, and length is 412 feet.

Mile 403.6. Big Ridge Overlook (3,815 feet)

Big Ridge is the mountain that gradually descends into the valley on the right side of the view.

Mile 403.6. Shut-In Trail [BRP 119] (from Big Ridge Overlook to Mills River Valley Overlook, BRP Mile 404.5) (N 35°27.023 W 82°42.541) Map 59

Length: 1.1 miles, one way; 2.2 miles, out-and-back
Difficulty: moderate

The Shut-In Trail now swings to the east to traverse a cross ridge of the main crest of the mountains. This provides a pleasant break from being right next to the parkway like much of the rest of the trail. The ascents are a little gentler than on the previous section.

.0   Descend the steps at the southern end of the overlook and enter the woods. (The Shut-In Trail also heads north by crossing the BRP, entering the woods, and going 1.2 miles to Stoney Bald Overlook, BRP mile 402.6.) Ascend gradually; a number of cancer roots and bloodroot line the trail.

.1   Solomon's seal and false Solomon's seal are abundant, as is lousewort.

.3   Cross over a flat ridge and continue with minor ups and downs. Blueberries, in season, may slow your progress. In fact, let them slow your progress. Take the time to enjoy a few.

.5   Begin to rise at a steadily increasing rate.

.7   Attain the ridgeline and follow it, slabbing to the right of a high knob.

.8   Walk along a narrowing ridgeline and gradually descend through a hardwood forest.

1.1   Arrive in Mills River Valley Overlook at BRP mile 404.5.

Mile 404. Fork Mountain Tunnel

The tunnel is 389 feet in length; minimum height is 14 feet.

Mile 404.2. Hominy Valley Overlook (3,975 feet)

A nice spot to watch the sun set over the mountain ridges to the west.

Mile 404.5. Mills Valley Overlook (4,085 feet)

This overlook has a view of the mountains to the east, making it a good sunrise observation point.

Mile 404.5. Shut-In Trail [BRP 120] (from Mills River Valley Overlook to Elk Pasture Gap, BRP Mile 405.5) (N 35°26.564 W 82°43.187) Map 59

> *Length: 1.2 miles, one way; 2.4 miles, out-and-back*
> *Difficulty: moderate*

There is only one short, steep ascent on this section of the Shut-In Trail. Once you complete this climb, the pathway follows a wavy ridge-line with very minor changes in elevation. A spring will supply liquid refreshment.

.0   Follow the trail from the southern end of the overlook and immediately begin a stiff climb. (The Shut-In Trail also leaves from the northern end of the overlook. It will reach Big Ridge Overlook, BRP mile 403.6, in 1.1 miles.) False hellebore, star chickweed, and Solomon's seal grow well here. Pass by a splendid array of lily of the valley.

.15   Slab to the left of a knob, going by a cluster of white trillium.

.3   Come to a spring.

.5   Cross onto the ridgeline and now continue with only slight ups and downs.

.9   The trail-building techniques are striking here, as the rock walls supporting the trail are solid and well built.

1.0   Cross over a small rise and parallel the BRP.

1.2   Cross the parkway in Elk Pasture Gap and arrive beside NC RT 151 at BRP mile 405.5.

Mile 405.5. Shut-In Trail [BRP 121] (from Elk Pasture Gap to Mount Pisgah Trailhead, BRP Mile 407.6) (N 35°26.050 W 82°43.828) Map 59

> *Length: 1.9 miles, one way; 3.8 miles, out-and-back*
> *Difficulty: strenuous*

Elk Pasture Gap is at an elevation of 4,200 feet. The Mount Pisgah Trail-head lies at almost 5,000 feet. You will gain that elevation in the final section of the Shut-In Trail. However, you will also be able to enjoy several outstanding views of Mount Pisgah and numerous other peaks and valleys. In addition, in late summer a large berry patch awaits those who expend the energy to reach it.

.0 Enter the woods to the south from NC RT 151 and pass by violets and wood anemone. (The Shut-In Trail also goes to the north. Cross the BRP and follow the trail 1.2 miles to Mills River Valley Overlook, BRP mile 404.5.) Steeply ascend by bloodroot and white trillium.

.2 Come into a large patch of mayapple.

.35 Finally reach the top of the knob and the end of a stiff climb. However, begin immediately to descend.

.45 Arrive in a wide, flat gap.

.5 The BRP is almost directly below; large-flowered trillium and wood anemone abound.

.7 Rise steeply once again.

.8 A break in the vegetation permits a view to the east overlooking Mills River Valley. Continue with the steady ascent.

.9 Level out somewhat as you enter a large patch of delicious berries.

1.1 The climb begins in earnest once again and will become even steeper as you progress. Note that with a change in elevation also comes a change in vegetation.

1.5 Finally reach the ridgeline, where there is a nice view to the east. Also, Mount Pisgah soars high above on your right.

1.6 Attain a small knob with limited views to the north and east. Descend into a thicket of mountain laurel.

1.9 Arrive at the Mount Pisgah Trailhead parking area and the southern terminus of the Shut-In Trail on the Mount Pisgah extension road. The Mount Pisgah Trail [BRP 122] begins to your right.

Mile 406.9. Little Pisgah Tunnel

The tunnel is 576 feet long; minimum height is 13 feet, 10 inches.

Mile 406.9. Big Creek Trail [FS 102] (N 35°25.232 W 82°44.610) Map 59

Length: 5.2 miles, one way; 10.4 miles, out-and-back
Difficulty: moderate if done one-way from the parkway; moderately strenuous if hiked from Hendersonville Reservoir Road

There is a very small parking area at the southern end of the Little Pisgah Ridge Tunnel. From here, the unmarked and unsigned (making it hard to find from the parkway) trail descends 5.2 miles to the Hendersonville Reservoir Road in the Pisgah National Forest's North Mills River area. The first portion is steep, with the route losing 2,000 feet within 2 miles. After this, the trail follows the course of Big Creek along the bed of an old railroad grade, where there are good campsites, some of them near old railroad camps. Be aware that your feet may get wet, as some of the stream crossings are not bridged. The trail connects with the Spencer Branch Trail [FS 140] just before it ends at the reservoir road.

Mile 407.3. Buck Spring Tunnel

The tunnel is 462 feet long; minimum height is 13 feet, 8 inches.

Trails of the Mount Pisgah Area, Blue Ridge Parkway
Miles 407.6–408.8

According to the Bible, Moses first sighted the "promised land of milk and honey" from a land mass called Mount Pisgah. Local folklore maintains that in 1776, the Reverend James Hall ascended a North Carolina peak and delighted in the beauty of the surrounding countryside. Remembering the biblical account of Moses, he named the summit Mount Pisgah and proclaimed that he, too, had been privileged to look out upon a land of milk and honey.

Near the turn of the twentieth century, Mount Pisgah was a part of George W. Vanderbilt's 125,000-acre estate. He and his associates often wandered over the mountainsides to spend time at his Buck Spring Hunting Lodge. Hired to manage the vast timber resources of the estate, Gifford Pinchot developed many forestry practices that are still in use today. In 1895, Vanderbilt employed Dr. Carl A. Schenck, who established the first forestry school in America in the valley below Mount Pisgah. (See BRP mile 411.9 for more information.) Many of his students became some of the initial forest service employees.

In 1914, upon Vanderbilt's death, his heirs sold a huge tract of land, including Mount Pisgah, to the federal government. This property became the basis of the Pisgah National Forest.

The Mount Pisgah area presents many wonderful opportunities for walking and hiking experiences. The Shut-In Trail, of course, may be followed for more than 16 miles from the eastern side of Mount Pisgah to the banks of the French Broad River. Those with stout legs and healthy lungs may climb to the observation platform on Mount Pisgah for their own view of a promised land. Easy and short, but also pleasurable, pathways provide links to the picnic area, campground, and lodge. Several forest service trails snake eastward along sloping ridge-lines into Pisgah National Forest to permit lengthy overnight trips and interesting campsites.

The Mount Pisgah area contains a park service picnic area, camp-ground, camp store, gift shop, restaurant, and the Pisgah Inn.

Mile 407.7. Mount Pisgah Trail [BRP 122] (4,990 feet)
(N 35°25.099 W 82°44.879) Map 60

> *Length: 2.5 miles, out-and-back*
> *Difficulty: strenuous*

The view of a "land of milk and honey" from the summit of Mount Pisgah certainly lives up to its descriptive name. Be forewarned, how-ever; this is not an excursion for those who are out of shape. The final .75 mile is, more or less, one long set of steep stairs. The trail builders deserve praise and appreciation for the planning and hard work that obviously went into creating this pathway over such rugged terrain.

Notwithstanding the warning, do take at least the first half of the Mount Pisgah Trail. The pathway is wide, level, and, in springtime, lined with more than its fair share of wildflowers.

.0   Begin at the trail sign at the end of the Mount Pisgah exten-sion road. (The Mount Pisgah Trailhead to the Picnic Area Con-nector Trail [BRP 123] immediately drops off to the left.) Walk very gently, ascending on a wide pathway and admiring the abundance of wildflowers—bedstraw, lousewort, star chick-weed, white violet, jewelweed, and ragwort.

.15   Pass by a large rock facing; rhododendron and mountain laurel close in on the trail.

.4   Come to a gushing double spring.

.55   The ascent becomes less gradual as you walk onto a narrow-ing ridgeline.

.8   Pass by an old bench. The tangy smell of galax will become apparent as you begin huffing and puffing up the rougher and steeper trail.

1.0   Arrive at a bench with a limited view. Good spot to take a break, as the trail will become even steeper and more rugged.

1.1   Note that the vegetation becomes stunted as you gain eleva-tion. The trail is now very rough and eroded.

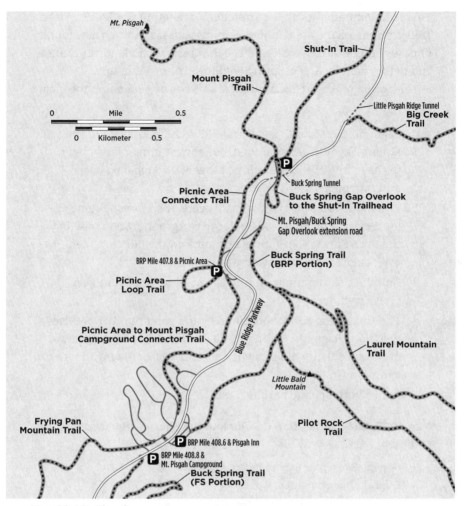

Map 60. Mt. Pisgah

1.25 Arrive at the observation platform on the 5,721-foot summit of Mount Pisgah. Rest, relax, and savor the fruits of your labors—a 360-degree view of the land of milk and honey. Retrace steps.

Mile 407.7. Mount Pisgah Trailhead to Picnic Area Connector Trail
[BRP 123] (N 35°25.099 W 82°44.879) Map 60

Length: .5 mile, one way; 1 mile, out-and-back
Difficulty: easy leg stretcher

This is an extended easy leg stretcher connecting the Mount Pisgah Trail with the picnic area. In just .5 mile it passes through several distinct vegetation areas—oak and beech forest, rhododendron tunnels, and damp, marshy areas. Spring wildflowers are abundant.

This would make a relaxing stroll after a hearty cookout in the picnic area.

.0 Begin on the Mount Pisgah Trail [BRP 122] at the end of the Mount Pisgah extension road, but almost immediately bear to the left on the descending pathway through oak, beech, and rhododendron.

.1 The rhododendron gives way to a very open forest. Bluets, lousewort, and violets add color to the ground. Soon pass by the Buck Spring Gap Tunnel entrance on the BRP and then walk below the parkway on a narrow trail.

.3 Galax is the dominant ground cover. Painted trillium also grows well here.

.4 The trailside is almost obscured by the great number of false hellebore. Begin ascending through a field, looking for a few of the succulent wild strawberries sure to be growing in late summer.

.5 Arrive in the picnic parking area.

Mile 407.7. Buck Spring Gap Overlook to the Shut-In Trailhead [BRP 124] (4,980 feet) (N 35°24.911 W 82°44.925) Map 60

> Length: .3 mile, one way; .5 mile, circuit
> Difficulty: moderately easy

The Mountains-to-Sea Trail (see Chapter 1) and this trail start together, separate for a short distance, and then rejoin. They would make a quick but energetic circuit walk of .5 mile. There are a couple of limited views along the way.

This is one of the shortest sections of the Mountains-to-Sea Trail. Therefore, you may want to walk it just to be able to brag to friends that you have walked a portion of this soon-to-be-famous trail.

Also be aware that the Buck Spring Gap Overlook is the northern trailhead for the Buck Spring Trail (BRP Portion) [BRP 127]—see mile 408.6.

.0   Ascend the steps at the northern end of the Buck Spring Gap Overlook from the Mount Pisgah extension road. Rise steeply, passing numerous strawberry plants.

.1   The Mountains-to-Sea Trail bears to the left; keep right.

.15   Reach the top of the knob for a somewhat limited view. Bear left and descend.

.2   Rejoin the Mountains-to-Sea Trail.

.3   Come to the Mount Pisgah extension road. The Shut-In Trail [BRP 121] (which the Mountains-to-Sea Trail follows) is a few feet ahead. The Mount Pisgah Trail [BRP 122] is to your left at the end of the road.

Mile 407.8. Picnic Area Loop Trail [BRP 125]

(N 35°24.747 W 82°45.069) Map 60

Length: .3 mile, circuit
Difficulty: easy

Following the Picnic Area Loop Trail is the only way to reach the accommodations (tables, restrooms, and water fountain) in Mount Pisgah's picnic area. Of course, you would not have to walk the whole trail just to enjoy your outdoor meal, but the pathway would make a pleasant after-lunch jaunt. You might even let nature supply your dessert. Blueberries may be found along a section of the trail in mid- to late summer.

.0   Begin near the middle of the picnic parking area next to the gated road. Ascend very gradually on a paved trail through rhododendron.

.05   Come into the open field of the picnic area and pass by the restrooms. Continue on a dirt road.

.1   Bear right at the intersection and walk by picnic tables hidden among the rhododendron and mountain laurel. Be watching for your chance to savor a few wild blueberries.

.2   Do not follow the dirt road into the open meadow; rather, take the trail into the rhododendron tunnel.

.3   Return to the parking area.

Mile 407.8. Picnic Area to Mount Pisgah Campground Connector Trail

[BRP 126] (N 35°24.747 W 82°45.069) Map 60

Length: 1 mile, one way; 2 miles, out-and-back
Difficulty: moderately easy

This connector pathway, a part of the Mountains-to-Sea Trail (see Chapter 1) turns out to be a real surprise. On trail maps of the Mount Pisgah area it looks like a dull, noisy, right-next-to-the-highway type of trail. However, the route quickly drops below the BRP into a dense forest of hemlock and rhododendron. If you didn't know you were so close to the Pisgah Inn, you might believe you were walking through a hidden and isolated cove. The rhododendron forms long, dark tunnels, and the extensive evergreens muffle much of the road noise. Moss, growing right on the treadway, bears witness to the fact that this trail receives little use.

- .0   Begin at the trail post just past the southern end of the picnic area parking lot and descend into a deep forest of hemlock and rhododendron where galax spreads across the earth.
- .25   Pass by galax and a few painted trillium and cross a couple of small water runs.
- .35   Emerge from the rhododendron into a more open forest and ascend gradually.
- .6   Cross over the campground loop trail and continue straight. (The campground loop trail is just what its name says—it encircles the campground to provide access to the various campsites.)
- .7   Pass steps leading up to the BRP. Continue straight, crossing a stone-paved drainage ditch.
- .9   Arrive at and follow the campground road. Reach the campground entrance station, BRP mile 408.8 (N 35°24.161 W 82°45.39.

Mile 408.3. Parking area

Mile 408.6. Pisgah Inn

Lodging, dining, gift shop, and camp store. 828-235-8228; www.pisgah inn.com.

Mile 408.6. Buck Spring Trail (FS Portion) [FS 104]

(N 35°24.182 W 82°45.244) Map 61

> *Length: 6 miles, one way; 12 miles, out-and-back*
> *Difficulty: moderate*
> *Highly recommended*

This just may be the world's most perfect walking path! The route descends from the Pisgah Inn to US RT 276. After a short distance of moderate descent along switchbacks, the grade is so gradual that you can barely perceive that you are dropping. However, your body appreciates it. There are no jolts to your ankles as there would be if you were dropping at a rapid pace, no pressure on your knees from trying to keep yourself from going downhill too fast, and no fatigue to your calf muscles from having to ascend for long periods of time. The one or two ascents are short and extremely gradual. They, in fact, provide a sort of welcome change from the ever-descending trail.

There are no appreciable views along the way, but the many little waterfalls, cascades, and wildflowers make up for that. Shade, courtesy of rhododendron and mountain laurel groves and a thick hardwood forest, will keep the hot summer sun off your brow.

You enter Pisgah National Forest in a couple of tenths of a mile after leaving the Pisgah Inn. Camping is allowed anywhere in the national forest. Although water is plentiful along this route, you would be very hard pressed to find more than one suitable, level campsite.

The Mountains-to-Sea Trail (see Chapter 1) follows the Buck Spring Trail from the Pisgah Inn to mile point 5.1.

To reach the far trailhead by automobile, drive south on the parkway to BRP mile 411.9. Descend east on US RT 276 for almost 2.3 miles to arrive at the wide trailhead parking area on the left side of the road.

.0 Park at the southern end of the Pisgah Inn parking lot, take the concrete walkway between the inn's office and restaurant, descend steps, and turn right on the wide, grassy roadway. The trail may or may not be signed. There are excellent views to the east and out across the ridge you will be descending.

.2 The roadbed comes to an end. Descend on a series of switchbacks. Cancer root is prevalent.

.4 Cross a small water run (that could be dry in summer) and continue via switchbacks.

.5 Recross the same water run and continue on a gently sloping pathway.

.6   Cross another small stream.

.8   Blackberries and raspberries abound!

.9   Cross over a small water run that has an especially pretty little waterfall.

1.0   Cross a water run lined by rhododendron.

1.1   False hellebore grows well around another water run you need to cross.

1.4   Swing around a spur ridge, enjoying the bountiful blueberries.

1.7   As you cross this water run, be sure to look uphill to see the water tumbling down a 40- to 50-foot rock facing.

1.9   Bellflowers appear in great numbers around the trail.

2.1   Cross another water run with small cascades uphill.

2.2   Pass by a large patch of lousewort and enter a blueberry and mountain laurel tunnel.

2.3   Cross a rhododendron-lined stream.

2.5   Cross the largest water run so far; bloodroot and Solomon's seal make an occasional appearance.

2.9   In the early spring, the azalea stands out and the dogwood trees' leaf bracts add a splash of white in an otherwise green forest.

3.0   Cross a rhododendron-crowned spur ridge that might provide a few small tent sites.

3.3   Cross a stream.

3.5   Cross another stream. The trail becomes a little rough and overgrown.

4.2   Cross a large stream.

4.5   Swing around a spur ridge that is covered in dogwood and azalea. Soon cross another stream.

4.9   Intersection.

▶ The Barnett Branch Trail [FS 618] veers off to the left and goes 3.9 miles to its trailhead on FSR 1206.

Stay right to continue on the Buck Spring Trail.

5.1   Cross stream; intersection.

▶ The Mountains-to-Sea Trail takes it leave of the Buck Spring Trail and ascends the steps to the right.

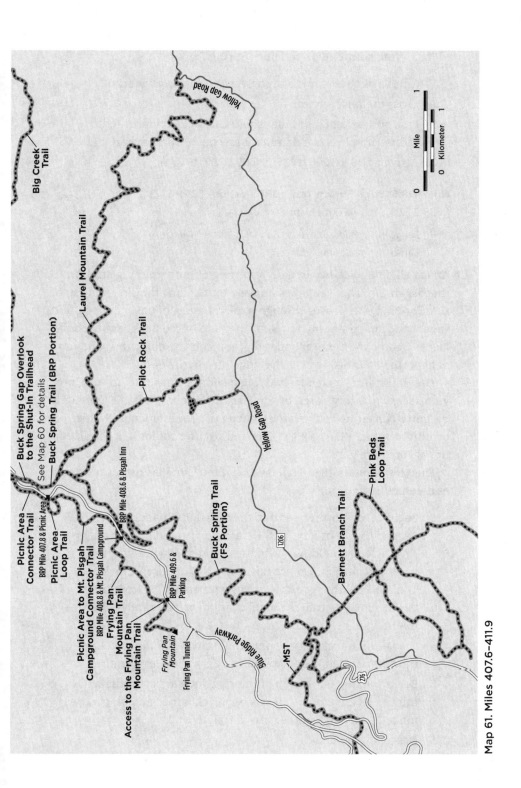

Map 61. Miles 407.6–411.9

Stay left to continue on the Buck Spring Trail.

5.5 Cross a large stream that possesses a rushing waterfall.

5.7 Cross the final stream.

5.8 Pass by a field of giant mayapple and wake robin trillium. Striped maple is the dominant low bush. Begin a gradual rise.

6.0 Arrive at US RT 276 (N 35°22.099 W 82°46.771).

Mile 408.6. Buck Spring Trail (BRP Portion) [BRP 127]
(N 35°24.215 W 82°45.200) Maps 60 & 61

> *Length: 1.1 miles, one way; 2.2 miles, out-and-back*
> *Difficulty: moderately easy*

An excellent choice for an early morning or early evening stroll from the Pisgah Inn. The trail takes an easy route along the side and top of East Fork Ridge. It passes through a mixed forest of oak, hemlock, and rhododendron on its way to the former site of the Buck Spring Lodge. Just as George W. Vanderbilt once did, you, too, can enjoy the panorama of a morning sun rising over the ridgelines in the east.

The trail is intersected by two forest service trails that, in turn, provide access to a large area of the Pisgah National Forest. Camping is permitted on either of the routes, giving rise to several possibilities for overnight hikes. (See BRP 411.9 for more information on Pisgah National Forest trails.)

The Mountains-to-Sea Trail (see Chapter 1) makes use of the route of the Buck Spring Trail.

.0 Begin at the northern end of the Pisgah Inn parking lot. Ascend the steps next to the trail sign, bear left, and pass by several lodge buildings. Rise into a forest of wind-stunted trees and shrubs. (Do not take the old Thompson Creek Trail [FS 602] that goes off to the right about 150 from the parking lot. The trail is rough, overgrown, and rarely—if ever— maintained.)

.15 Cross over a rock outcropping that provides limited winter-time views. Slab the steep hillside on a wide, level trail.

.3 Begin walking on the top of the ridgeline and continue with minor ups and downs. In season, blackberries and blueberries make this a delicious section of trail to walk.

.45 Descend gradually.

.6 Intersection.

▶ The Pilot Rock Trail [FS 321] goes to the right .2 mile to the summit of Little Bald Mountain and 2.3 miles more to end on Yellow Gap Road (FSR 1206). The far trailhead can be reached by car by following the parkway south and exiting at BRP mile 411.9. Descend on US RT 276 for several miles and turn left onto FSR 1206. Continue for almost 4 miles to reach the trailhead.

Bear to the left and descend into rhododendron tunnels to continue on the Buck Spring Trail.

.7 Intersection.

▶ The Laurel Mountain Trail [FS 121] bears to the right for 7.1 miles to Yellow Gap Road. The far trailhead may be reached by following the above directions to the far trailhead of Pilot Rock Trail. Continue 4.5 miles beyond the Pilot Rock Trailhead on FSR 1206 to reach the Laurel Mountain Trailhead.

Bear left and walk on a galax-lined trail to continue on the Buck Spring Trail.

.9 Enter a thick rhododendron tunnel.

1.0 Arrive at the site of Vanderbilt's Buck Spring Lodge, which was used as a hunting and entertaining retreat around the turn of the twentieth century. You'll find pleasing views to the east. Continue straight; the Mountains-to-Sea Trail drops to the left.

1.1 Arrive at the Buck Spring Gap Overlook (N 35°24.911 W 82°44.925) on the Mount Pisgah extension road.

Mile 408.8. Mount Pisgah campground (4,850 feet)

Mile 408.8. Frying Pan Mountain Trail [BRP 128]
(N 35°24.161 W 82°45.392) Map 61

Length: 3.8 miles, out-and-back
Difficulty: moderately strenuous

Along this route you can observe the effects of the harsher weather of an upland environment. The vegetation is strong and healthy near the campground but becomes gnarled and stunted as you cross over an exposed knob.

The Frying Pan Mountain Trail would be a suitable walk to the fire tower to enjoy either sunrise or sunset. In the morning, you could watch the sunlight slowly spread across the Mills River and Davidson River Valleys. In the evening, dark shadows begin to creep up from the Pigeon River to cover Frying Pan Mountain and Mount Pisgah.

You could decrease the length of the hike by 2.2 miles (out-and-back) by starting from the very short (a few feet) connector trail from the small parking area at BRP mile 409.6.

.0   Begin at the trail sign on the campground entrance road. Pass by a couple of service buildings and ascend into an oak forest.

.2   Follow the ridgeline to the left.

.4   Coming close to the edge of the ridge, obtain a limited view to the southeast. The trees become smaller and wind-gnarled as you ascend.

.6   Passing by a few evergreens, begin to descend.

.8   Your objective, the fire tower, can be seen through the vegetation.

1.1   Drop into Frying Pan Gap, so named because local herders used to camp and cook here. The parkway (BRP mile 409.6) is just to your left. Follow the dirt road uphill.

1.3   Avoid the old road that bears right.

1.5   Cross under a utility line and by a gated dirt road to the right.

1.6   The road levels out for a short distance; the fire tower is directly ahead.

1.9   Arrive at the fire tower for a 360-degree view that includes the BRP almost directly below and Mount Pisgah to the north. Retrace steps.

Mile 409.3. Funnel Top Overlook (4,925 feet)

Funnel Top is the appropriately named high point visible from the overlook.

Mile 409.6. Access to Frying Pan Mountain Trail [BRP 129] (4,931 feet)
(N 35°28.713 W 82°46.109) Map 61

A short trail of just a few feet provides access to the Frying Pan Mountain Trail, connecting at the 1.1-mile point of the description above (BRP mile 408.8). Be sure you do not block the road that emanates from the parkway here in Frying Pan Gap.

Mile 410.2. Frying Pan Tunnel

The tunnel is 577 feet long; minimum height is 13 feet, 8 inches.

Mile 410.3. The Pink Beds Overlook (4,825 feet)

Named for the hundreds of thousands of mountain laurel, rhododendron, and azalea that bloom in the lands below the parkway in spring and early summer.

Mile 411. The Cradle of Forestry Overlook (4,710 feet)

The view eastward is of the forest that was a part of America's first school of forestry. See BRP mile 411.9 for more information.

Mile 411.8. Cold Mountain Overlook (4,542 feet)

The 6,030-foot mountain is the high point in the distance and was made famous by Charles Frazier's book of the same name. Frazier lived near the foot of the mountain when he wrote the book, which is based on true events. Incidentally, the 2003 movie with Nicole Kidman and Jude Law was not filmed here, but in the Carpathian Mountains of Romania.

Mile 411.9. Wagon Road Gap. US RT 276 (4,535 feet)

Access to Waynesville (22 miles; full services) and Brevard (18 miles; full services).

Three miles to the west on US RT 276 will bring you to the trailheads of Old Butt Knob [FS 332], Shining Creek [FS 363], and Big East Fork [FS 357] Trails. All of these trails intersect other pathways in the Shining Rock Wilderness (see BRP mile 420.2).

Along its winding descent from the Blue Ridge Parkway eastward toward Brevard, US RT 276 provides access to a succession of worthwhile attractions:

The Pink Beds, described at BRP mile 410.3, can be explored via the moderately easy 4.5-mile circuit Pink Beds Loop Trail [FS 118].

America's first school of forestry is commemorated at the Cradle of Forestry's Forest Discovery Center. Dioramas and exhibits inside tell of the beginning of forestry and provide examples of how conservation has advanced in the past century. An easy 1-mile interpretive trail takes you by structures that were used by Dr. Carl Schenck and his students as they learned how to best manage the country's natural resources. Another 1-mile trail leads to an old sawmill and steam engine. There is a fee to visit.

Why spend big bucks to go to a manufactured water park? Give the forest service a dollar and they will let you spend all day going down a naturally occurring 60-foot waterslide. Looking Glass Creek rushes over a slick, granite face at about 11,000 gallons a minute, dropping you into the 7-foot pool at its base. Of course, you'll have to wait until the summer season to do this, when bathrooms are open and lifeguards are on duty. A bit of natural fun not to be missed.

You can't slide down Looking Glass Falls, but you also don't have to take more than two or three steps from your car to see the creek tumble 60 feet down a rocky chute. If you're feeling energetic, take the dozens of steps to its base and be cooled by the misty spray.

You learned about the trees of the forest at the Forestry Center; now gain knowledge of the creatures that inhabit it at the Pisgah Center for Wildlife Education. Inside displays introduce you to the diversity of wildlife found throughout North Carolina, and an accessible pathway &. has educational exhibits that focus on wildlife and fish management, law enforcement, and conservation education. The kids will enjoy feeding the brook, rainbow, and brown trout in the adjacent fish hatchery.

Possibly the highlight of this side trip from the BRP is the monolithic Looking Glass Rock, its exposed granite surfaces encircling the mountain and reflecting the slanted rays of a low-hanging winter sun. Accessed from US RT 276 via FSR 475, a 3.2-mile (6.4 miles out-and-back), moderately strenuous trail rises, along the rugged terrain (some of the most spectacular scenes in the movie *Last of the Mohicans* were filmed here) to a grand vista from the summit.

More information about all of the attractions along US RT 276 (except Pisgah Center for Wildlife Education—828-877-4423) may be obtained by contacting

> Pisgah Ranger District
> 1600 Pisgah Highway
> Pisgah Forest, NC 28768
> 828-877-3265
> www.fs.usda.gov

Mile 412.2. Wagon Road Gap Overlook (4,550 feet)

Walk a few feet from the parking area to view US RT 276, which was originally nothing more than a footpath across the mountains. Come here in late summer/early fall to witness a most spectacular natural event. At an elevation of 4,535 feet, this area is one of the few, if only, places along the parkway to witness the migration of the monarch butterflies.

Mile 412.2. Mountains-to-Sea Trail (N 35°22.206 W 82°47.493). See Chapter 1.

Mile 413.2. Pounding Mill Overlook (4,700 feet)

There's no mistaking Looking Glass Mountain on the right side of the viewpoint. Frying Pan Mountain is to the left.

Mile 415.7. Cherry Cove Overlook (4,327 feet)

Cherry Cove, named for the abundant black cherry trees that grow there, is directly below the overlook.

Mile 415.7. Mountains-to-Sea Trail (N 35°20.153 W 82°48.898). See Chapter 1.

This section is often referred to as Pisgah Ledges as the trail passes through the Shining Rock Wilderness on the way to an access point on FSR 816 at mile 420.2.

Mile 415.9. Case Camp Ridge Trail [FS 119]
(N 35°20.153 W 82°48.898) Map 62

> *Length: 1.5 miles, one way; 3 miles, out-and-back*
> *Difficulty: moderate*

This little-used trail drops eastward along a ridgeline for slightly over 1.5 miles to FSR 475B. (The closest place to park on the parkway is .2 mile to the north at Cherry Cove Overlook, BRP mile 415.7.) Since it is on national forest land, camping is allowed anywhere along the route. Suitable sites and water, however, may be hard to locate.

The far trailhead may be reached by driving north on the parkway to BRP mile 411.9. Descend east on US RT 276 and, soon after the Cradle of Forestry Visitor Center, turn right onto FSR 475B. The trailhead is .9 mile out this road.

Mile 416.3. Log Hollow Overlook (4,445 feet)

Just as it can be seen from BRP mile 413.2, there is no mistaking Looking Glass Mountain from here. The overlook is named for the major logging operations that took place in this area in the late 1800s.

Mile 417. Looking Glass Rock Overlook (4,493 feet)

The mountain receives its name from the way its granite walls glisten in the sunlight when wet. Like Stone Mountain, visible from BRP mile 232.5, Looking Glass Mountain is a pluton and received its distinctive look when overlying layers of rocks eroded, letting the lower rock swell upward and break off, creating the dome shape.

Mile 417. Skinny Dip Falls and Mountains-to-Sea Trail Access [BRP 130]
(N 35°19.314 W 82°49.677) Map 62

Length: .8 mile, out-and-back to the falls
Difficulty: moderately easy

The three-tiered, 30-foot Skinny Dip Falls is an impressive sight and a recommended outing since you can reach it with such a small amount of effort. Do be aware that this is a popular destination throughout the year, especially on warm summer weekends.

A connector trail enters the forest just north of the Looking Glass Rock Overlook and comes to a junction with the Mountains-to-Sea Trail (See Chapter 1) in .2 mile. (To the right that pathway continues northward to connect with the Bridges Camp Gap Trail [FS 307]. It, in turn, has a junction with the Big East Fork Trail [FS 357], which has nice campsites along its lower reaches.)

To reach Skinny Dip Falls, stay to the left at the original junction and continue on the Mountains-to-Sea Trail to pass through a forest of birch trees as you begin to hear the sounds of the falls. Jewelweed and stinging nettle crowd the trail at .35 mile, just before you descend a steep set of wooden steps to a footbridge at the base of the falls. Plan to spend some time here, wading or swimming in one of the pools just above or below the bridge.

It's possible to continue beyond the falls on the Mountains-to-Sea Trail to gain access to the pathways of the Shining Rock Wilderness. See BRP mile 420.2 for information on those trails.

Mile 418.3. East Fork Overlook (4,995 feet)

The view ahead looks into the valley created by the East Fork of the Pigeon River, which contains Yellowstone Falls. The rugged terrain of the Shining Rock Wilderness is to the left.

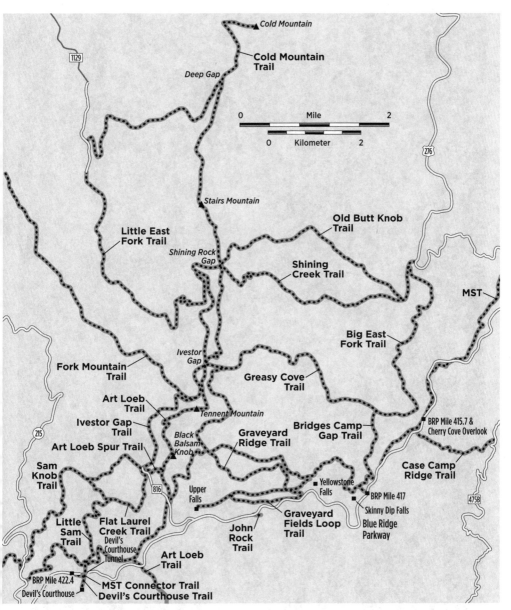

Map 62. Miles 411.9–422.4

Skinny Dip Falls.

Mile 418.8. Graveyard Fields Overlook (4,995 feet)

The fields obtained their name from the hundreds of dead tree trunks lying on the ground, resembling gravestones, after a fire swept across more than 25,000 acres in 1925.

Mile 418.8. Graveyard Fields Loop Trail [BRP 131] (5,120 feet)
(N 35°19.219 W 82°50.824) Map 63

> *Length: 2.2 miles, circuit*
> *Difficulty: moderately easy*

Much of the Shining Rock Wilderness is somewhat reminiscent of the Rocky Mountains along the Continental Divide, and Graveyard Fields is no exception. Even the name of the stream and falls, Yellowstone, evokes the Rockies.

The trail parallels the wide and shallow river, winding through mountain laurel, rhododendron, serviceberry, and open grasslands. A short side trail drops to the base of impressive Yellowstone Falls. Also, the Graveyard Ridge Trail [FS 336] intersects the loop trail to provide easy access to the wilderness.

.0   Descend through mountain laurel and rhododendron on the steps at the northern end of the overlook. Follow a paved trail.

.1   The pavement ends.

.15 Cross the cascading waters of a small creek.

.3   Pass by a rock outcropping with a small cave; the trail then switches back rather precipitously on a badly eroded pathway. Cross the river on a footbridge and turn right on a short side trail to see Yellowstone Falls. Retrace your steps back to the footbridge.

.5   Do not recross the bridge; follow the trail upstream and ascend where serviceberry blossoms dot the trail. Intersection.

▶ Almost immediately the Graveyard Ridge Trail [FS 336] bears to the right, ascending gradually on an old logging road to connect with the Art Loeb Trail [FS 146] (see mile 420.2) at the edge of the Shining Rock Wilderness in about 3 miles. Nice campsites possible along this route.

Keep left to continue on the Graveyard Loop Trail.

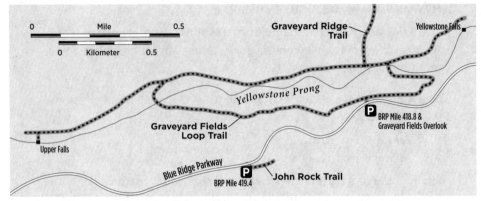

Map 63. Graveyard Fields Loop Trail (mile 418.8)

.6   Walk along the bank where the river is wide and shallow.

.85 Pass by a rock dam that has created a shallow wading pool. Cross a side stream and wind through rhododendron and mountain laurel.

1.0 Cross a small side stream twice. Galax covers the ground like ivy.

1.2 The valley is very wide and open here, affording a view of the surrounding bald mountains.

1.4 Intersection.

   ▶ An unmaintained trail goes right for about .5 mile to the Upper Falls. These falls are impressive, but be aware that the trail is rough and rocky and gains considerable elevation.

Bear left, boulder-hop part of the river, and cross the rest of the stream on a wooden footbridge. Cross a second bridge to continue on the Graveyard Loop Trail.

1.6 Pass through a damp and muddy area and gradually ascend into rhododendron thickets. Continue with minor ups and downs.

2.0 Cross a marshy spot on a 100-foot-long log bridge. The trail then becomes rough and rocky.

2.2 Ascend the steps and return to the overlook.

Mile 419.4. John Rock Trail [BRP 132] (5,330 feet)

(N 35°18.992 W 82°51.300) Map 63

Several short, leg-stretcher trails emanate from the overlook to the edge of the ridgeline for a view into the Davidson River Valley. The official route ascends for .15 mile from the north end of the overlook parking area. For safety's sake, and to prevent erosion, do not take any of the unauthorized trails that descend steeply over the mountainside.

Mile 420.2. FSR 816 (5,550 feet) (N 35°18.934 W 82°52.162)

FSR 816 in Balsam Gap permits access to the Mountains-to-Sea Trail (see Chapter 1) and the Art Loeb Trail [FS 146] with intersecting trails in the Shining Rock Wilderness, an area intensely beautiful and well suited for overnight hiking. (See below for details about the Shining Rock Wilderness trails that all connect, in some fashion, with the Art Loeb Trail.) Some trails lace the open bald mountains, created by logging at the turn of the century and catastrophic fires in 1925 and again in 1942. Other pathways cross over narrow ridgelines, some of which have peaks attaining heights over 5,000 and 6,000 feet. All of the trails connect in some way and even permit access to additional routes in other portions of Pisgah National Forest. The unique conditions in this area make it a highly recommended place to spend some time.

Also connecting with FSR 816 is the Flat Laurel Creek Trail [FS 346] (Map 62), a connector between the Little Sam Trail [FS 347] (Map 62), which intersects the Mountains-to-Sea Trail in 1.4 miles, and the 3-mile Sam Knob Trail [FS 350] (Map 62), which follows old roads and railroad grades from FSR 816 to NC RT 215.

Further information on Shining Rock Wilderness may be obtained by contacting

> Pisgah Ranger District
> 1600 Pisgah Highway
> Pisgah Forest, NC 28768
> 828-877-3265

Mile 420.2. Art Loeb Trail [FS 146], western section

(N 35°18.934 W 82°52.162) Map 62

The 30-mile-long Art Loeb Trail, a National Recreation Trail, connects with the myriad of trails in the Shining Rock Wilderness and Pisgah National Forest, providing many options for extended overnight excursions.

The Art Loeb Trail traverses miles of open heath and grass balds through the Shining Rock Wilderness.

On the western side of the BRP, the trail crosses FSR 816 about .8 mile from the parkway and passes through wonderfully open heath and grass balds to traverse the main ridgeline in the Shining Rock Wilderness for close to 12 miles. The trail ends at a Boy Scout camp on NC RT 1129. Access this far trailhead by automobile by exiting the parkway at BRP mile 423.2. Follow NC RT 215 for 13 miles to the west, and turn right onto NC RT 1129 for 4 miles to the Boy Scout camp.

It is probably best to look at Map 62 when reading this description, as the plethora of intersecting routes can be quite confusing. It will also help you plan some great circuit hikes in the wilderness.

.0   Ascend from FSR 816.

.25   Intersection.

> The Art Loeb Spur Trail (sometimes referred to as Black Balsam Ridge Trail) descends to the left .3 mile to end at FSR 816 and the Ivestor Gap Trail [FS 101].

Stay to the right to continue on the Art Loeb Trail.

.4   Cross the 6,214-foot open summit of Black Balsam and revel in the beauty and space around you.

1.5 Continuing to enjoy the vast views, cross 6,046-foot Tennent Mountain.

2.2 Descend into Ivestor Gap and the intersection with a number of trails.

▶ To the right the Graveyard Ridge Trail [FS 336] gradually descends along an old railroad grade (with good campsites) for 3 miles and intersects with Graveyard Fields Loop Trail [BRP 116] near BRP mile 418.8.

▶ In .2 mile from its intersection with the Art Loeb Trail, the Graveyard Ridge Trail intersects with the 3.2-mile Greasy Cove Trail [FS 362], which has flat spots for camping before it begins to descend to terminate at the junction with 3.6-mile Big East Fork Trail [FS 357]. That route parallels the large stream, passing by some great cascades and swimming holes to end on US RT 276, 3 miles west of BRP 411.9.

▶ Also in Ivestor Gap, the Art Loeb Trail connects with the Ivestor Gap Trail [FS 101], an easy grade that goes off to the left and terminates at the parking area at the end of FSR 816. Great views along its full length of 1.9 miles. With nearly continuous views, a spectacular circuit hike of not quite 5 miles would include the Ivestor, Art Loeb, and Art Loeb Spur Trails.

▶ A little over a mile along the Ivestor Gap Trail, the 7-mile Fork Mountain Trail [FS 109] goes off to the right. That rugged route follows the ups and downs of a major ridgeline with few views in summer to descend to its terminus on NC 215, 8.4 miles from BRP mile 423.2.

▶ In addition, the Ivestor Gap Trail continues straight ahead from Ivestor Gap for 2 miles to end at another maze of intersections in Shining Rock Gap. Along this route, it intersects with the Little East Fork Trail [FS 107], which switchbacks to descend along its namesake stream and end at the Daniel Boone Scout Camp on NC RT 1129.

In Ivestor Gap, bear just barely to the right to continue on the Art Loeb Trail along the main crest of the mountains.

4.0 Arrive in Shining Rock Gap, a large flat area that bears the scars of too many campers. It is also the site of another, almost bewildering intersection of several trails.

▶ Just as it comes into Shining Rock Gap, the Art Loeb Trail contacts the Shining Creek Trail [FS 363], which descends to the right, steeply in places, for 3 miles to end on RT US 276, 3 miles west of BRP mile 411.9. Along its upper portion, the tumbling stream, rocks thickly covered in neon green moss, and a woodland of towering spruce trees call to mind the evergreen forests of New England.

▶ Just a short distance into Shining Rock Gap, the 3.2-mile Old Butt Knob Trail [FS 332] goes right and follows a spur ridge, going over a few knobs to reach Old Butt Knob, where it makes a steep descent of almost 1,500 feet to end at the Shining Creek Trail, about .5 mile from that route's terminus on US RT 276.

▶ The Ivestor Gap Trail departs the Art Loeb Trail to the left on its way back to the parking area on FSR 816.

The Art Loeb Trail continues straight out of Shining Rock Gap, initially on an old railroad grade.

4.8 Reach the top of Stairs Mountain (5,869 feet), the final high point of the Art Loeb Trail before it begins to descend.

6.9 Deep Gap and an intersection.

▶ To the right, the lesser-used Cold Mountain Trail [FS 141] goes 1.5 miles to the 6,030-foot summit made famous by Charles Frazier's best-selling book.

The Art Loeb Trail makes a hard left and descends, sometimes via switchbacks, through a lush cove forest full of wildflowers in the spring.

10.9 The trail ends at Daniel Boone Scout Camp at NC RT 1129.

Mile 420.2. Art Loeb Trail [FS 146], eastern section
(N 35°18.934 W 82°52.162) Map 64

Heading southward from FSR 816, the Art Loeb Trail crosses to the east side of the parkway at mile 421.2 (N 35°18.419 W 82°52.888; no parking) and intersects the 3-mile Farlow Gap [FS 106], 3.6-mile Cat Gap [FS 120], 1-mile Cedar Rock [FS 124], 2.9-mile Butter Gap [FS 123], and 3.5-mile

North Slope [FS 359] Trails on its 19-mile length to arrive at US RT 276 just east of the Pisgah Ranger Station near the Davidson River Campground. (US RT 276 connects with the parkway at BRP mile 411.9.) All of the mentioned trails connect with other forest service trails, providing many miles of hiking and campsites.

More information may be obtained from

Pisgah Ranger District
1600 Pisgah Highway
Pisgah Forest, NC 28768
828-877-3265
www.fs.usda.gov

Mile 421.2. Old Silver Mine

A silver mine operated near here around the turn of the twentieth century.

Mile 421.2. Art Loeb Trail [FS 146] crosses the BRP (no parking)

Mile 421.7. Fetterbush Overlook (5,494 feet)

Nice place for sunset. The fetterbush, a member of the heath family, has long clusters of tiny white blossoms that bloom early in the spring, appearing about a month before the mountain laurel's flower. Drying up later in the year, they resemble small brown peppercorns hanging from the tips of the branches.

Mile 422.1. Devil's Courthouse Tunnel

The tunnel is 665 feet long; minimum height is 14 feet, 2 inches.

Mile 422.4. Devil's Courthouse Overlook (5,462 feet)

The view from the overlook is nearly as spectacular as that from the top of the rock formation at the end of the Devil's Courthouse Trail [BRP 133]. Do not miss stopping at this overlook! See Devil's Courthouse Trail mile point .45 below to know what you are looking at.

Mile 422.4. Devil's Courthouse Trail [BRP 133] (5,462 feet)
(N 35°18.309 W 82°53.962) Map 65

> *Length: .9 mile, out-and-back*
> *Difficulty: moderately strenuous*
> *Highly recommended*

The Cherokees believed that the evil spirit Judaculla once held court inside this massive rock outcropping. You won't have to face this giant devil to enjoy the magnificent view, but the mountain will make you huff and puff to attain it. Fortunately the trail is fairly short and the effort worthwhile.

The trail passes through a highland forest of spruce and fir. The Fraser fir trees here have been as devastated by the woolly adelgid as those near Richland Balsam (BRP mile 431).

The viewpoint is a favorite spot with the locals for watching hawks (and an occasional eagle or falcon) riding the hot air currents that rise from the valleys below.

A short side trail provides access to the Mountains-to-Sea Trail (see Chapter 1).

.0 Walk next to the parkway on the paved sidewalk.

.1 Turn away from the BRP, enter the woods, and ascend rather steeply into a forest of stately evergreens. This is a good spot to enjoy several different songbirds early in the morning. Pass by a bench.

.2 A second bench.

.3 Arrive at another bench—a nice spot to watch the hawks soaring high above. Intersection.

▶ A short trail to the left connects with the Mountains-to-Sea Trail.

Bear right and ascend to continue on the Devil's Courthouse Trail.

.4 Ascend on stone steps. Rhododendron and other shrubs close in on the trail.

.45 Attain the high point of the trail for a grand 360-degree view from which you can see three different states. To the south is South Carolina; to the southwest, Georgia; and to the west, Snow Bird Mountain in Tennessee. The BRP snakes southward onto the Balsam Range. Nearby are Sam Knob in the Shining Rock Wilderness, Richland Balsam, Rich Mountain, and Pilot Mountain. There are almost no signs of civilization! Retrace steps.

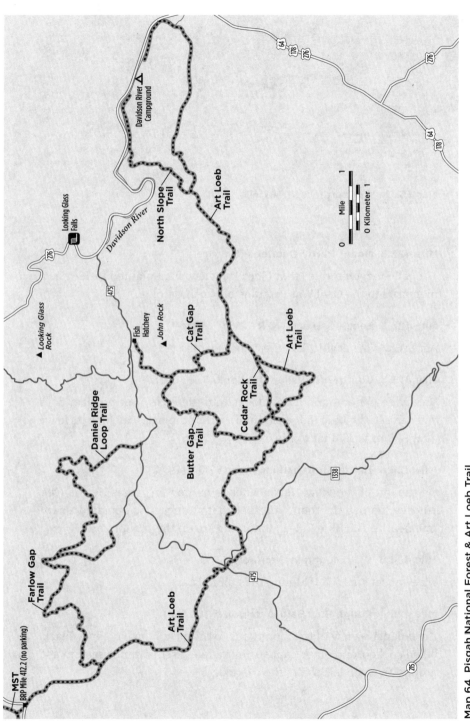

Map 64. Pisgah National Forest & Art Loeb Trail

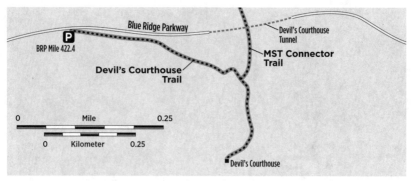

Map 65. Devil's Courthouse Trail (mile 422.4)

Mile 422.8. Mount Hardy Overlook (5,415 feet)

The tall evergreen trees that block the view were planted in 1942 as a memorial to the Civil War veterans of North Carolina.

Mile 423.3. Beech Gap and NC RT 215 (5,340 feet)

Access to Waynesville (23 miles) and Rosman (18 miles).

Mile 423.5. Courthouse Valley Overlook (5,362 feet)

This wide panorama not only looks into the valley, but on clear days you can see the Blue Ridge Mountains (that the parkway took its leave of at BRP mile 354) far to the east.

Mile 424.4. Herrin Knob parking area (5,510 feet)

On the left of the view, Herrin Knob is named for James Herren (yes, whoever named the mountain spelled it wrong), who operated a sawmill nearby. The Blue Ridge Mountains are on the far horizon.

Mile 424.8. Wolf Mountain Overlook (5,500 feet)

Nice sunset spot. Wolf Mountain is directly ahead.

Mile 425.4. Rough Butt Bald Overlook (5,300 feet)

An expansive view of the mountains to the east. Brown creeper, black-billed cuckoo, and black-capped chickadee are sometimes seen in and around the woods close to the overlook.

Mile 425.4. Mountains-to-Sea Trail access [BRP 134]

(N 35°18.250 W 82°56.557) Map 66

> *Length: .15 mile, one way; .3 mile, out-and-back*
> *Difficulty: moderately easy*

A short leg stretcher through a cool, shaded forest, this pathway inter-
sects the Mountains-to-Sea Trail (see Chapter 1). The Mountains-to-Sea
Trail in this area provides access to many of the trails in the Middle
Prong Wilderness, where camping is allowed along any of the routes.

.0 Begin across the BRP from the southern end of the Rough
    Butt Overlook. Enter a cool, shaded forest whose understory
    includes rhododendron and trillium.

.05 Cross a murmuring brook and ascend.

.1 The forest floor becomes very open.

.15 Intersect the Mountains-to-Sea Trail.

Mile 426.5. Haywood Gap Trail [FS 142] Map 66

The closest parkway parking area to this trailhead is Bear Pen parking
area, BRP mile 427.6 (N 35°19.292 W 82°57.894). The Haywood Gap Trail
enters the Middle Prong Wilderness and descends west from the parkway for 3 miles to end at FSR 97. FSR 97 is gated and must be walked
2.5 miles to arrive at the forest service's Sunburst Recreation Area and
campground on NC RT 215. The recreation area may be reached by
exiting the parkway at BRP mile 423.2 and driving west on NC RT 215
for 8.5 miles.

Along the way, Haywood Gap Trail passes by the Mountains-to-Sea
Trail (see Chapter 1) and 2.75-mile Buckeye Gap Trail [FS 126], which
provides access to the Green Mountain Trail [FS 113]. That strenuous,
5-mile route follows a ridgeline with frequent open views to end near
the Sunburst Recreation Area on NC 215.

Mile 427.6. Bear Pen Gap parking area (5,560 feet)

View into the Tuckaseigee River Valley. A good place to hear the whistled too too-too of the small northern saw-whet owl.

Mile 427.6. Bear Pen Gap Trail [BRP 135] (N 35°19.292 W 82°57.894) Map 66

> *Length: 2.8 miles, one way; 5.6 miles, out-and-back*
> *Difficulty: moderate*

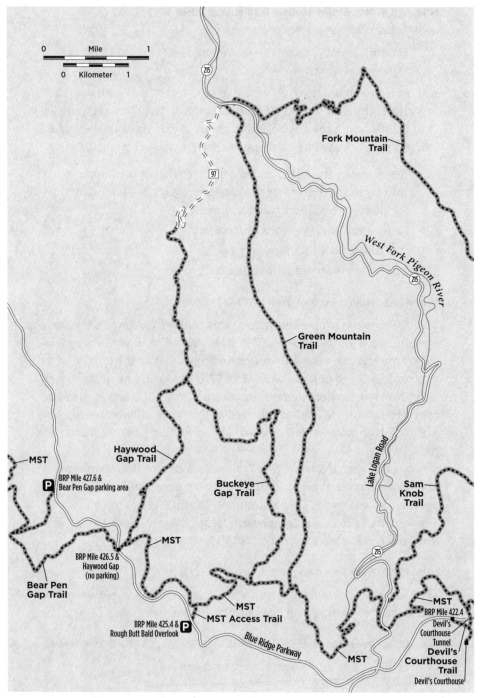

Map 66. Miles 422.4–427.6

Only the first portion of this trail is actually the BRP's Bear Pen Gap Trail. The rest is a part of the Mountains-to-Sea Trail (see Chapter 1). It is a most pleasant walk, as the first half is on an old, almost level roadway lined, in early spring, by abundant wildflowers. The remainder of the route slabs the side of a knob rich with hemlock and rhododendron. There are also two excellent campsites along the route.

.0 Begin on the unmarked trail at the northern end of the overlook. Descend on a well-established trail.

.1 The trail develops into an old woods road.

.2 Spring beauties, trailing arbutus, and trout lilies abound.

.4 Cross a moss-lined water run that descends in small cascades.

.6 A dirt road, the Mountains-to-Sea Trail, comes in from the right. Bear left to continue on the trail.

.7 Pass through a forest service gate and be alert! Make a left turn uphill at the road intersection.

.8 Descend very gradually.

1.0 Begin a gentle rise.

1.2 Be alert! As you enter an open field, the trail leaves the road, makes a hard left, and descends. (The field would be an excellent campsite. The lack of water is compensated by flat land to pitch a tent and wonderfully open views to the east and south. Also, the meadow provides wild strawberries for a snack or dessert.) The route now continues as a narrow pathway bordered by bluets. Slab around the steep hillside. Cross a rock slide in which the builders of this trail have done an excellent job of smoothing the way for you.

1.6 The trail makes a couple of quick, short switchbacks.

1.7 Cross a second rock field and ascend via switchbacks.

1.8 The route levels out and then gradually descends into an evergreen forest.

2.0 Come into a small meadow that also provides a couple of vistas and a few nice, dry campsites. Enter a hemlock forest and ascend.

2.3 Leave the evergreens behind and gradually descend through a hardwood forest.

2.7 Rhododendron closes in on the pathway.

2.8 Arrive at the parkway in Haywood Gap, BRP mile 426.5 (N 35°18.820 W 82°57.248); no parking available. The Mountains-to-Sea Trail crosses the parkway and continues via the Haywood Gap Trail [FS 142].

Mile 427.8. Spot Knob Overlook (5,652 feet)

The spruce and birch forest visible from the westward-looking overlook is good habitat for the Carolina northern flying squirrel.

Mile 428. Caney Fork Overlook (5,650 feet)

The woodlands near the far-reaching eastward-looking vista are also the home of the Carolina northern flying squirrel.

Mile 428.5. Beartrap Gap Overlook (5,580 feet)

Obviously named for the early settlers' practice of trapping bears. A signpost provides information about the black bears that inhabit the lands around the full length of the parkway.

Mile 430.4. Beartrail Ridge parking area (5,872 feet)

Like the forest near mile 427.6, this is a good place to possibly encounter American woodcocks, northern saw-whet owls, and Blackburnian warblers.

Mile 430.7. Cowee Mountains Overlook (5,960 feet)

Receding from the overlook, the Cowee Mountains extend through Jackson, Macon, and Swain Counties. Another good place to hear the whistled *too-too-too* of the small northern saw-whet owl.

Mile 431. Haywood-Jackson Overlook (6,020 feet)

The Balsam Range is ahead, with the Pisgahs on the right.

Mile 431. Richland Balsam Self-Guiding Trail [BRP 136]

(N 35°21.584 W 82°59.214) Map 67

> *Length: 1.4 miles, circuit*
> *Difficulty: moderate*

Here is a chance to observe a forest in transition. Fraser fir was once the dominant tree on this lofty peak. Sadly, perhaps weakened by acid rain and the balsam woolly adelgid, these stately giants are crashing to the

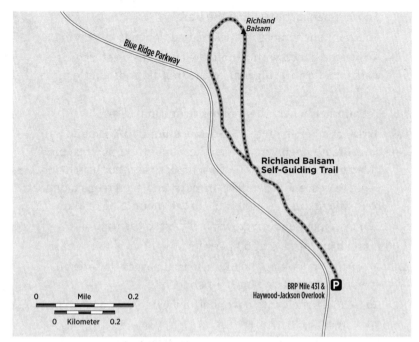

Map 67. Mile 431

forest floor. Some scientists estimate 80 percent of the Fraser firs along this portion of the parkway have succumbed. Plants (such as certain mosses) that depended on the moist conditions the firs provided are dying and being replaced by shrubs and briers.

A brochure keyed to numbered stations on the trail is available at the beginning of the route. It describes plants and trees and discusses the effects of the change in the forest.

A walk along the Richland Balsam Self-Guiding Trail may raise many questions in your mind. Is this a natural process taking place? Could it have been prevented? Will the Fraser firs eventually reestablish themselves? If not, what type of environment will nature now provide?

.0 Begin on a paved trail at the southern end of the Haywood-Jackson Overlook and ascend through an amazingly thick undergrowth.

.1 Arrive at a bench just after the pavement ends.

.15 At the loop trail intersection, bear right and ascend a little more steeply.

.2   Another bench; bluets line the trail.

.3   Another bench; moss is thick and fiddleheads appear in May.

.4   Arrive at a bench with a limited view to the west. Begin to walk on a narrow ridgeline as the trail ascends a little more gradually.

.5   Yet another bench; the trail begins its final climb.

.6   Arrive at a bench on the 6,292-foot summit of Richland Balsam. Breath deeply and enjoy the wonderful fragrance provided by the fir trees. You will soon pass another bench and begin to descend. The rocks, mosses, and evergreens along the route may remind you of trails in the mountains of Maine.

.75 Bench. Rhododendron grows well next to the trail.

1.0 A break in the vegetation permits a slight view to the east.

1.1 A bench overlooking the BRP. The trail passes through an evergreen tunnel and makes a short rise.

1.2 Come to a bench with a wonderful view to the east. Descend once more.

1.3 Return to the loop trail intersection. Bear right.

1.4 Arrive back at the overlook.

Mile 431.4. Richland Balsam Overlook (6,053 feet)

Highest point on the BRP.

Mile 432.7. Lone Bald Overlook (5,635 feet)

Covered by a grassy meadow at the time it was named, Lone Bald, to the right of the overlook, is now overgrown with bushes, windswept trees, and a few spruce trees.

♿ Mile 433.3. Roy A. Taylor Overlook Trail [BRP 137]
(N 35°22.752 W 83°01.009) Map 68

At an elevation of a little more than 5,500 feet, this is a recommended walk. The easy leg stretcher is a paved pathway lined by spiderwort, white bergamot, and jewelweed. It is all of 150 feet long and leads to a constructed elevated platform that juts into space and provides a view of the green expanse of the more than 30,000-acre Roy A. Taylor Memorial Forest. Taylor was the chairman of the U.S. Congress' National Parks and Recreation Committee from 1967 to 1977.

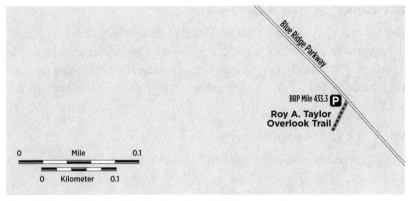

Map 68. Roy A. Taylor Overlook (mile 433.3)

Mile 435.3. Double Top Mountain Overlook (5,365 feet)

Dark Ridge is on the right, Snaggy Bald is to the left, and Deep Ridge Creek flows between the two.

Mile 435.3. Mountains-to-Sea Trail (N 35°23.450 W 83°02.236).
See Chapter 1.

Mile 435.7. Licklog Gap Overlook (5,135 feet)

Be watching for an abundance of birds, including grosbeaks, juncos, towhees, warblers, downy and hairy woodpeckers, blue jays, catbirds, cedar waxwings, and solitary vireos.

Mile 435.7. Mountains-to-Sea Trail (N 35°23.874 W 83°02.564).
See Chapter 1.

Mile 436.8. Grassy Ridge Mine Overlook (5,250 feet)

The mine referred to was a mica mine located below the overlook that operated from the mid-1800s to the mid-1900s. In addition to the birds identified at BRP mile 435.7, yellow-bellied sapsuckers and black-billed cuckoos have been seen in the yellow birch and northern red oak forest near this overlook.

Mile 436.8. Mountains-to-Sea Trail (N 35°24.605 W 83°02.709).
See Chapter 1.

Mile 438.9. Steestachee Bald Overlook (4,780 feet)

Steestachee Bald is the knob to the right in the view.

Mile 439.4. Cove Field Ridge Overlook (4,620 feet)

A large tract of land on Coal Field Ridge was saved from any future development when the Conservation Trust for North Carolina was able to purchase it from willing sellers not long after the turn of the twenty-first century. The organization subsequently deeded the land to the parkway.

Mile 439.7. Pinnacle Ridge Tunnel

At 813 feet, this is the BRP's second-longest tunnel. Minimum height 13 feet, 10 inches.

Mile 440. Saunook Overlook (4,375 feet)

The small Saunook settlement and Pinnacle Ridge can be seen from the overlook.

Mile 440.9. Waynesville Overlook (4,110 feet)

The view of Waynesville is more expansive when the leaves are off the trees.

Mile 441.4. Standing Rock Overlook (3,915 feet)

Look to the southern end of the overlook to see where the name comes from.

Mile 441.9. Rabb Knob Overlook (3,725 feet)

The view is of the Richland Creek Valley and Balsam Gap.

Mile 442.2. Balsam Gap Overlook (3,630 feet)

Black-capped chickadees, not all that common along the BRP, have been spotted in the area around the overlook.

Mile 442.8. BRP maintenance facilities

Mile 443.1. Balsam Gap. US RT 74 and US RT 23 (3,370 feet)

Access to Waynesville (8 miles; full services) and Sylva (12 miles; full services).

Mile 444.6. Mountains-to-Sea Trail (N 35°26.516 W 83°05.815). See Chapter 1.

Mile 444.6. The Orchards Overlook (3,810 feet)

The overlook is named for apple orchards located in the Richland Creek area, although they are not visible from the parkway.

Mile 445.2. Mount Lynn Lowry Overlook (4,000 feet)

The Reverend Billy Graham dedicated the cross located at the summit of the mountain in 1962. The cross honors, Lynn, the daughter of General Sumter Lowry, who died of leukemia that year. Private donations and work by the Conservation Trust of North Carolina permitted land around the summit to be conveyed to the parkway in 2010. Although Sumter Lowry was a champion of land preservation as early as the 1920s, he is most remembered for his political career; he ran for governor of Florida in the 1950s on a segregationist platform.

Woodfin Cascades may be seen from the overlook when the leaves are off the trees.

Mile 446. Woodfin Valley Overlook (4,325 feet)

Birds often seen in the oak forest next to the overlook include the tufted titmouse, solitary vireo, towhee, junco, and several warblers.

Mile 446.7. Woodfin Cascades Overlook (4,535 feet)

The cascades may be heard but not seen from the overlook.

Mile 448.1. Wesner Bald Overlook (4,912 feet)

The Great Balsam Mountains tower above the trees of the overlook to the south and east. Listen for the sound of a saw-whet owl in the early evening.

Mile 448.5. Scott Creek Overlook (5,050 feet)

At 5,050 feet, the overlook is a place to see and hear birds found in the spruce-fir forests and rhododendron thickets of the parkway's higher elevations. It offers a good chance to observe ravens, cedar waxwings, Canada warblers, and golden-crowned kinglets in spring and summer.

Mile 449. Fork Ridge Overlook (5,280 feet)

Below the evergreens next to the overlook (which is exactly 1 mile above sea level) is the Scott Creek Valley. In spring and summer, be watching for brown creepers, red-breasted nuthatches, and black-capped chickadees.

Mile 450.2. Yellow Face Overlook (5,610 feet)

The mountain visible from the overlook has rocks that have a yellowish tint to them, thus the name.

Mile 451.2. Waterrock Knob Visitor Center

A .3 mile access road leads to the visitor center and gift shop, as well as restrooms and water. About .1 mile along the access road is the Browning Knob Overlook, honoring R. Gentry Browning, who was influential in helping locate the BRP in this area of North Carolina.

Mile 451.2. Waterrock Knob Trail [BRP 138] (5,820 feet)
(N 35°27.599 W 83°08.442) Map 69

> *Length: 1.1 miles, out-and-back*
> *Difficulty: moderately strenuous*
> *Very highly recommended*

While the view from the parking area is breathtaking, it will pale in comparison with the exhilaration of ascending the Waterrock Knob Trail. Every step upward reveals a new vista or perspective overlooking the expanse of Pisgah National Forest. Ridgelines rise and fall far into the distance, unspoiled by any signs of human activity. Hiking up the moderately strenuous pathway, you will smell—almost taste—the rich aroma of red spruce and Fraser fir with each breath.

An additional attraction of the Waterrock Knob Trail is that it attains the highest elevation of all of the BRP trails. The summit is higher than the surrounding ground, giving you a free and soaring feeling. The knob is the joining point of the Plott Balsam and Great Balsam ranges.

Don't miss this one!

The Mountains-to-Sea Trail (see Chapter 1) makes use of a portion of the Waterrock Knob Trail.

.0 Follow the paved trail steeply uphill. In 200 feet, the eastbound Mountains-to-Sea Trail goes off to the right.

.1 Pass by a bench.

.15 Come to a second bench and a set of steps overlooking the BRP. The pavement ends soon at a vista to the south and east.

.19 The westbound Mountains-to-Sea Trail goes off to the left.

.35 Come to a bench with a view to the west. The trail now becomes eroded and steeper.

The Waterrock Knob Trail is worth hiking even on inclement days, as it provides views of the parkway snaking through the mists.

.45 Pass by a rock facing and switchback to the right on a set of steps.

.55 Just before the summit, the Plott Balsams Traverse (see the next entry below) goes off to the left. The 6,400-foot summit of Waterrock Knob provides views to the southeast of the Cowee and Nantahala Mountains. To the northeast are the Newfound Mountains. Retrace steps.

Mile 451.2. Plott Balsams Traverse (N 35°27.599 W 83°08.442) Map 69

Length: 8 miles, out-and-back
Difficulty: strenuous

Around 2015, more than 5,300 acres adjoining Waterrock Knob were protected by land purchases through a joint effort of the federal government and a group of conservation organizations. Plans are to incorporate this property into the Blue Ridge Parkway, creating the Waterrock Knob Park.

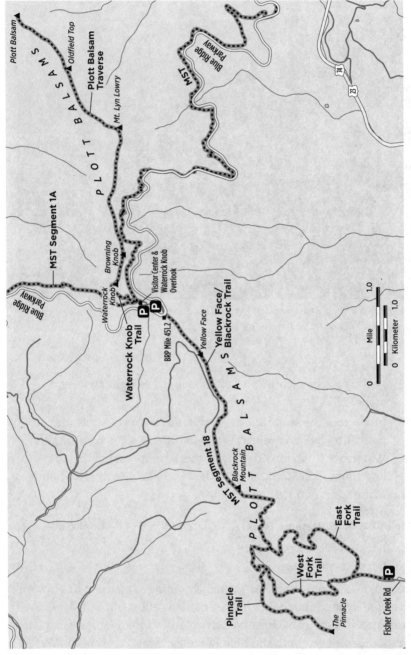

Map 69. Mile 451.2

The purchased land includes some of the highest terrain close to the parkway, with several spots rising above 6,000 feet. As this book went to press, there was no official BRP trail across these summits, but there is what some have described as a "manway," a route that has been used through the years to reach these high points. This description is included for those of you who are comfortable hiking without any markings (although individuals have tried to mark the way by various methods throughout the years) on a route that can be quite steep and strenuous in places. Check at the Waterrock Knob Visitor Center for the most current information.

.0   Follow Waterrock Knob Trail [BRP 138] almost to the summit of the knob.

.55 Just before taking the last set of steps to the top of Waterrock Knob, bear left onto the pathway that begins the Plott Balsams Traverse. Almost immediately begin a rocky and steep descent with a 40 percent grade, followed by an ascent.

1.1 Arrive at the top of Browning Knob above 6,000 feet in elevation. Continue along the undulating ridgeline.

2.2 Arrive at the 6,240-foot summit of Mount Lyn Lowry, topped by a large cross that is visible from miles around (see BRP mile 445.2 for more information). The wide-ranging view from here is similar to that from Waterrock Knob. Beyond the summit, the route descends more than 500 feet in less than .5 mile to a woods road. With other intersecting roads, it may be hard to determine which to take.

3.2 Cross over Oldfield Top (a little lower than 6,000 feet in elevation) with additional views.

3.75 Be on the lookout for the (possibly unmarked) trail that makes the final ascent to Plott Balsam.

4   Reach the wooded 6,088-foot summit. Retrace steps.

8   Arrive back at the Waterrock Knob Visitor Center parking.

Mile 451.2. Mountains-to Sea Trail (N 35°27.417 W 83°08.541) See Chapter 1.

Please Note: The Mountains-to-Sea Trail has two alternate routes to its southern terminus in the Great Smoky Mountains National Park that begin on the Waterrock Knob Trail [BRP 138].

Segment 1A is 68.9 miles long and leaves the Waterrock Knob Trail at .19 mile from that pathway's parking lot. From there, it parallels the

BRP on trail and dirt roads (touching the parkway at Soco Gap Over-look—BRP mile 455.5) before turning westward to follow the length of Heintooga Road (BRP mile 548.2). It then enters the Great Smokies to follow a series of trails to the end point atop Clingman's Dome.

Segment 1B is 49.5 miles long and descends from the Waterrock Knob Trail along the Waterrock Knob access road and makes use of the Yellow Face/Blackrock Trail and pathways in Pinnacle Park (see a description of those trails below). It then passes through the towns of Sylva and Dillsboro, parallels the Tuckasegee River, and finishes by fol-lowing trails in the Great Smokies to Clingman's Dome.

Mile 451.2. Yellow Face/Blackrock Trail and the trails of Pinnacle Park
(N 35°27.417 W 83°08.541) Map 69

A network of pathways on land owned by conservation organizations and the city of Sylva is accessed from the BRP, providing an exploration of another section of the Plott Balsams, this time along the mountain range's more southern peaks.

Park your automobile at the Browning Knob Overlook on the access road to the Waterrock Knob Visitor Center to begin the outings from the parkway. To reach the far trailhead in Pinnacle Park, you will take the parkway's exit ramp at Balsam Gap (mile 443.1) and turn onto US 23/74 to follow it for 8.2 miles toward Sylva for a right turn onto Steeple Road. In just another .2 mile, turn left onto Skyland Road, go an additional .5 mile, make a right onto Fisher Creek Road, and continue 2.2 more miles to the trailhead. Be aware that everyone, even day hikers, must fill out the registration form available at the trailhead kiosk.

Yellow Face/Blackrock Trail (N 35°27.417 W 83°08.541)

> Length: 1.4 miles out-and-back to Yellow Face; 4.4 miles out-and-back to Blackrock; 3.5 miles one way if you are going to join up with and continue on the West Fork Trail
>
> Difficulty: moderate to Yellow Face; strenuous beyond Yellow Face

This primitive but well-used trail runs along the crest of the ridgeline to cross over Yellow Face and Blackrock Mountains for soaring views from elevations of 5,000 to 6,000 feet above sea level. It is possible to continue beyond Blackrock on the trails of Sylva's Pinnacle Park to ad-ditional views from the Pinnacle, or follow descending pathways to the park's trailhead outside the town.

.0 Walk downhill along the Waterrock Knob Visitor Center access road from Browning Knob Overlook.

.1 Cross the BRP and enter the woods on a trail marked by occasional purple and gold blazes (and sometimes blue blazes).

.7 After passing two short side trails with views to the southeast, attain the 6,032-foot summit of Yellow Face with some views southward.

1.5 It may be possible to make camp on the right side of the trail at this point, where you may find rusting machinery parts left over from old logging days. From here, the ridgeline is narrow, less than 10 feet wide in some places.

2.2 After negotiating an ascent by scrambling over roots and rocks that may require the use of both feet and hands, reach the top of Blackrock Mountain at 5,745 feet above sea level. It's time to stop and enjoy the spectacular view: Waterrock Knob is that pyramid-shaped mountain in the near distance, while the two conical mountains further away are Mount Pisgah and Cold Mountain. Almost due south is the town of Sylva with the Cowhee Mountains behind it. To the west are the Great Smoky Mountains. From the summit, the trail descends very steeply—more than 800 feet in .6 mile, without any switchbacks to alleviate the stress on your knees and ankles.

2.8 The narrow trail comes to an end as you meet up with an old woods road.

3.5 The Yellow Face/Blackrock Trail comes to end as the woods road comes to the junction of the West Fork and East Fork Trails.

West Fork Trail (N 35°25.262 W 83°11.436)

> *Length: 1.9 miles, one way (3.8 miles out-and-back) to the junction with the Pinnacle Trail; 2.5 miles one way (5 miles out-and-back) to the junction with the Yellow Face/Blackrock Trail*
> *Difficulty: strenuous*

The West Fork Trail follows old roads along its full length, but be aware that it is an unrelenting ascent of close to 2,000 feet before you reach the main ridgeline.

.0 Follow the quickly rising old woods road from Pinnacle Park's parking area.

.3 Stay to the left when the East Fork Trail goes off the right. (The East Fork Trail rises steadily for a little over 2 miles to meet back up with the West Fork Trail at the 2.5 mile point.)

.5 Cross Fisher Creek, the last reliable source of water on this hike.

.7 The side trail to the left goes .1 mile to Campsite #1.

1.6 The side trail to the right goes to Campsite #2.

1.9 Junction with the Pinnacle Trail. Keep to the right to stay on the West Fork Trail.

2.5 The West Fork Trail comes to an end at the junction of the East Fork and Yellow Face/Blackrock Trails.

The Pinnacle Trail (N 35°26.284 W 83°11.132)

> *Length: 2.8 miles out-and back from the junction with the West Fork Trail*
> *Difficulty: Moderate (with a strenuous .2 mile just before the Pinnacle)*

The Pinnacle has such an awe-inspiring view that reaching it has almost become a rite of passage for students of nearby Western Carolina University.

.0 From the junction of the West Fork Trail and the Pinnacle Trail, continue on the Pinnacle Trail along an old woods road gradually ascending the ridgeline to the south.

.6 Pinnacle Park's Campsite #3 is to the right. The woods road soon comes to an end, and the trail continues along a narrow pathway.

1.4 Break out into the open on the multiple rock outcroppings that make up the Pinnacle and provide soaring views in all directions. The town of Sylva is almost directly below you, nearly 2,500 lower in elevation. To the north are Blackrock and Yellow Face, while to the northeast it is possible to trace US 74 along Scott Creek Valley to Balsam Gap, the dividing point of the Great Balsam and Plott Balsam Mountains. Retrace your steps.

2.8 Return to the West Fork Trail.

Mile 452.1. Cranberry Ridge Overlook (5,475 feet)

The high elevation makes this a place to watch for spring and summer birds, such as a winter wren, veery, or dark-eyed junco.

Mile 452.3. Woollyback Overlook (5,420 feet)

The ridge below and to the right of the overlook receives its name from the thick growths of mountain laurel and rhododendron shrubs that give it a "woolly" look. Since the ridge was named, a number of spruce trees have become established, breaking through the shrubs and growing above them.

Mile 453.4. Hornbuckle Valley Overlook (5,105 feet)

Descending the eastern side of the Blue Ridge Mountains, Hornbuckle Creek flows into the Qualla Reservation. It's named for John Hornbuckle, a Cherokee who fought for the Union during the Civil War and later farmed the area.

Mile 454.4. Thunder Struck Ridge Overlook (4,780 feet)

The ridge, whose name origin should be quite obvious, is located about 100 feet below the overlook.

Mile 455.1. Fed Cove Overlook (4,550 feet)

The cove purportedly received its moniker from a settler who was known only as "Fed."

Mile 455.5. Soco Gap Overlook (4,570 feet)

Unless the vegetation has been cut down, this is a parking area more than an overlook.

Mile 455.5. Mountains-to-Sea Trail (N 35°29.656 83°09.348 W)
See Chapter 1.

Mile 455.7. Soco Gap and US RT 19 (4,340 feet)

Access to Dellwood (8 miles) and Cherokee (12 miles).

Mile 456.2. Jonathan Creek Overlook (4,460 feet)

Like Soco Gap Overlook at mile 455.5, this is more of a parking area than an overlook. The creek is named for early pioneer Jonathan McPeters, who lived for a short while near where the creek empties into the Pigeon River.

Mile 457.7. Enter Cherokee Indian Qualla Reservation

Mile 457.9. Plott Balsam Overlook (5,020 feet)

The Plott Balsam Mountains are named for a family of 1700s settlers who emigrated from Germany. Geographically, the mountain range stretches, more or less, from the Tuckaseigee River to the southwest to Maggie Valley to the northeast. The range is bordered by the Great Balsam and the Great Smoky Mountains.

Mile 458.2. Heintooga Spur Road (5,100 feet) (N 35°30.599 W 83°10.739)

The 8.9-mile-long Heintooga Spur Road provides access from the parkway to a southeastern corner of the Great Smoky Mountains National Park.

1.3 Mile High Overlook (5,250 feet). A spectacular view of the Great Smoky Mountains. The highest point of the entire 2,100+-mile Appalachian Trail, Clingmans Dome, is on the far left of the vista. A little more to the right is Mount LeConte hiding behind the mass of Mount Kephart. Farther right is Mount Guyot. The valley below the overlook is Bog Cove in the Qualla Reservation.

1.4 Maggie Valley Overlook (5,215 feet). At one time, Maggie Valley was an isolated outpost and lumber camp. Today, the lights shining at night show just popular and populated it has become.

2.3 Lake Junaluska Overlook (5,030 feet). Good luck seeing the lake in spring and summer, but you do have the opportunity to see a hairy woodpecker, red-eyed vireo, eastern wood-pewee, and white-breasted nuthatch.

3.3 Horsetrough Ridge parking area (4,540 feet). Named for horse-troughs that had been carved from a hollow tree.

3.6 Black Camp Gap parking area (4,500 feet). Boundary of the Great Smoky Mountains National Park.

3.6 ♿ Masonic Marker Trail [BRP 139] (N 35°32.081 W 83°10.296) Map 70. A paved leg-stretcher of 250 feet that leads to an interesting monument. Erected in 1938, the marker contains more than 600 stones from 41 countries and every one of the earth's continents. Assemblies of Masons have taken place here every year since 1935, and the monument was erected to symbolize the universality of the organization. The notable construction of the monument makes a stop here worthwhile,

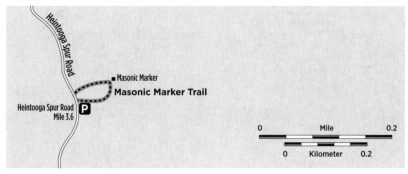

Map 70. Masonic Marker Trail

even if you have no interest in the Masons. Elk are often seen grazing (and, unfortunately, being fed by visitors) here.

3.9 Parking overlook (4,540 feet). Listen for the sound of the saw-whet owl from April into June.

4.8 Parking overlook (4,475 feet). It may be possible to see Flat Creek Falls when the leaves are off the trees.

5.3 Parking area and southern trailhead of the Flat Creek Trail—see mile 8.9 below for more information about the trail.

6.0 Parking area (5,130 feet) (N 35°33.800 W 83°09.700). Pathways leading to a network of the Great Smokies' trails, most notably the Cataloochee Divide, Rough Fork, Hemphill, and Polls Gap Trails, emanate from the parking area. Blackburnian warblers may be seen here in spring and summer.

6.2 Parking area.

8.4 Balsam Mountain campground (5,340 feet) (N 35°34.079 W 83°10.547).

8.9 Heintooga Ridge picnic area (5,335 feet) (N 35°34.390 W 83°10.818). Two trails (Map 71) emanate from the picnic area. The Flat Creek Trail winds for 2.5 miles through a spruce and birch forest. It passes by Flat Creek Falls and ends at a point (N 35°33.249 W 83°09.828) on the spur road 3.6 miles from the picnic area (and 5.3 miles from the parkway). The self-guiding Balsam Mountain Nature Trail (.6 mile) connects the picnic area with the campground.

9.0 Parking area (5,323 feet). End of paved road. A one-way motor nature road (gravel) continues into Great Smoky Mountains National Park.

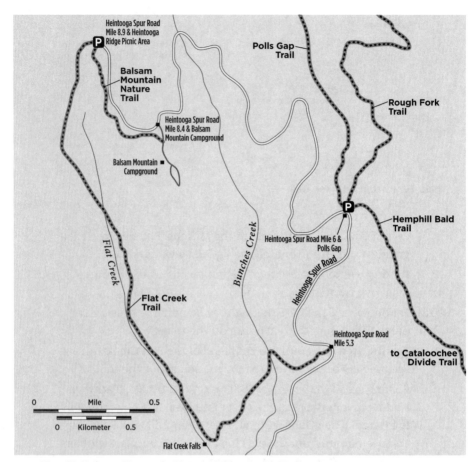

Map 71. Balsam Mountain Nature & Flat Creek Trails

Mile 458.8. Lickstone Ridge Tunnel

The tunnel is 402 feet long; minimum height is 11 feet, 1 inch.

Mile 458.9. Lickstone Overlook (5,150 feet)

Grand view of the mountains to the southeast. Coyotes have been heard yipping in the distance on a number of occasions from this overlook.

Mile 459.3. Bunches Bald Tunnel

It is only 255 feet long and is the BRP's lowest tunnel, with a minimum height of 10 feet, 6 inches.

Mile 459.5. Bunches Bald Overlook (4,925 feet)

Bunches Bald rises about 600 feet higher than the overlook.

Mile 460.8. Jenkins Ridge Overlook (4,445 feet)

Jenkins Ridge, to the left, is named for an early settler. Look for least flycatchers and yellow-bellied sapsuckers in spring and summer.

Mile 461.2. Big Witch Tunnel

Its length is 348 feet; minimum height is 11 feet, 3 inches.

Mile 461.6. Big Witch Gap, Indian Road, and Bunches Creek Road
(4,160 feet)

Mile 461.9. Big Witch Overlook (4,150 feet)

Excellent view of the Great Smoky Mountains. Big Witch is the anglicized name of a famous Cherokee medicine man who lived to be more than 90 years old.

Mile 462.3. Barnett Fire Tower Road

Mile 463.9. Thomas Divide Overlook (3,735 feet)

Thomas Divide is the ridge to the left. Sourwood, red maple, and black locust grow near the overlook. The locust leafminer feeds on a number of trees, including apples, cherries, beech, birch, and oaks, but it favors black locust. The adult leafminers overwinter in bark crevices and feed on and skeletonize the lower surface of newly emerged spring leaves. Soon they deposit eggs from which the larvae emerge to bore into a leaf and feed. By midsummer, they begin the season's second generation, causing early browning and dropping of leaves, sometimes as soon as late August.

Mile 465.6. Rattlesnake Mountain Tunnel

The tunnel has a length of 395 feet and a minimum height of 14 feet, 5 inches.

Mile 466.2. Sherill Cove Tunnel

It is 550 feet long. Minimum height is 14 feet, 4 inches.

Mile 467.4. Ballhoot Scar Overlook (2,550 feet)

"Ballhoot!" is what loggers would yell when a tree they had cut was sent sliding down the mountain, creating a scar on the hillside. Some of these scars are still visible along parkway trails.

Mile 467.9. Raven Fork Overlook (2,400 feet)

The view is onto the eastern side of the Great Smoky Mountains National Park. Just below the overlook are the meadows of Floyd Bottoms, within the park.

Mile 468.4. Oconaluftee Overlook (2,200 feet)

It is interesting to think about the journey that water takes. The Oconaluftee River rises within the heights of the Great Smoky Mountains and flows into the Tuckaseigee River, which enters Fontana Lake and the Little Tennessee River. The latter flows into the Tennessee River, which empties into the Ohio River, which, in turn, makes its way to the Mississippi River. So a drop of rain that falls on the eastern side of the Great Smokies might travel all the way to the Gulf of Mexico.

Mile 469.1. US RT 441 and the southern terminus of the Blue Ridge Parkway

Access to Cherokee, North Carolina (2 miles), and Gatlinburg, Tennessee (29 miles). The Great Smoky Mountains National Park Oconaluftee Visitor Center is located on US RT 441. The Great Smokies, of course, offer a large network of hiking and walking trails.

More information on the Great Smoky Mountains National Park may be obtained by contacting

> Great Smoky Mountains National Park
> 107 Park Headquarters Road
> Gatlinburg, TN 37738
> 865-436-1200
> www.nps.gov/grsm

There is a wide variety of guides to the trails of the Great Smoky Mountains National Park. Several are available in the Oconaluftee Visitor Center or may be obtained through the Great Smoky Mountains Natural History Association.

> Great Smoky Mountains Natural History Association
> 115 Park Headquarters Road
> Gatlinburg, TN 37738
> 865-436-7318; 888-898-9102
> www.smokiesstore.com

APPENDIXES

Appendix A. Blue Ridge Parkway Offices

Blue Ridge Parkway Central Office

> Blue Ridge Parkway
> 199 Hemphill Knob Road
> Asheville, NC 28803
> 828-271-2779
> For emergencies: 800-PARKWATCH (800-727-5928)
> Recorded information: 828-298-0398
> TDD 828-298-0358
> www.nps.gov/blri

Blue Ridge Parkway Ranger Offices

The ranger offices are sometimes better equipped to supply you with detailed information about trails and conditions in their own districts than the central BRP office in Asheville. However, these offices are not staffed twenty-four hours a day. If you find an office closed in an emergency, you should call 911 and then PARKWATCH at 800-727-5928.

Ridge District (Miles 0–106)

Mile 29	Montebello Office 133 Whetstone Ridge Drive Vesuvius, VA 24483 540-377-2105
Mile 66.3	James River/Big Island Office P.O. Box 345 Big Island, VA 24525 434-299-5941
Mile 85.9	Peaks of Otter Office 85919 Blue Ridge Parkway Bedford, VA 24523 540-586-4357

Plateau District (Miles 106–216.7)

Mile 112   Vinton Office
2551 Mountain View Road
Vinton, VA 24179
540-857-2213

Mile 167.1   Rocky Knob Office
1670 Blue Ridge Parkway
Floyd, VA 24091
540-745-9660

Mile 199.4   Fancy Gap Office
134 Ranger Road
Fancy Gap, VA 24328
276-728-4511

Highland District (Miles 216.7–303)

Mile 245.5   Laurel Springs Office
49800 Blue Ridge Parkway
Laurel Springs, NC 28644
336-372-8568

Mile 294.4   Sandy Flats Office
Route 1, Box 565
Blowing Rock, NC 28605
336-372-8568

Pisgah District (Miles 305–469.1)

Mile 330.9   Gillespie Gap Office
Route 1, Box 798
Spruce Pine, NC 28777
828-765-6082

Mile 382.3   Oteen Ranger Station
51 Ranger Drive
Asheville, NC 28805
828-298-0281

Mile 442.8   Balsam Gap Office
Balsam Gap
Waynesville, NC 28786
828-456-9530

Appendix B. Inns, Lodges, and Cabins on the Blue Ridge Parkway

These facilities are operated by private concessionaires under contract with the park service. Contact the particular facility to make reservations or obtain detailed information.

Mile 85.6   Peaks of Otter Lodge
85554 Blue Ridge Parkway
Bedford, VA 24523
866-387-9905
www.peaksofotter.com

Mile 169   Rocky Knob Cabins

Please Note: As this book went to press, the cabins were closed, and it is in doubt if they will repopen. Contact BRP Main Office for up-to-date information.

Mile 241.1   Bluffs Lodge

Please Note: Bluffs Lodge was closed as this book went to press. Contact BRP Main Office for up-to-date information.

Mile 408.6   Pisgah Inn
P.O. Drawer 749
Waynesville, NC 28786
828-235-8228
www.pisgahinn.com

The Blue Ridge Parkway Association publishes a very complete directory of commercial accommodations, services, and attractions within easy driving range of the BRP. The directory is available free of charge at most parkway facilities or by contacting

Blue Ridge Parkway Association
P.O. Box 2136
Asheville, NC 28802
828-670-1924
www.blueridgeparkway.org

Appendix C. Campgrounds on the Blue Ridge Parkway

BRP campgrounds are usually open from May through October. Some sites do stay open year-round, but these can change from year to year. Call 828-298-0398 for the most up-to-date information. Camping is permitted only in the designated campgrounds. Drinking water and restrooms are provided. Shower and laundry facilities are not available, except at Mount Pisgah Campground. (There are plans to provide showers in other campgrounds as funds become available.) There are no hookups, but each campground does have a sanitary dumping station. Advance reservations for all of the campgrounds except Crabtree Falls, which is on a first-come, first-serve basis, may be made by calling 877-444-6777 or through www.recreation.com. Please remember that camping is prohibited along all of the "official" BRP trails, except in the three designated backcountry areas noted below.

Mile 60.9	Otter Creek (779 feet)
Mile 86	Peaks of Otter (2,875 feet)
Mile 167	Rocky Knob (2,995 feet). Backcountry camping (1,790 feet) also available; required permits (free) can be obtained at the ranger station (mile 167; 540-745-9661) or the campground office.
Mile 239.2	Doughton Park (3,650 feet). Backcountry camping (1,555 feet) also available; free permits may be obtained from the ranger station (49800 Blue Ridge Parkway, Laurel Springs, NC 28644; 336-372-8568) at BRP mile 245.4.
Mile 296	Johns River Road Trail [BRP 84]. Backcountry camping only (3,350 feet); from mid-May until the end of October, permits must be obtained at Julian Price Memorial Park Campground (mile 296.9; 828-963-5911). Off-season permits can be obtained at the Sandy Flats Ranger Office (5580 Shulls Mill Road—mile 294.6; 828-295-7591).
Mile 297.1	Julian Price Memorial Park (3,440 feet)
Mile 316.4	Linville Falls (3,197 feet)
Mile 339.5	Crabtree Falls (3,760 feet)
Mile 408.6	Mount Pisgah (4,850 feet)

Appendix D. Blue Ridge Parkway Roadside Bloom Calendar

This is a general guideline of the common and/or showy plants on the parkway. There are other flowers on the BRP not listed here, and blooming times will vary from year to year according to the weather. Usually flowers will appear in Virginia before they do in North Carolina, because of Virginia's lower average elevation. Use this guide whenever you can; seeking out and identifying certain plants will no doubt add to your enjoyment of the parkway.

The plants are organized by blooming time, starting in February. The abbreviation "PA" indicates a picnic area.

This information is supplied courtesy of the U.S. National Park Service, Blue Ridge Parkway.

Flower	Peak Bloom	Mile Point or General Location
Skunk Cabbage *Symplocarpus foetidus*	February–March	176.1, 185.8, 217.0
Dandelion *Taraxacum officinale*	February–June	Common along road
Dwarf Iris *Iris verna*	March–April	260.5
Mayapple *Podophyllum peltatum*	March–April	76.2–76.4, 296–297, 315–317, 320.8, 339.5
Spring Beauty *Claytonia caroliniana*	March–April	Craggy Gardens PA
Birdfoot Violet *Viola pedata*	March–May	147.4, 202, 260.5, 379
Serviceberry-Sarvis *Amelanchier arborea*	March–May	241–242, 294–297, 308.3, 347.6, 368–370
Silver-Bell Tree *Halesia carolina*	March–May	344.1–355.3
Buttercups *Ranunculus hispidus*	March–June	Common along road
Wild Strawberry *Fragaria virginiana*	March–June	Common along road
Bloodroot *Sanguinaria canadensis*	April–May	85.6, 191–193, 198.7, 294
Crested Dwarf Iris *Iris cristata*	April–May	195, 198, 210, 250.8, 273.4, 379
Fringed Phacelia *Phacelia fimbriata*	April–May	365–370

Flower	Peak Bloom	Mile Point or General Location
Golden Groundsel *Senecio aureus*	April–May	29.1, 85.8 (PA), 330–340
Great Chickweed *Stellaria pubera*	April–May	Common in rich, moist woods
Indian Paintbrush *Castilleja coccinea*	April–May	369–371
Pinxter Flower *Rhododendron nudiflorum*	April–May	4, 92–97, 138.6, 145.5, 154.5 (PA), 162.9, 211.6
Princess Tree *Paulownia tomentosa*	April–May	100–123, 381–382, 396, 400
Solomon's Seal *Polyganatum biflorum*	April–May	Common in moist, wooded slopes and coves
Squirrel Corn *Dicentra canadensis*	April–May	Craggy Gardens PA, 458.2 (Heintooga Spur Road)
Trillium *Trillium spp.*	April–May	175, 200–216, 339–340, 364.6
Tulip Poplar *Liriodendron tulipifera*	April–May	Common in low woods and coves
Heal All *Prunella vulgaris*	April–frost	Common along road
Fetterbush Late *Leucothoe racemosa*	April–May	241.1, 379
Redbud *Cercia canadensis*	Late April–May	54–68
Black Locust *Robina pseudo-acacia*	April–June	100–123, 367–368, 383
Dutchman's Breeches *Dicentra cucullaria*	April–June	367.8 (PA), 458.2 (Heintooga Spur Road)
False Solomon's Seal *Smilacina racemosa*	April–June	Common along road
Foam Flower *Tiarella cordifolia*	April–June	269.9, 339.5, 369.7 (PA)
Witch Hobble-Hobblebush *Viburnum alnofolium*	April–June, August (fruit)	295.5, 362–367, higher elevations in rich, moist woods
Carolina Rhododendron *Rhododendron minus*	Late April–June	308–310, 404–411

Flower	Peak Bloom	Mile Point or General Location
Dogwood *Cornus florida*	May	6, 85.8 (PA), 154.5 (PA), 217–219, 230–232, 378–382
Fraser Magnolia *Magnolia fraseri*	May	173–174, 252–253
Large-Flowered Trillium *Trillium grandiflorum*	May	3–7, 64–85, 154.5 (PA), 168–169, 175, 330–340, 370–375
Allegheny Blackberry *Rubus allegheniensis*	May–June	6, 167.2, 239.9, 305–315, 339.5, 367.6 (PA)
Bead Lily *Clintonia umbellulata*	May–June	Common in rich, moist deciduous woods
Bittersweet *Calastrus orbiculatus*	May–June	242.4, 383, 394, 396
Bluets *Houstonia spp.*	May–June	200.2, 355–368 (PA)
Bowman's Root *Gillenia trifoliata*	May–June	24–45, 149.5, 260, 332, 368–369
Bristly Locust *Robinia hispida*	May–June	167–174, 308.3, 347.9
Field Hackweed *Hieracilum pratense*	May–June	6, 78.4, 165.5, 229.5, 325–330
Fire Pink *Silene virginica*	May–June	1–2, 85.8 (PA), 154.5 (PA), 241 (PA), 339.3 (PA), 367–375, 404–408
Flame Azalea *Rhododendron calendulaceum*	May–June	138.6, 144–145, 149.5, 164–166, 217–221, 308–310, 368–380, 412–423
Galax *Galax aphylla*	May–June	Common in deciduous forests and open rocky areas
Hawthorne *Crataegus spp.*	May–June	155–176, 365.6, 368
New Jersey Tea *Caenothus americanus*	May–June	42–43, 91–100, 138.4, 197, 211, 241, 328.6
Pinkshell *Rhododendron vaseyi*	May–June	305.2, 342–343, 349–351, 419–424
Red-Berried Elder *Sambucus pubens*	May–June	355–360, 369, 412–425, higher elevations in rich, moist woods
Small's Groundsel *Senecio smallii*	May–June	29.1, 85.8 (PA), 330–340

Flower	Peak Bloom	Mile Point or General Location
Staghorn Sumac *Rhus typhina*	May–June	Common along road in dry, rocky areas
Wild Geranium *Geranium maculatum*	May–June	84–86, 170–172, 211.6, 375
Columbine *Aquilegia canadensis*	May–July	74–75, 339.3 (PA), 370–378
Fly Poison *Amianthium muscaetoxicum*	May–July	210–216, 406–408
Phlox *Phlox carolina*	May–July	4, 79–82, 163–164, 200–202, 219–221, 339.3 (PA), 370–380
Bladder Campion *Silene cucubalus*	May–August	376–381
Queen Anne's Lace *Daucus carota*	May–September	Common along open fields and road
Mountain Laurel *Kalmia latifolia*	Late May–June	130.5, 162.9, 347.9, 380, 400
Virginia Spiderwort *Tradescantia subaspera*	Late May–July	85.8 (Sharp Top Trail), 380–381
Catawba Rhododendron *Rhododendron catawbiense*	June	44.9, 77–83, 130.5, 138.6, 239, 247, 266.8, 348–350, 364.1
Goat's Beard *Aruncus dioicus*	June	10–11, 24, 240, 337.6, 370–375
Sundrop *Oenothera fruticosa*	June	8–10, 89–91, 229, 270.6, 351–352, 355–360, 370–375
Tree of Heaven *Ailanthus altissima*	June	Common along road in Virginia, 382
Viper's Bugloss *Echium vulgare*	June	5–40
American Elder *Sambucus canadensis*	June–July	29, 85.8 (PA), 136–138, 272–275, 311.2
Beard Tongue *Penstemmon spp.*	June–July	44.4, 89–91, 154.5 (PA), 254.5, 339–340, 370–372
Fragrant Thimbleberry *Rubus odoratus*	June–July	18, 74.7, 339.3 (PA), 369–372, 406–408
Mountain Ash *Sorbus americana*	June–July	Higher elevation spruce-fir forests, Mount Mitchell, Mount Pisgah

Flower	Peak Bloom	Mile Point or General Location
Sourwood *Oxydendrum arboretum*	June–July	102–106, 231–232, 321–327, 375–380
Spirea *Spirea japonica*	June–July	368–378
White Rhododendron *Rhododendron maximum*	June–July	162.9, 169 (PA), 232–233, 339.3 (PA), 352–353, 455–456
Butter and Eggs *Linaria superbum*	June–August	Common along road and waste places
Butterfly Weed *Asclepias tuberosa*	June–August	63–65, 238–246
Coreopsis *Coreopsis pubescens*	June–August	29.6, 77, 157, 190, 306
Deptford Pink *Dianthus armeria*	June–August	Common along grassy roadsides
False Hellebore *Veratrum viride*	June–August	346.6, Craggy Gardens Nature Trail
Turkscap Lily *Lilium superbum*	June–August	187.6, 364–368, 406–411
Mullein *Verbascumthapsus*	June–September	Common along road on dry banks
Bull Thistle *Carduus lanceolatus*	Late June–frost	Common along road and pastures at lower elevations
Black Cohosh *Cimicifuga racemosa*	July	6, 85.8 (PA), 169 (PA), 374
Black-Eyed Susan *Rudbeckia hirta*	July	Common in fields and along road
Fleabane *Erigeron strigosus*	July	Common in fields and along road
Ox-Eye Daisy *Chrysanthemum leucanthemum*	July	Common in fields and along road
Tall Meadow-Rue *Thalictrum polyganum*	July	85.8 (PA), 155.2, 248
Yarrow *Achillea millefolium*	July	Common in fields and along road
Bergamot or Beebalm *Monarda fistulosa*	July–August	38.8, 368–374
Common Milkweed *Asclepias syriaca*	July–August	85–86, 167–176

Flower	Peak Bloom	Mile Point or General Location
Oswego Tea *Monarda didyma*	July–August	Common in wet areas at higher elevations
Tall Coneflower *Rudbeckia laciniata*	July–August	36, 161.2, 228.1, 314, 359–368
Bellflower *Campanula americana*	July–September	370–375
Starry Campion *Silene stellata*	July–September	378–380
White Snakeroot *Eupatorium rugosum*	July–October	Common along road
Boneset *Eupatorium perfoliatum*	August	29.1, 85.8 (PA), 151, 247, 314
Cardinal Flower *Lobelia cardinalis*	August	Infrequently in wet areas
Ironweed *Vernonia noveboracensis*	August	245, 248
Jewel Weed *Impatiens capensis*	August	Common along road in wet areas
Joe-Pye-Weed *Eupatorium purpureum*	August	6, 85.8 (PA), 146, 248, 339.3 (PA), 357–359
Pokeberry *Phytolacca americana*	August	6, 74.7, 151, 239.9, 323, 376.9
Virgins Bower *Clematis virginiana*	August	13.1, 85.8 (PA), 176.1, 285–289, 313–314
Angelica *Angelica triquinata*	August–September	295.7, 339.5, 355, Craggy Gardens Nature Trail
Blazing Star *Liatris spicata*	August–September	305.1, 369–370
Dodder or Love Vine *Cuscuta rostrata*	August–September	Common along road
Sneezeweed *Helenium autumnale*	August–September	29.1, 85.8 (PA), 176.1, 229, 313–314
Nodding Lady Tresses *Spiranthes cernua*	August–frost	365–368
Gentian *Gentiana quinquefolia*	Late August–frost	85.8, 363–368

Flower	Peak Bloom	Mile Point or General Location
Aster *Aster spp.*	September	Common in fields and along road
Goldenrod *Solidago spp.*	September	Common in fields and along road
Yellow Ironweed *Actinomeris alternifolia*	September–October	6, 88, 154.5, 271.9, 330.8
Witch Hazel *Hamamelis virginiana*	Late September–October	130.5, 293.3, 295, 305.1, 308.3, 339.5, 347.6, 367.7

Appendix E. Forest Service Maps

The maps included in this book will serve you well for hikes along the parkway and most of the forest service trails. It might be helpful, though, to have a national forest map or two with you when driving along the parkway, as they provide a number of details, such as optional roadways, additional trails, and possible campsites and campgrounds.

If you are going to do any extensive hiking on trails of the national forests, it is suggested you obtain a map. These maps will give you an overview of the area you will be hiking and present the options available to you. However, be aware that many of the trails in the national forests are not well maintained or marked and are also used less than BRP trails. Except for the first one, all of the maps listed below may be ordered through www. nationalforestmapstore.com; 406-329-3024.

The *National Geographic Trails Illustrated Map #789, Lexington, Blue Ridge Mountains* covers the parkway from BRP Mile 0 to 104.3 and is available from www.natgeomaps.com; 800-962-1643.

The *Pisgah National Forest Grandfather, Toecane, and French Broad Ranger Districts Map* covers the parkway from BRP mile 295.4 to 367.6.

The *Pisgah National Forest, Pisgah Ranger District Map* covers the parkway from BRP mile 393.6 to 431.4.

The Pisgah National Forest also offers a number of detailed trail maps of the following sections of the national forest:

The *Linville Gorge Wilderness Map*, with trails accessible from BRP miles 312.2 and 317.5 (Grandfather Ranger District)

The *South Toe, Mount Mitchell, and Big Ivy Trail Map*, with trails accessible from BRP miles 350.4 and 355.4 (Appalachian Ranger District)

The *Shining Rock Wilderness and Middle Prong Wilderness Map*, covering parkway miles 393.6–431.4 (Pisgah Ranger District)

Appendix F. Bicycling the Blue Ridge Parkway

Bicycling the parkway is an excellent way to enjoy the scenic highway. You are able to cover quite a few miles during the course of a day, but because you are moving at a slower rate than if you were in an automobile, you are able to take in more of the sights, sites, and smells. There are no commercial trucks to contend with, the BRP stays close to the crest of the mountains for grandstand views, and pullouts and picnic areas provide shaded resting spots and drinking water. Deer and other wildlife may be seen on a regular basis, while wildflowers bloom profusely by the roadside. Restaurants, camp stores, campgrounds, and lodges on and near BRP property make it convenient to refuel or rest for the night.

Bicyclists on the parkway need to be aware of special regulations. Bicycles may be ridden only on paved road surfaces and parking areas and are not permitted on trails or walkways. You must ride single file, stay to the right on the road, and comply with all applicable state and federal motor vehicle traffic regulations. Between sunset and sunrise; in times of rain, fog, or other periods of low visibility; and while traveling through a tunnel you are required to have a white light or reflector visible at least 500 feet to the front and a red light or reflector visible at least 200 feet to the rear. You must ride at a speed reasonable for control with regard to traffic, weather, road, and light conditions.

The chart below (reprinted by permission of the park service with statistics by Tom DeVaughn of Troutville, Virginia) provides an idea of the elevation changes to expect while cycling various parkway sections.

	Major Uphills NORTHBOUND			Major Uphills SOUTHBOUND		
Milepost	Total Elev. Climbed	Between Milepost	Elev. Change	Total Elev. Climbed	Between Milepost	Elev. Change
0–24	1,450 ft.	13.7–10.7	563 ft.	2,180 ft.	0–3	391
		9.2–8.5	222 ft.		3.7–8.5	1,100 ft.
		4.7–3.0	300 FT.		9.2–10.7	322 ft.
					18.5–23.0	785 ft.
24.0–48.0	2,670 ft.	46.4–43.9	627 ft.	1,742 ft.	37.4–38.8	229 ft.
		40.0–38.8	331 ft.		42.0–43.9	570 ft.
		37.4–34.0	951 ft.		47.0–48.0	177 ft.
48.0–63.0	1,870 ft.	63.0–49.3	1,852 ft.	250 ft.	48.0–49.3	228 ft.
63.0–76.7	0			3,305 ft.	63.0–76.7	3,305 ft.
76.7–96.0	2,865 ft.	93.1–91.6	374 ft.	1,360 ft.	89.1–91.6	569 ft.
		89.1–87.3	634 ft.		93.1–95.4	428 ft.
		85.6–84.7	230 ft.			
		83.5–76.7	1,490 ft.			
96.0–120.4	2,680 ft.	115.0–113.0	280 ft.	1,657 ft.	118.1–120.4	426 ft.
		106.0–103.6	500 ft.			
		102.5–99.8	820 ft.			
120.4	Mill Mountain Spur—Length to summit is 3.1 miles. Elevation climb from BRP to summit is 580 ft. The elevation climb from summit to BRP is 330 ft.					
120.4–144.0	2,006 ft.	140.1–139.3	229 ft.	3,200 ft.	127.0–132.5	1,400 ft.
		136.0–134.9	285 ft.		134.0–134.9	195 ft.
		124.6–123.1	320 ft.		136.4–138.2	275 ft.
121.4–144.0	265 ft.					
144.0–168.0	1,840 ft.	159.4–157.6	389 ft.	2,530 ft.	150.6–152.1	278 ft.
		150.6–149.8	226 ft.		157.0–157.6	195 ft.
					164.7–168.0	830 ft.
168.0–192.0	2,455	189.4–188.7	220 ft.	1,745 ft.	169.5–170.1	260 ft.
		175.1–171.9	575 ft.		176.2–177.0	212 ft.
		168.9–168.0	185 ft.		186.6–188.8	360 ft.
192.0–216.0	2,225 ft.	215.6–214.0	260 ft.	2,047 ft.	195.0–196.2	235 ft.
		210.6–209.4	220 ft.		197.6–198.7	210 ft.
		199.4–198.7	165 ft.		200.5–201.5	335 ft.
216.0–240.0	1,566 ft.	240.0–239.3	160 ft.	2,530 ft.	216.6–217.7	240 ft.
		238.5–237.2	270 ft.		231.3–233.1	550 ft.
		220.8–220.1	205 ft.		233.7–235.2	280 ft.
					235.2–236.9	365 ft.

| | Major Uphills NORTHBOUND | | | Major Uphills SOUTHBOUND | | |
Milepost	Total Elev. Climbed	Between Milepost	Elev. Change	Total Elev. Climbed	Between Milepost	Elev. Change
204.0–264.6	2,625 ft.	257.8–256.8	200 ft.	2,680 ft.	240.0–240.8	170 ft.
		248.0–244.5	495 ft.		249.0–249.8	235 ft.
		243.8–242.9	270 ft.		251.3–252.8	300 ft.
		242.4–241.5	300 ft.		263.6–264.6	360 ft.
264.6–288.0	3,050 ft.	285.2–283.8	400 ft.	3,160 ft.	265.2–266.8	270 ft.
		279.6–278.8	270 ft.		269.8–271.1	330 ft.
		276.4–273.1	910 ft.		271.4–273.1	575 ft.
		269.8–268.6	315 ft.		276.4–277.4	375 ft.
		268.1–266.8	380 ft.		281.7–282.4	280 ft.
					282.7–283.8	255 ft.
					286.0–287.8	500 ft.
288.0–312.0	2,185 ft.	309.9–306.5	460 ft.	2,210 ft.	288.7–289.9	250 ft.
		305.6–305.0	200 ft.		291.8–293.8	400 ft.
		295.8–293.8	555 ft.		298.6–302.1	1,005 ft.
		291.8–289.9	275 ft.			
312.0–336.3	3,120 ft	336.3–335.7	215 ft.	2,705 ft.	316.4–318.2	380 ft.
		327.4–325.8	290 ft.		318.5–320.7	590 ft.
		325.0–320.7	1,210 ft.		330.9–332.1	410 ft.
		316.4–312.4	520 ft.		332.6–334.5	545 ft.
336.3–358.5	1,705 ft.	351.9–349.9	565 ft.	4,060 ft.	336.3–338.9	540 ft.
		334.1–341.8	530 ft.		345.4–349.9	1,480 ft.
		339.8–338.9	260 ft.		351.9–355.0	920 ft.
					355.4–358.5	520ft.
355.4	The spur road to Mt. Mitchell is 4.8 miles. Total elevation climb from BRP is 1,390 ft.					
385.5–384.0	4,265 ft.	383.5–376.7	1,135 ft.	680 ft.	361.1–364.1	500 ft.
		375.3–364.1	2,535 ft.			
		361.1–358.5	540 ft.			
384.0–408.0	850 ft.	No major uphills		3,705 ft.	393.8–396.4	920 ft.
					397.3–399.7	430 ft.
					400.3–405.5	965 ft.
					405.7–407.7	745 ft.

	Major Uphills NORTHBOUND			Major Uphills SOUTHBOUND		
Milepost	Total Elev. Climbed	Between Milepost	Elev. Change	Total Elev. Climbed	Between Milepost	Elev. Change
408.0–431.4	1,835 ft.	426.5–424.8	315 ft.	2,775 ft.	416.8–420.2	1,100 ft.
		423.2–412.6	250 ft.		423.2–424.8	230 ft.
		415.6–413.2	385 ft.		426.5–428.2	405 ft.
		411.9–409.6	400 ft.		429.0–431.4	600 ft.
431.4–469.1	7,470 ft.	469.1–262.2	2,240 ft.	2,450 ft.	443.1–451.2	2,450 ft.
		461.6–458.9	1,000 ft.		455.7–458.9	810 ft.
		455.7–415.2	1,480 ft.			
		443.1–435.5	2,020 ft.			
		433.3–431.4	475 ft.			
458.2	From end of Heintooga Spur Road to BRP	3.6–1.0	860 ft.	From BRP to end of Heintooga Spur Road	0.0–1.0	255 ft.
TOTAL	UPHILL CLIMB NORTHBOUND IS 48,722 FT.			UPHILL CLIMB SOUTHBOUND IS 48,601 FT.		

Appendix G. Become a Blue Ridge Trail Master

Become a recognized Blue Ridge Trail Master by hiking every one of the more than 130 official Blue Ridge Parkway trails. Simply keep a record of the date of each of your hikes and write a report (doesn't need to be more than one or two sentences) for each trail, providing your feelings about the trail, its condition, and if anything has changed since this book was published. In return, receive the suitable-for-framing Blue Ridge Trail Master certificate of recognition. Join a very elite club—as of the publication of this book, the author, Leonard M. Adkins, is the only person to have reported having hiked all of the parkway's trails. Send reports to habitualhiker@verizon.net.

Blue Ridge Trail Master

✳ ✳ ✳ ✳ ✳

Presented To

✳ ✳ ✳ ✳ ✳

for hiking and reporting on every one of the more than 130 official park service trails along the 469-mile Blue Ridge Parkway. This award recognizes the dedication it took to accomplish this task.

Leonard M. Adkins, Author
Hiking and Traveling the Blue Ridge Parkway

ACKNOWLEDGMENTS

I never could have completed this book by myself. Because of their invaluable assistance, I wish to gratefully acknowledge the following:

Cindy Carpenter, information assistant, Pisgah National Forest—thanks for your help;

Paul Carson and Jonathan Bennett—thanks for the information about the Overmountain Victory National Historic Trail;

Art Frederick, Blue Ridge Parkway ranger—I would have been unable to follow the route of the Roanoke Valley Horse Trail without his assistance;

Peter Hamel, Mindy DeCesar, Peter Givens, Elizabeth Faison, Leesa Brandon, Dawn Leonard, and the numerous other Blue Ridge Parkway employees—thank you for looking over the manuscript and providing suggestions. Your help was invaluable and any mistakes that may remain are mine and not yours;

Ann Messick—fewer wildflowers would have been identified without her help;

Phil Noblitt, former Blue Ridge Parkway staff interpretive specialist—a most patient person who cheerfully answered any question I asked;

Mary Ann Peckham, former Blue Ridge Parkway staff interpretive specialist—her encouragement helped me decide to write the book;

West Virginia Scenic Trails Association—for use of the association's measuring wheel;

Bob Ellenwood, Laurie and Bill Foot, Cheryl Maynard, Marti McCallister—thanks, folks, for your friendship and for opening your homes to me;

J. Richard Wells—for the kind words in the Foreword;

Mark Simpson-Vos, Stephanie Wenzel, Zachary Read, Beth Lassiter, Susan Garrett, and David Perry, University of North Carolina Press—thank you.

The Blue Ridge Parkway, with its hundreds of miles of meandering pathways, has provided me with innumerable days of walking pleasure. I would like to thank all of the people, past and present, who have worked long and hard to make my amblings possible.

SUGGESTED READINGS AND FIELD GUIDES

Adkins, Leonard M. *The Appalachian Trail: A Visitor's Companion*. Birmingham, Ala.: Menasha Ridge Press, 2000.

———. *50 Hikes in Northern Virginia: Walks, Hikes, and Backpacks from the Allegheny Mountains to the Chesapeake Bay*. 4th ed. Woodstock, Vt.: Backcountry Publications, 2015.

———. *50 Hikes in Southern Virginia: From the Cumberland Gap to the Atlantic Ocean*. 2nd ed. Woodstock, Vt.: Backcountry Guides, 2007.

———. *Wildflowers of the Appalachian Trail*. 3rd ed. Birmingham, Ala.: Menasha Ridge Press, 2017.

———. *Wildflowers of the Blue Ridge and Great Smoky Mountains*. Birmingham, Ala.: Menasha Ridge Press, 2005.

Beane, Jeffrey C., Alvin L. Braswell, Joseph C. Mitchell, William M. Palmer, and Julian R. Harrison III. *Amphibians and Reptiles of the Carolinas and Virginia*. 2nd ed., revised and updated. Chapel Hill: University of North Carolina Press, 2010.

Brewer, Carson, et al. *Hiking Trails of the Smokies*. Gatlinburg, Tenn.: Great Smoky Mountains Natural History Association, 2012.

Brooks, Maurice. *The Appalachians*. Morgantown, W.Va.: Seneca Books, 1995.

Bull, John, and John Farrand, Jr. *The Audubon Society Field Guide to North American Birds, Eastern Region*. New York: Alfred A. Knopf, 2001.

Byrd, Nathan, ed. *A Forester's Guide to Observing Animal Use in the South*. Atlanta, Ga.: Forest Service, U.S. Department of Agriculture, 1981.

Catlin, David T. *A Naturalist's Blue Ridge Parkway*. Knoxville: University of Tennessee Press, 1984.

de Hart, Allen. *North Carolina Hiking Trails*. Boston: AMC Books, 2005.

———. *The Trails of Virginia: Hiking the Old Dominion*. Chapel Hill: University of North Carolina Press, 2006.

Fletcher, Colin, and Chip Rawlins. *The Complete Walker IV*. New York: Alfred A. Knopf, 2002.

Graf, Irma S., and Brian B. King, eds. *Appalachian Trail Guide to Central Virginia*. 2nd ed. Harpers Ferry, W.Va.: Appalachian Trail Conservancy, 2014.

Gupton, Oscar W., and Fred W. Swope. *Fall Wildflowers of the Blue Ridge and Great Smoky Mountains*. Charlottesville: University Press of Virginia, 1989.

———. *Wildflowers of the Shenandoah Valley and Blue Ridge Mountains*. Charlottesville: University Press of Virginia, 2002.

Jolley, Harley E. *The Blue Ridge Parkway*. Knoxville: University of Tennessee Press, 1997.

Justice, William S., C. Ritchie Bell, and Anne H. Lindsey. *Wild Flowers of North Carolina*. 2nd ed. Chapel Hill: University of North Carolina Press, 2005.

Kephart, Horace. *Our Southern Highlanders*. 1929. Reprint. Knoxville: University of Tennessee Press, 1976, 1984.

Little, Elbert L. *The Audubon Society Field Guide to North American Trees*. New York: Alfred A. Knopf, 1980.

Logue, Frank, Nicole Blouin, and Victoria Logue. *Guide to the Blue Ridge Parkway*. Birmingham, Ala.: Menasha Ridge Press, 2010.

Lord, William. *Blue Ridge Parkway Guide*. Birmingham, Ala.: Menasha Ridge, 1992.

Peterson, Roger T. *Peterson Field Guide to Birds of Eastern and Central North America*. 6th ed. Boston: Houghton Mifflin, 2010.

Petrides, George A. *A Field Guide to Trees and Shrubs*. Boston: Houghton Mifflin, 1988.

Potter, Eloise F., James F. Parnell, Robert P. Teulings, and Ricky Davis. *Birds of the Carolinas*. 2nd ed. Chapel Hill: University of North Carolina Press, 2006.

Prueshner, Bill, and Mary Ann Prueshner, eds. *Appalachian Trail Guide to Southwest Virginia*. Harpers Ferry, W. Va.: Appalachian Trail Conservancy, 2015.

Radford, Albert E., Harry E. Ahles, and C. Ritchie Bell. *Manual of the Vascular Flora of the Carolinas*. Chapel Hill: University of North Carolina Press, 1976.

Rives, Margaret R. *Blue Ridge Parkway: The Story Behind the Scenery*. Las Vegas, Nev.: KC Publications, 1982.

Simpson, Marcus B., Jr. *Birds of the Blue Ridge Mountains: A Guide for the Blue Ridge Parkway, Great Smoky Mountains, Shenandoah National Park, and Neighboring Areas*. Chapel Hill: University of North Carolina Press, 1992.

Stokes, Donald W. *The Natural History of Wild Shrubs and Vines*. New York: Harper and Row, 1989.

Webster, William David, James F. Parnell, and Walter C. Biggs Jr. *Mammals of the Carolinas, Virginia, and Maryland*. Chapel Hill: University of North Carolina Press, 2004.

Whisnant, Anne Mitchell. *Super-Scenic Motorway: A Blue Ridge Parkway History*. Chapel Hill: University of North Carolina Press, 2010.

INDEX

Bold page numbers indicate the detailed description of a trail.

About the Author

Leonard M. Adkins has logged more than 20,000 miles hiking the world's backcountry. Each hiking season finds him on some new adventure. He has hiked the entire Appalachian Trail five times; traversed the Continental Divide Trail from Canada to Mexico; followed the full Pacific Northwest Trail through Montana, Idaho, and Washington; and walked Canada's Great Divide Trail. He has also trekked the full length of the Pyrenees High Route from the Atlantic to the Mediterranean and has explored Iceland's interior. With his wife, Laurie, he hiked West Virginia's Allegheny Trail and the Mid-Atlantic's Tuscarora Trail. Together, they tramped New Zealand's Milford Track, along with a number of the country's other Great Walks. And, of course, he has hiked every one of the official parkway trails in this book—with a surveyor's measuring wheel to ensure the accuracy of the mileage and the description.

Leonard is the author of more than 20 books and over 200 articles on the outdoors, nature, and travel and is the walking columnist for *Blue Ridge Country* magazine. He has also been a Natural Heritage Monitor for the Appalachian Trail Conservancy, helping to observe and protect rare and endangered plants, and has been on the boards of directors of two Appalachian Trail maintaining clubs. As FRIENDS of the Blue Ridge Parkway's Adopt-an-Overlook volunteers, Leonard and Laurie work to maintain the quality of the visitor experience to the Greenstone Overlook, the spot that inspired him to walk all of the parkway's official trails in the first place.

Other **Southern Gateways Guides** you might enjoy